American Attitudes

**Look for these other books from New Strategist Publications,
specialists in unlocking and analyzing consumer trends**

American Attitudes: Who Thinks What about
the Issues That Shape Our Lives, 3rd ed.

American Consumers: Trends and Projections 1950–2050

American Generations: Millennials, Generation X, Baby Boom,
Swing, & WWII Generations, 3rd ed.

American Incomes: Demographics of Who Has Money, 3rd ed.

American Marketplace: Demographics and Spending Patterns, 4th ed.

American Men and Women: Demographics of the Sexes

Americans 55 and Older: A Changing Market, 2nd ed.

Americans and Their Homes: Demographics of Homeownership

Americans at Play: Demographics of Outdoor Recreation and Travel

The Baby Boom: Americans Aged 35 to 54, 2nd ed.

Best Customers: Demographics of Consumer Demand

Best of Health: Demographics of Health Care Consumers, 2nd ed.

Generation X: The Young Adult Market, 2nd ed.

Household Spending: Who Spends How Much on What, 5th ed.
(also available on CD-ROM)

Racial and Ethnic Diversity: Asians, Blacks, Hispanics,
Native Americans, and Whites, 3rd ed.

Regional Markets: Demographics of Growth and Decline

Wise Up to Teens: Insights into Marketing
and Advertising to Teenagers, 2nd ed.

American Attitudes

Who Thinks What about the Issues That Shape Our Lives

BY SUSAN MITCHELL

3rd EDITION

New Strategist Publications, Inc.
Ithaca, New York

New Strategist Publications, Inc.
P.O. Box 242, Ithaca, New York 14851
800-848-0842
www.newstrategist.com

Copyright 2000. NEW STRATEGIST PUBLICATIONS, INC.

ISBN 1-885070-30-6

Printed in the United States of America

For Lorraine, Joe, Emily, and Skylar
and, of course, for Sam

Table of Contents

List of Tables

Chapter 3. Personal Outlook

Chapter 4. Public Arena

Chapter 5. Race

Chapter 6. Religion

Chapter 7. Sexual Attitudes and Behavior

Chapter 8. Women's Roles

Chapter 9. Work and Money

Introduction

Change has been a constant in the United States for more than 200 years, but the pace of change has accelerated since the mid-1900s. New technologies have radically altered the way we live and work. The traditional household of the 1950s, made up of a stay-at-home mother, working father, and children, has fractured into dual-income families, single parents, and single-person households. We are more racially and ethnically diverse than ever before.

It is no surprise, then, that over the past 20 years Americans have changed their minds about many issues. Some of the biggest changes are in opinions about race and the roles of women. Twenty years ago, far more Americans believed in separate societies for blacks and whites and separate spheres for men and women. Since then, men and women, blacks and whites, old and young, the most and the least educated have changed their minds about race and women's roles.

Racial tension is still very real, but the most overtly racist attitudes and forms of discrimination are greatly diminished. Few Americans now favor laws that prevent people of different races from marrying. The idea that blacks have less innate ability than whites has lost credibility, although some racial stereotypes persist. People are more likely to rate whites than blacks as hardworking and intelligent, for example.

Likewise, most Americans matter-of-factly accept women's participation in politics and business. Compared with 20 years ago, far fewer Americans believe women should be homemakers, leaving politics and breadwinning to men. The public has also changed its mind about working mothers. Most now believe children don't suffer if their mother works, although they are divided about the impact on the family in general.

Families have changed, but Americans still value family life. Most married people say their marriage is very happy. Given a choice, Americans would spend more time with their family and friends and less time doing housework. The time they spend with their family is focused on fewer children as family size has shrunk. The majority of Americans now consider two the ideal number of children.

Most Americans say they are happy and they are in better health than they were 20 years ago. They trust their physicians, but they have a poor opinion of HMOs. Americans are split on whether other people are generally helpful or selfish, and barely half think others try to be fair. The majority no longer trust other people.

Most Americans are religious, but there is more religious diversity than there was 20 years ago when Protestants were in the majority. Especially among the young, a growing share of people say they have no religious preference. Reflecting the nation's increased religious diversity, the majority of the public believes there are basic truths in many religions.

Americans have less confidence in religious leaders than they had 20 years ago and want them to stay out of politics. They don't mind if athletes give thanks to God in public, but they don't want to see religious images in advertising.

Americans continue to be concerned about crime. Support for gun control is at an all-time high. The public has a much more negative view of the nation's leaders—especially elected officials—than it did in 1978. Americans want a less activist government, but still believe government has some responsibility to help the poor and make sure people can pay for medical care. Americans are divided on whether the federal government should help fund the arts, but most say state and local governments should assist arts organizations.

More Americans now identify themselves as independent rather than Republican or Democrat. But the percentage of people who say they are liberal, moderate, or conservative is virtually unchanged from 20 years ago.

Americans want secure and interesting jobs, preferably being their own boss. Increasing numbers would rather work in the private sector, especially for a small company. The proportion of those who say hard work is the key to success is higher than in the past, but the percentage of those unwilling to let work interfere with other aspects of their lives has also increased. People are more likely than they were a decade ago to say they work hard but not at the expense of the rest of their lives.

Most people would continue to work even if they did not need the money. Americans want Social Security to be there for them when they retire, however. Most do not want to see the system privatized, although they believe Social Security has serious problems and will need major changes.

Sexual mores have changed since the 1970s. Support for sex education in the schools is higher than ever. The growing acceptance of premarital sex and homosexuality continue the liberalization of attitudes that began in the "free love" era of the 1960s. Attitudes toward adultery and pornography, however, have become more conservative.

Men and Women

Men and women agree on many issues. Even when they disagree, their differences of opinion often are smaller than in other demographic segments. On some issues, however, men and women disagree sharply.

Conventional wisdom holds that women are more liberal than men, and there is some truth in it. Women are more likely to identify themselves as Democrats, and on some issues they are more likely to take the liberal position. They are less supportive of the death penalty and more supportive of gun control, for example. They are more likely to believe discrimination and lack of education are behind the lower socioeconomic status of blacks. Women are more likely than men to want government to play an active role in solving a variety of problems, such as making sure people can pay for health care and reducing income differences between rich and poor.

Men are more accepting of premarital sex and sex between teens. Men and women are equally likely to favor sex education in the schools. Men support restricting pornography to adults, while women are divided between wanting it outlawed entirely and restricted to adults.

Men and women have changed their opinions about women's roles, and there is now little disagreement about the appropriateness of women in the workplace or in government. But men are more skeptical than women about the impact of working mothers on the family, particularly the effect on children.

The sexes differ in their attitude about work. More men than women would choose self-employment. Women want job security, a chance to help others, and socially useful work. Men are more likely to think work is a person's most important activity. Women are more likely to be exhausted at the end of the workday.

The Races

The different experiences of blacks and whites over hundreds of years have clearly left their mark on attitudes. Blacks and whites hold different opinions about many issues, and people of "other" race have yet another set of opinions. Most people who identify themselves as a race other than black or white are Hispanic or Asian. Most are first- or second-generation Americans. Their attitudes are sometimes influenced by their experience as immigrants or the children of immigrants. They are far more likely to believe America offers the opportunity to improve one's standard of living, for example. And they are most likely to think that their children will have a much better standard of living than they themselves have.

Socioeconomics also play a role in differences of opinion by race. Whites have, on average, a higher socioeconomic status than blacks and others. This difference is one reason why whites are most likely to be satisfied with their financial situation. While most whites consider themselves middle or upper class, most blacks and other races say they are working class.

It should surprise no one that there is considerable difference of opinion on racial issues. Whites are more likely than blacks and others to say "blacks shouldn't push where they are not wanted" and to support laws against interracial marriage. Blacks and other races are most likely to believe discrimination is one reason for the lower socioeconomic status of blacks. People of other race, however, are most likely to believe lack of motivation is a factor.

Whites are most likely to support the death penalty, while blacks and other races are most likely to favor requiring a police permit to purchase a gun. Blacks and other races think government should do more to solve the nation's problems while whites think government already does too much. Whites are more likely to think Social Security has major problems and will need a major overhaul. Blacks and other races are more likely to want the system to continue as is rather than privatizing it.

Money may not buy happiness, but it can go a long way in that direction. The higher socioeconomic status of whites is one factor in their greater likelihood of saying they are very happy, find life exciting, and are in excellent health. Blacks and other races have much less faith in other people than whites do—they are far more likely to say people take advantage of others, are not trustworthy, and are selfish.

The races are religiously diverse. Blacks are most likely to be Protestant, while other races are most likely to be Catholic. In many respects, blacks are more religious than whites and other races. They are more likely to believe in heaven, hell, and miracles. They are most likely to say they try to carry their religious beliefs into other arenas of life.

Majorities of all races support women's participation in business and politics. Blacks have a more positive attitude toward working mothers, however, while people of other race are slightly more inclined to support traditional sex roles.

The Generations

The generation gap, which was so divisive in the 1960s, is still apparent today. Times and attitudes have changed, but on many issues older and younger Americans still do not see eye to eye. On some issues, each successive age cohort is more likely to agree or disagree. On other issues, there is a dividing line at age 50 or 60 with a wide difference of opinion separating baby boomers and Generation Xers from older generations. Younger generations are more comfortable with much of the ongoing social change than are older generations.

The enormous changes in attitudes about race over the past 20 years are apparent in the differences of opinion between young and old. Older generations are more likely to say "blacks shouldn't push where they aren't wanted" and to support laws against interracial marriage.

The women's movement shaped the attitudes of younger generations about women's roles. Baby boomers and younger adults are less likely than older people to believe men and women should adhere to traditional roles at home, at work, and in politics. Younger generations also have a more positive view of working mothers.

There are also differences in religious attitudes by age. The young are more diverse in their religious preferences and more likely to have no religion. Older generations are more likely to attend religious services and to have confidence in the leaders of organized religion. The older people are the more they favor school prayer and think we trust too much in science and not enough in religious faith

Older generations continue to be appalled by many of the changes in sexual mores, while the young are more accepting of homosexuality, premarital sex, pornography, and sex education in the schools.

When it comes to work and money, attitudes are linked to lifestage. The young are least satisfied with their financial situation but most likely to say it is improving. Older Americans are most satisfied with their personal finances but least likely to say their finances are improving. Younger generations are more likely to consider themselves working class, while older people are more likely to say they are middle class.

Younger generations have an entrepreneurial spirit—they are more likely to want to be their own boss and to work in the private sector. Older workers are more likely to let work interfere with other areas of their lives, while younger workers are more likely to try to keep a balance between work and personal life.

Older generations are more likely to defer to authority, and this applies to their relationship with their physicians. They are more likely to trust their doctor's judgment and to think doctors always treat patients with respect. The middle-aged are the most cynical about physicians and HMOs. At this age, people are beginning to confront more serious illnesses, and as boomers have moved into the age group, they are demanding more of the health care system.

The Role of Education

Education clearly influences attitudes on some issues, but its role is less clear in other areas. The relationships between age and education (younger Americans are better educated) and between income and education (the well educated have higher incomes) make it difficult to ascertain whether education, age, or socioeconomic status is the most important determinant of attitudes.

Differences of opinion by education on pocketbook issues are undoubtedly influenced by income differences. College graduates are more satisfied with their financial situation than those with less education, and they are more likely to say their financial situation has improved over the past few years. Most college graduates consider themselves middle class, while the majority of those with less education say they are working class. The less education people have the more likely they are to think that a job is just a way to earn money.

Education seems to be one factor in attitudes about women's roles. Those with less education are more likely to favor traditional sex roles and less likely to vote for a female presidential candidate.

Education has its advantages, but it also has disadvantages. People with more education are more pressed for time. They are more likely to say they would like to spend more time with their family and friends and pursuing leisure activities. College graduates want to spend less time at work, while those with less education—who need the money—want to spend more time working.

People with less education are more likely to believe government has a responsibility to help the poor and the sick and that it should provide jobs for people who want them. College graduates are more likely to favor privatizing the Social Security system.

Attitudes about racial issues are also linked to education. College graduates are more likely to view education as the cause of socioeconomic differences between blacks and whites, while the less educated are more likely to blame a lack of motivation. Those with less education are more likely to support laws against interracial marriage and to believe "blacks shouldn't push where they are not wanted."

Religious attitudes and practices differ somewhat by education. Those with less education are more likely to support school prayer and to interpret the Bible literally. People with less education are more likely to believe in heaven and hell. College graduates are more likely to think people with strong religious beliefs are often too intolerant of others. But this doesn't mean college graduates are less religious. In fact, they are more likely than those with less education to attend religious services at least once a week.

Education makes a big difference in personal outlook. Those with more education are more likely to be very happy, to have excellent health, and to find life exciting. They are more likely to think others are trustworthy, fair, and helpful.

College graduates are more supportive of the arts. They are more likely than those with less education to have attended an arts performance or visited an art museum in the past year and to volunteer time for arts organizations. The more education people have the more likely they are to support government funding of the arts.

About This Book

The third edition of *American Attitudes* examines ongoing changes in the opinions of Americans and analyzes the social and demographic trends behind those changes.

The data in *American Attitudes* are from the General Social Survey of the University of Chicago's National Opinion Research Center. NORC is the oldest nonprofit, university-affiliated national survey research facility in the nation. It conducts the GSS through face-to-face interviews with an independently drawn, representative sample of 1,500 to 3,000 noninstitutionalized English-speaking people aged 18 or older who live in the United States. The sample size for the 1998 survey, on which this book is based, was approximately 2,800 people, although interviewers asked some respondents fewer questions. NORC took the first GSS in 1972, and then conducted it annually through 1994 (except for the years 1979, 1981, and 1992). It now conducts the survey every two years, and 1998 is the latest year for which data are available.

Until publication of the first edition of *American Attitudes* in 1996, social scientists and other researchers were the only ones with ready access to the wealth of information collected by the GSS—which was available only to those with the computing skills to mine the data. New Strategist's publication of *American Attitudes* now gives the public regular access to this rich database. The book contains cross-tabulations—performed by the author—of the latest attitudinal data by sex, age, race, and education. Whenever possible, responses to the same attitudinal questions are shown at 10-year intervals back to the 1970s, allowing readers to see how attitudes have changed over the past two decades and to track attitudinal change within 10-year age cohorts. The book also includes the author's insightful examination of why Americans think the way they do and how their opinions might change in the future.

The third edition of *American Attitudes* is organized into nine chapters: The Arts, Health and Medicine, Personal Outlook, Public Arena, Race, Religion, Sexual Behavior, Women's Roles, and Work and Money. Although interviewers asked certain core questions in every survey, the GSS also includes modules on topics that differ from survey to survey. These inquiries provide in-depth data on subjects such as work, religion, and the roles of women.

Each chapter in *American Attitudes* includes tables and text describing the differences and similarities in the attitudes of Americans by demographic characteristic in 1998, 1988, and 1978. The author selected the questions presented here from the hundreds included in the GSS for their timeliness and ability to present a broad perspective on the attitudes of Americans toward the most important public and private issues. In the cases of questions asked in the 1998 survey but omitted in the 1988 or 1978 surveys, the author substituted responses from the closest available year. Although some were edited for space or clarity, the questions appearing above each table are generally worded as they appear in the survey. GSS researchers have changed the wording of some questions over the years (for example, substituting "black" for "Negro"), but this has not affected the continuity of the results.

Although "other race" is included as a category in the 1998 tables, it is not included as a category in the trend tables. Several factors make it difficult to compare the responses of people of other race across time. One problem is the small sample size of the other race category in past years. Another problem is the change in the way Hispanics identify themselves. Twenty years ago, many people of Hispanic origin identified themselves as white, but today a larger share identify themselves as other race.

The GSS is an invaluable road map to American thought, but remember that the mental landscape can be foggy at times. Many factors, such as current events and the wording of questions, can influence opinion. Some attitudes and behaviors are notoriously hard to measure, such as those surrounding race and sexuality. Respondents may give answers they consider socially acceptable rather than their honest opinions. It is hard to know, for example, if everyone who answers "yes" to the abstract question, "Would you vote for a black presidential candidate?" would actually do so in the voting booth.

Nevertheless, a well-designed and properly executed survey such as the GSS minimizes these problems. And by looking at broad categories of Americans, it is possible to get a feeling for where we agree and disagree as a nation. The longitudinal nature of many of the survey questions offers an especially valuable look at how attitudes have changed over the past two decades and, by examining the attitudes of younger age groups, what the future may hold.

For more information about the General Social Survey, contact the National Opinion Research Center, University of Chicago, 1155 East 60th Street, Chicago, IL 60637; telephone (773) 753-7500; Internet site <www.norc.uchicago.edu>. The Roper Center for Public Opinion Research, 341 Mansfield Road, U-1164, Storrs, CT 06269-1164, also distributes GSS data.

1

The Arts

Most people think truly talented artists should be able to support themselves, but this doesn't mean they want government support for the arts to be eliminated. Americans are divided on whether or not the federal government should provide financial assistance to arts organizations, but most believe state and local governments should fund the arts.

Although most people support the arts in theory, far fewer support them in practice. Few Americans attended a ballet, dance, classical music, or opera performance or visited an art museum in the past year. Only a small minority of Americans volunteered for an arts organization.

The majority of Americans think art should express the artist's personal thoughts and emotions rather than being limited to expressing the beauty of the world and the human spirit. Few agree that modern art is just "slapped on" or think only the elite are qualified to judge art.

Women are slightly more supportive of the arts than men are, but the differences by sex are small. A slightly higher percentage of women than men think state and local governments should support the arts, while men are slightly more likely than women to think the federal government should not fund the arts. Men are more likely to believe we spend too much on the arts. Not coincidentally, men are also more likely to believe artists should be self-supporting. Women are more likely to trust the judgment of teachers in assigning reading material, while men are more likely to think few people are qualified to judge art.

The only issue on which women and men differ substantially is the aim of art. Women are considerably more likely to think art should celebrate what is most beautiful about the world and the human spirit. Men are more likely to believe art should express the artist's thoughts and emotions.

Whites are less likely than blacks and "other" races to think government should provide financial assistance to the arts. Whites are also less likely to trust teachers to decide what students should read and to believe that only a few people are qualified to judge art. Blacks are least likely to have attended a music or dance performance or to have visited an art museum in the past year. Blacks are more likely than whites and other races to think art should express the beauty of the world and the human spirit.

The older people are the more they believe the aim of art is to express the world's beauty rather than the artist's personal thoughts and feelings.

People in their forties and fifties are the most reliable patrons of the arts. They are most likely among all age groups to have visited an art museum and to have attended a dance or classical music performance in the past year. Those in their forties are most likely to have volunteered for an arts organization and to think we spend too little on the arts. People aged 60 or older are least likely to support government funding of the arts, although they are only slightly more likely than other age groups to oppose it. Many say they simply don't know. Older Americans are also more likely than younger adults to think modern painting is no better than a child's drawing.

Education has the greatest influence on attitudes toward art. The reason for this correlation is simple. The more education people have, the more likely they are to have been exposed to and developed an appreciation for the arts.

College graduates are far more likely than those with less education to think we spend too little on the arts and to support government funding for arts organizations. They are also much more likely to have volunteered their time to arts groups and to have attended dance or music performances and visited art museums in the past year. College graduates have a much higher opinion of modern art and much lower expectations about artists' ability to support themselves.

Visited Art Museum in Past Year

The growing number of college graduates bodes well for art museums.

Although most Americans did not visit an art museum in the past year, a sizable minority (37 percent) have done so. Those most likely to visit art museums are those with the most education. As the level of education among Americans increases, attendance at art museums is likely to rise.

Fully 71 percent of people with a graduate degree and 66 percent of those with a bachelor's degree visited an art museum in the past year. In contrast, only 28 percent of high school graduates and 16 percent of those with less education went to an art museum.

Blacks are less likely than whites and "other" races to visit an art museum. While 38 to 39 percent of whites and others went to an art museum, only 24 percent of blacks did. Women and men are equally likely to have gone to an art museum.

People in their forties and fifties are the biggest art patrons. Nearly half of people in their fifties (48 percent) and 43 percent of those in their forties visited an art museum in the past year. Least likely to go to an art museum are people aged 70 or older, and only one-quarter of them did.

Visited Art Museum in Past Year, 1998

"Have you visited an art museum or gallery in the past twelve months?"

(percent of people aged 18 or older responding by sex, race, age, and education, 1998)

	yes	no
Total	**37%**	**63%**
Men	37	63
Women	37	63
Black	24	76
White	39	61
Other	38	63
Aged 18 to 29	34	66
Aged 30 to 39	36	64
Aged 40 to 49	43	57
Aged 50 to 59	48	52
Aged 60 to 69	30	70
Aged 70 or older	24	76
Not a high school graduate	16	83
High school graduate	28	72
Bachelor's degree	66	34
Graduate degree	71	29

Note: Numbers may not add to 100 because "don't know" is not shown.
Source: General Social Survey, National Opinion Research Center, University of Chicago; calculations by the author

Attended Classical Music, Opera, or Dance Performances

College graduates are the primary audience for dance and music performances.

Only 20 percent of Americans attended a dance performance and just 17 percent attended a classical music or opera performance in the past year. Although lack of interest is no doubt one factor, access to performances is another. Outside metropolitan areas, there are few opportunities to attend dance or music performances.

Men and women are equally likely to have attended a classical music or opera performance, but women are more likely than men to have attended a ballet or dance performance. Twenty-three percent of women attended a dance performance in the past year compared with only 16 percent of men.

By race, whites are most likely to have attended a classical music or opera performance, while blacks are least likely. Twenty percent of whites and 24 percent of "other" races attended a performance of ballet or other dance compared with only 14 percent of blacks.

People in their forties and fifties are more likely to be in the audiences of music and dance performances than older or younger people. Being in their peak earning years, people in those age groups can better afford the ticket price. In addition, the middle-aged are less likely to have small children, whereas the need for a babysitter is often a limiting factor for younger adults.

Education is the most important factor in determining attendance at dance and music performances. Although arts education is minimal in most schools and even many colleges, the more education people have, the more likely they are to develop an appreciation for the arts. Nearly half of people with a graduate degree attended a dance or music performance in the past year, as did about one-third of those with a bachelor's degree. Among people with a high school diploma or less education, fewer than 15 percent attended a music or dance performance.

Attended Classical Music or Opera Performance in Past Year, 1998

"Have you gone to a classical music or opera performance, not including school performances, in the past year?"

(percent of people aged 18 or older responding by sex, race, age, and education, 1998)

	yes	no
Total	**17%**	**83%**
Men	17	83
Women	17	83
Black	9	91
White	19	81
Other	13	88
Aged 18 to 29	17	83
Aged 30 to 39	14	86
Aged 40 to 49	18	82
Aged 50 to 59	23	77
Aged 60 to 69	17	83
Aged 70 or older	13	87
Not a high school graduate	5	95
High school graduate	11	89
Bachelor's degree	32	68
Graduate degree	48	52

Note: Numbers may not add to 100 because "don't know" is not shown.
Source: General Social Survey, National Opinion Research Center, University of Chicago; calculations by the author

Attended Dance Performance in Past Year, 1998

"Have you gone to a live ballet or dance performance, not including school performances in the past twelve months?"

(percent of people aged 18 or older responding by sex, race, age, and education, 1998)

	yes	no
Total	**20%**	**80%**
Men	16	84
Women	23	77
Black	14	86
White	20	80
Other	24	76
Aged 18 to 29	16	84
Aged 30 to 39	19	81
Aged 40 to 49	25	75
Aged 50 to 59	22	78
Aged 60 to 69	18	82
Aged 70 or older	16	84
Not a high school graduate	6	94
High school graduate	14	86
Bachelor's degree	34	66
Graduate degree	47	53

Note: Numbers may not add to 100 because "don't know" is not shown.
Source: General Social Survey, National Opinion Research Center, University of Chicago; calculations by the author

Volunteer Work in the Arts

College graduates are most likely to support the arts with their time.

Only 16 percent of Americans did volunteer work for organizations involved in the arts, culture, or humanities in the past year. For working-age people, lack of time is a good excuse for not volunteering, but may not be the main hindrance since people of retirement age are even less likely to volunteer. Most Americans are simply not well versed in the arts and are more likely to volunteer for agencies with greater connection to their lives, such as school or church organizations.

Those most likely to volunteer are the college educated, who are also the ones most exposed to and educated about the arts. More than one-quarter of college graduates did volunteer work for arts organizations in the past year compared with only 15 percent of high school graduates and 6 percent of those with less education.

Blacks are least likely to have done volunteer work for arts agencies, although the differences by race are small. Twelve percent of blacks, 16 percent of whites, and 19 percent of "other" races donated their time to arts agencies.

People in their forties are more likely than other age groups to be volunteers. Twenty-one percent of people aged 40 to 49 were arts volunteers in the past year, as were 17 percent of people under age 30. Only 12 to 15 percent of other age groups volunteered in the arts.

Volunteer Work in the Arts, 1998

"Last year, did you do any volunteer work for organizations involved in the arts, culture, or the humanities?"

(percent of people aged 18 or older responding by sex, race, age, and education, 1998)

	yes	*no*
Total	**16%**	**84%**
Men	16	84
Women	16	84
Black	12	88
White	16	84
Other	19	81
Aged 18 to 29	17	83
Aged 30 to 39	14	86
Aged 40 to 49	21	79
Aged 50 to 59	15	85
Aged 60 to 69	14	85
Aged 70 or older	12	88
Not a high school graduate	6	94
High school graduate	15	85
Bachelor's degree	26	74
Graduate degree	27	73

Note: Numbers may not add to 100 because "don't know" is not shown.
Source: General Social Survey, National Opinion Research Center, University of Chicago; calculations by the author

Spending on the Arts

College graduates are most likely to think we spend too little on the arts.

The plurality of Americans think spending on the arts is about right, while 21 percent say it is too little and 19 percent say it is too much. Sixteen percent say they don't know. The differences of opinion by sex and race are small, but people of different ages and levels of education disagree substantially.

The older people are the more likely they are to believe we spend too much on the arts. Only 14 percent of people under age 30 believe we spend too much on the arts, but the proportion rises to 26 percent among those aged 70 or older. Only 6 percent of the oldest Americans believe we spend too little. People in their forties are most likely to feel this way (29 percent).

One-third of college graduates say we spend too little on the arts compared with 13 to 17 percent of those with less education. Only 12 to 14 percent of college graduates say we spend too much compared with 20 to 22 percent of those with less education. Twenty-nine percent of people who did not complete high school say they don't know.

Spending on the Arts, 1998

"Are we spending too much, too little, or about the right amount on the arts?"

(percent of people aged 18 or older responding by sex, race, age, and education, 1998)

	too little	*about right*	*too much*	*don't know*
Total	**21%**	**44%**	**19%**	**16%**
Men	21	44	22	14
Women	22	45	16	18
Black	21	40	16	22
White	21	45	19	14
Other	17	41	17	24
Aged 18 to 29	25	44	14	16
Aged 30 to 39	20	45	17	18
Aged 40 to 49	29	40	19	12
Aged 50 to 59	23	45	19	13
Aged 60 to 69	16	46	22	16
Aged 70 or older	6	46	26	22
Not a high school graduate	13	37	22	29
High school graduate	17	48	20	15
Bachelor's degree	34	40	14	11
Graduate degree	33	49	12	6

Source: General Social Survey, National Opinion Research Center, University of Chicago; calculations by the author

Should Federal, State, and Local Governments Support the Arts?

College graduates are most likely to believe government should fund arts.

Americans are divided on whether or not the federal government should fund arts organizations, with 45 percent saying "yes" and 45 percent saying "no." Eleven percent are undecided. More than half of adults support state and local funding for the arts, however.

Whites are less likely than blacks and "other" races to support government funding of the arts. Only 43 percent of whites believe the federal government should aid arts organizations compared with 51 percent of blacks and 53 percent of other races. Barely half of whites believe state and local governments should fund the arts, but 59 percent of blacks and 67 percent of other races support state funding of the arts. Sixty-three percent of blacks and 61 percent of other races support local funding of the arts.

Support for government funding of the arts falls with age. Over half of people under age 30 believe federal, state, and local governments should provide financial assistance to arts organizations, but fewer than half of those aged 60 or older agree. Older Americans are more supportive of local and state funding of the arts than of federal funding.

College graduates are considerably more likely than those with less education to support government funding of the arts. Only 35 percent of people who did not complete high school support federal arts funding, but the figure rises to 63 percent among people with a graduate degree. Three-quarters of college graduates think local governments should help arts organizations compared with only 42 percent of people who did not complete high school.

Should the Federal Government Support the Arts? 1998

"If arts organizations, such as art museums, dance, operas, theater groups, and symphony orchestras, need financial assistance to operate, do you feel that the federal government should provide assistance or not?"

(percent of people aged 18 or older responding by sex, race, age, and education, 1998)

	yes	no	don't know
Total	**45%**	**45%**	**11%**
Men	44	49	8
Women	46	42	13
Black	51	36	13
White	43	47	10
Other	53	32	15
Aged 18 to 29	54	37	9
Aged 30 to 39	45	44	11
Aged 40 to 49	48	45	7
Aged 50 to 59	41	50	10
Aged 60 to 69	34	50	16
Aged 70 or older	36	49	15
Not a high school graduate	35	47	18
High school graduate	42	47	10
Bachelor's degree	57	35	8
Graduate degree	63	31	7

Source: General Social Survey, National Opinion Research Center, University of Chicago; calculations by the author

Should State Governments Support the Arts? 1998

"Should state governments provide financial assistance to arts organizations?"

(percent of people aged 18 or older responding by sex, race, age, and education, 1998)

	yes	no	don't know
Total	**54%**	**35%**	**11%**
Men	51	40	9
Women	56	31	13
Black	59	27	14
White	52	38	10
Other	67	21	12
Aged 18 to 29	59	33	9
Aged 30 to 39	54	36	10
Aged 40 to 49	59	33	8
Aged 50 to 59	55	34	10
Aged 60 to 69	45	37	18
Aged 70 or older	43	40	17
Not a high school graduate	40	40	20
High school graduate	53	36	11
Bachelor's degree	65	29	7
Graduate degree	71	23	6

Source: General Social Survey, National Opinion Research Center, University of Chicago; calculations by the author

Should Local Governments Support the Arts? 1998

"Should municipal or county governments assist arts organizations financially?"

(percent of people aged 18 or older responding by sex, race, age, and education, 1998)

	yes	no	don't know
Total	**55%**	**34%**	**11%**
Men	53	39	8
Women	57	30	13
Black	63	27	11
White	53	36	11
Other	61	27	12
Aged 18 to 29	55	34	11
Aged 30 to 39	55	35	9
Aged 40 to 49	60	33	7
Aged 50 to 59	58	31	11
Aged 60 to 69	49	35	16
Aged 70 or older	47	37	16
Not a high school graduate	42	38	21
High school graduate	52	37	12
Bachelor's degree	75	21	4
Graduate degree	73	24	3

Source: General Social Survey, National Opinion Research Center, University of Chicago; calculations by the author

Who Is Qualified to Judge Art?

Most Americans don't believe only the elite are qualified to judge art.

Americans have a general aversion to elitism, and this dislike is evident in their beliefs about the ability of people to judge art. Slightly more than half of Americans say they don't believe only the elite can judge excellence in the arts. Thirty-eight percent believe it does require special knowledge and ability to judge art.

Men are more likely than women to believe few people are qualified to judge art. The difference in opinion is greater by race than by sex, however. Only 35 percent of whites think few are qualified to judge art compared with 42 percent of blacks and 53 percent of "other" races.

People in their fifties and those aged 70 or older are more likely than other age groups to believe it takes a professional to judge art. The biggest differences of opinion, however, are by education. The more education people have, the less likely they are to believe judging art requires special knowledge and ability. Seventy-six percent of people with a graduate degree disagree with the statement that only the select few can judge art, the figure drops to just 39 percent among people who did not complete high school. The least educated are also the ones most likely to say they do not know who is qualified to judge art.

Who Is Qualified to Judge Art? 1998

"Only a few people have the knowledge and ability to judge excellence in the arts. Do you agree or disagree?"

(percent of people aged 18 or older responding by sex, race, age, and education, 1998)

	strongly agree	agree	disagree	strongly disagree	don't know	agree, total	disagree, total
Total	**7%**	**31%**	**37%**	**15%**	**11%**	**38%**	**52%**
Men	8	32	35	15	9	40	50
Women	5	30	38	14	12	35	52
Black	7	35	29	10	19	42	39
White	6	29	40	16	9	35	56
Other	12	41	19	14	13	53	33
Aged 18 to 29	5	28	40	14	13	33	54
Aged 30 to 39	4	29	37	19	10	33	56
Aged 40 to 49	7	28	45	14	7	35	59
Aged 50 to 59	12	34	31	14	9	46	45
Aged 60 to 69	7	28	35	15	15	35	50
Aged 70 or older	9	40	26	10	15	49	36
Not a high school graduate	6	33	32	7	23	39	39
High school graduate	8	34	34	12	12	42	46
Bachelor's degree	6	24	44	24	2	30	68
Graduate degree	6	16	52	24	2	22	76

Source: General Social Survey, National Opinion Research Center, University of Chicago; calculations by the author

Trusting Teachers' Judgment in Assigning Reading

Most people trust teachers to decide what students should be reading.

Despite frequent criticism of the nation's educational system, most Americans trust teachers to decide what students should be reading. Fifty-nine percent trust teachers, while only 37 percent say they do not.

Women are slightly more likely than men to trust the judgment of teachers. Whites are slightly less likely than blacks and "other" races to trust teachers to decide what students should read. There is little variation by age in the percentage of those who say they trust teachers.

Interestingly, the group that includes most of the nation's teachers and professors (college graduates) is no more likely than people who did not complete high school to trust teachers' judgment in assigning reading to students. High school graduates are slightly less likely to trust teachers.

Trusting Teachers' Judgment in Assigning Reading, 1998

"I trust the judgment of the teachers and professors who decide what high school and college students should be reading. Do you agree or disagree?"

(percent of people aged 18 or older responding by sex, race, age, and education, 1998)

	strongly agree	agree	disagree	strongly disagree	don't know	agree, total	disagree, total
Total	**5%**	**54%**	**29%**	**8%**	**5%**	**59%**	**37%**
Men	5	51	30	9	5	56	39
Women	4	57	27	7	5	61	34
Black	7	55	24	6	8	62	30
White	4	54	30	8	5	58	38
Other	10	55	23	8	5	65	31
Aged 18 to 29	4	55	26	10	5	59	36
Aged 30 to 39	4	52	29	9	5	56	38
Aged 40 to 49	3	54	34	6	2	57	40
Aged 50 to 59	5	55	28	9	3	60	37
Aged 60 to 69	4	55	25	9	7	59	34
Aged 70 or older	6	54	26	4	11	60	30
Not a high school graduate	5	58	22	5	11	63	27
High school graduate	5	52	31	9	4	57	40
Bachelor's degree	4	57	27	8	4	61	35
Graduate degree	5	57	30	4	5	62	34

Source: General Social Survey, National Opinion Research Center, University of Chicago; calculations by the author

Is Modern Art Child's Play?

Most people have an appreciation for modern art.

Americans are not quite the Philistines they are often accused of being. Most have enough appreciation of modern art to know that it is not just slapped on. Only 27 percent think a child could do as well as a modern painter. Sixty-two percent disagree with this notion.

The greatest gulf in opinions on this issue is by education. People with more education are more likely to disagree that modern art is just paint randomly slapped on a canvas. Fully 87 percent of people with a graduate degree disagree with this point of view as do 69 percent of those with a bachelor's degree and 60 percent of high school graduates. Among people who did not complete high school, however, only 47 percent disagree with the statement while 33 percent agree and 19 percent say they don't know.

Age also divides people on this question. Among people under age 60, 63 to 69 percent disagree that modern art is just slapped on. A smaller 51 percent of people in their sixties and only 46 percent of people aged 70 or older disagree.

Blacks and whites are more likely than people of "other" race to reject the idea that modern art is something a child could do. While 61 to 62 percent of blacks and whites say this notion is false, a smaller 54 percent of other races concur.

Is Modern Art Child's Play? 1998

"Modern painting is just slapped on; a child could do it. Do you agree or disagree?"

(percent of people aged 18 or older responding by sex, race, age, and education, 1998)

	strongly agree	agree	disagree	strongly disagree	don't know	agree, total	disagree, total
Total	**4%**	**23%**	**49%**	**13%**	**11%**	**27%**	**62%**
Men	4	22	50	13	11	26	63
Women	4	25	47	13	11	29	60
Black	3	18	52	9	19	21	61
White	4	24	49	13	9	28	62
Other	7	28	36	18	11	35	54
Aged 18 to 29	3	25	48	16	8	28	64
Aged 30 to 39	4	23	51	14	9	27	65
Aged 40 to 49	2	22	56	13	7	24	69
Aged 50 to 59	4	19	47	16	13	23	63
Aged 60 to 69	3	28	42	9	17	31	51
Aged 70 or older	11	27	39	7	17	38	46
Not a high school graduate	6	27	43	4	19	33	47
High school graduate	4	25	49	11	11	29	60
Bachelor's degree	4	21	48	21	6	25	69
Graduate degree	2	7	62	25	4	9	87

Source: General Social Survey, National Opinion Research Center, University of Chicago; calculations by the author

Artists Should Be Self-Supporting

The college educated are more skeptical of artists' ability to support themselves.

The majority of Americans (57 percent) believe truly excellent artists can support themselves through their art alone. One-third disagree, and 12 percent say they don't know.

Men are more likely than women to think artists should be able to support themselves (61 versus 52 percent).

Fifty-seven percent of whites and 54 percent of blacks say artists should be able to support themselves compared with 49 percent of "other" races. One-quarter of blacks disagree compared with one-third of whites and other races. Only 10 percent of whites, but 20 percent of blacks and 18 percent of other races, say they don't know.

Similar percentages of people in all age groups say artists should be able to support themselves (54 to 59 percent). People aged 70 or older are most likely to say they don't know, however.

The largest difference of opinion on this issue is by education. The college educated are more skeptical than those with less education about the ability of artists to support themselves. Only 39 percent of people with a graduate degree and 46 percent of those with a bachelor's degree believe artists should be able to support themselves with their art. In contrast, 58 to 61 percent of people with less education say artists should be self-supporting.

Artists Should Be Self-Supporting, 1998

"Artists and performers who are truly excellent will be able to support themselves by selling artworks or tickets to performances. Do you agree or disagree?"

(percent of people aged 18 or older responding by sex, race, age, and education, 1998)

	strongly agree	agree	disagree	strongly disagree	don't know	agree, total	disagree, total
Total	**8%**	**49%**	**27%**	**5%**	**12%**	**57%**	**32%**
Men	10	51	25	4	10	61	29
Women	6	46	28	5	14	52	33
Black	8	46	24	1	20	54	25
White	7	50	28	5	10	57	33
Other	10	39	24	9	18	49	33
Aged 18 to 29	9	46	29	5	11	55	34
Aged 30 to 39	8	49	26	5	13	57	31
Aged 40 to 49	9	47	30	4	10	56	34
Aged 50 to 59	6	50	28	4	12	56	32
Aged 60 to 69	5	49	31	6	·10	54	37
Aged 70 or older	5	54	17	6	18	59	23
Not a high school graduate	7	51	16	3	22	58	19
High school graduate	7	54	25	3	12	61	28
Bachelor's degree	7	39	36	12	6	46	48
Graduate degree	10	29	46	6	8	39	52

Source: General Social Survey, National Opinion Research Center, University of Chicago; calculations by the author

What Should Be the Aim of Art?

Most Americans say art does not have to be beautiful.

Although most people may prefer to look at art that they consider beautiful, they don't believe the primary aim of art should be the expression of beauty. Rather, most adults believe art should be a personal expression of the artist's thoughts and emotions. Three out of five Americans say works of art should express the artist's deepest thoughts and emotions, while only 38 percent believe art should celebrate the beauty of the world and the human spirit. There are disagreements, however, by demographics.

Men are more likely than women to think art should be a personal expression by the artist (68 versus 54 percent). While 61 to 62 percent of whites and "other" races believe art should be a personal expression, a smaller 50 percent of blacks agree.

The proportion of people believing art should be a personal expression of the artist falls with age. While three-quarters of people under age 30 say it should be, the figure drops to only 39 percent among people aged 70 or older. The majority of the oldest Americans say art should express what is most beautiful about the world and the human spirit.

Seven out of ten college graduates feel art should express the thoughts and emotions of the artist, but only 59 percent of people with a high school diploma and 48 percent of those who did not complete high school agree.

What Should Be the Aim of Art? 1998

"I'm going to read two statements about what works of art should do. Please tell me which statement comes closest to your opinion. Art works should celebrate what is most beautiful about the world and the human spirit. Art works should freely express the artist's deepest thoughts and emotions, good and bad."

(percent of people aged 18 or older responding by sex, race, age, and education, 1998)

	express beauty of world and human spirit	artist's personal expression
Total	**38%**	**60%**
Men	31	68
Women	44	54
Black	47	50
White	36	62
Other	39	61
Aged 18 to 29	23	75
Aged 30 to 39	35	64
Aged 40 to 49	39	60
Aged 50 to 59	42	57
Aged 60 to 69	47	50
Aged 70 or older	57	39
Not a high school graduate	50	48
High school graduate	39	59
Bachelor's degree	28	70
Graduate degree	26	72

Note: Numbers may not add to 100 because "don't know" is not shown.
Source: General Social Survey, National Opinion Research Center, University of Chicago; calculations by the author

2

Health and Medicine

The days of the kindly physician who made house calls and the relatively uninformed, compliant patient are long gone. Americans are increasingly knowledgeable consumers of health care. And they are not particularly pleased with many aspects of health and medicine in the U.S. today.

Americans dislike the idea that people may lack the health care they need simply because they can't afford it. Nearly half of Americans believe the federal government should be primarily responsible for making sure people have help paying their medical bills. About one-third think both individuals and government bear this responsibility.

Although physician-assisted suicide still provokes controversy, the majority of Americans favor allowing physicians to help the incurably ill end their lives. Americans are more likely to approve of physician-assisted suicide now than they were in 1978.

Most Americans say they are in good or excellent health. They are divided in their opinions of the medical system, however, as equal percentages of adults say they have a great deal of confidence and only some confidence in medicine.

People generally have good opinions about their physician, but they aren't as happy with health care leaders and health maintenance organizations. About half of adults think that HMOs help control costs, but fewer than one-quarter believe they improve the quality of care patients receive. Pluralities think HMOs take important medical decisions out of the hands of physicians and prevent people from getting the tests and care they need. But they are divided on whether HMOs undermine the trust between doctors and patients.

Although Americans are critical of HMOs, they are positive in the assessment of their own physician. Solid majorities trust their doctor's judgment and believe he or she puts their medical needs above all other considerations. Smaller majorities say they are not worried that their doctor will be prevented from telling them all their treatment options and that they will be denied the treatment or services they need.

Only half of Americans think doctors try not to worry patients and always treat their patients with respect. About half say they think doctors are not as thorough as they should be and do not always avoid unnecessary expenses. Americans are divided on whether or not doctors sometimes take unnecessary risks or cause worry by failing to explain medical problems. Fewer than half are confident that doctors won't recommend surgery unless it is absolutely necessary.

Women have more contact with the health care system than men do. Their greater familiarity may not have bred outright contempt, but it has influenced their opinion of the health-care system. Women are generally less positive than men in their assessments of physicians and HMOs and have less confidence in health care leaders. Women's lower opinion of the health care system may be one reason why they are less likely than men to support physician-assisted suicide.

Women are more likely than men to think HMOs limit the ability of doctors to make decisions, damage trust between doctors and patients, and prevent patients from getting needed care—including tests and mental-health services. They are also less likely than men to think HMOs help control costs and improve the quality of health care.

Majorities of women and men have good opinions about their physician. Women express more discontent on some issues, however. They are less likely than men to think doctors always treat their patients with respect and are as thorough as they should be. Women are also less likely to say they believe doctors recommend surgery only when no other option is available and more likely to think that doctors cause people to worry because they don't explain medical problems. Men are more likely to think doctors always do their best to keep the patient from worrying.

Men are more likely than women to say they rarely see the same doctor twice when they go for medical care. This difference occurs because men are more likely to wait to see a doctor until they have an acute health problem that needs immediate attention, limiting their ability to specify a particular physician.

The lower socioeconomic status of blacks is the major reason why they are most likely to say their health is only fair or poor. Whites are most likely to say they are in excellent health. Socioeconomic differences also influence opinions about who should be responsible for health care costs. Blacks and other races are much more likely than whites to believe the federal government should make sure people can pay their doctor and hospital bills. The percentage of blacks who say government should have primary responsibility is lower now than it was in 1978, however.

Whites are more likely than blacks and other races to say they don't worry that their doctor will put cost considerations above care. They are also most likely to trust their doctors to reveal treatment mistakes. But whites are not as impressed with the bedside manner of doctors. Whites are less likely than blacks and other races to believe doctors try not to worry patients and always treat patients with respect.

Whites and blacks are less likely than other races to think doctors recommend surgery only as a last resort. Blacks are less likely than whites and other races to think doctors need to be more thorough, but they are more likely to believe doctors sometimes take unnecessary risks.

Whites have a much lower opinion of HMOs than blacks and people of other races do, but blacks and other races are more likely than whites to say they don't know about the HMO issues examined here. Whites are much more likely to disagree that HMOs improve the quality of care and to believe they limit doctors and prevent patients from getting the care they need.

As people get older, their need for health care increases. But in the past two decades, the percentage of older people whose health is only fair or poor has declined as Americans have become more health conscious and as new treatments for the chronic and life-threatening diseases of aging have emerged.

Generational differences abound in opinions about health and medicine. Younger generations are more likely to support physician-assisted suicide, although majorities of all ages favor it. The younger people are the more likely they are to believe the government should be primarily responsible for ensuring that people can pay for health care. Older generations are more likely to think it should be up to the individual or the responsibility of both government and the individual.

Older generations are products of an era when patients did not second-guess their doctors. This attitude is one reason why the percentage of people who say they trust their doctor's judgment rises with age. Older generations are also more likely to believe profits are not a factor in health care decisions. The older people are the more likely they are to believe doctors avoid unnecessary expenses and to say they don't think their doctor considers cost over care. The percentage of those who say they don't worry about being denied treatment or that their doctor won't be allowed to tell them all the treatment options also rises with age.

The oldest Americans are most likely to think doctors try not to worry patients and always treat patients with respect. People in their forties and fifties are most likely to feel doctors do not always treat patients with respect and aren't as thorough as they should be.

They are most likely to think that doctors sometimes recommend surgery although there is another way. They are much more likely than other age groups to say HMOs make it difficult to see a specialist for mental or emotional problems and take important medical decisions out of the hands of physicians. People in their fifties are most likely to say HMOs limit necessary tests, and nearly half believe HMOs prevent people from getting the care they need. The majority of people in their fifties don't believe that HMOs improve the quality of health care. People aged 40 to 69 are most likely to say HMOs undermine trust between doctors and patients. Health care providers should be concerned about these negative assessments from the middle-aged. They are the leading edge of younger, more informed generations and they are just beginning to confront serious medical problems. As they do, they will demand more from the health care system.

Higher education increases the likelihood of being employed and having health insurance. Some of the differences of opinion by education are influenced by this fact. But people with more education are also more demanding consumers, and this attitude frequently creates conflicts between patients and health care providers.

College graduates are far more likely than people with less education to say they are in excellent health. People who did not complete high school, many of whom are older, are most likely to say they are in only fair or poor health.

People with more education also have a more negative view of medical care in the U.S. today, particularly HMOs. The more education people have, the more likely they are to say HMOs control costs. But the proportion of those who say they don't believe HMOs improve the quality of health care also increases with education. People with more education are more likely to think HMOs prevent people from getting the care they need, including mental health care. They are more likely to believe HMOs take important medical decisions out of the hands of physicians and that they undermine trust between doctors and patients.

The less education people have the more likely they are to think doctors always do their best to keep patients from worrying and always treat patients with respect. People who did not complete high school are most likely to trust their doctor to reveal any mistakes made in their treatment and to think doctors always avoid unnecessary expenses. More than half of people with at least a high school diploma disagree.

Confidence in the Leaders of Medicine

Fewer than half of Americans have a great deal of confidence in medical leaders.

Only 44 percent of Americans say they have a great deal of confidence in the leaders of medicine, whereas another 45 percent say they have only some confidence. While this is hardly a strong endorsement of the medical profession, people have even less confidence in government, education, business, labor, and most of the nation's other important institutions. The percentage of people saying they have a great deal of confidence in medical leaders is not much different from what it was in 1978, but it is lower than the 51 percent who expressed a great deal of confidence in 1988.

Women have more contact with the health care system than men, but this has not boosted their confidence. In fact, women are less likely than men to say they have a great deal of confidence in medical leaders (40 versus 49 percent). Ten percent of women have hardly any confidence in the medical establishment.

People aged 40 to 69 are less likely than those older or younger to have a great deal of confidence in medical leaders. The percentage of people under age 30 who have a great deal of confidence fell from 53 percent in 1978 to 49 percent in 1998. Forty-five percent of people in their forties had a great deal of confidence in medicine in 1978, but the figure had dropped to 40 percent by 1998. Among people in their sixties, however, the proportion of those who have a great deal of confidence rose from 35 to 41 percent during those years.

In 1978, 42 percent of people who did not complete high school said they had a great deal of confidence in medical leaders, but by 1998 the figure had risen to 49 percent. The proportion of people with a bachelor's degree who feel a great deal of confidence rose from 43 to 52 percent during those years. Among high school graduates, the proportion of adults who feel confident fell from 50 to 41 percent between 1978 and 1998. Fourteen percent of people who did not complete high school have hardly any confidence in medicine compared with 5 to 9 percent of people with more education.

Confidence in the Leaders of Medicine, 1998

"As far as the people running medicine are concerned, would you say you have a great deal of confidence, only some confidence, or hardly any confidence at all in them?"

(percent of people aged 18 or older responding by sex, race, age, and education, 1998)

	great deal	only some	hardly any
Total	**44%**	**45%**	**9%**
Men	49	42	7
Women	40	48	10
Black	44	44	11
White	44	46	8
Other	44	45	10
Aged 18 to 29	49	41	8
Aged 30 to 39	46	45	8
Aged 40 to 49	40	50	9
Aged 50 to 59	41	49	9
Aged 60 to 69	41	49	9
Aged 70 or older	46	40	11
Not a high school graduate	49	34	14
High school graduate	41	48	9
Bachelor's degree	52	42	5
Graduate degree	45	47	8

Note: Numbers may not add to 100 because "don't know" is not shown.
Source: General Social Survey, National Opinion Research Center, University of Chicago; calculations by the author

Confidence in the Leaders of Medicine, 1978 to 1998

"As far as people running medicine are concerned, would you say you have a great deal of confidence, only some confidence, or hardly any confidence at all in them?"

(percent of people aged 18 or older responding by sex, race, age, and education, 1978–98)

	a great deal			only some			hardly any		
	1998	1988	1978	1998	1988	1978	1998	1988	1978
Total	**44%**	**51%**	**46%**	**45%**	**42%**	**44%**	**9%**	**6%**	**9%**
Men	49	55	47	42	38	44	7	6	9
Women	40	48	45	48	45	44	10	6	9
Black	44	55	45	44	40	47	11	4	8
White	44	51	46	46	42	44	8	6	9
Aged 18 to 29	49	61	53	41	34	41	8	3	6
Aged 30 to 39	46	49	48	45	44	43	8	6	8
Aged 40 to 49	40	51	45	50	43	48	9	5	7
Aged 50 to 59	41	46	41	49	49	47	9	6	11
Aged 60 to 69	41	44	35	49	47	50	9	8	13
Aged 70 or older	46	49	43	40	40	39	11	9	15
Not a high school graduate	49	52	42	34	39	42	14	8	15
High school graduate	41	49	50	48	44	43	9	6	7
Bachelor's degree	52	53	43	42	45	51	5	2	6
Graduate degree	45	59	44	47	37	52	8	4	5

Note: Numbers may not add to 100 because "don't know" is not shown.
Source: General Social Survey, National Opinion Research Center, University of Chicago; calculations by the author

Whose Responsibility Are Health Care Costs?

Few people think government has no role in paying for health care.

Forty-seven percent of Americans think government should be primarily responsible for making sure people can pay their health care bills. About one-third believe it is the combined responsibility of government and the individual. Only 18 percent think government has little or no role in paying for health care. In 1975, Americans were slightly more likely to say it should be left up to the individual (21 percent).

In 1975, men were more likely than women to place responsibility with the government. By 1998, however, this correlation was reversed, as 49 percent of women said government should be responsible compared with 44 percent of men.

Blacks are more likely than whites to say government should have the most responsibility, but the gap is smaller than it was in 1975. In that year, 69 percent of blacks and 46 percent of whites assigned government the most responsibility. In 1998, however, a smaller 59 percent of blacks felt this way compared with 44 percent of whites. Twenty percent of whites, but only 10 percent of blacks, think it should be the individual's responsibility.

Older Americans are less likely than younger people to believe government should be primarily responsible for making sure people can pay for health care. This result is an interesting twist, since people aged 65 or older are almost universally covered by the government's largest health care program, Medicare. More than half of people under age 30 and 47 to 49 percent of those aged 40 to 59 take the position that the government should pay, but a much smaller 35 to 37 percent of people aged 60 or older agree. In 1975, a larger 48 to 51 percent of people aged 60 or older thought government should be primarily responsible for health care.

People who did not complete high school are least likely to believe the individual should have primary responsibility for paying health care costs. Only 13 percent feel this way compared with 19 to 21 percent of people with more education.

Whose Responsibility Are Health Care Costs? 1998

"In general, some people think that it is the responsibility of the government in Washington to see to it that people have help in paying for doctors and hospital bills. Others think that these matters are not the responsibility of the federal government and that people should take care of these things themselves. Where would you place yourself on a scale of 1 to 5 or haven't you made up your mind on this?"

(percent of people aged 18 or older responding by sex, race, age, and education, 1998)

	government 1	2	agree with both 3	4	take care of self 5
Total	25%	22%	32%	10%	8%
Men	22	22	32	11	11
Women	27	22	32	9	6
Black	37	22	28	5	5
White	22	22	33	11	9
Other	30	22	25	8	9
Aged 18 to 29	27	27	29	9	4
Aged 30 to 39	23	27	31	10	6
Aged 40 to 49	26	23	28	12	9
Aged 50 to 59	26	21	31	7	11
Aged 60 to 69	20	15	41	11	12
Aged 70 or older	25	12	40	8	12
Not a high school graduate	33	15	33	4	9
High school graduate	24	23	32	10	9
Bachelor's degree	20	26	32	13	7
Graduate degree	24	26	28	14	7

Note: Numbers may not add to 100 because "don't know" is not shown.
Source: General Social Survey, National Opinion Research Center, University of Chicago; calculations by the author

Whose Responsibility Are Health Care Costs? 1975 to 1998

"In general, some people think that it is the responsibility of the government in Washington to see to it that people have help in paying for doctors and hospital bills. Others think that these matters are not the responsibility of the federal government and that people should take care of these things themselves. Where would you place yourself on a scale of 1 to 5 or haven't you made up your mind on this?"

(percent of people aged 18 or older responding by sex, race, age, and education, 1975–98)

	government (1 and 2)			agree with both (3)			take care of self (4 and 5)		
	1998	*1988*	*1975*	*1998*	*1988*	*1975*	*1998*	*1988*	*1975*
Total	**47%**	**48%**	**49%**	**32%**	**35%**	**29%**	**18%**	**15%**	**21%**
Men	44	47	51	32	33	26	22	18	21
Women	49	49	46	32	36	30	15	13	21
Black	59	74	69	28	19	22	10	4	7
White	44	44	46	33	37	29	20	17	23
Aged 18 to 29	54	49	56	29	36	25	13	13	16
Aged 30 to 39	50	55	52	31	29	25	16	15	22
Aged 40 to 49	49	47	40	28	37	34	21	14	23
Aged 50 to 59	47	51	39	31	28	33	18	18	26
Aged 60 to 69	35	41	48	41	41	28	23	13	23
Aged 70 or older	37	43	51	40	37	29	20	18	16
Not a high school graduate	48	50	53	33	35	28	13	12	15
High school graduate	47	46	44	32	35	29	19	16	25
Bachelor's degree	46	50	46	32	32	29	20	17	24
Graduate degree	50	47	52	28	33	20	21	20	24

Note: Numbers may not add to 100 because "don't know" is not shown.
Source: General Social Survey, National Opinion Research Center, University of Chicago; calculations by the author

Physician-Assisted Suicide

Support for physician-assisted suicide for the terminally ill has grown.

Support for allowing the incurably ill to hasten the end of their lives has grown over the past few decades. The majority of Americans (68 percent) favor giving the incurably ill the option of having a doctor end their lives. This is a larger majority than the 58 percent who favored it in 1978.

Women, blacks, the elderly, and people who did not complete high school are not as willing as others to allow doctors to end the life of a terminally ill patient. Seventy-three percent of men, but a smaller 63 percent of women, support physician-assisted suicide. Both men and women are more likely to favor the measure than they were in 1978, however.

Only 51 percent of blacks believe physicians should be allowed to help the terminally ill end their lives, compared with 70 percent of whites and 66 percent of "other" races. Historical experiences, such as the Tuskegee Syphilis Experiment—in which blacks with syphilis were left untreated so physicians could observe the progression of the disease— have left many blacks suspicious that practices such as physician-assisted suicide will be used against them.

Among people aged 60 or older, 58 to 59 percent support physician-assisted suicide compared with 67 to 73 percent of other age groups. With the exception of Americans in their sixties, support grew within all age groups between 1978 and 1998.

People who did not complete high school (a group in which older Americans are over-represented) are less likely than those with more education to believe doctors should be able to help the terminally ill end their lives. While 67 percent of high school graduates and 71 percent of college graduates support it, a smaller 60 percent of the least educated agree.

Physician-Assisted Suicide, 1998

"When a person has a disease that cannot be cured, do you think doctors should be allowed by law to end the patient's life by some painless means if the patient and his family request it?"

(percent of people aged 18 or older responding by sex, race, age, and education, 1998)

	yes	no	don't know
Total	**68%**	**27%**	**6%**
Men	73	23	4
Women	63	30	7
Black	51	44	5
White	70	24	6
Other	66	27	7
Aged 18 to 29	73	22	5
Aged 30 to 39	69	25	6
Aged 40 to 49	67	28	5
Aged 50 to 59	72	22	6
Aged 60 to 69	58	36	6
Aged 70 or older	59	34	7
Not a high school graduate	60	34	6
High school graduate	67	26	6
Bachelor's degree	71	23	6
Graduate degree	71	25	4

Source: General Social Survey, National Opinion Research Center, University of Chicago; calculations by the author

Physician-Assisted Suicide, 1978 to 1998

"When a person has a disease that cannot be cured, do you think doctors should be allowed by law to end the patient's life by some painless means if the patient and his family request it?"

(percent of people aged 18 or older responding by sex, race, age, and education, 1978–98)

	yes			no		
	1998	**1988**	**1978**	**1998**	**1988**	**1978**
Total	**68%**	**66%**	**58%**	**27%**	**29%**	**38%**
Men	73	70	62	23	25	35
Women	63	62	55	30	33	41
Black	51	47	44	44	47	54
White	70	68	59	24	27	36
Aged 18 to 29	73	73	69	22	23	28
Aged 30 to 39	69	70	62	25	24	35
Aged 40 to 49	67	65	51	28	33	47
Aged 50 to 59	72	62	46	22	32	46
Aged 60 to 69	58	58	59	36	36	37
Aged 70 or older	59	57	45	34	36	49
Not a high school graduate	60	58	50	34	37	45
High school graduate	67	69	59	26	27	37
Bachelor's degree	71	67	66	23	26	30
Graduate degree	71	70	71	25	23	26

Note: Numbers may not add to 100 because "don't know" is not shown.
Source: General Social Survey, National Opinion Research Center, University of Chicago; calculations by the author

Health Status

Most Americans say they are in good or excellent health.

The large majority of Americans (79 percent) rate their health as excellent or good. The plurality of 48 percent rate their health as good, while 31 percent say it is excellent. Since 1977, the percentage of people who say their health is good or excellent has grown despite the continued aging of the population.

Whites are more likely than blacks or "other" races to say they are in excellent health (33 percent compared with 24 percent of blacks and 26 percent of other races). About one-fifth of blacks say their health is only fair compared with 16 percent of whites. Both blacks and whites were less likely to say their health was only fair or poor in 1998 than in 1977.

As one would expect, the percentage of people rating their health as excellent declines with age. Among people under age 40, 37 to 39 percent consider themselves to be in excellent health. A smaller 31 percent of people aged 40 to 59 think their health is excellent. Among people in their sixties, only 22 percent rate their health as excellent. The figure falls to 15 percent among people aged 70 or older. Significantly, however, the proportion of people aged 60 or older who say their health is only fair or poor declined between 1977 and 1998.

The college educated are far more likely than those with less education to say they are in excellent health (45 to 46 percent compared with 28 percent of high school graduates and 13 percent of people with less education). People with lower levels of education generally have lower incomes and less access to health care than those with more education. In addition, many less educated Americans are older people with age-related health problems.

Health Status, 1998

"Would you say your own health, in general, is excellent, good, fair, or poor?"

(percent of people aged 18 or older responding by sex, race, age, and education, 1998)

	excellent	good	fair	poor
Total	**31%**	**48%**	**17%**	**5%**
Men	31	48	17	4
Women	31	48	16	5
Black	24	48	21	7
White	33	47	16	4
Other	26	51	16	6
Aged 18 to 29	39	47	13	1
Aged 30 to 39	37	51	12	1
Aged 40 to 49	31	49	16	3
Aged 50 to 59	31	44	17	8
Aged 60 to 69	22	46	23	9
Aged 70 or older	15	46	26	13
Not a high school graduate	13	43	30	13
High school graduate	28	51	18	4
Bachelor's degree	46	45	6	2
Graduate degree	45	41	11	2

Note: Numbers may not add to 100 because "don't know" is not shown.
Source: General Social Survey, National Opinion Research Center, University of Chicago; calculations by the author

Health Status, 1977 to 1998

"Would you say your own health, in general, is excellent, good, fair, or poor?"

(percent of people aged 18 or older responding by sex, race, age, and education, 1977–98)

	excellent			good			fair			poor		
	1998	1988	1977	1998	1988	1977	1998	1988	1977	1998	1988	1977
Total	31%	31%	32%	48%	45%	41%	17%	18%	20%	5%	6%	7%
Men	31	35	32	48	47	42	17	15	20	4	3	7
Women	31	28	32	48	44	40	16	20	21	5	9	7
Black	24	26	27	48	44	37	21	21	25	7	9	11
White	33	32	32	47	45	42	16	17	20	4	6	6
Aged 18 to 29	39	36	40	47	50	44	13	13	13	1	1	2
Aged 30 to 39	37	41	43	51	48	44	12	10	12	1	1	2
Aged 40 to 49	31	32	32	49	51	45	16	13	16	3	4	6
Aged 50 to 59	31	26	25	44	39	41	17	25	27	8	9	8
Aged 60 to 69	22	26	19	46	36	29	23	28	35	9	11	17
Aged 70 or older	15	13	17	46	37	34	26	30	33	13	20	16
Not a high school graduate	13	15	19	43	40	36	30	29	31	13	16	14
High school graduate	28	29	35	51	50	45	18	17	16	4	4	3
Bachelor's degree	46	53	56	45	40	32	6	6	10	2	1	2
Graduate degree	45	62	41	41	34	45	11	3	11	2	2	3

Note: Numbers may not add to 100 because "don't know" is not shown.
Source: General Social Survey, National Opinion Research Center, University of Chicago; calculations by the author

HMOs Help Control Costs

Almost half of Americans agree that HMOs keep health care costs down.

Many health care consumers are unhappy with health maintenance organizations, but nearly half (48 percent) agree that HMOs help control health care costs. Only 22 percent disagree, while 15 percent say they don't know.

Among men, 52 percent believe HMOs control costs, but among women a smaller 46 percent agree. Women are more likely to say they don't know. Whites are most likely to say they do not think HMOs help control costs. Twenty-three percent of whites disagree with that premise compared with 19 percent of blacks and 16 percent of "other" races.

The middle-aged are most likely to think HMOs control costs. More than half of people in their forties and fifties believe HMOs control costs compared with 49 percent of people under age 40 and 43 percent of those in their sixties. Only 34 percent of people aged 70 or older agree, while 31 percent of this age group say they don't know.

College graduates are considerably more likely than those with less education to credit HMOs with controlling costs. More than 60 percent of college graduates think this claim is true compared with 46 percent of high school graduates and only 37 percent of those with less education. One-third of the least educated say they don't know.

HMOs Help Control Costs, 1998

"Health Maintenance Organizations (HMOs) help to control costs.
How much do you agree or disagree?"

(percent of people aged 18 or older responding by sex, race, age, and education, 1998)

	strongly agree	agree	neither	disagree	strongly disagree	don't know	agree, total	disagree, total
Total	**6%**	**42%**	**15%**	**18%**	**4%**	**15%**	**48%**	**22%**
Men	7	45	14	19	3	12	52	22
Women	5	41	15	18	4	17	46	22
Black	4	41	19	15	4	17	45	19
White	6	43	14	19	4	14	49	23
Other	9	40	10	15	1	24	49	16
Aged 18 to 29	5	44	18	14	3	16	49	17
Aged 30 to 39	7	42	19	18	3	11	49	21
Aged 40 to 49	9	47	11	19	6	8	56	25
Aged 50 to 59	7	44	15	19	3	12	51	22
Aged 60 to 69	3	40	13	19	3	20	43	22
Aged 70 or older	2	32	8	22	4	31	34	26
Not a high school graduate	6	31	12	16	3	32	37	19
High school graduate	6	40	15	20	5	15	46	25
Bachelor's degree	8	52	16	17	2	6	60	19
Graduate degree	8	55	16	11	4	5	63	15

Note: Numbers may not add to 100 because "don't know" is not shown.
Source: General Social Survey, National Opinion Research Center, University of Chicago; calculations by the author

Do HMOs Damage Doctor-Patient Trust?

Americans are not sure if trust between doctors and patients suffers in HMOs.

Americans are divided on whether HMOs damage the trust between doctors and patients, with 36 percent saying they agree that they do and 30 percent saying they do not. The remainder neither agree nor disagree or say they don't know.

Women are slightly more likely to think the doctor-patient relationship suffers because of HMOs, while men are slightly more likely to say it does not. There is a larger difference of opinion by race. While 39 percent of whites believe HMOs damage trust between doctors and patients, a smaller 25 to 26 percent of blacks and "other" races agree.

Between 43 and 47 percent of people aged 40 to 69 feel that HMOs damage doctor-patient trust. Only one-third of people in their thirties and those aged 70 or older agree. Adults under age 30 are least likely to feel this way, and only 24 percent agree.

Only 29 percent of people who did not complete high school think HMOs damage trust between doctors and patients, and the same percentage think they do not. Thirty percent say they don't know. A larger 37 to 38 percent of high school graduates and people with a bachelor's degree believe HMOs damage doctor-patient trust. People with a graduate degree are most likely to believe they do (42 percent).

Do HMOs Damage Doctor-Patient Trust? 1998

"Health Maintenance Organizations (HMOs) damage the trust between doctors and patients. How much do you agree or disagree?"

(percent of people aged 18 or older responding by sex, race, age, and education, 1998)

	strongly agree	agree	neither	disagree	strongly disagree	don't know	agree, total	disagree, total
Total	**9%**	**27%**	**19%**	**27%**	**3%**	**13%**	**36%**	**30%**
Men	8	26	21	29	4	12	34	33
Women	10	28	18	26	2	15	38	28
Black	4	22	20	31	4	17	26	35
White	10	29	20	26	3	12	39	29
Other	7	18	17	29	7	22	25	36
Aged 18 to 29	4	20	24	33	4	15	24	37
Aged 30 to 39	8	25	22	30	3	11	33	33
Aged 40 to 49	12	31	19	27	4	7	43	31
Aged 50 to 59	14	32	18	25	3	8	46	28
Aged 60 to 69	14	33	17	16	2	18	47	18
Aged 70 or older	6	27	12	25	1	29	33	26
Not a high school graduate	8	21	13	24	5	30	29	29
High school graduate	10	28	20	27	2	14	38	29
Bachelor's degree	8	29	23	31	3	6	37	34
Graduate degree	13	29	29	21	4	4	42	25

Note: Numbers may not add to 100 because "don't know" is not shown.
Source: General Social Survey, National Opinion Research Center, University of Chicago; calculations by the author

HMOs Deny Needed Care and Limit Necessary Tests

The plurality thinks HMOs keep people from getting the tests and treatments they need.

About two in five people think health maintenance organizations prevent people from getting the care they need and prevent doctors from prescribing tests necessary for treatment. Only 24 percent think HMOs do not limit tests and just 29 percent think they do not deny needed care.

More women than men agree that HMOs limit tests and deny care. Women are more likely than men to have had treatments and tests denied because they have more contact with the health care system.

More than 40 percent of whites think HMOs deny needed care and limit tests. In contrast, only 27 percent of blacks and 29 percent of "other" races think HMOs deny necessary care. Twenty-nine percent of blacks and 33 percent of other races agree that HMOs prevent doctors from prescribing necessary tests. Blacks and people of other races are considerably more likely than whites to say they don't know whether HMOs limit tests and treatments.

There are large differences of opinion on these issues by education. College graduates are most likely to believe HMOs prevent people from getting the care they need and prevent doctors from ordering necessary tests. Although fewer high school graduates agree, the plurality of them believes HMOs limit tests and care. People who did not graduate from high school are least likely to agree, but roughly equal numbers say they agree, disagree, or don't know.

HMOs Deny Needed Care, 1998

"Health Maintenance Organizations (HMOs) prevent people from getting the care they need. How much do you agree or disagree?"

(percent of people aged 18 or older responding by sex, race, age, and education, 1998)

	strongly agree	agree	neither	disagree	strongly disagree	don't know	agree, total	disagree, total
Total	9%	31%	17%	26%	3%	14%	40%	29%
Men	6	28	21	30	3	12	34	33
Women	10	33	15	24	3	15	43	27
Black	4	23	21	30	4	18	27	34
White	9	33	16	26	3	12	42	29
Other	7	22	20	21	9	22	29	30
Aged 18 to 29	5	23	25	30	4	15	28	34
Aged 30 to 39	7	34	20	25	4	10	41	29
Aged 40 to 49	10	34	15	30	4	7	44	34
Aged 50 to 59	12	36	16	22	3	11	48	25
Aged 60 to 69	14	29	15	23	1	18	43	24
Aged 70 or older	7	27	9	25	3	29	34	28
Not a high school graduate	6	23	12	24	5	30	29	29
High school graduate	10	29	17	27	4	13	39	31
Bachelor's degree	7	36	20	28	2	7	43	30
Graduate degree	10	39	24	21	2	4	49	23

Note: Numbers may not add to 100 because "don't know" is not shown.
Source: General Social Survey, National Opinion Research Center, University of Chicago; calculations by the author

HMOs Limit Necessary Tests, 1998

"Health Maintenance Organizations (HMOs) prevent doctors from prescribing tests necessary for treatment. How much do you agree or disagree?"

(percent of people aged 18 or older responding by sex, race, age, and education, 1998)

	strongly agree	agree	neither	disagree	strongly disagree	don't know	agree, total	disagree, total
Total	**9%**	**33%**	**18%**	**22%**	**2%**	**16%**	**42%**	**24%**
Men	8	31	21	24	2	15	39	26
Women	10	34	15	21	3	17	44	24
Black	5	24	18	30	2	21	29	32
White	10	35	17	21	2	15	45	23
Other	10	23	26	13	2	25	33	15
Aged 18 to 29	6	27	25	23	2	16	33	25
Aged 30 to 39	8	35	19	22	3	13	43	25
Aged 40 to 49	14	33	16	26	2	9	47	28
Aged 50 to 59	11	45	13	18	1	13	56	19
Aged 60 to 69	13	32	18	14	2	22	45	16
Aged 70 or older	5	26	11	22	3	32	31	25
Not a high school graduate	7	22	17	21	2	32	29	23
High school graduate	9	31	18	22	2	17	40	24
Bachelor's degree	10	40	20	20	2	8	50	22
Graduate degree	14	45	16	19	3	4	59	22

Note: Numbers may not add to 100 because "don't know" is not shown.
Source: General Social Survey, National Opinion Research Center, University of Chicago; calculations by the author

HMOs Do Not Improve Quality of Care

Two in five adults do not believe HMOs improve health care.

Only 23 percent of Americans think health maintenance organizations improve the quality of care. Forty-one percent disagree. Nearly one-quarter neither agree nor disagree.

Forty-four percent of women, but only 37 percent of men, do not believe HMOs make health care better. Only 20 percent of women and 24 percent of men believe they do.

Blacks are more likely than whites and "other" races to think HMOs improve care (31 percent versus 20 percent of whites and 26 percent of other races). Whites are most likely to disagree. Forty-five percent of whites say HMOs do not improve the quality of health care compared with 27 percent of blacks and 24 percent of other races.

Young adults, who generally have less contact with the health care system than the population at large, are most likely to believe HMOs improve care. One-third of people under age 30 think HMOs improve the quality of health care. In contrast, 25 percent or fewer of older people agree. More than half of people in their fifties say they don't believe that HMOs improve the quality of care.

The percentage of people who disagree that HMOs make health care better rises with education, from only 28 percent among the least educated to 56 percent among the most educated. People who did not complete high school are most likely to say they don't know if HMOs improve health care.

HMOs Do Not Improve Quality of Care, 1998

"Health Maintenance Organizations (HMOs) improve the quality of care. How much do you agree or disagree?"

(percent of people aged 18 or older responding by sex, race, age, and education, 1998)

	strongly agree	agree	neither	disagree	strongly disagree	don't know	agree, total	disagree, total
Total	**3%**	**20%**	**23%**	**29%**	**12%**	**13%**	**23%**	**41%**
Men	3	21	26	29	8	12	24	37
Women	2	18	22	29	15	14	20	44
Black	5	26	24	20	7	18	31	27
White	2	18	23	32	13	12	20	45
Other	3	23	29	18	6	21	26	24
Aged 18 to 29	4	29	29	18	5	14	33	23
Aged 30 to 39	2	18	26	31	12	10	20	43
Aged 40 to 49	3	22	21	32	14	7	25	46
Aged 50 to 59	2	13	18	37	19	11	15	56
Aged 60 to 69	3	19	24	25	13	16	22	38
Aged 70 or older	2	13	20	28	10	28	15	38
Not a high school graduate	4	23	17	21	7	29	27	28
High school graduate	2	20	24	28	11	14	22	39
Bachelor's degree	1	20	25	34	14	6	21	48
Graduate degree	3	9	29	33	23	3	12	56

Note: Numbers may not add to 100 because "don't know" is not shown.
Source: General Social Survey, National Opinion Research Center, University of Chicago; calculations by the author

HMOs Limit Doctors' Decision Making

Americans worry that HMOs don't let doctors decide the best treatment for patients.

People worry that doctors in health maintenance organizations don't have the freedom to decide which treatment is best for patients. Nearly half of Americans (46 percent) agree that HMOs take important medical decisions out of the hands of physicians. Only 22 percent disagree, while 16 percent neither agree nor disagree and 15 percent say they don't know.

Women are slightly more likely than men to believe HMOs limit doctors' decision making (48 versus 43 percent). More substantial differences exist by race. While 49 percent of whites believe HMOs take away the autonomy of physicians, only 34 percent of blacks and 37 percent of "other" races agree.

More than half of people aged 40 to 59 believe HMOs take medical decisions out of the hands of physicians. Forty-five percent of people in their thirties and 47 percent of those in their sixties agree. In contrast, only 38 percent of people under age 30 think doctors' hands are tied by HMOs.

Education makes the biggest difference in opinion on this issue. Only one-third of people who did not complete high school think HMOs limit doctors' decision making, but the proportion rises to 61 percent among people with a graduate degree. However, those with the least education do not necessarily disagree—one-third say they don't know.

HMOs Limit Doctors' Decision Making, 1998

"Health Maintenance Organizations (HMOs) take important medical decisions out of the hands of physicians. How much do you agree or disagree?"

(percent of people aged 18 or older responding by sex, race, age, and education, 1998)

	strongly agree	agree	neither	disagree	strongly disagree	don't know	agree, total	disagree, total
Total	**13%**	**33%**	**16%**	**20%**	**2%**	**15%**	**46%**	**22%**
Men	11	32	18	23	3	14	43	26
Women	14	34	14	19	2	17	48	21
Black	6	28	16	26	3	20	34	29
White	14	35	15	19	2	14	49	21
Other	15	22	20	18	1	24	37	19
Aged 18 to 29	7	31	20	23	3	16	38	26
Aged 30 to 39	13	32	20	21	2	12	45	23
Aged 40 to 49	16	38	14	21	3	8	54	24
Aged 50 to 59	20	34	12	21	2	12	54	23
Aged 60 to 69	16	31	18	12	3	20	47	15
Aged 70 or older	7	33	7	19	1	33	40	20
Not a high school graduate	7	26	13	18	4	33	33	22
High school graduate	14	33	15	21	2	16	47	23
Bachelor's degree	13	36	20	23	2	7	49	25
Graduate degree	20	41	18	18	1	3	61	19

Note: Numbers may not add to 100 because "don't know" is not shown.
Source: General Social Survey, National Opinion Research Center, University of Chicago; calculations by the author

HMOs Limit Mental Health Care

Nearly half of Americans think HMOs make it more difficult to get mental health care.

Traditionally, health insurance plans have offered minimal coverage, if any, for mental health care. Health maintenance organizations have not improved on this record, according to about half of Americans. Only 19 percent say they disagree that HMOs make it more difficult to see a specialist for mental health problems.

Fifty-one percent of women think HMOs make it more difficult to get mental health care. A smaller 43 percent of men agree. Half of whites think HMOs limit mental health care compared with 41 percent of blacks and "other" races. Nearly one-quarter of blacks disagree, however, compared with 18 to 19 percent of whites and other races. People of other race are most likely to say they don't know.

The proportion of people who think HMOs limit mental health care rises with education. Only 33 percent of people who did not complete high school think HMOs make it more difficult to get treatment for mental health problems. But among people with a graduate degree, 62 percent feel this way. People with less education are considerably more likely to say they don't know.

HMOs Limit Mental Health Care, 1998

"HMOs make it more difficult to see a specialist for problems like emotional, nervous, and mental health problems. How much do you agree or disagree?"

(percent of people aged 18 or older responding by sex, race, age, and education, 1998)

	strongly agree	agree	neither	disagree	strongly disagree	don't know	agree, total	disagree, total
Total	**14%**	**34%**	**14%**	**17%**	**2%**	**18%**	**48%**	**19%**
Men	12	31	17	20	2	18	43	22
Women	15	36	13	15	2	19	51	17
Black	11	30	15	21	3	19	41	24
White	15	35	14	16	2	18	50	18
Other	13	28	15	18	1	25	41	19
Aged 18 to 29	9	32	20	19	3	18	41	22
Aged 30 to 39	14	33	16	20	1	16	47	21
Aged 40 to 49	19	41	11	14	3	12	60	17
Aged 50 to 59	18	35	12	19	1	14	53	20
Aged 60 to 69	16	31	16	11	2	25	47	13
Aged 70 or older	7	28	10	16	3	35	35	19
Not a high school graduate	7	26	13	17	3	34	33	20
High school graduate	14	33	14	17	2	20	47	19
Bachelor's degree	15	41	15	18	1	10	56	19
Graduate degree	25	37	16	14	1	6	62	15

Note: Numbers may not add to 100 because "don't know" is not shown.
Source: General Social Survey, National Opinion Research Center, University of Chicago; calculations by the author

Concern That Necessary Treatment Will Be Denied

Retirees are most likely to have health insurance and least likely to worry about being denied treatment.

As health care companies try to contain costs, stories of people who were injured or died because they were denied treatment occasionally surface in the media. Most Americans, however, are not worried that they will be denied the treatment or services they need. Sixty-two percent do not worry about this, while about one-quarter say they are concerned and another 13 percent are uncertain.

There is little difference of opinion between men and women on this issue. Whites are slightly more likely than blacks and "other" races to say they worry about not getting treatment, while people of other race are less likely than blacks and whites to say they are not worried.

Older Americans have more faith in the health care system than younger people do. They are also the ones most likely to have health insurance, thanks to Medicare. Only 11 percent of people aged 70 or older and 18 percent of those in their sixties worry that they won't get needed treatment compared with 23 to 29 percent of younger people.

Concern That Necessary Treatment Will Be Denied, 1998

"I worry that I will be denied the treatment or services I need. Do you agree or disagree?"

(percent of people aged 18 or older responding by sex, race, age, and education, 1998)

	strongly agree	agree	uncertain	disagree	strongly disagree	agree, total	disagree, total
Total	4%	19%	13%	53%	9%	23%	62%
Men	4	17	13	55	8	21	63
Women	4	20	13	52	9	24	61
Black	4	17	13	60	5	21	65
White	4	20	13	53	9	24	62
Other	6	16	21	42	9	22	51
Aged 18 to 29	4	25	15	50	4	29	54
Aged 30 to 39	4	19	17	50	7	23	57
Aged 40 to 49	6	21	12	52	9	27	61
Aged 50 to 59	5	21	10	56	8	26	64
Aged 60 to 69	3	15	15	54	13	18	67
Aged 70 or older	3	8	9	63	14	11	77
Not a high school graduate	9	16	13	48	9	25	57
High school graduate	3	19	15	54	7	22	61
Bachelor's degree	3	18	10	58	11	21	69
Graduate degree	5	20	12	46	15	25	61

Note: Numbers may not add to 100 because "don't know" is not shown.
Source: General Social Survey, National Opinion Research Center, University of Chicago; calculations by the author

Rarely See Same Doctor Twice

Three-quarters of Americans say this is not their experience.

The solo practitioner is nearly extinct in America. Most doctors now practice in groups, saving money on office space, support staff, and equipment. But for patients, this development can mean they see different doctors each time they seek medical care. So far, however, few patients believe they are passed around from doctor to doctor. Only 19 percent agree that they rarely see the same doctor twice, while three-quarters of Americans disagree with that statement.

Nearly one-quarter of men say they rarely see the same doctor twice compared with only 15 percent of women. One reason for this discrepancy may be that men tend to postpone seeking medical care until they have an urgent problem, thus reducing the likelihood that they will be able to see their usual physician.

This is also the case with younger adults, who don't normally schedule regular appointments for checkups. Twenty-seven percent of people under age 30 and 21 to 22 percent of those aged 30 to 49 say they rarely see the same doctor twice. The proportion drops to 15 percent among people in their fifties, to 11 percent among those in their sixties, and to only 5 percent among people aged 70 or older.

There is also a relationship between education and the likelihood of seeing the same physician on consecutive visits. While 22 percent of people who did not complete high school rarely see the same doctor twice, the proportion falls to only 9 percent among those with a graduate degree. Finances may play a role here. People with more money are better able to afford the services of smaller practices and specialists.

Rarely See Same Doctor Twice, 1998

"I hardly ever see the same doctor when I go for medical care. Do you agree or disagree?"

(percent of people aged 18 or older responding by sex, race, age, and education, 1998)

	strongly agree	agree	uncertain	disagree	strongly disagree	agree, total	disagree, total
Total	**3%**	**16%**	**4%**	**57%**	**18%**	**19%**	**75%**
Men	4	19	6	55	14	23	69
Women	2	13	3	58	22	15	80
Black	3	20	4	59	12	23	71
White	3	14	4	57	20	17	77
Other	5	21	12	49	13	26	62
Aged 18 to 29	3	24	5	53	10	27	63
Aged 30 to 39	3	18	7	54	15	21	69
Aged 40 to 49	4	18	3	54	19	22	73
Aged 50 to 59	2	13	4	59	22	15	81
Aged 60 to 69	4	7	2	59	26	11	85
Aged 70 or older	1	4	2	66	25	5	91
Not a high school graduate	4	18	5	55	16	22	71
High school graduate	3	16	4	58	17	19	75
Bachelor's degree	2	14	6	54	23	16	77
Graduate degree	3	6	6	57	25	9	82

Note: Numbers may not add to 100 because "don't know" is not shown.
Source: General Social Survey, National Opinion Research Center, University of Chicago; calculations by the author

Trust Doctor's Judgment

The overwhelming majority trust their doctor's judgment.

Americans are more critical than ever about the nation's health care system, but they have not lost faith in their physicians. Four in five adults trust their doctor's judgment about their medical care needs. Only 7 percent say they do not trust their doctor's judgment, while 11 percent are uncertain.

There is almost no difference of opinion by race or sex on this question. Agreement varies by age, however. The tendency of younger generations to distrust authority extends to physicians, it seems. Only 9 percent of people under age 40 and 11 to 12 percent of those aged 40 to 59 strongly agree that they trust their doctor's judgment. The proportion rises to 18 and 19 percent among people aged 60 or older.

People who did not complete high school are most likely to trust their doctor's judgment. Nineteen percent strongly feel this way compared with 10 to 13 percent of people with more education.

Trust Doctor's Judgment, 1998

"I trust my doctor's judgments about my medical care. Do you agree or disagree?"

(percent of people aged 18 or older responding by sex, race, age, and education, 1998)

	strongly agree	agree	uncertain	disagree	strongly disagree	agree, total	disagree, total
Total	**12%**	**69%**	**11%**	**6%**	**1%**	**81%**	**7%**
Men	12	69	10	6	1	81	7
Women	12	68	12	6	1	80	7
Black	9	71	12	6	2	80	8
White	13	68	11	6	1	81	7
Other	8	71	15	2	1	79	3
Aged 18 to 29	9	69	11	7	2	78	9
Aged 30 to 39	9	66	15	9	1	75	10
Aged 40 to 49	12	70	11	4	2	82	6
Aged 50 to 59	11	68	14	7	0	79	7
Aged 60 to 69	18	66	8	4	2	84	6
Aged 70 or older	19	72	4	3	1	91	4
Not a high school graduate	19	62	9	5	2	81	7
High school graduate	10	69	12	6	1	79	7
Bachelor's degree	11	71	10	6	2	82	8
Graduate degree	13	63	14	8	0	76	8

Note: Numbers may not add to 100 because "don't know" is not shown.
Source: General Social Survey, National Opinion Research Center, University of Chicago; calculations by the author

Trust Doctors to Reveal Mistakes

Three in five adults think their doctor would tell them about a mistake.

Doctors carry liability insurance for a reason. Medical mistakes frequently result in lawsuits. But most Americans believe that if their doctor made a mistake, he or she would tell them. Sixty percent say they trust their doctor to tell them if a mistake was made. Only 21 percent believe their doctor would conceal it from them.

Whites are slightly more likely than blacks and "other" races to believe their doctor would let them know if a mistake was made. Sixty percent of both men and women agree.

Older generations have more confidence than younger adults that their physicians would reveal mistakes in treatment. Fully 70 percent of people aged 70 or older and 67 percent of people aged 60 to 69 agree that their doctors would reveal mistakes. People in their thirties are least likely to believe this (54 percent). People aged 30 to 59 are most likely to think doctors would conceal a mistake (21 to 25 percent).

People who did not complete high school (many of whom are older adults) are more likely than those with more education to think doctors would tell them about mistakes (65 percent compared with 57 to 60 percent of those with more education). Fourteen percent of the least educated strongly agree compared with only 4 to 7 percent of people with more education.

Trust Doctors to Reveal Mistakes, 1998

"I trust my doctor to tell me if a mistake was made about my treatment. Do you agree or disagree?"

(percent of people aged 18 or older responding by sex, race, age, and education, 1998)

	strongly agree	agree	uncertain	disagree	strongly disagree	agree, total	disagree, total
Total	**7%**	**53%**	**16%**	**16%**	**5%**	**60%**	**21%**
Men	8	52	16	15	5	60	20
Women	7	53	16	17	4	60	21
Black	7	48	17	18	5	55	23
White	7	54	15	16	5	61	21
Other	13	43	23	13	2	56	15
Aged 18 to 29	7	53	17	15	4	60	19
Aged 30 to 39	6	48	19	19	5	54	24
Aged 40 to 49	7	55	15	16	5	62	21
Aged 50 to 59	6	51	15	20	5	57	25
Aged 60 to 69	12	55	15	13	3	67	16
Aged 70 or older	10	60	13	11	2	70	13
Not a high school graduate	14	51	12	14	4	65	18
High school graduate	7	53	15	18	4	60	22
Bachelor's degree	7	50	22	14	5	57	19
Graduate degree	4	55	18	15	5	59	20

Note: Numbers may not add to 100 because "don't know" is not shown.
Source: General Social Survey, National Opinion Research Center, University of Chicago; calculations by the author

Doctors Treat Patients with Respect

Half of Americans thinks doctors treat their patients with respect.

Physicians may be technically competent, but many could use some help with their people skills. Only half the populace thinks doctors treat patients with respect. One-third believe doctors do not treat patients with respect, while 14 percent are uncertain.

Thirty-seven percent of women say they do not think doctors treat their patients with respect compared with a smaller 30 percent of men. Men are more likely to say they are not certain whether doctors are respectful.

Whites are most likely to think doctors do not treat patients with respect (36 percent compared with 27 percent of blacks and 23 percent of "other" races). While 57 percent of blacks and 60 percent of other races agree that doctors show respect to patients, a smaller 49 percent of whites agree.

The oldest Americans are most likely to think doctors are respectful toward patients. Fully 73 percent think this true compared with 45 to 55 percent of other age groups. Fourteen percent of the oldest adults strongly agree, compared with 10 percent of people in their sixties and 3 to 6 percent of younger adults.

Only one-quarter of people who did not complete high school, many of whom are older, disagree that doctors treat patients with respect. In contrast, 33 percent of high school graduates, 38 percent of people with a bachelor's degree, and 47 percent of those with a graduate degree do not believe doctors are respectful.

Doctors Treat Patients with Respect, 1998

"Doctors always treat their patients with respect. Do you agree or disagree?"

(percent of people aged 18 or older responding by sex, race, age, and education, 1998)

	strongly agree	agree	uncertain	disagree	strongly disagree	agree, total	disagree, total
Total	**6%**	**45%**	**14%**	**30%**	**4%**	**51%**	**34%**
Men	6	46	17	27	3	52	30
Women	6	44	12	33	4	50	37
Black	7	50	15	24	3	57	27
White	5	44	14	32	4	49	36
Other	12	48	16	21	2	60	23
Aged 18 to 29	4	46	15	31	2	50	33
Aged 30 to 39	3	43	17	32	4	46	36
Aged 40 to 49	6	39	14	35	5	45	40
Aged 50 to 59	4	41	13	36	5	45	41
Aged 60 to 69	10	45	14	26	4	55	30
Aged 70 or older	14	59	7	16	3	73	19
Not a high school graduate	11	48	12	20	5	59	25
High school graduate	5	47	14	30	3	52	33
Bachelor's degree	4	39	18	34	4	43	38
Graduate degree	9	32	11	42	5	41	47

Note: Numberxs may not add to 100 because "don't know" is not shown.
Source: General Social Survey, National Opinion Research Center, University of Chicago; calculations by the author

Doctors Ignore Patient History

Most Americans don't think doctors ignore their medical history.

Knowing a patient's medical history is important in diagnosing and treating current illnesses. Most Americans are confident that health care professionals are, in fact, taking their medical history into account. Sixty-four percent say they disagree that past medical problems are ignored when they seek treatment for new problems. Only 18 percent agree.

The youngest adults are most likely to feel their medical history is ignored. Nearly one-quarter (23 percent) agree compared with 17 percent of people aged 30 to 69 and only 11 percent of those aged 70 or older. This disparity may be the result of the different perceptions of people by lifestage. But it is also possible that many physicians assume young adults don't have a relevant medical history.

People who did not complete high school are far more likely to think that health care professionals ignore their medical history. Fully 30 percent of the least educated agree compared with only 11 to 17 percent of those with more education. Just over half of people without a high school diploma do not believe past medical problems are ignored compared with 63 percent of high school graduates and 65 percent of people with a graduate degree. People with a bachelor's degree are most likely to disagree (71 percent).

Doctors Ignore Patient History, 1998

"The medical problems I've had in the past are ignored when I seek care for a new medical problem. Do you agree or disagree?"

(percent of people aged 18 or older responding by sex, race, age, and education, 1998)

	strongly agree	agree	uncertain	disagree	strongly disagree	agree, total	disagree, total
Total	**3%**	**15%**	**14%**	**57%**	**7%**	**18%**	**64%**
Men	3	14	16	57	6	17	63
Women	2	15	13	57	8	17	65
Black	3	16	14	59	4	19	63
White	3	14	14	57	8	17	65
Other	2	18	17	49	7	20	56
Aged 18 to 29	2	21	16	53	3	23	56
Aged 30 to 39	3	14	17	54	6	17	60
Aged 40 to 49	3	14	15	58	9	17	67
Aged 50 to 59	2	15	12	59	9	17	68
Aged 60 to 69	3	14	13	61	8	17	69
Aged 70 or older	2	9	12	62	10	11	72
Not a high school graduate	7	23	11	49	4	30	53
High school graduate	2	15	16	57	6	17	63
Bachelor's degree	0	11	14	61	10	11	71
Graduate degree	2	9	18	54	11	11	65

Note: Numbers may not add to 100 because "don't know" is not shown.
Source: General Social Survey, National Opinion Research Center, University of Chicago; calculations by the author

Doctors Don't Explain Medical Problems

Some people believe doctors don't explain enough, while others are satisfied with what they hear.

Americans are divided on whether doctors cause people to worry because they don't explain medical problems to their patients. Forty-one percent think doctors do cause people to worry, while 43 percent think they do not. Sixteen percent say they are uncertain.

Women are slightly more likely than men to think doctors do not explain medical problems (42 versus 38 percent). Men are more likely to say they are uncertain.

About two in five blacks and whites think doctors don't explain medical problems, but the same percentage think they do. People of "other" races are less likely to think doctors don't explain medical issues, and more likely to say they are uncertain.

Nearly half of people aged 60 or older disagree that doctors cause patients to worry by not explaining medical problems to them. But almost half of people in their fifties think doctors don't explain enough. Among people under age 50, a smaller 38 to 41 percent agree.

People who did not complete high school are most likely to strongly agree that doctors do not explain medical problems (12 percent compared with 4 to 6 percent of people with more education). Only 32 percent of people with a bachelor's degree think doctors cause worry by not explaining medical problems compared with a larger 41 to 44 percent of people with a high school diploma or less education and an even larger 46 percent of those with a graduate degree.

Doctors Don't Explain Medical Problems, 1998

"Doctors cause people to worry a lot because they don't explain medical problems to patients. Do you agree or disagree?"

(percent of people aged 18 or older responding by sex, race, age, and education, 1998)

	strongly agree	agree	uncertain	disagree	strongly disagree	agree, total	disagree, total
Total	7%	34%	16%	38%	5%	41%	43%
Men	5	33	18	38	4	38	42
Women	7	35	14	38	5	42	43
Black	9	33	15	38	4	42	42
White	6	35	16	38	5	41	43
Other	3	25	22	41	6	28	47
Aged 18 to 29	6	35	20	34	3	41	37
Aged 30 to 39	5	33	19	38	3	38	41
Aged 40 to 49	8	33	14	40	5	41	45
Aged 50 to 59	6	41	14	36	3	47	39
Aged 60 to 69	8	32	10	40	8	40	48
Aged 70 or older	7	30	13	40	8	37	48
Not a high school graduate	12	32	14	34	4	44	38
High school graduate	6	35	15	37	4	41	41
Bachelor's degree	5	27	19	44	5	32	49
Graduate degree	4	42	20	29	4	46	33

Note: Numbers may not add to 100 because "don't know" is not shown.
Source: General Social Survey, National Opinion Research Center, University of Chicago; calculations by the author

Doctors Don't Give All Treatment Options

Only one person in five agrees.

There is genuine concern among many Americans that physicians are limited in what they can say and do by companies that consider profits over patient care. Most people, however, do not worry that their doctor is being prevented from telling them the full range of treatment options. Only 21 percent worry about this issue, while 58 percent are not concerned. Seventeen percent are uncertain whether there is cause for concern or not.

Majorities of blacks and whites do not worry that they aren't fully informed about treatment options, but fewer than half the people of "other" races agree. Whites are less likely than blacks and others to say they are uncertain.

The proportion of people who don't believe that their doctors are prevented from telling them all their treatment options rises with age, from 50 percent among people under age 30 to 70 percent among those aged 70 or older. Younger generations are more likely to say they agree or are uncertain.

People with at least a high school diploma are more likely than people who did not graduate from high school to trust their doctors to tell them all their options. The most and the least educated are most likely to worry that their doctor doesn't reveal all the options.

Doctors Don't Give All Treatment Options, 1998

"I worry that my doctor is being prevented from telling me the full range of options for my treatment. Do you agree or disagree?"

(percent of people aged 18 or older responding by sex, race, age, and education, 1998)

	strongly agree	agree	uncertain	disagree	strongly disagree	agree, total	disagree, total
Total	**3%**	**18%**	**17%**	**50%**	**8%**	**21%**	**58%**
Men	3	21	17	48	8	24	56
Women	3	17	17	51	9	20	60
Black	3	15	21	51	6	18	57
White	3	19	16	51	8	22	59
Other	3	20	23	34	11	23	45
Aged 18 to 29	4	19	22	46	4	23	50
Aged 30 to 39	3	19	22	47	7	22	54
Aged 40 to 49	5	20	15	51	8	25	59
Aged 50 to 59	2	22	11	52	10	24	62
Aged 60 to 69	2	18	12	53	12	20	65
Aged 70 or older	2	10	14	56	14	12	70
Not a high school graduate	6	20	19	43	8	26	51
High school graduate	3	18	18	50	8	21	58
Bachelor's degree	3	18	14	55	9	21	64
Graduate degree	4	23	12	44	14	27	58

Note: Numbers may not add to 100 because "don't know" is not shown.
Source: General Social Survey, National Opinion Research Center, University of Chicago; calculations by the author

Doctors Avoid Unnecessary Surgery

The plurality agrees that doctors recommend surgery only when there are no other options.

The good news for the medical profession is that people are more likely to agree than to disagree that physicians recommend surgery only if it there is no alternative. The bad news is that the proportion of those who agree (43 percent) is less than a majority. A substantial one-third do not believe doctors avoid unnecessary surgery, while 19 percent are uncertain.

For women, the issue of unnecessary surgery is hardly academic. Until recently, doctors often told women they needed hysterectomies and mastectomies without offering any alternatives. No doubt this situation is one reason for the discrepancy in attitudes between men and women on this question. Thirty-eight percent of women, but a smaller 31 percent of men, disagree that doctors avoid unnecessary surgery.

Thirty-six percent of whites disagree that physicians avoid unnecessary surgery compared with 32 percent of blacks and only 16 percent of "other" races. Forty-two percent of blacks and whites agree that doctors do not recommend surgery unless there are no other options compared with the 51 percent majority of other races.

There is considerable variation by age on this question. The oldest adults are most likely to agree (54 percent of those aged 70 or older) that doctors avoid unnecessary surgery. People in their fifties and those in their thirties are least likely to agree (37 to 38 percent).

There is a significant gap between the opinions of college graduates and those with less education. Only 32 to 36 percent of college graduates think doctors never recommend surgery when another treatment is available compared with a larger 44 percent of high school graduates and 52 percent of those with less education.

Doctors Avoid Unnecessary Surgery, 1998

"Doctors never recommend surgery (an operation) unless there is no other way to solve the problem. Do you agree or disagree?"

(percent of people aged 18 or older responding by sex, race, age, and education, 1998)

	strongly agree	agree	uncertain	disagree	strongly disagree	agree, total	disagree, total
Total	**4%**	**39%**	**19%**	**31%**	**3%**	**43%**	**34%**
Men	3	42	21	27	4	45	31
Women	4	37	18	35	3	41	38
Black	6	36	22	27	5	42	32
White	3	39	19	33	3	42	36
Other	7	44	24	15	1	51	16
Aged 18 to 29	4	44	21	26	2	48	28
Aged 30 to 39	5	33	21	35	2	38	37
Aged 40 to 49	2	39	18	34	6	41	40
Aged 50 to 59	2	35	20	36	5	37	41
Aged 60 to 69	6	36	19	34	2	42	36
Aged 70 or older	5	49	17	21	3	54	24
Not a high school graduate	6	46	19	22	2	52	24
High school graduate	4	40	20	30	4	44	34
Bachelor's degree	2	34	22	36	4	36	40
Graduate degree	1	31	16	45	3	32	48

Note: Numbers may not add to 100 because "don't know" is not shown.
Source: General Social Survey, National Opinion Research Center, University of Chicago; calculations by the author

Doctors Take Unnecessary Risks

There is a great deal of uncertainty on the issue of risk.

No one wants to think his or her physician would take an unnecessary risk when treating a medical condition. But Americans are divided on the question whether doctors do or not. Only 39 percent think doctors avoid unnecessary risks, while 34 percent think doctors are willing to take risks. One-quarter are uncertain.

Women are slightly more likely than men to believe doctors will take unnecessary risks (35 versus 31 percent). Forty-one percent of blacks agree that doctors take unnecessary risks compared with a smaller 33 percent of whites and "other" races.

People in their sixties are most likely to believe doctors will take unnecessary risks (40 percent) while people aged 70 or older are least likely to think so (28 percent). People under age 40 are most likely to say they are uncertain (28 percent compared with 20 to 22 percent of older people).

The percentages of those who believe doctors do not take unnecessary risks rises with education. While only 30 percent of people who did not complete high school believe doctors do not take unnecessary risks, the proportion rises to 44 to 45 percent among college graduates.

Doctors Take Unncessary Risks, 1998

"Sometimes doctors take unnecessary risks in treating their patients. Do you agree or disagree?"

(percent of people aged 18 or older responding by sex, race, age, and education, 1998)

	strongly agree	agree	uncertain	disagree	strongly disagree	agree, total	disagree, total
Total	**4%**	**30%**	**24%**	**35%**	**4%**	**34%**	**39%**
Men	3	28	25	34	5	31	39
Women	4	31	24	35	3	35	38
Black	4	37	27	25	6	41	31
White	4	29	24	37	4	33	41
Other	7	26	29	25	5	33	30
Aged 18 to 29	2	32	28	31	3	34	34
Aged 30 to 39	4	27	28	36	3	31	39
Aged 40 to 49	5	32	22	34	5	37	39
Aged 50 to 59	4	30	23	37	3	34	40
Aged 60 to 69	6	34	20	35	4	40	39
Aged 70 or older	3	25	20	36	7	28	43
Not a high school graduate	8	31	25	27	3	39	30
High school graduate	4	30	25	34	4	34	38
Bachelor's degree	2	26	24	38	7	28	45
Graduate degree	1	34	19	41	3	35	44

Note: Numbers may not add to 100 because "don't know" is not shown.
Source: General Social Survey, National Opinion Research Center, University of Chicago; calculations by the author

Doctors Try Not to Worry Patients

The percentage of those who agree declines with education.

Under the best of circumstances, medical problems are worrisome. Physicians can easily add to a patient's concerns if they are careless. Half of Americans think physicians try not to worry patients, however. Only 28 percent disagree, while 20 percent are uncertain.

Men and women disagree on this question. Among men, 55 percent think doctors always do their best to keep patients from worrying, but a smaller 48 percent of women agree. The difference of opinion by race is even greater. Only 49 percent of whites believe that physicians try not to worry patients compared with 63 percent of blacks and 57 percent of "other" races.

Americans aged 70 or older are more likely than other age groups to think doctors try not to worry patients (69 percent). People in their fifties are least likely to agree (45 percent). Among other age groups, 49 to 51 percent agree.

The widest gap in opinion is by education. Among people who did not complete high school, 62 percent think doctors try not to worry patients. But the proportion of those who feel this way declines to only 34 percent among people with a graduate degree.

Doctors Try Not to Worry Patients, 1998

"Doctors always do their best to keep the patient from worrying. Do you agree or disagree?"

(percent of people aged 18 or older responding by sex, race, age, and education, 1998)

	strongly agree	agree	uncertain	disagree	strongly disagree	agree, total	disagree, total
Total	**4%**	**47%**	**20%**	**25%**	**3%**	**51%**	**28%**
Men	5	50	19	23	2	55	25
Women	3	45	20	26	3	48	29
Black	2	61	15	17	2	63	19
White	4	45	20	27	3	49	30
Other	6	51	21	18	2	57	20
Aged 18 to 29	2	47	23	24	1	49	25
Aged 30 to 39	3	47	20	27	3	50	30
Aged 40 to 49	4	45	20	27	4	49	31
Aged 50 to 59	3	42	21	32	2	45	34
Aged 60 to 69	6	45	17	26	3	51	29
Aged 70 or older	9	60	14	12	3	69	15
Not a high school graduate	6	56	14	17	3	62	20
High school graduate	3	49	19	25	3	52	28
Bachelor's degree	3	44	21	29	2	47	31
Graduate degree	6	28	30	32	3	34	35

Note: Numbers may not add to 100 because "don't know" is not shown.
Source: General Social Survey, National Opinion Research Center, University of Chicago; calculations by the author

Doctors Aren't Thorough Enough

Many Americans think doctors need to be more thorough.

A common complaint among users of the health care industry is that patients wait forever to get into the examining room, but when the doctor finally arrives, he or she is in and out in the blink of an eye. This complaint is reflected in the fact that half of Americans agree that doctors are not as thorough as they should be. Only one-third disagree, while 14 percent are uncertain.

Women are slightly more likely than men to feel doctors need to be more thorough. Among blacks, 46 percent believe doctors are not thorough enough compared with a larger 50 percent of whites and 56 percent of "other" races. Blacks are more likely to say they are uncertain.

By age, similar percentages of people agree that doctors are not thorough enough. The highest percentage is found among people in their fifties (54 percent) and the lowest percentage among people aged 70 or older (48 percent).

Slightly more than half of people with a graduate degree and a similar percentage of those with a high school diploma or less think doctors need to be more thorough. A smaller 42 percent of people with a bachelor's degree feel this way. They are most likely to say they are uncertain or disagree.

Doctors Aren't Thorough Enough, 1998

"Doctors aren't as thorough as they should be. Do you agree or disagree?"

(percent of people aged 18 or older responding by sex, race, age, and education, 1998)

	strongly agree	agree	uncertain	disagree	strongly disagree	agree, total	disagree, total
Total	**9%**	**41%**	**14%**	**31%**	**3%**	**50%**	**34%**
Men	9	39	15	32	3	48	35
Women	9	43	13	30	4	52	34
Black	8	38	18	29	2	46	31
White	9	41	13	31	4	50	35
Other	9	47	11	25	3	56	28
Aged 18 to 29	8	43	19	26	2	51	28
Aged 30 to 39	8	41	14	32	2	49	34
Aged 40 to 49	9	40	14	33	3	49	36
Aged 50 to 59	9	45	11	28	4	54	32
Aged 60 to 69	10	43	9	27	9	53	36
Aged 70 or older	12	36	11	35	5	48	40
Not a high school graduate	12	40	12	29	3	52	32
High school graduate	10	44	13	29	3	54	32
Bachelor's degree	5	37	20	32	6	42	38
Graduate degree	11	41	13	31	2	52	33

Note: Numbers may not add to 100 because "don't know" is not shown.
Source: General Social Survey, National Opinion Research Center, University of Chicago; calculations by the author

Doctors Put Medical Needs First

Seven in ten Americans trust their doctors to put their medical needs above all other considerations.

Many people worry that the profit motive encourages health care providers to cut corners when treating patients. But seven in ten Americans trust their doctor to put their medical needs above all other considerations. Only 11 percent disagree with this notion.

Whites have the most faith in their physicians. Seventy-three percent trust their doctor to put their medical needs first compared with 70 percent of blacks and 66 percent of "other" races.

People aged 60 or older are more likely than younger people to believe their doctors put their medical needs above all other considerations. Fully 79 to 80 percent of people aged 60 or older agree. People in their forties are almost as likely to agree (76 percent). Least likely to agree are people in their thirties, only 65 percent of whom believe their doctors put their medical needs first.

People with the most education are least certain that doctors put their medical needs first. Twenty percent of people with a graduate degree are uncertain compared with 14 to 17 percent of people with less education. Among people with a high school diploma or a bachelor's degree, 72 to 73 percent agree that their doctor puts their medical needs first compared with 64 percent of people with a graduate degree and 69 percent of those who did not complete high school.

Doctors Put Medical Needs First, 1998

"I trust my doctor to put my medical needs above all other considerations when treating my medical problems. Do you agree or disagree?"

(percent of people aged 18 or older responding by sex, race, age, and education, 1998)

	strongly agree	agree	uncertain	disagree	strongly disagree	agree, total	disagree, total
Total	10%	62%	15%	10%	1%	72%	11%
Men	8	63	15	10	1	71	11
Women	11	62	15	9	1	73	10
Black	8	62	15	11	2	70	13
White	10	63	15	9	1	73	10
Other	13	53	15	13	0	66	13
Aged 18 to 29	7	63	16	9	2	70	11
Aged 30 to 39	7	58	19	13	0	65	13
Aged 40 to 49	10	66	14	8	1	76	9
Aged 50 to 59	11	60	14	11	1	71	12
Aged 60 to 69	13	66	11	9	0	79	9
Aged 70 or older	15	65	10	7	1	80	8
Not a high school graduate	14	55	14	9	2	69	11
High school graduate	9	64	15	10	1	73	11
Bachelor's degree	9	63	17	8	1	72	9
Graduate degree	8	56	20	13	0	64	13

Note: Numbers may not add to 100 because "don't know" is not shown.
Source: General Social Survey, National Opinion Research Center, University of Chicago; calculations by the author

Worry That Doctors Consider Costs over Care

Only one-quarter of Americans worry that their doctors will put costs first.

Most Americans are aware that some health care companies reward doctors for keeping costs down to improve the company's bottom line. But the 59 percent majority do not worry that their own doctor will consider profits before care. About one-quarter, however, agree that their doctor might consider cost over care.

Among whites, 62 percent say they don't think doctors put costs first compared with 57 percent of blacks and a much smaller 42 percent of "other" races. Only 23 to 24 percent of blacks and whites think doctors consider cost over care compared with 32 percent of other races.

People aged 60 or older have more faith in their physicians than younger generations do. While 72 to 74 percent of the oldest adults do not believe their doctors would consider cost over care, the proportion drops to 61 to 62 percent among people aged 40 to 59 and to only 51 to 53 percent among adults under age 40.

College graduates are least concerned that their doctors consider cost before care. Among college graduates, 65 to 67 percent trust their doctors to put care above cost. This share compares with a smaller 59 percent of high school graduates and just 51 percent of people who did not complete high school.

Worry That Doctors Consider Costs over Care, 1998

"I worry that my doctor will put cost considerations above the care I need. Do you agree or disagree?"

(percent of people aged 18 or older responding by sex, race, age, and education, 1998)

	strongly agree	agree	uncertain	disagree	strongly disagree	agree, total	disagree, total
Total	4%	20%	15%	51%	8%	24%	59%
Men	3	22	15	50	8	25	58
Women	4	19	14	52	8	23	60
Black	5	19	17	51	6	24	57
White	3	20	14	53	9	23	62
Other	2	30	18	34	8	32	42
Aged 18 to 29	4	24	18	45	6	28	51
Aged 30 to 39	3	26	17	46	7	29	53
Aged 40 to 49	4	19	13	54	8	23	62
Aged 50 to 59	4	21	13	54	7	25	61
Aged 60 to 69	4	14	10	60	12	18	72
Aged 70 or older	3	10	12	59	15	13	74
Not a high school graduate	7	19	18	43	8	26	51
High school graduate	3	21	15	51	8	24	59
Bachelor's degree	3	18	11	56	11	21	67
Graduate degree	1	18	15	55	10	19	65

Note: Numbers may not add to 100 because "don't know" is not shown.
Source: General Social Survey, National Opinion Research Center, University of Chicago; calculations by the author

Doctors Avoid Unnecessary Patient Expenses

Most Americans do not think physicians avoid unnecessary expenses.

Health care costs have been rising rapidly. Concern over the cost of care is not limited to people without health insurance, because even the insured are finding themselves responsible for a growing share of costs. Consequently, many people want physicians to avoid unnecessary expenses. Unfortunately, only 22 percent of Americans agree that doctors always avoid unnecessary patient charges, while the 55 percent majority disagree.

There is little difference between the opinions of men and women on this issue. By race, more than half of blacks and whites disagree that physicians avoid unnecessary expenses, but fewer than half of "other" races agree. Other races are most likely to feel uncertain about this.

Older generations tend to have a higher opinion of physicians than younger people do. Only 17 to 19 percent of people under age 50 think doctors avoid unnecessary charges. Among people aged 50 to 69, a larger 24 to 27 percent agree that doctors try to limit costs. Among people aged 70 or older, fully 38 percent agree.

College graduates are more likely to think doctors may be careless about limiting costs. Only 15 to 16 percent agree that doctors avoid unnecessary expenses compared with 22 percent of high school graduates and 35 percent of those with less education.

Doctors Avoid Unnecessary Patient Expenses, 1998

"Doctors always avoid unnecessary patient expenses. Do you agree or disagree?"

(percent of people aged 18 or older responding by sex, race, age, and education, 1998)

	strongly agree	agree	uncertain	disagree	strongly disagree	agree, total	disagree, total
Total	**2%**	**20%**	**20%**	**47%**	**8%**	**22%**	**55%**
Men	2	18	21	48	7	20	55
Women	2	21	20	46	9	23	55
Black	2	20	19	43	12	22	55
White	2	20	20	48	8	22	56
Other	3	15	28	44	2	18	46
Aged 18 to 29	2	16	25	47	7	18	54
Aged 30 to 39	1	16	21	51	8	17	59
Aged 40 to 49	2	17	18	51	10	19	61
Aged 50 to 59	3	21	19	45	7	24	52
Aged 60 to 69	3	24	20	43	8	27	51
Aged 70 or older	6	32	18	34	7	38	41
Not a high school graduate	5	30	22	30	7	35	37
High school graduate	2	20	18	48	9	22	57
Bachelor's degree	1	15	25	51	7	16	58
Graduate degree	2	13	23	54	6	15	60

Note: Numbers may not add to 100 because "don't know" is not shown.
Source: General Social Survey, National Opinion Research Center, University of Chicago; calculations by the author

3

Personal Outlook

Most Americans say they are happy and have happy marriages. About equal shares say their lives are exciting and pretty routine. Life might be a little more exciting if people could change the way they spend their time, however. Given a choice, solid majorities would spend more time with family and friends and engaged in leisure activities. The plurality would spend less time doing housework. Since 1989, the percentages of people who want to spend more time with friends, family, or at play have increased. So has the percentage of Americans who want to spend less time doing housework.

Most people consider themselves very trusting, but they don't think other people merit their trust. The majority believes you can't be too careful in dealing with others. Nearly half, however, think most people try to be helpful, and slightly more than half say most people try to be fair. While this is good news, the bad news is that people are less likely to think others are fair and helpful than they were 20 years ago.

Unlike people in many other countries, Americans are not constrained by rigid social castes that limit their opportunities. Solid majorities of adults think they can change the course of their life and that it is up to each individual to make his or her own fate.

The belief in the individual is also reflected in the characteristics people think are most important to instill in children. Half say it is most important for children to learn to think for themselves, while the remainder are divided between thinking it is most important for children to be obedient, hard working, and helpful.

Men and women have similar opinions about most of the issues examined in this chapter. If there are differences, they are generally small. Men are slightly more likely than women to find life exciting, while women are more likely to say their lives are pretty routine.

Both men and women would reallocate their time given the opportunity, but they have somewhat different preferences for how they would spend their days. Men are slightly more likely than women to want to spend more time at work. Women are considerably more likely to want to spend more time with friends and less time doing housework.

Men and women are equally likely to think most people can be trusted, but majorities of both sexes believe you can't be too careful in dealing with other people. Women are considerably more likely than men to think most people try to be helpful, while men are more likely to say other people just look out for themselves. Majorities of men and women believe most people try to be fair. But the percentage of those who feel this way has declined among both sexes in the past 20 years.

Men are much more likely to think it is all right for unmarried couples to live together and more likely to think it's a good idea to do so before marrying. Men and women also disagree on childrearing issues. Women are more likely than men to think it is most important for children to think for themselves. Men are more likely than women to think it is sometimes necessary to discipline children with a hard spanking.

Money may not buy happiness, but lower socioeconomic status and a history of discrimination clearly make a difference in the attitudes of Americans by race. Whites are more likely than blacks and "other" races to be happy, to have a happy marriage, and to think life is exciting. Whites are also more likely to believe other people are generally fair, helpful, and trustworthy. Blacks are most likely to think others would take advantage if they got a chance, are selfish rather than helpful, and are not to be trusted. But the gap between the percentages of blacks and whites who think people are fair and helpful is smaller than it was two decades ago because the percentage of whites who think so has dropped.

The societal barriers blacks and people of other race have had to overcome is undoubtedly one reason why they are more likely than whites to believe people cannot change the course of their lives. If they could change how they spend their time, however, majorities of all races would spend more time with family and engaged in leisure pursuits. But blacks are less likely to say this than whites and other races. Whites, on the other hand, are least likely to want to spend more time at work.

There are also differences of opinion by race on issues relating to children. Whites are far more likely than blacks and other races to believe it is most important for children to learn to think for themselves. Blacks are most likely to say children should learn to obey. Blacks and other races are more likely than whites to say children should learn to work hard.

Whites are least likely to prefer large families. Substantial shares of blacks and people of other race think three or more children is ideal. Blacks are most likely to think spanking is necessary to discipline children, while people of other race are least likely to think so.

While being young has its advantages, sometimes older Americans have the edge. People aged 70 or older are most likely to say their marriage is happy. People in their forties are least likely to have happy marriages. People under age 60 are more likely to say their lives are exciting. After age 60, the majority says life is pretty routine.

Younger generations may have more exciting lives, but the excitement comes at a price. People in their thirties and forties are much more likely than other age groups to want more leisure time and more time with their family. The percentage of people in their forties who want more family time has increased considerably since 1989. People aged 70 or older, on the other hand, are content with the amount of time they spend with friends, engaged in leisure activities, and doing housework. Most would like more time with family, but they are less likely than younger people to feel this way.

The younger people are, the more likely they are to have a negative opinion of others. Younger generations are far more likely to say people take advantage rather than try to be fair, and are selfish rather than helpful. The percentage of people who think you can't be too careful when dealing with other people also declines with age, with the exception of the oldest Americans. People aged 70 or older are more likely than the middle-aged to think you have to be careful. This watchfulness is not surprising since many elderly people have been taken advantage of by unscrupulous businesses and individuals.

Most people aged 30 to 59 think it is most important that children learn to think for themselves. The youngest adults, perhaps responding to the highly competitive economy in which they came of age, are more likely than their elders to say it is most important for children to learn to work hard. People aged 60 or older are much more likely than younger generations to believe it is most important that children learn obedience.

Obedience would certainly be a valuable characteristic in the large families favored by older Americans. People aged 60 or older are much more likely than younger generations to think families should have at least four children.

The largest difference of opinion by age is over the issue of cohabitation. Majorities of people under age 40 think it is all right for a couple to live together even if they don't intend to marry. Most people under age 30 think couples should live together before they marry. But the proportion of people who approve of unmarried couples living together falls sharply with age. The majority of people aged 70 or older disapprove.

People who did not complete high school are, on average, older and less likely to be employed than people with more education. While education influences people's opinions about many issues, these other factors also play a role.

A lower rate of employment, for example, means more free time. That is why people with lower levels of education are least likely to want more time with their family, friends, or in leisure activities. They are also far less likely to want to reduce the time they spend doing housework. College graduates, on the other hand, are much more likely than those with less education to want more time off from work.

People who did not complete high school are at a distinct disadvantage in today's economy, which is one reason why they are far more likely than people with more education to believe there is little people can do to change the course of their life. This fact also contributes to the substantial rise during the past two decades in the percentage of the least educated who say they are not too happy.

People with a high school diploma or less are more likely than college graduates to consider themselves very trusting. But apparently they think few people deserve their trust. The majority of college graduates think most people can be trusted, but most of those with less education think you can't be too careful in dealing with other people. College graduates also have more faith in the fairness and helpfulness of others.

Opinions about childrearing also differ by education. The more educated people are the more they believe children must learn to think independently and the less importance they place on obedience or hard work. People without a college degree are also more likely to prefer large families and to think spanking is a necessary part of disciplining children.

Personal Happiness

High school dropouts are most likely to say they are not too happy.

Americans are neither dancing in the streets nor wallowing in despair. The majority (56 percent) are "pretty happy." One-third are "very happy," and only 12 percent are "not too happy."

About one-third of men and women are very happy. Men were a little less likely in 1998 than in 1978 to say they were very happy. The percentage of women who are not too happy increased slightly over the past 20 years.

One-third of whites say they are very happy compared with only 22 percent of blacks and 28 percent of "other" races. Twenty percent of blacks and 18 percent of others, but only 10 percent of whites, are not too happy.

Young adults and people in their forties are less likely than other age groups to say they are very happy. The proportion of young adults who are very happy fell from 33 to 26 percent between 1978 and 1998. Concurrently, there was a rise in the proportion of those who are not too happy, from 11 percent in 1978 to 15 percent in 1998. Fourteen percent of people aged 70 or older were not too happy in 1998, up from 9 percent in 1978.

The economy is not as favorable for people without a college degree as it once was. This is one factor behind the rise in the percentage of less educated adults who say they are not too happy. In 1978, 9 to 12 percent of people without a college degree were not too happy, but by 1998 fully 23 percent of people who did not complete high school were not too happy. Nearly half of people with a graduate degree (46 percent) are very happy compared with 34 percent of people with a bachelor's degree and 28 to 31 percent of people without a college degree.

Personal Happiness, 1998

"Taken all together, how would you say things are these days—would you say that you are very happy, pretty happy, or not too happy?"

(percent of people aged 18 or older responding by sex, race, age, and education, 1998)

	very happy	pretty happy	not too happy
Total	**32%**	**56%**	**12%**
Men	31	58	11
Women	33	54	13
Black	22	58	20
White	34	56	10
Other	28	53	18
Aged 18 to 29	26	59	15
Aged 30 to 39	34	57	9
Aged 40 to 49	28	58	13
Aged 50 to 59	33	56	11
Aged 60 to 69	39	49	11
Aged 70 or older	35	51	14
Not a high school graduate	31	46	23
High school graduate	28	60	12
Bachelor's degree	34	57	8
Graduate degree	46	48	5

Note: Numbers may not add to 100 because "don't know" is not shown.
Source: General Social Survey, National Opinion Research Center, University of Chicago; calculations by the author

Personal Happiness, 1978 to 1998

"Taken all together, how would you say things are these days—would you say that you are very happy, pretty happy, or not too happy?"

(percent of people aged 18 or older responding by sex, race, age, and education, 1978–98)

	very happy			pretty happy			not too happy		
	1998	*1988*	*1978*	*1998*	*1988*	*1978*	*1998*	*1988*	*1978*
Total	**32%**	**33%**	**34%**	**56%**	**58%**	**56%**	**12%**	**10%**	**10%**
Men	31	32	35	58	59	55	11	9	10
Women	33	33	34	54	57	57	13	10	9
Black	22	19	22	58	62	58	20	19	21
White	34	34	36	56	57	56	10	9	8
Aged 18 to 29	26	30	33	59	60	57	15	10	11
Aged 30 to 39	34	32	36	57	60	58	9	8	7
Aged 40 to 49	28	30	31	58	61	59	13	10	10
Aged 50 to 59	33	38	36	56	50	54	11	12	9
Aged 60 to 69	39	36	35	49	55	52	11	9	13
Aged 70 or older	35	34	36	51	56	55	14	10	9
Not a high school graduate	31	28	34	46	52	54	23	20	12
High school graduate	28	35	34	60	59	57	12	7	9
Bachelor's degree	34	33	35	57	61	59	8	6	6
Graduate degree	46	33	35	48	57	55	5	11	10

Note: Numbers may not add to 100 because "don't know" is not shown.
Source: General Social Survey, National Opinion Research Center, University of Chicago; calculations by the author

Is Life Exciting?

Few Americans say life is dull.

Americans are divided between those who find life exciting (45 percent) and those who find it pretty routine (49 percent). Almost no one says life is dull.

Life is more exciting for men than for women. Nearly half of men (48 percent) find life exciting compared with 42 percent of women. Women are more likely to say their lives are pretty routine (50 versus 47 percent). Whites are considerably more likely than blacks and "other" races to say life is exciting. Forty-six percent of whites say so compared with 38 to 39 percent of blacks and other races.

People in their retirement years have more time to do what they want, but this doesn't seem to make life more exciting. Only 39 percent of people in their sixties and 34 percent of people aged 70 or older say life is exciting. Among people under age 60, 45 to 48 percent find life exciting. Twelve percent of people aged 70 or older say life is dull compared with 3 to 7 percent of younger adults.

The proportion of people who say life is exciting rises sharply with education. This was true in earlier years as well. Only 29 percent of people who did not complete high school say life is exciting, but the proportion rises to 40 percent among high school graduates. Fully 60 percent of people with a bachelor's degree and 77 percent of those with a graduate degree say life is exciting.

Is Life Exciting? 1998

"In general, do you find life exciting, pretty routine, or dull?"

(percent of people aged 18 or older responding by sex, race, age, and education, 1998)

	exciting	routine	dull
Total	**45%**	**49%**	**5%**
Men	48	47	4
Women	42	50	6
Black	39	53	7
White	46	48	5
Other	38	54	7
Aged 18 to 29	45	47	7
Aged 30 to 39	47	48	4
Aged 40 to 49	48	47	4
Aged 50 to 59	47	49	3
Aged 60 to 69	39	54	5
Aged 70 or older	34	52	12
Not a high school graduate	29	57	13
High school graduate	40	55	5
Bachelor's degree	60	36	3
Graduate degree	77	21	1

Note: Numbers may not add to 100 because "don't know" is not shown.
Source: General Social Survey, National Opinion Research Center, University of Chicago; calculations by the author

Is Life Exciting? 1977 to 1998

"In general, do you find life exciting, pretty routine, or dull?"

(percent of people aged 18 or older responding by sex, race, age, and education, 1977–98)

	exciting			routine			dull		
	1998	*1988*	*1977*	*1998*	*1988*	*1977*	*1998*	*1988*	*1977*
Total	**45%**	**44%**	**44%**	**49%**	**50%**	**49%**	**5%**	**5%**	**7%**
Men	48	47	47	47	49	45	4	4	7
Women	42	43	42	50	51	52	6	6	6
Black	39	29	41	53	60	47	7	11	11
White	46	46	44	48	48	49	5	5	6
Aged 18 to 29	45	49	50	47	47	46	7	4	5
Aged 30 to 39	47	50	51	48	46	45	4	4	4
Aged 40 to 49	48	49	47	47	46	45	4	4	6
Aged 50 to 59	47	44	40	49	51	50	3	5	8
Aged 60 to 69	39	37	34	54	57	57	5	6	9
Aged 70 or older	34	29	32	52	59	55	12	11	12
Not a high school graduate	29	23	31	57	62	56	13	15	12
High school graduate	40	42	46	55	54	50	5	3	4
Bachelor's degree	60	67	71	36	31	25	3	2	4
Graduate degree	77	80	67	21	20	32	1	0	1

Note: Numbers may not add to 100 because "don't know" is not shown.
Source: General Social Survey, National Opinion Research Center, University of Chicago; calculations by the author

Consider Self a Trusting Person

More than 9 in 10 Americans say they are at least somewhat trusting.

Americans have a low opinion of the trustworthiness of their fellow human beings, but few say this is because they themselves are distrusting. Half of adults (53 percent) say they are very trusting and another 39 percent say they are somewhat trusting. Only 8 percent admit they are not trusting.

Women are slightly more likely than men to be very trusting (55 versus 51 percent). People aged 70 or older are more likely than younger adults to say they are very trusting (63 percent compared with 50 to 53 percent of people under age 70).

The largest differences of opinion on this issue are by race and education. Fully 60 percent of blacks say they are very trusting, but only 52 percent of whites and 46 percent of "other" races consider themselves very trusting.

College graduates are less likely to think of themselves as very trusting people. Only 46 to 49 percent say they are very trusting compared with 53 percent of high school graduates and 64 percent of people who did not complete high school.

Consider Self a Trusting Person, 1998

"Do you think of yourself as a trusting person? Are you very trusting, somewhat trusting, somewhat distrusting, or very distrusting?"

(percent of people aged 18 or older responding by sex, race, age, and education, 1998)

	very trusting	somewhat trusting	somewhat distrusting	very distrusting
Total	**53%**	**39%**	**6%**	**2%**
Men	51	41	5	2
Women	55	37	7	1
Black	60	32	4	3
White	52	40	6	1
Other	46	43	10	0
Aged 18 to 29	52	41	5	2
Aged 30 to 39	50	42	7	1
Aged 40 to 49	52	39	7	2
Aged 50 to 59	53	39	6	2
Aged 60 to 69	53	38	8	2
Aged 70 or older	63	31	5	1
Not a high school graduate	64	28	5	3
High school graduate	53	38	6	2
Bachelor's degree	46	48	6	0
Graduate degree	49	46	4	0

Note: Numbers may not add to 100 because "don't know" is not shown.
Source: General Social Survey, National Opinion Research Center, University of Chicago; calculations by the author

Trustworthiness of People

Most Americans say you can't be too careful in dealing with other people.

Americans have a low opinion of the trustworthiness of other people. Only 38 percent say most people can be trusted, while 56 percent say you can't be too careful in dealing with people.

Whites are far more trusting than blacks and people of "other" races. Forty-two percent of whites say most people can be trusted compared with a much smaller 17 percent of blacks and 23 percent of other races. Fully 77 percent of blacks say you can't be too careful in dealing with others compared with 52 percent of whites and 66 percent of other races.

The percentage of Americans who believe most people can be trusted rises with age to peak among people in their sixties, then drops sharply among those aged 70 or older. Unscrupulous businesses that prey on the elderly have made older Americans wary. Only 39 percent of people aged 70 or older think you can trust most people compared with 48 to 49 percent of people aged 50 to 69 and 43 percent of those in their forties. Young adults are most likely to think other people are not trustworthy, however. Only 35 percent of people in their thirties and 20 percent of those under age 30 think most people can be trusted.

College graduates are more trusting than those with less education. About half of people with a bachelor's degree and 69 percent of those with a graduate degree think most people can be trusted, but only 33 percent of high school graduates and 22 percent of those without a high school diploma agree.

Trustworthiness of People, 1998

"Generally speaking, would you say that most people can be trusted or that you can't be too careful in dealing with people?"

(percent of people aged 18 or older responding by sex, race, age, and education, 1998)

	most people can be trusted	you can't be too careful	depends*
Total	**38%**	**56%**	**6%**
Men	39	55	5
Women	37	57	6
Black	17	77	5
White	42	52	6
Other	23	66	10
Aged 18 to 29	20	72	7
Aged 30 to 39	35	59	6
Aged 40 to 49	43	51	5
Aged 50 to 59	48	47	4
Aged 60 to 69	49	46	5
Aged 70 or older	39	53	8
Not a high school graduate	22	73	4
High school graduate	33	62	5
Bachelor's degree	53	38	8
Graduate degree	69	24	7

* Volunteered response.
Note: Numbers may not add to 100 because "don't know" is not shown.
Source: General Social Survey, National Opinion Research Center, University of Chicago; calculations by the author

Trustworthiness of People, 1978 to 1998

"Generally speaking, would you say that most people can be trusted or that you can't be too careful in dealing with people?"

(percent of people aged 18 or older responding by sex, race, age, and education, 1978–98)

	most people can be trusted			you can't be too careful		
	1998	*1988*	*1978*	*1998*	*1988*	*1978*
Total	**38%**	**41%**	**39%**	**56%**	**55%**	**57%**
Men	39	41	44	55	54	52
Women	37	41	35	57	56	60
Black	17	14	15	77	82	82
White	42	45	42	52	51	53
Aged 18 to 29	20	27	34	72	69	61
Aged 30 to 39	35	42	42	59	54	52
Aged 40 to 49	43	46	40	51	47	54
Aged 50 to 59	48	48	50	47	50	48
Aged 60 to 69	49	48	31	46	51	63
Aged 70 or older	39	43	36	53	52	61
Not a high school graduate	22	25	23	73	71	72
High school graduate	33	40	42	62	56	54
Bachelor's degree	53	60	59	38	35	36
Graduate degree	69	70	66	24	25	27

Note: Numbers may not add to 100 because "depends" and "don't know" are not shown.
Source: General Social Survey, National Opinion Research Center, University of Chicago; calculations by the author

Fairness of People

Americans are less likely to think others are fair.

One-half of Americans say most people try to be fair, down from 64 percent who felt that way in 1978. Thirty-eight percent believe most people will try to take advantage of others if they get a chance, up from 30 percent in 1978.

Whites are much more inclined than blacks and people of "other" race to believe most people try to be fair. Only one-third of blacks and others believe in people's fairness compared with a 57 percent majority of whites.

Young people are less likely than their elders to have faith in the fairness of others. Only 36 percent of people under age 30 think most people are fair compared with 52 percent of people in their thirties and 56 to 60 percent of older adults. The percentage of people who think most people are fair has declined within every age group since 1978.

Well-educated people are far more likely than those with less education to have faith in the motives of others. While 62 to 77 percent of college graduates say most people try to be fair, only 50 percent of high school graduates and 38 percent of those who did not complete high school agree.

Fairness of People, 1998

"Do you think most people would try to take advantage of you if they got a chance, or would they try to be fair?"

(percent of people aged 18 or older responding by sex, race, age, and education, 1998)

	would try to be fair	would take advantage	depends*
Total	**52%**	**38%**	**9%**
Men	52	40	8
Women	53	37	10
Black	34	57	10
White	57	34	8
Other	33	48	17
Aged 18 to 29	36	54	9
Aged 30 to 39	52	37	10
Aged 40 to 49	56	37	5
Aged 50 to 59	60	33	8
Aged 60 to 69	58	30	11
Aged 70 or older	59	29	11
Not a high school graduate	38	51	9
High school graduate	50	41	9
Bachelor's degree	62	28	10
Graduate degree	77	10	10

* *Volunteered response.*
Note: Numbers may not add to 100 because "don't know" is not shown.
Source: General Social Survey, National Opinion Research Center, University of Chicago; calculations by the author

Fairness of People, 1978 to 1998

"Do you think most people would try to take advantage of you if they got a chance, or would they try to be fair?"

(percent of people aged 18 or older responding by sex, race, age, and education, 1978–98)

	would try to be fair			would take advantage		
	1998	*1988*	*1978*	*1998*	*1988*	*1978*
Total	**52%**	**58%**	**64%**	**38%**	**36%**	**30%**
Men	52	55	63	40	40	32
Women	53	60	66	37	34	28
Black	34	34	32	57	62	63
White	57	62	68	34	33	26
Aged 18 to 29	36	40	54	54	51	40
Aged 30 to 39	52	65	65	37	31	29
Aged 40 to 49	56	59	63	37	35	29
Aged 50 to 59	60	56	70	33	39	25
Aged 60 to 69	58	63	69	30	30	26
Aged 70 or older	59	72	77	29	24	19
Not a high school graduate	38	47	52	51	45	42
High school graduate	50	57	67	41	37	28
Bachelor's degree	62	77	80	28	18	15
Graduate degree	77	74	81	10	26	8

Note: Numbers may not add to 100 because "depends" and "don't know" are not shown.
Source: General Social Survey, National Opinion Research Center, University of Chicago; calculations by the author

Helpfulness of People

Older generations still believe most people try to be helpful.

In 1978, 59 percent of Americans believed other people try to be helpful most of the time. By 1998, however, the proportion of those who felt this way had declined to less than half (48 percent). The proportion of adults who say other people are just looking out for themselves rose from 35 to 43 percent between 1978 and 1998.

Women have more faith in others than men do. More than half of women think people try to be fair compared with 42 percent of men. Both men and women are less likely to think others try to be fair now than 20 years ago.

Blacks are more likely than whites and people of "other" race to believe most people are just looking out for themselves. More than half of blacks say people are just looking out for themselves compared with 40 percent of whites and 47 percent of "other" races.

Younger generations are more cynical than their elders. Fifty-six percent of people under age 30 think people are just looking out for themselves, while only 35 percent think people try to be helpful. People in their thirties are divided, with 43 percent saying people try to be helpful and 46 percent saying they just look out for themselves. Most people aged 40 or older believe others try to be helpful. This perspective is highest among people aged 70 or older. Sixty percent of the oldest Americans think people try to be helpful, while only 28 percent think they are just looking out for themselves.

The more education people have, the higher their opinion of others. Only 40 to 46 percent of people with a high school diploma or less education think most people try to be helpful compared with 53 to 65 percent of college graduates.

Helpfulness of People, 1998

"Would you say that most of the time people try to be helpful, or that they are mostly just looking out for themselves?"

(percent of people aged 18 or older responding by sex, race, age, and education, 1998)

	try to be helpful	just look out for themselves	depends*
Total	**48%**	**43%**	**9%**
Men	42	48	9
Women	52	38	9
Black	39	53	9
White	50	40	9
Other	41	47	11
Aged 18 to 29	35	56	8
Aged 30 to 39	43	46	11
Aged 40 to 49	51	42	8
Aged 50 to 59	54	39	7
Aged 60 to 69	53	36	11
Aged 70 or older	60	28	12
Not a high school graduate	40	51	9
High school graduate	46	43	10
Bachelor's degree	53	38	8
Graduate degree	65	26	8

* Volunteered response.
Note: Numbers may not add to 100 because "don't know" is not shown.
Source: General Social Survey, National Opinion Research Center, University of Chicago; calculations by the author

Helpfulness of People, 1978 to 1998

"Would you say that most of the time people try to be helpful, or that they are mostly just looking out for themselves?"

(percent of people aged 18 or older responding by sex, race, age, and education, 1978–98)

	try to be helpful			just look out for themselves		
	1998	*1988*	*1978*	*1998*	*1988*	*1978*
Total	**48%**	**50%**	**59%**	**43%**	**44%**	**35%**
Men	42	46	52	48	48	42
Women	52	53	65	38	41	30
Black	39	35	31	53	60	61
White	50	53	63	40	42	32
Aged 18 to 29	35	39	51	56	54	46
Aged 30 to 39	43	52	64	46	44	31
Aged 40 to 49	51	52	57	42	43	35
Aged 50 to 59	54	53	67	39	44	28
Aged 60 to 69	53	58	58	36	38	34
Aged 70 or older	60	54	65	28	37	28
Not a high school graduate	40	40	49	51	53	44
High school graduate	46	51	63	43	44	33
Bachelor's degree	53	58	70	38	40	24
Graduate degree	65	65	73	26	32	19

Note: Numbers may not add to 100 because "depends" and "don't know" are not shown.
Source: General Social Survey, National Opinion Research Center, University of Chicago; calculations by the author

Change Time Spent in Leisure Activities?

People in the parenting age groups are most likely to want more leisure time.

Here's a surprise: seven in ten Americans would like to spend more time pursuing leisure activities if they could. About one-quarter are lucky enough to feel they have the right amount of leisure time, while only 3 percent want to spend less time enjoying leisure activities. The proportion of people who would like more time for leisure rose slightly between 1989 and 1998.

Among whites, 73 percent would like more leisure time compared with 67 percent of blacks and 70 percent of "other" races. The proportions of blacks and whites who want more time to play are higher than they were in 1989, when 60 percent of blacks and 67 percent of whites said they would like more leisure time.

The people most likely to want more leisure time are working parents. More than 80 percent of people aged 30 to 49—the ages at which most people are working and raising children—would spend more time on leisure activities if they could. Work interferes with leisure whether you have children or not, however, and that is why 71 percent of people under age 30 and 74 percent of those in their fifties would like more leisure time. Just 58 percent of people in their sixties and 45 percent of those aged 70 or older would spend more time on leisure activities.

Only 52 percent of people who did not complete high school, many of whom are older, would like to spend more time on leisure activities. In contrast, 71 percent of high school graduates and 79 to 82 percent of college graduates want more time to play.

Change Time Spent in Leisure Activities? 1998

"Suppose you could change the way you spend your time, spending more on some things and less on others. Which of the things on the following list would you like to spend more time on, which would you like to spend less time on, and which would you like to spend the same amount of time on as now: Time in leisure activities."

(percent of people aged 18 or older responding by sex, race, age, and education, 1998)

	much more time	a little more time	same as now	a bit less time	much less time	more time, total	less time, total
Total	**30%**	**41%**	**23%**	**2%**	**1%**	**71%**	**3%**
Men	32	39	22	3	2	71	5
Women	29	43	23	2	1	72	3
Black	27	40	23	5	3	67	8
White	32	41	23	2	1	73	3
Other	19	51	24	1	3	70	4
Aged 18 to 29	33	38	23	5	0	71	5
Aged 30 to 39	34	46	17	1	2	80	3
Aged 40 to 49	35	48	13	2	2	83	4
Aged 50 to 59	29	45	20	2	1	74	3
Aged 60 to 69	27	31	33	3	0	58	3
Aged 70 or older	15	30	46	3	2	45	5
Not a high school graduate	24	28	35	6	3	52	9
High school graduate	30	41	23	3	1	71	4
Bachelor's degree	35	47	17	0	0	82	0
Graduate degree	34	45	17	1	1	79	2

Note: Numbers may not add to 100 because "can't choose" is not shown.
Source: General Social Survey, National Opinion Research Center, University of Chicago; calculations by the author

Change Time Spent in Leisure Activities? 1989 and 1998

"Suppose you could change the way you spend your time, spending more on some things and less on others. Which of the things on the following list would you like to spend more time on, which would you like to spend less time on, and which would you like to spend the same amount of time on as now: Time in leisure activities."

(percent of people aged 18 or older responding by sex, race, age, and education, 1989–98)

	more time		same as now		less time	
	1998	*1989*	*1998*	*1989*	*1998*	*1989*
Total	**71%**	**66%**	**23%**	**28%**	**3%**	**4%**
Men	71	69	22	26	5	4
Women	72	64	23	30	3	4
Black	67	60	23	29	8	8
White	73	67	23	29	3	3
Aged 18 to 29	71	78	23	19	5	3
Aged 30 to 39	80	76	17	19	3	4
Aged 40 to 49	83	71	13	26	4	2
Aged 50 to 59	74	67	20	28	3	5
Aged 60 to 69	58	48	33	41	3	8
Aged 70 or older	45	36	46	56	5	6
Not a high school graduate	52	45	35	45	9	6
High school graduate	71	69	23	26	4	4
Bachelor's degree	82	80	17	17	0	2
Graduate degree	79	78	17	22	2	0

Note: Numbers may not add to 100 because "can't choose" is not shown.
Source: General Social Survey, National Opinion Research Center, University of Chicago; calculations by the author

Change Time Spent at Work?

College graduates would like to work fewer hours.

It's not surprising that 27 percent of adults would like to spend less time at work or even that 31 percent are satisfied with the amount of time they spend at work now. What is remarkable is that nearly one-quarter of adults would like to spend more time at work.

Twenty-six percent of men, but only 21 percent of women, want to work more. Twenty-seven percent of men and women want to work less. But fully one-quarter of women say they can't choose.

Whites generally have higher incomes than blacks and "other" races, and that may be the major reason for the differences in opinion on this issue by race. Only 19 percent of whites would like to spend more time at work compared with a much larger 37 to 38 percent of blacks and other races. One-quarter of blacks would like to spend much more time at work.

Young adults usually have more time than money, which is why 39 percent of 18-to-29-year-olds would like to spend more time working while only 17 percent want to work less. People aged 30 to 59, on the other hand, are most likely to want to work fewer hours.

The more education people have the more employable they are. College graduates might wish they were a little less employable. Thirty-seven percent of people with a bachelor's degree and almost half of those with a graduate degree want to work less. In contrast, only 17 to 23 percent of people with less education want to work fewer hours. One-quarter to 28 percent of people without a college degree would like to spend more hours at work compared with only 10 to 16 percent of college graduates.

Change Time Spent at Work? 1998

"Suppose you could change the way you spend your time, spending more on some things and less on others. Which of the things on the following list would you like to spend more time on, which would you like to spend less time on, and which would you like to spend the same amount of time on as now: Time in a paid job."

(percent of people aged 18 or older responding by sex, race, age, and education, 1998)

	much more time	a little more time	same as now	a bit less time	much less time	can't choose	more time, total	less time, total
Total	10%	13%	31%	18%	9%	20%	23%	27%
Men	11	15	32	18	9	14	26	27
Women	9	12	29	18	9	24	21	27
Black	25	12	25	14	6	19	37	20
White	6	13	31	19	10	20	19	29
Other	19	19	35	10	4	13	38	14
Aged 18 to 29	17	22	33	14	3	11	39	17
Aged 30 to 39	9	16	31	21	11	11	25	32
Aged 40 to 49	8	8	37	24	13	10	16	37
Aged 50 to 59	12	11	26	21	13	16	23	34
Aged 60 to 69	2	11	33	11	6	37	13	17
Aged 70 or older	5	7	16	5	5	62	12	10
Not a high school graduate	15	13	19	12	5	36	28	17
High school graduate	10	15	31	15	8	20	25	23
Bachelor's degree	5	11	32	20	17	14	16	37
Graduate degree	4	6	29	39	10	13	10	49

Source: General Social Survey, National Opinion Research Center, University of Chicago; calculations by the author

Change Time Spent at Work? 1989 and 1998

"Suppose you could change the way you spend your time, spending more on some things and less on others. Which of the things on the following list would you like to spend more time on, which would you like to spend less time on, and which would you like to spend the same amount of time on as now: Time in a paid job."

(percent of people aged 18 or older responding by sex, race, age, and education, 1989–98)

	more time		same as now		less time	
	1998	1989	1998	1989	1998	1989
Total	**23%**	**21%**	**31%**	**41%**	**27%**	**27%**
Men	26	20	32	42	27	31
Women	21	22	29	39	27	25
Black	37	34	25	32	20	24
White	19	19	31	42	29	28
Aged 18 to 29	39	35	33	39	17	22
Aged 30 to 39	25	18	31	46	32	33
Aged 40 to 49	16	22	37	39	37	37
Aged 50 to 59	23	17	26	41	34	29
Aged 60 to 69	13	17	33	36	17	24
Aged 70 or older	12	11	16	41	10	14
Not a high school graduate	28	29	19	34	17	18
High school graduate	25	22	31	42	23	25
Bachelor's degree	16	14	32	49	37	34
Graduate degree	10	11	29	36	49	48

Note: Numbers may not add to 100 because "can't choose" is not shown.
Source: General Social Survey, National Opinion Research Center, University of Chicago; calculations by the author

Change Time Spent on Housework?

The plurality of Americans would rather spend less time doing housework.

Most people like having a clean home, but few people like cleaning the house. Given the opportunity, 41 percent of Americans would spend less time on housework, presumably by having someone else do it. One-third are satisfied with the amount of time they spend on housework right now. One-quarter would like to spend more time cleaning. This doesn't necessarily mean they enjoy housework. Many would simply like their homes to be in better shape. Since 1989, the percentage of those who say they would like to spend less time doing housework has grown slightly.

Women still do more housework than men, and this fact is reflected in the differences of opinion on this issue by sex. Forty-five percent of women want to spend less time doing housework compared with 34 percent of men. Thirty-six percent of men would not change the amount of time they spend on housework compared with 30 percent of women. Women were far more likely in 1998 than in 1989 to want to spend less time doing housework.

Young adults are more likely than older ones to want more time to clean. People aged 60 or older, the majority of whom are retired, are the ones most satisfied with the amount of time they spend on housework. Forty-four to 51 percent of people aged 30 to 59, many of whom are cleaning up after children and teenagers, would like to spend less time doing housework compared with a smaller 29 to 33 percent of people under age 30 and those aged 60 or older.

People who did not complete high school, many of whom are older adults, are most likely to say they wouldn't change the amount of time they spend on housework (41 percent compared with 28 to 32 percent of those with more education). While 41 to 48 percent of people with at least a high school diploma would like to spend fewer hours cleaning, a much smaller 29 percent of those with less education feel that way.

Change Time Spent on Housework? 1998

"Suppose you could change the way you spend your time, spending more on some things and less on others. Which of the things on the following list would you like to spend more time on, which would you like to spend less time on, and which would you like to spend the same amount of time on as now: Time doing household work."

(percent of people aged 18 or older responding by sex, race, age, and education, 1998)

	much more time	a little more time	same as now	a bit less time	much less time	more time, total	less time, total
Total	**5%**	**20%**	**33%**	**21%**	**20%**	**25%**	**41%**
Men	5	20	36	18	16	25	34
Women	5	19	30	23	22	24	45
Black	10	18	34	14	20	28	34
White	4	20	32	23	19	24	42
Other	7	26	30	13	23	33	36
Aged 18 to 29	5	26	39	16	13	31	29
Aged 30 to 39	6	21	29	23	21	27	44
Aged 40 to 49	4	20	27	23	24	24	47
Aged 50 to 59	5	16	24	28	23	21	51
Aged 60 to 69	6	12	44	19	14	18	33
Aged 70 or older	2	17	41	14	19	19	33
Not a high school graduate	7	18	41	10	19	25	29
High school graduate	6	19	32	23	18	25	41
Bachelor's degree	1	22	28	23	25	23	48
Graduate degree	2	23	30	20	21	25	41

Note: Numbers may not add to 100 because "can't choose" is not shown.
Source: General Social Survey, National Opinion Research Center, University of Chicago; calculations by the author

Change Time Spent on Housework? 1989 and 1998

"Suppose you could change the way you spend your time, spending more on some things and less on others. Which of the things on the following list would you like to spend more time on, which would you like to spend less time on, and which would you like to spend the same amount of time on as now: Time doing household work."

(percent of people aged 18 or older responding by sex, race, age, and education, 1989–98)

	more time		same as now		less time	
	1998	1989	1998	1989	1998	1989
Total	**25%**	**24%**	**33%**	**38%**	**41%**	**37%**
Men	25	20	36	38	34	39
Women	24	27	30	38	45	35
Black	28	29	34	35	34	36
White	24	23	32	38	42	37
Aged 18 to 29	31	30	39	35	29	34
Aged 30 to 39	27	27	29	32	44	40
Aged 40 to 49	24	22	27	37	47	40
Aged 50 to 59	21	17	24	41	51	40
Aged 60 to 69	18	18	44	45	33	35
Aged 70 or older	19	21	41	47	33	28
Not a high school graduate	25	26	41	38	29	33
High school graduate	25	23	32	39	41	36
Bachelor's degree	23	26	28	35	48	38
Graduate degree	25	9	30	38	41	52

Note: Numbers may not add to 100 because "can't choose" is not shown.
Source: General Social Survey, National Opinion Research Center, University of Chicago; calculations by the author

Change Time Spent with Family?

People with young children are most likely to want more family time.

There is no doubt what the number one priority of Americans would be if they could choose how they spend their time. They would spend more time with their family. Four in five want more family time, while only 18 percent are content with the amount of time they spend with their family. Forty-one percent would like to spend much more time with their family.

There is little difference by sex or race on this issue. There are sizable differences by age, however. People aged 30 to 49 are most likely to want to spend more time with their family. Half of people in their thirties and 43 percent of those in their forties want to spend much more time with their family. This reflects both lifestage—at these ages most have children—and the desire for a better balance between work and the rest of life. Among people under age 30 and those aged 50 to 69, 76 to 78 percent would like to spend more time with their family. It is particularly interesting that only 60 percent of people aged 70 or older would like to spend more time with their family. Older adults rarely live with grown children anymore, and with the busy lives of younger generations, many older adults don't spend a lot of time with their family. But many are obviously content with this arrangement. Thirty-one percent don't want to change the amount of time they spend with their family.

The percentage of people who want to spend more time with their family rises with education. Only 69 percent of people who did not complete high school want more family time, but the proportion increases to 88 percent among people with a graduate degree. One reason for the rise with education is that the best-educated people are more likely to be employed and working long hours.

Change Time Spent with Family? 1998

"Suppose you could change the way you spend your time, spending more on some things and less on others. Which of the things on the following list would you like to spend more time on, which would you like to spend less time on, and which would you like to spend the same amount of time on as now: Time with your family."

(percent of people aged 18 or older responding by sex, race, age, and education, 1998)

	much more time	*a little more time*	*same as now*	*a bit less time*	*much less time*	*more time, total*	*less time, total*
Total	**41%**	**38%**	**18%**	**1%**	**1%**	**79%**	**2%**
Men	40	39	17	0	2	79	2
Women	42	37	19	1	0	79	1
Black	39	37	21	0	1	76	1
White	41	38	17	1	1	79	2
Other	44	34	17	1	1	78	2
Aged 18 to 29	37	39	22	1	1	76	2
Aged 30 to 39	51	33	15	0	0	84	0
Aged 40 to 49	43	43	11	0	1	86	1
Aged 50 to 59	39	39	18	1	1	78	2
Aged 60 to 69	34	44	18	1	1	78	2
Aged 70 or older	30	30	31	1	3	60	4
Not a high school graduate	39	30	22	1	5	69	6
High school graduate	44	35	18	0	1	79	1
Bachelor's degree	39	41	18	0	0	80	0
Graduate degree	32	56	10	0	0	88	0

Note: Numbers may not add to 100 because "can't choose" is not shown.
Source: General Social Survey, National Opinion Research Center, University of Chicago; calculations by the author

Change Time Spent with Family? 1989 and 1998

"Suppose you could change the way you spend your time, spending more on some things and less on others. Which of the things on the following list would you like to spend more time on, which would you like to spend less time on, and which would you like to spend the same amount of time on as now: Time with your family."

(percent of people aged 18 or older responding by sex, race, age, and education, 1989–98)

	more time		same as now		less time	
	1998	*1989*	*1998*	*1989*	*1998*	*1989*
Total	**79%**	**74%**	**18%**	**22%**	**2%**	**3%**
Men	79	74	17	21	2	3
Women	79	75	19	22	1	2
Black	76	71	21	24	1	4
White	79	75	17	22	2	2
Aged 18 to 29	76	73	22	22	2	4
Aged 30 to 39	84	82	15	15	0	2
Aged 40 to 49	86	76	11	23	1	1
Aged 50 to 59	78	79	18	17	2	2
Aged 60 to 69	78	64	18	32	2	3
Aged 70 or older	60	66	31	28	4	3
Not a high school graduate	69	70	22	25	6	3
High school graduate	79	74	18	22	1	3
Bachelor's degree	80	75	18	22	0	3
Graduate degree	88	82	10	17	0	0

Note: Numbers may not add to 100 because "can't choose" is not shown.
Source: General Social Survey, National Opinion Research Center, University of Chicago; calculations by the author

Change Time Spent with Friends?

Most Americans wish they could spend more time hanging out with friends.

Given a choice, 64 percent of Americans would spend more time with their friends. Only 30 percent are content with the amount of time they spend with friends now.

Sixty-six percent of women would like to spend at least a little more time with their friends compared with 62 percent of men. Fully 21 percent of women would like to spend much more time with their friends compared with 17 percent of men.

Whites are more likely than blacks and people of "other" race to say they would like a lot more time with friends. Twenty-one percent of whites say so compared with 13 percent of blacks and 17 percent of others. Thirty-five percent of blacks are content with the amount of time they spend with friends compared with 30 percent of whites and others. Blacks are most likely to say they want less time with friends (12 percent compared with 2 percent of whites and others).

By age 70, few Americans are still in the work force, giving them more control over how they spend their time. This explains why nearly half (47 percent) of people aged 70 or older are content with the amount of time they spend with friends. Only 25 to 27 percent of people under age 50 and 30 to 37 percent of those aged 50 to 69 think they get enough time with their friends. Among people under age 50, most of whom have time-consuming work and family obligations, 68 to 70 percent want at least a little more time with their friends.

The percentage of people who would like to see their friends more often rises with education. This is so not only because people with more education are more likely to be working, but also because many of the less-educated Americans are older. Only 52 percent of people who did not complete high school would choose to spend more time with friends compared with 61 percent of high school graduates and 78 to 80 percent of college graduates.

Change Time Spent with Friends? 1998

"Suppose you could change the way you spend your time, spending more on some things and less on others. Which of the things on the following list would you like to spend more time on, which would you like to spend less time on, and which would you like to spend the same amount of time on as now: Time with your friends."

(percent of people aged 18 or older responding by sex, race, age, and education, 1998)

	much more time	a little more time	same as now	a bit less time	much less time	more time, total	less time, total
Total	**19%**	**45%**	**30%**	**2%**	**1%**	**64%**	**3%**
Men	17	45	33	3	1	62	4
Women	21	45	29	2	1	66	3
Black	13	37	35	6	6	50	12
White	21	47	30	2	0	68	2
Other	17	46	30	1	1	63	2
Aged 18 to 29	23	45	27	4	1	68	5
Aged 30 to 39	20	48	27	1	2	68	3
Aged 40 to 49	19	51	25	3	1	70	4
Aged 50 to 59	20	45	30	2	1	65	3
Aged 60 to 69	18	40	37	2	1	58	3
Aged 70 or older	13	35	47	3	1	48	4
Not a high school graduate	23	29	37	6	3	52	9
High school graduate	18	43	35	2	1	61	3
Bachelor's degree	25	55	19	1	0	80	1
Graduate degree	21	57	20	1	0	78	1

Note: Numbers may not add to 100 because "can't choose" is not shown.
Source: General Social Survey, National Opinion Research Center, University of Chicago; calculations by the author

Change Time Spent with Friends? 1989 and 1998

"Suppose you could change the way you spend your time, spending more on some things and less on others. Which of the things on the following list would you like to spend more time on, which would you like to spend less time on, and which would you like to spend the same amount of time on as now: Time with your friends."

(percent of people aged 18 or older responding by sex, race, age, and education, 1989–98)

	more time		same as now		less time	
	1998	*1989*	*1998*	*1989*	*1998*	*1989*
Total	**64%**	**62%**	**30%**	**33%**	**3%**	**4%**
Men	62	60	33	34	4	5
Women	66	64	29	32	3	3
Black	50	41	35	44	12	13
White	68	65	30	31	2	2
Aged 18 to 29	68	70	27	26	5	3
Aged 30 to 39	68	65	27	30	3	4
Aged 40 to 49	70	62	25	35	4	3
Aged 50 to 59	65	61	30	34	3	4
Aged 60 to 69	58	55	37	40	3	4
Aged 70 or older	48	55	47	39	4	4
Not a high school graduate	52	53	37	37	9	7
High school graduate	61	62	35	34	3	3
Bachelor's degree	80	76	19	23	1	1
Graduate degree	78	69	20	31	1	0

Note: Numbers may not add to 100 because "can't choose" is not shown.
Source: General Social Survey, National Opinion Research Center, University of Chicago; calculations by the author

Ability to Change the Course of Life

Few people think they cannot change how their lives turn out.

Americans generally believe their destiny is in their own hands. Only 10 percent believe that there is little a person can do to change the course of his or her life. Fully 79 percent say they disagree with the statement, including more than one-third who strongly disagree.

The socioeconomic conditions of whites are generally better than those of blacks and "other" races, and this disparity is probably a significant factor in the differences of opinion on this question by race. Fully 20 percent of blacks and other races, but only 9 percent of whites, think there is little people can do to change the course of their life. Eighty-three percent of whites disagree with this statement compared with only 67 to 68 percent of blacks and other races.

Most people aged 30 to 59 have comfortable incomes and good health, two factors which undoubtedly influence their opinion on this issue. Fully 82 to 83 percent of people in this age group do not believe that people are powerless to change the course of their life. Among those under age 30, a slightly smaller 78 percent say people cannot control how their life turns out. The proportion of people who believe they can control their destiny is a smaller 74 percent among people in their sixties and stands at just 71 percent among those aged 70 or older. Many older Americans have lower incomes and, more important, poorer health—factors over which they have little control.

The least educated Americans are most likely to feel people cannot change the course of their life (26 percent compared with 10 percent or fewer of people with at least a high school diploma). One reason for this perspective is the disproportionate number of older people among the least educated. Another reason is the difficulty the poorly educated have in getting ahead in today's economy.

Ability to Change the Course of Life, 1998

"There is little that people can do to change the course of their lives. Do you agree or disagree?"

(percent of people aged 18 or older responding by sex, race, age, and education, 1998)

	strongly agree	agree	neither	disagree	strongly disagree	agree, total	disagree, total
Total	**3%**	**7%**	**7%**	**43%**	**36%**	**10%**	**79%**
Men	3	8	7	43	36	11	79
Women	4	7	7	44	36	11	80
Black	7	13	10	42	25	20	67
White	3	6	6	45	38	9	83
Other	7	13	10	31	37	20	68
Aged 18 to 29	4	8	7	40	38	12	78
Aged 30 to 39	3	3	9	40	42	6	82
Aged 40 to 49	5	7	4	42	40	12	82
Aged 50 to 59	1	10	4	48	35	11	83
Aged 60 to 69	6	6	10	46	28	12	74
Aged 70 or older	2	14	9	52	19	16	71
Not a high school graduate	5	21	15	37	14	26	51
High school graduate	4	6	7	46	35	10	81
Bachelor's degree	2	3	6	34	54	5	88
Graduate degree	1	1	0	47	51	2	98

Note: Numbers may not add to 100 because "can't choose" is not shown.
Source: General Social Survey, National Opinion Research Center, University of Chicago; calculations by the author

We Give Meaning to Our Lives

The plurality of Americans believe they, personally, must provide the meaning in their life.

Is life inherently meaningful for divine or other reasons? Or is life only meaningful if we make it so? Forty-four percent agree that we personally provide the meaning in our lives, while 34 percent disagree. Eighteen percent neither agree nor disagree.

Men are slightly more likely than women to think we give our life meaning (47 versus 43 percent). A somewhat larger difference of opinion is found by race. Among whites and blacks, 44 to 45 percent say we personally give meaning to life, but a larger 56 percent of people of "other" races feel this way.

People in their forties are least likely to think we personally give meaning to life (39 percent compared with 43 to 49 percent of other age groups). Younger generations are most likely to say they neither agree nor disagree (20 to 22 percent of people under age 40 compared with 13 to 16 percent of older people).

The most educated Americans are also the most divided on this issue. Forty percent of people with a graduate degree say we give meaning to life, but 41 percent do not feel this way. Among people with less education, 44 to 45 percent think we personally give our lives meaning, while a smaller percentage think this is not the case.

We Give Meaning to Our Lives, 1998

"Life is only meaningful if you provide the meaning yourself. Do you agree or disagree?"

(percent of people aged 18 or older responding by sex, race, age, and education, 1998)

	strongly agree	agree	neither	disagree	strongly disagree	agree, total	disagree, total
Total	10%	34%	18%	21%	13%	44%	34%
Men	11	36	17	19	13	47	32
Women	10	33	18	22	12	43	34
Black	12	33	20	16	14	45	30
White	10	34	18	22	13	44	35
Other	16	40	18	18	2	56	20
Aged 18 to 29	10	39	22	16	8	49	24
Aged 30 to 39	13	31	20	21	13	44	34
Aged 40 to 49	11	28	16	23	19	39	42
Aged 50 to 59	9	38	15	23	9	47	32
Aged 60 to 69	7	36	13	24	17	43	41
Aged 70 or older	7	40	16	20	9	47	29
Not a high school graduate	7	38	20	16	10	45	26
High school graduate	10	35	17	22	13	45	35
Bachelor's degree	12	32	21	19	12	44	31
Graduate degree	14	26	15	27	14	40	41

Note: Numbers may not add to 100 because "can't choose" is not shown.
Source: General Social Survey, National Opinion Research Center, University of Chicago; calculations by the author

We Make Our Own Fate

Most people think we personally are responsible for how our lives turn out.

In the end, how our lives turn out is up to us, according to the majority of Americans. Fifty-eight percent agree that we make our own fate. Only 18 percent think this is not the case.

Men are more likely than women to think individuals are responsible for how their life turns out (62 versus 55 percent). Twenty-two percent of women, but only 15 percent of men, do not think we make our own fate.

While 56 to 58 percent of blacks and whites think we are responsible for our own fate, a larger 67 percent of "other" races believe this to be true. Fully 26 percent of other races, but only 16 percent of blacks and whites, strongly agree. Many people of other race are first- or second-generation immigrants. They, or their parents, have succeeded in making their own fate by immigrating.

Among people aged 60 or older, 53 percent think we make our own fate. Among those under age 60, a larger 58 to 60 percent agree. Declining health may influence the attitudes of older Americans, making them feel they have less control over their fate.

The most and the least educated disagree somewhat on this issue. Sixty-two percent of people who did not complete high school agree that we make our own fate. Among people with a high school diploma or a bachelor's degree, 57 to 58 percent think we make our own fate. Among those with a graduate degree, however, only 54 percent say individuals are responsible for the way their life turns out.

We Make Our Own Fate, 1998

"We each make our own fate. Do you agree or disagree?"

(percent of people aged 18 or older responding by sex, race, age, and education, 1998)

	strongly agree	agree	neither	disagree	strongly disagree	agree, total	disagree, total
Total	**16%**	**42%**	**19%**	**12%**	**6%**	**58%**	**18%**
Men	18	44	20	9	6	62	15
Women	15	40	19	15	7	55	22
Black	16	40	18	14	6	56	20
White	16	42	20	12	7	58	19
Other	26	41	15	10	3	67	13
Aged 18 to 29	18	42	19	10	5	60	15
Aged 30 to 39	20	40	23	10	5	60	15
Aged 40 to 49	18	40	16	15	10	58	25
Aged 50 to 59	13	46	18	12	7	59	19
Aged 60 to 69	11	42	20	19	6	53	25
Aged 70 or older	11	42	20	13	4	53	17
Not a high school graduate	19	43	17	10	4	62	14
High school graduate	17	41	19	13	6	58	19
Bachelor's degree	16	41	19	12	9	57	21
Graduate degree	15	39	27	10	8	54	18

Note: Numbers may not add to 100 because "can't choose" is not shown.
Source: General Social Survey, National Opinion Research Center, University of Chicago; calculations by the author

Marital Happiness

Blacks are least likely to say their marriage is very happy.

Most married people describe their marriage as "very happy" (64 percent). One-third say their marriage is "pretty happy," while few say their marriage is "not too happy."

The greatest disparity in the percentages of people with a very happy marriage is by race. Two-thirds of whites say their marriage is very happy compared with a much smaller 47 percent of blacks and 58 percent of "other" races. In 1978, an even smaller 40 percent of blacks said their marriage was very happy.

The oldest Americans are most likely to have a very happy marriage. Nearly three-quarters of people aged 70 or older say their marriage is very happy compared with 67 percent of people in their sixties and 65 percent of those in their twenties. Among those aged 30 to 59, a smaller 61 to 63 percent have a very happy marriage.

College graduates are most likely to say their marriage is very happy. Only 61 percent of people with a high school diploma or less education have a very happy marriage compared with 68 to 71 percent of college graduates.

Marital Happiness, 1998

"Taking all things together, how would you describe your marriage? Would you say that your marriage is very happy, pretty happy, or not too happy?"

(percent of people aged 18 or older responding by sex, race, age, and education, 1998)

	very happy	*pretty happy*	*not too happy*
Total	**64%**	**33%**	**3%**
Men	64	33	2
Women	64	33	3
Black	47	47	6
White	66	32	2
Other	58	37	5
Aged 18 to 29	65	32	3
Aged 30 to 39	63	36	1
Aged 40 to 49	61	36	3
Aged 50 to 59	63	33	4
Aged 60 to 69	67	29	3
Aged 70 or older	72	26	2
Not a high school graduate	61	32	6
High school graduate	61	37	2
Bachelor's degree	71	27	2
Graduate degree	68	29	3

Note: Asked only of those currently married. Numbers may not add to 100 because "don't know" is not shown. Source: General Social Survey, National Opinion Research Center, University of Chicago; calculations by the author

Marital Happiness, 1978 to 1998

"Taking all things together, how would you describe your marriage? Would you say that your marriage is very happy, pretty happy, or not too happy?"

(percent of people aged 18 or older responding by sex, race, age, and education, 1978–98)

	very happy			pretty happy			not too happy		
	1998	*1988*	*1978*	*1998*	*1988*	*1978*	*1998*	*1988*	*1978*
Total	**64%**	**60%**	**65%**	**33%**	**37%**	**32%**	**3%**	**2%**	**3%**
Men	64	64	66	33	34	32	2	1	2
Women	64	57	65	33	39	32	3	4	3
Black	47	44	40	47	49	51	6	7	8
White	66	62	67	32	35	30	2	2	2
Aged 18 to 29	65	58	67	32	39	31	3	3	1
Aged 30 to 39	63	61	64	36	37	34	1	2	2
Aged 40 to 49	61	59	57	36	38	37	3	3	5
Aged 50 to 59	63	63	69	33	34	29	4	3	2
Aged 60 to 69	67	56	70	29	40	28	3	2	2
Aged 70 or older	72	65	67	26	30	31	2	2	3
Not a high school graduate	61	57	61	32	35	35	6	6	4
High school graduate	61	61	67	37	37	31	2	2	2
Bachelor's degree	71	65	65	27	35	33	2	0	1
Graduate degree	68	58	64	29	37	33	3	5	2

Note: Asked only of those currently married. Numbers may not add to 100 because "don't know" is not shown.
Source: General Social Survey, National Opinion Research Center, University of Chicago; calculations by the author

Living Together

Cohabitation will become more acceptable.

Since the 1960s, the number of unmarried couples who live together has increased sharply. Americans have become more accepting of this practice, but there is still considerable disagreement on whether it is right or not. Forty-three percent say it is okay for a couple to live together without intending to get married. One-third do not think it is right.

Men and women are miles apart on this issue. Half of men agree that it is all right to live together compared with only 37 percent of women. Women are considerably more likely than men to say they neither agree nor disagree (23 versus 17 percent) and that they disagree (37 versus 31 percent).

There is disagreement on this issue by race as well. Only 33 percent of blacks think it is okay to cohabit compared with 44 to 47 percent of whites and "other" races. Forty-one percent of blacks disapprove compared with 34 percent of whites and 26 percent of others.

The differences of opinion by age point to a future in which most people will accept cohabitation. As older generations die off, the opinions of younger generations will become the norm, and younger generations are far more accepting of cohabitation. Fully 61 percent of people under age 30 think it is all right to live together, but the proportion drops to only 17 percent among people aged 70 or older.

Among college graduates, 47 to 51 percent think it is okay for a couple to live together. In contrast, only 41 to 42 percent of those with less education agree. People without a college degree are most likely to say they neither agree nor disagree.

Living Together, 1998

"It is alright for a couple to live together without intending to get married. Do you agree or disagree?"

(percent of people aged 18 or older responding by sex, race, age, and education, 1998)

	strongly agree	agree	neither	disagree	strongly disagree	agree, total	disagree, total
Total	**17%**	**26%**	**20%**	**16%**	**18%**	**43%**	**34%**
Men	18	32	17	13	18	50	31
Women	16	21	23	18	19	37	37
Black	15	18	24	19	22	33	41
White	17	27	20	16	18	44	34
Other	18	29	25	8	18	47	26
Aged 18 to 29	25	36	16	10	12	61	22
Aged 30 to 39	19	33	18	15	14	52	29
Aged 40 to 49	18	25	19	13	21	43	34
Aged 50 to 59	13	22	27	15	20	35	35
Aged 60 to 69	8	16	27	21	25	24	46
Aged 70 or older	7	10	22	30	26	17	56
Not a high school graduate	17	25	20	18	17	42	35
High school graduate	15	26	21	17	18	41	35
Bachelor's degree	18	29	18	12	21	47	33
Graduate degree	22	29	16	14	17	51	31

Note: Numbers may not add to 100 because "can't choose" is not shown.
Source: General Social Survey, National Opinion Research Center, University of Chicago; calculations by the author

"Trial" Marriage Is a Good Idea

Americans are divided on this issue.

With divorce rates at an all-time high, you might think Americans would support cohabitation as a sort of "trial" marriage before tying the knot. But Americans are divided on this question, as 39 percent say they think it is a good idea and 33 percent say they do not.

Men are more likely than women to want to try before they buy. Forty-three percent of men agree that it is a good idea for a couple to live together before marriage compared with 36 percent of women. Blacks and whites are less likely than "other" races to think a trial marriage is a good idea (38 to 39 percent compared with 51 percent of other races).

The largest difference of opinion is found by age. The older people are the less likely they are to think couples should live together before marriage. Fully 58 percent of adults under age 30 think cohabiting before marriage is a good idea, but the proportion falls to just 14 percent among people aged 70 or older. Only 19 percent of people under age 30 do not believe cohabiting before marriage is a good thing compared with 54 percent of people aged 70 or older.

Interestingly, the less education people have the more likely they are to support trial marriages. Forty-four percent of people who did not complete high school say they think it is a good idea, but the proportion drops to just 30 percent among people with a graduate degree. The percentage of those who say they disagree does not increase with education, however. Rather, people with more education are more likely to say they neither agree nor disagree.

"Trial" Marriage Is a Good Idea, 1998

"It's a good idea for a couple who intend to get married to live together first. Do you agree or disagree?"

(percent of people aged 18 or older responding by sex, race, age, and education, 1998)

	strongly agree	agree	neither	disagree	strongly disagree	agree, total	disagree, total
Total	**15%**	**24%**	**26%**	**17%**	**16%**	**39%**	**33%**
Men	16	27	24	16	16	43	32
Women	15	21	28	18	16	36	34
Black	19	20	24	20	16	39	36
White	14	24	27	17	16	38	33
Other	18	33	23	11	12	51	23
Aged 18 to 29	26	32	22	7	12	58	19
Aged 30 to 39	18	28	25	15	12	46	27
Aged 40 to 49	14	25	27	14	18	39	32
Aged 50 to 59	11	19	31	22	16	30	38
Aged 60 to 69	5	15	30	21	24	20	45
Aged 70 or older	4	10	26	33	21	14	54
Not a high school graduate	19	25	19	18	16	44	34
High school graduate	15	25	27	16	15	40	31
Bachelor's degree	13	21	28	15	21	34	36
Graduate degree	6	24	35	16	17	30	33

Note: Numbers may not add to 100 because "don't know" is not shown.
Source: General Social Survey, National Opinion Research Center, University of Chicago; calculations by the author

Ideal Number of Children

Two is the most popular number.

American families have been shrinking for decades, and this trend is reflected in the number of children people believe is ideal. For the majority of Americans (56 percent), the ideal family has two children. Twenty percent think three is best. Only 11 percent think four or more children is ideal.

Men and women have similar opinions about the ideal number of children, but opinions differ by race. Whites are most likely to favor two children (58 percent compared with 48 to 51 percent of blacks and "other" races). Four children is ideal according to 16 percent of blacks and 12 percent of other races, but only 8 percent of whites. The number of blacks who think four children is ideal fell from 23 percent in 1978, however.

Older Americans still cling to the ideal of a large family. Fully 18 percent of people in their sixties and 22 percent of people aged 70 or older believe four or more children is ideal, compared with 10 percent or fewer of those under age 60. The percentage of those who favor large families was smaller in most age groups in 1998 than it was in 1978.

The more education people have the less likely they are to favor large families. Twenty-two percent of people who did not complete high school believe four or more children is ideal, compared with 12 percent of high school graduates and 5 percent of college graduates.

Ideal Number of Children, 1998

"What do you think is the ideal number of children for a family to have?"

(percent of people aged 18 or older responding by sex, race, age, and education, 1998)

	none	one	two	three	four	five or more	as many as you want
Total	**1%**	**3%**	**56%**	**20%**	**9%**	**2%**	**9%**
Men	2	2	56	22	8	2	9
Women	1	4	56	19	10	2	9
Black	1	4	48	19	16	5	7
White	2	2	58	21	8	1	9
Other	0	4	51	18	12	5	10
Aged 18 to 29	2	4	57	23	9	1	5
Aged 30 to 39	0	4	55	22	8	2	9
Aged 40 to 49	2	3	56	18	6	2	12
Aged 50 to 59	2	1	64	17	5	1	11
Aged 60 to 69	1	1	56	20	16	2	4
Aged 70 or older	0	1	47	21	18	4	9
Not a high school graduate	2	2	49	18	16	6	8
High school graduate	2	3	55	21	10	2	8
Bachelor's degree	1	2	62	21	4	1	9
Graduate degree	1	3	54	21	5	0	16

Note: Numbers may not add to 100 because "don't know" is not shown.
Source: General Social Survey, National Opinion Research Center, University of Chicago; calculations by the author

Ideal Number of Children, 1978 to 1998

"What do you think is the ideal number of children for a family to have?"

(percent of people aged 18 or older responding by sex, race, age, and education, 1978–98)

	two			three			four		
	1998	1988	1978	1998	1988	1978	1998	1988	1978
Total	**56%**	**53%**	**49%**	**20%**	**21%**	**23%**	**9%**	**9%**	**13%**
Men	56	55	50	22	21	20	8	9	12
Women	56	52	48	19	22	25	10	9	14
Black	48	37	35	19	22	18	16	17	23
White	58	55	51	21	21	24	8	8	11
Aged 18 to 29	57	55	56	23	25	23	9	9	11
Aged 30 to 39	55	56	57	22	20	20	8	8	7
Aged 40 to 49	56	58	51	18	21	18	6	5	16
Aged 50 to 59	64	52	39	17	19	29	5	10	14
Aged 60 to 69	56	50	44	20	17	27	16	14	16
Aged 70 or older	47	42	34	21	24	24	18	10	18
Not a high school graduate	49	47	39	18	16	21	16	14	18
High school graduate	55	55	53	21	23	25	10	8	11
Bachelor's degree	62	49	58	21	27	22	4	6	8
Graduate degree	54	61	55	21	13	21	5	5	5

Note: Numbers may not add to 100 because "don't know" is not shown.
Source: General Social Survey, National Opinion Research Center, University of Chicago; calculations by the author

Most Important Qualities in Children

Most Americans want kids to be independent.

We are a nation of individualists, and we are raising our children to carry on this tradition. Half of Americans (49 percent) say it is most important that children learn to think for themselves. People are far more likely to rank independent thinking first in importance than obedience, hard work, helping others, or being popular. Since 1988, however, the proportion of people choosing independent thinking as the most important quality declined slightly, while the proportion of those who say children should learn to work hard has risen slightly.

Women are more likely than men to put the highest value on independent thinking (52 versus 47 percent). The gap is narrower than it was in 1986, however. Whites are more likely than blacks and "other" races to say thinking for oneself is most important (53 versus 37 to 39 percent of blacks and other races). Blacks are more likely to say it is most important that children learn to obey. Only 16 percent of whites rank learning to work hard most important compared with 22 to 26 percent of blacks and other races.

There are substantial differences by age in the rankings. People aged 30 to 59 are more likely than older and younger age groups to say teaching children to think for themselves is most important. Older Americans are far more likely to say obedience is most important, while people under age 30 are more likely than other age groups to believe children need to learn to work hard.

People with different levels of education have substantially different views on the qualities children need to succeed. Only 23 percent of people who did not complete college (many of whom are older) ranked independent thinking as the most important quality in children. The figure rises to 71 percent among those with a graduate degree. The proportion of adults who say obedience is most important is highest among those with the least education (33 percent compared with 8 to 19 percent of people with a high school diploma or more).

Most Important Qualities in Children, 1998

"If you had to choose, which thing on this list would you pick as the most important for a child to learn to prepare him or her for life?"

(percent of people aged 18 or older choosing a quality as most important by sex, race, age, and education, 1998)

	to think for himself or herself	to obey	to work hard	to help others	to be popular
Total	**49%**	**19%**	**17%**	**13%**	**1%**
Men	47	20	19	14	1
Women	52	18	16	13	1
Black	37	30	22	8	2
White	53	17	16	14	1
Other	39	18	26	16	2
Aged 18 to 29	46	16	21	17	1
Aged 30 to 39	53	16	19	11	1
Aged 40 to 49	56	14	16	13	1
Aged 50 to 59	52	19	15	14	0
Aged 60 to 69	43	26	19	9	2
Aged 70 or older	40	32	12	15	1
Not a high school graduate	23	33	23	19	2
High school graduate	50	19	16	14	1
Bachelor's degree	65	10	16	10	0
Graduate degree	71	8	11	7	2

Note: Numbers may not add to 100 because "don't know" is not shown.
Source: General Social Survey, National Opinion Research Center, University of Chicago; calculations by the author

Most Important Qualities in Children, 1988 and 1998

"If you had to choose, which thing on this list would you pick as the most important for a child to learn to prepare him or her for life?"

(percent of people aged 18 or older choosing a quality as most important by sex, race, age, and education, 1988–98)

	to think for himself/herself		to obey		to work hard		to help others		to be popular	
	1998	1988	1998	1988	1998	1988	1998	1988	1998	1988
Total	**49%**	**53%**	**19%**	**20%**	**17%**	**14%**	**13%**	**12%**	**1%**	**1%**
Men	47	48	20	22	19	15	14	13	1	1
Women	52	56	18	18	16	13	13	12	1	1
Black	37	38	30	27	22	19	8	15	2	1
White	53	55	17	19	16	13	14	12	1	1
Aged 18 to 29	46	48	16	16	21	19	17	16	1	1
Aged 30 to 39	53	56	16	13	19	16	11	13	1	1
Aged 40 to 49	56	62	14	15	16	9	13	13	1	1
Aged 50 to 59	52	59	19	16	15	13	14	11	0	1
Aged 60 to 69	43	55	26	25	19	12	9	6	2	2
Aged 70 or older	40	34	32	46	12	8	15	11	1	2
Not a high school graduate	23	37	33	32	23	14	19	14	2	2
High school graduate	50	52	19	20	16	15	14	12	1	1
Bachelor's degree	65	71	10	6	16	12	10	10	0	1
Graduate degree	71	71	8	7	11	11	7	11	2	0

Note: Numbers may not add to 100 because "don't know" is not shown.
Source: General Social Survey, National Opinion Research Center, University of Chicago; calculations by the author

Spanking Children

Most people still believe in spanking, but the percentage is down from a decade ago.

While "time out" has become the discipline of choice for many parents in recent years, spanking still remains popular. Nearly three-quarters of Americans say a spanking is sometimes necessary for disciplining children. Studies by social researchers indicating that spanking may do more harm than good may be influencing parents, however. The proportion of the public that favors spanking is down from 77 percent in 1988.

Women are more likely than men to want to spare the rod. While 78 percent of men agree that a spanking is sometimes necessary, a smaller 69 percent of women feel this way. There are even stronger differences of opinion by race. Fully 83 percent of blacks think children must sometimes be spanked compared with 72 percent of whites and 65 percent of "other" races.

Enthusiasm for spanking declines with education. Among people who did not complete high school, fully 81 percent agree that children must sometimes be spanked. Among people with a high school diploma or a bachelor's degree, 70 to 74 percent think spanking is sometimes necessary. But a much smaller 58 percent of people with a graduate degree feel this way.

Spanking Children, 1998

"It is sometimes necessary to discipline a child with a good, hard spanking—do you agree or disagree?"

(percent of people aged 18 or older responding by sex, race, age, and education, 1998)

	strongly agree	agree	disagree	strongly disagree	agree, total	disagree, total
Total	**26%**	**47%**	**18%**	**7%**	**73%**	**25%**
Men	30	48	15	5	78	20
Women	23	46	20	9	69	29
Black	32	51	11	4	83	15
White	25	47	19	7	72	26
Other	28	37	23	12	65	35
Aged 18 to 29	20	52	19	6	72	25
Aged 30 to 39	24	48	17	9	72	26
Aged 40 to 49	28	43	19	8	71	27
Aged 50 to 59	27	46	19	7	73	26
Aged 60 to 69	33	47	15	5	80	20
Aged 70 or older	28	46	19	5	74	24
Not a high school graduate	30	51	18	2	81	20
High school graduate	28	46	17	7	74	24
Bachelor's degree	20	50	20	9	70	29
Graduate degree	21	37	24	16	58	40

Note: Numbers may not add to 100 because "don't know" is not shown.
Source: General Social Survey, National Opinion Research Center, University of Chicago; calculations by the author

Spanking Children, 1988 and 1998

"It is sometimes necessary to discipline a child with a good, hard spanking—do you agree or disagree?"

(percent of people aged 18 or older responding by sex, race, age, and education, 1988–98)

	agree/strongly agree		disagree/strongly disagree	
	1998	1988	1998	1988
Total	**73%**	**77%**	**25%**	**22%**
Men	78	81	20	18
Women	69	73	29	26
Black	83	84	15	15
White	72	76	26	23
Aged 18 to 29	72	73	25	26
Aged 30 to 39	72	79	26	21
Aged 40 to 49	71	76	27	24
Aged 50 to 59	73	80	26	20
Aged 60 to 69	80	77	20	21
Aged 70 or older	74	77	24	20
Not a high school graduate	81	79	20	20
High school graduate	74	78	24	21
Bachelor's degree	70	76	29	24
Graduate degree	58	60	40	39

Note: Numbers may not add to 100 because "don't know" is not shown.
Source: General Social Survey, National Opinion Research Center, University of Chicago; calculations by the author

4

Public Arena

Everyone has an opinion about "public-arena" issues—gun control, the death penalty, taxes, Social Security, and so on. These opinions, often inflamed by the media or by politicians, can be well-informed or seriously misinformed. Many think gun control is a controversial issue, for example, but the public is remarkably united on it. The overwhelming majority believe people should have to obtain a police permit before buying a gun.

Concern about crime unites people on other issues as well. Most people support the death penalty and feel their local courts are not harsh enough on criminals. Two in five people are afraid to walk at night in their own neighborhood, a fear which undoubtedly contributes to conservative opinions about punishment for criminals.

The perennial complaint of Americans is, of course, taxes. In 1998, most people thought their taxes were too high, as they did in 1988 and 1977. They may not like paying them, but there is solid consensus that cheating on taxes is wrong. Republicans have tried to capitalize on tax aversion but this tactic hasn't boosted membership in the GOP. Loyalty toward both major parties is on the decline. Independents now outnumber both Republicans and Democrats.

Although Americans support cutbacks in social programs, they still believe government should aid some segments of society. The plurality thinks government should help the poor, but that individuals are equally responsible for helping themselves. Most people do not believe, however, that it is government's responsibility to make sure everyone has a job.

One problem that demands government attention is Social Security. Most Americans think the system has serious problems that will require major changes. But only one-third of the public would privatize it.

Americans may not hold much hope that government can fix Social Security, however. The vast majority have little confidence in Congress and the White House. Few of the nation's major institutions fare any better. Only about one-quarter or fewer Americans have a great deal of confidence in major corporations, organized labor, banks and financial institutions, and education. The press is at rock bottom in public opinion; only one in ten has a great deal of confidence in it.

Women are far more likely than men to feel vulnerable to crime in their own neighborhood, so it is no surprise that they are more concerned about preventing crime than punishing criminals. Women are much more likely than men to favor requiring a permit to purchase a gun, while men are stronger supporters of the death penalty. Solid majorities of both sexes believe the courts are not harsh enough with criminals.

Men have stronger opinions about the nation's leaders. They are more likely than women to express a great deal of confidence in the Supreme Court, the scientific community, and the military. On the other hand, men are more likely to have hardly any confidence in Congress, the executive branch of the federal government, and unions. Women tend to take the middle ground, most often expressing only some confidence in the leaders of the nation's major institutions.

Men's low regard for government may play a role in their greater opposition to an activist government. Women are more likely than men to believe government should help the poor, provide jobs to all who want them, and reduce income differences between the rich and the poor. Men are much more likely to say government is already doing too many things that should be left up to businesses and individuals. They are also more likely than women to say the government keeps too many secrets.

The gender gap that emerges in elections is unlikely to disappear any time soon. Men are more likely to consider themselves conservative, while women are more likely to say they are moderate or liberal. Women are much more likely than men to identify themselves as Democrats, while men prefer to be labeled Republican or independent.

On average, women have longer life spans and greater need for a secure retirement income. Their relative longevity is one reason why women are less likely than men to believe the current Social Security system should be phased out and replaced with private retirement accounts. Men are less likely than women to say it is wrong to underreport income to lower one's tax bill.

The races disagree sharply on many public arena issues. Whites are most likely to say they have a great deal of confidence in the Supreme Court, the military, the scientific community, and major corporations. Blacks and "other" races are most likely to express great confidence in education and the media. Whites are more likely than blacks and other races to express little confidence in the executive branch of the federal government and organized labor. Blacks have the least confidence in the Supreme Court, banks and financial institutions, and big business.

The role of government provokes some of the most pointed disagreements between the races. Blacks are far more likely than whites and somewhat more likely than other races to believe government should alleviate poverty and provide jobs. Whites are far more likely than blacks and other races to think government does too much already. Whites are most likely to want government out of the retirement business, while blacks are more likely to think the Social Security program should continue more or less as it is now.

Blacks are more likely than whites and other races to say they are politically moderate, while whites tend to be conservative, and other races liberal. By a wide margin, blacks are more likely than whites and other races to consider themselves Democrats. Whites are far more likely to consider themselves Republicans, while people of other race are most likely to be independents.

Blacks and other races are more likely than whites to be fearful of walking in their own neighborhood at night. But this attitude does not translate into more support for a tough-on-crime approach. Blacks are most likely to think the courts sometimes deal too harshly with persons convicted of crimes and they are least likely to support the death penalty. Blacks and other races are considerably more likely than whites, however, to favor requiring people to obtain a police permit before buying a gun.

Solid majorities of all age groups support gun control, but there is some disagreement by age regarding the justice system. The youngest and the oldest adults are less likely than other age groups to feel the courts are not harsh enough on criminals—although young adults are most likely to be crime victims and the elderly are most likely to feel vulnerable to crime in their own neighborhood.

People in their thirties and forties have the greatest concerns about the Social Security system, while people aged 60 or older are most likely to think that, at worst, there are only minor problems with the system. People under age 50 are most likely to favor privatizing Social Security, although the plurality would prefer that the system continue as it is now.

People aged 30 to 59 are most likely to be disgruntled with their taxes. The percentage of people who think their taxes are too high peaks among people in their forties, who also tend to be the most dissatisfied with the leaders of the nation's government, businesses, and other major institutions.

Younger generations tend to be more individualistic and less civic-minded than their elders. One could also argue that they need to develop a stronger sense of ethics. The youngest adults are less likely than older people to say it is wrong to lie to obtain government benefits. Generation Xers and baby boomers are less likely than adults aged 50 or older to say it is wrong to cheat on one's taxes.

College graduates frequently disagree with less educated Americans on public-arena issues. People with college degrees are more likely to say they have a great deal of confidence in the scientific community, the Supreme Court, and major companies. Americans who did not complete high school are most likely to have a great deal of confidence in Congress, banks and financial institutions, organized labor, education, the media, and the military.

Democrats still command the most loyalty among people who did not complete high school. People with at least a high school diploma are more likely to identify themselves as independents than as Democrats or Republicans.

On some issues, opinions change as the level of education rises. The more education people have the more likely they are to support gun control. The percentage of people who say it is seriously wrong to cheat on taxes or to lie to obtain government benefits also rises with education.

Some differences of opinion by education reflect self-interest. Incomes rise with education, and this affluence influences attitudes on financial issues. People who did not complete high school (who also have the lowest incomes) are most likely to strongly agree that government should do everything possible to help the poor raise their standard of living, reduce the income disparity between rich and poor, and provide jobs. They are least likely to believe the government is doing too many things that should be left up to business and individuals.

College graduates are divided on whether Social Security should be privatized or continue in its present state. Majorities of people without a college degree, on the other hand, want to keep the Social Security system as it is.

Confidence in Leaders

Few of the nation's leaders inspire a great deal of confidence.

Americans are losing confidence in their leaders. Most people say they have only some confidence in the leaders of the nation's major institutions. A minority (and in some cases, a small minority) has a great deal of confidence in leaders. None of the institutions considered here instills a great deal of confidence in the majority of Americans.

Americans are most likely to have a great deal of confidence in the leaders of the military, the scientific community, and the Supreme Court. The lowest ratings go to the executive branch of the federal government and Congress.

Men are more likely than women to express a great deal of confidence in the Supreme Court, the scientific community, major corporations, the military, and even the press—which gets a particularly dismal assessment from all segments of the population. Men are more likely to have hardly any confidence in the executive branch, Congress, and organized labor. Women generally take the middle ground, with majorities saying they have some confidence in most of these institutions.

There are some strong differences of opinion by race. Whites are more likely than blacks and "other" races to express a great deal of confidence in the Supreme Court and the scientific community, but they are less likely to have a lot of confidence in education and the media. Whites are also more likely to say they have hardly any confidence in the executive branch of the federal government and organized labor. Blacks are most likely to have little confidence in the Supreme Court, banks and financial institutions, and big business.

The middle-aged are particularly disgruntled with the nation's government and institutions. People aged 40 to 59 are most likely to say they have hardly any confidence in Congress and the press. People in their forties are most likely to have little confidence in the executive branch, while those in their fifties and sixties have the least confidence in unions. The youngest and the oldest adults tend to have the most confidence in many of the institutions examined here.

College graduates are considerably more likely than those with less education to have a great deal of confidence in the leaders of the scientific community, the Supreme Court, and major companies. People who did not complete high school are most likely to have a great deal of confidence in financial institutions, the military, education, the press, organized labor, and Congress.

Confidence in Leaders, 1998

"As far as the people running the following institutions are concerned, would you say you have a great deal of confidence, only some confidence, or hardly any confidence at all in them?"

(percent of people aged 18 or older responding by sex, race, age, and education, 1998)

	executive branch of federal government			Congress			Supreme Court			banks and financial institutions		
	great deal	only some	hardly any	great deal	only some	hardly any	great deal	only some	hardly any	great deal	only some	hardly any
Total	**14%**	**48%**	**35%**	**11%**	**56%**	**30%**	**31%**	**50%**	**14%**	**26%**	**56%**	**16%**
Men	14	46	38	11	54	33	34	47	15	27	54	17
Women	13	49	33	10	58	28	28	52	13	24	58	15
Black	16	53	27	11	56	30	24	49	21	26	50	20
White	13	46	38	10	56	31	33	50	13	26	57	15
Other	24	52	19	14	57	21	26	51	14	25	52	18
Aged 18 to 29	15	48	33	15	53	29	38	45	14	29	52	17
Aged 30 to 39	12	54	32	9	61	27	30	52	13	25	58	15
Aged 40 to 49	11	45	42	10	56	32	27	55	15	19	59	20
Aged 50 to 59	16	47	36	8	55	36	32	49	16	24	57	17
Aged 60 to 69	13	49	35	10	62	25	29	51	13	23	64	11
Aged 70 or older	20	41	33	10	52	31	31	45	13	35	47	13
Not a high school graduate	21	40	30	16	46	29	26	40	19	31	46	16
High school graduate	12	47	39	10	55	32	27	54	15	24	57	18
Bachelor's degree	11	56	31	9	64	26	39	50	9	27	61	11
Graduate degree	20	55	25	4	72	23	49	47	4	24	65	10

(continued)

(continued from previous page)

	major companies			organized labor			scientific community			education		
	great deal	*only some*	*hardly any*	*great deal*	*only some*	*hardly any*	*great deal*	*only some*	*hardly any*	*great deal*	*only some*	*hardly any*
Total	**26%**	**56%**	**13%**	**11%**	**52%**	**29%**	**40%**	**45%**	**8%**	**27%**	**55%**	**17%**
Men	30	52	15	11	51	33	46	40	8	25	57	17
Women	23	60	11	11	53	26	35	49	8	29	54	16
Black	14	62	18	10	52	26	25	53	13	38	46	15
White	28	55	12	11	51	31	43	44	6	24	57	17
Other	26	58	11	13	65	16	38	42	12	32	57	8
Aged 18 to 29	28	59	10	14	60	18	46	42	7	31	56	12
Aged 30 to 39	25	59	13	10	54	27	43	44	7	25	55	19
Aged 40 to 49	27	58	13	9	50	33	34	50	9	22	58	20
Aged 50 to 59	24	55	16	7	50	36	38	48	8	21	58	20
Aged 60 to 69	32	52	13	8	51	35	36	47	7	29	56	14
Aged 70 or older	23	52	13	18	40	30	38	38	9	37	48	11
Not a high school graduate	20	52	17	17	45	25	28	40	14	40	43	13
High school graduate	24	60	13	10	52	30	35	49	9	24	57	19
Bachelor's degree	34	53	10	8	57	27	55	38	4	22	62	15
Graduate degree	37	53	9	6	55	36	60	39	1	29	63	8

(continued)

(continued from previous page)

	the press			the military		
	great deal	only some	hardly any	great deal	only some	hardly any
Total	**9%**	**46%**	**42%**	**36%**	**49%**	**12%**
Men	12	44	43	43	44	12
Women	7	48	42	31	52	13
Black	13	45	41	32	50	15
White	8	46	43	37	49	12
Other	11	45	40	38	39	16
Aged 18 to 29	12	46	40	35	46	16
Aged 30 to 39	8	47	42	34	52	11
Aged 40 to 49	8	43	47	34	49	14
Aged 50 to 59	7	46	45	30	54	14
Aged 60 to 69	12	53	35	40	47	10
Aged 70 or older	11	43	41	48	42	6
Not a high school graduate	15	41	37	49	34	10
High school graduate	9	46	44	35	50	13
Bachelor's degree	8	46	44	28	56	13
Graduate degree	5	60	34	28	57	15

Note: Numbers may not add to 100 because "don't know" is not shown.
Source: General Social Survey, National Opinion Research Center, University of Chicago; calculations by the author

Confidence in Banks and Financial Institutions

The oldest and youngest adults have the most confidence in banks.

Americans have relatively little confidence in government and business, and banks are no exception. Only one-quarter say they have a great deal of confidence in the leaders of banks and financial institutions. More than half (56 percent) have only some confidence, while 16 percent have hardly any. In 1978, a larger 33 percent said they had a great deal of confidence and a smaller 12 percent said they had hardly any.

The percentages of people who have a great deal, only some, or hardly any confidence in business are similar by demographic characteristic, with a few exceptions. People under age 30 and those aged 70 or older are more likely than other age groups to say they have a great deal of confidence in the leaders of banks and financial institutions (29 and 35 percent, respectively). People in their forties are least likely to say so (19 percent).

Among people with a high school diploma or more education, 24 to 27 percent have a great deal of confidence in banks and financial institutions. Among people who did not complete high school, a larger 31 percent have a great deal of confidence. But people with less education are also more likely to have hardly any confidence in financial institutions. Only 10 to 11 percent of college graduates say they have hardly any confidence in these institutions compared with 16 to 18 percent of people with less education.

Confidence in Banks and Financial Institutions, 1978 to 1998

"As far as people running banks and financial institutions are concerned, would you say you have a great deal of confidence, only some confidence, or hardly any confidence at all in them?"

(percent of people aged 18 or older responding by sex, race, age, and education, 1978–98)

	a great deal			only some			hardly any		
	1998	*1988*	*1978*	*1998*	*1988*	*1978*	*1998*	*1988*	*1978*
Total	**26%**	**27%**	**33%**	**56%**	**58%**	**54%**	**16%**	**13%**	**12%**
Men	27	26	35	54	57	50	17	14	14
Women	24	27	31	58	58	57	15	13	10
Black	26	30	31	50	56	53	20	13	15
White	26	27	33	57	58	54	15	14	11
Aged 18 to 29	29	30	23	52	53	56	17	15	20
Aged 30 to 39	25	25	28	58	56	61	15	15	11
Aged 40 to 49	19	20	34	59	65	56	20	15	10
Aged 50 to 59	24	28	39	57	58	53	17	12	7
Aged 60 to 69	23	29	40	64	54	52	11	12	4
Aged 70 or older	35	28	50	47	62	37	13	7	10
Not a high school graduate	31	28	35	46	55	50	16	11	11
High school graduate	24	28	33	57	56	54	18	15	13
Bachelor's degree	27	26	28	61	64	61	11	10	11
Graduate degree	24	18	37	65	69	58	10	12	3

Note: Numbers may not add to 100 because "don't know" is not shown.
Source: General Social Survey, National Opinion Research Center, University of Chicago; calculations by the author

Confidence in Major Companies

Most people have only some confidence in the nation's big businesses.

The majority of Americans (56 percent) say they have only some confidence in the leaders of big business. About one-quarter have a great deal of confidence. These figures are slighter better than in 1978, when a smaller 22 percent had a great deal of confidence in major companies.

Men are more likely than women to say they have a great deal of confidence in major companies (30 versus 23 percent). This is an improvement over 1978 when 27 percent of men and only 18 percent of women had solid confidence in major companies.

Whites have more confidence in big business than blacks do. Only 14 percent of blacks have a great deal of confidence in major companies compared with 28 percent of whites. Eighteen percent of blacks, but only 12 percent of whites, have hardly any confidence in the leaders of major companies. In 1978, an even larger 26 percent of blacks had hardly any confidence in business compared with 15 percent of whites.

Differences by age are slight, but people in their sixties are more likely than other age groups to say they have a great deal of confidence in the people running major companies. In 1978, the middle-aged were more likely than other age groups to say this.

College graduates are more likely than those with less education to have a great deal of confidence in big business. More than one-third of college graduates feel a great deal of confidence compared with 20 to 24 percent of people without a college degree. Seventeen percent of people who did not complete high school say they have hardly any confidence in big business compared with 13 percent of high school graduates and 9 to 10 percent of college graduates.

Confidence in Major Companies, 1978 to 1998

"As far as people running major companies are concerned, would you say you have a great deal of confidence, only some confidence, or hardly any confidence at all in them?"

(percent of people aged 18 or older responding by sex, race, age, and education, 1978–98)

	a great deal			only some			hardly any		
	1998	1988	1978	1998	1988	1978	1998	1988	1978
Total	**26%**	**25%**	**22%**	**56%**	**60%**	**58%**	**13%**	**11%**	**16%**
Men	30	29	27	52	57	55	15	11	15
Women	23	21	18	60	62	60	11	11	17
Black	14	12	8	62	67	60	18	16	26
White	28	27	23	55	59	58	12	10	15
Aged 18 to 29	28	28	15	59	61	64	10	8	19
Aged 30 to 39	25	22	22	59	64	58	13	11	18
Aged 40 to 49	27	26	28	58	58	57	13	13	12
Aged 50 to 59	24	24	30	55	61	57	16	12	11
Aged 60 to 69	32	20	23	52	61	60	13	13	12
Aged 70 or older	23	26	19	52	55	45	13	8	20
Not a high school graduate	20	19	16	52	56	54	17	14	21
High school graduate	24	23	22	60	63	62	13	11	14
Bachelor's degree	34	40	31	53	51	53	10	6	14
Graduate degree	37	25	45	53	65	45	9	8	6

Note: Numbers may not add to 100 because "don't know" is not shown.
Source: General Social Survey, National Opinion Research Center, University of Chicago; calculations by the author

Confidence in Congress

Congressional leaders inspire little confidence among Americans.

Only 11 percent of the public has a great deal of confidence in Congressional leaders. Most adults (56 percent) have only some confidence, while 30 percent have hardly any confidence in Congress. In 1978, a smaller 21 percent had hardly any confidence in Congress.

Men have a lower opinion of Congress than women do. One-third of men have hardly any confidence in Congressional leaders compared with 28 percent of women. Both men and women had less confidence in 1998 than in 1978.

The middle-aged (40-to-59-year-olds) and the oldest Americans are most likely to say they have hardly any confidence in Congressional leaders. The youngest adults have more faith than their elders. Fifteen percent of people under age 30 have a great deal of confidence in Congress compared with 10 percent or fewer of their elders.

The proportion of people saying they have a great deal of confidence in Congressional leaders declines with education. Only 4 percent of people with a graduate degree feel a great deal of confidence compared with 16 percent of people who did not complete high school. College graduates are most likely to say they have only some confidence in Congress.

Confidence in Congress, 1978 to 1998

**"As far as people running Congress are concerned, would you say you have
a great deal of confidence, only some confidence, or hardly any confidence at all in them?"**

(percent of people aged 18 or older responding by sex, race, age, and education, 1978–98)

	a great deal			only some			hardly any		
	1998	1988	1978	1998	1988	1978	1998	1988	1978
Total	11%	15%	13%	56%	62%	63%	30%	19%	21%
Men	11	16	14	54	60	61	33	21	23
Women	10	15	12	58	63	64	28	18	19
Black	11	14	14	56	67	64	30	12	19
White	10	15	13	56	61	63	31	21	21
Aged 18 to 29	15	24	13	53	57	60	29	16	25
Aged 30 to 39	9	14	12	61	65	67	27	17	19
Aged 40 to 49	10	13	14	56	66	67	32	20	16
Aged 50 to 59	8	18	16	55	59	58	36	19	23
Aged 60 to 69	10	8	9	62	64	64	25	23	21
Aged 70 or older	10	11	12	52	60	61	31	25	19
Not a high school graduate	16	13	14	46	61	58	29	19	21
High school graduate	10	18	12	55	58	64	32	21	21
Bachelor's degree	9	10	13	64	75	69	26	14	19
Graduate degree	4	12	13	72	65	63	23	24	21

Note: Numbers may not add to 100 because "don't know" is not shown.
Source: General Social Survey, National Opinion Research Center, University of Chicago; calculations by the author

Confidence in the Supreme Court

Whites have far more confidence than blacks in the nation's highest court.

Half of Americans say they have only some confidence in the Supreme Court. Thirty-one percent say they have a great deal of confidence in the Court, while 14 percent have hardly any. While this isn't an overwhelming vote of confidence, the Supreme Court enjoys a higher rating than Congress and the executive branch of government.

Men are more likely than women to say they have a great deal of confidence in the Supreme Court (34 versus 28 percent). One-third of whites, but only one-quarter of blacks, have a great deal of confidence in the nation's highest court. Twenty-one percent of blacks have hardly any confidence in the Supreme Court compared with only 13 percent of whites. By both sex and race, the percentages of people with a great deal of confidence in the court increased between 1978 and 1998.

People under age 30 are most likely to say they have a great deal of confidence in the high court (38 percent). People in their forties are least likely to feel this way (27 percent).

The college educated are more likely than those with less education to say they have a great deal of confidence in the Supreme Court. Conversely, people who did not complete college are more likely to say they have hardly any confidence in the Court.

Confidence in the Supreme Court, 1978 to 1998

"As far as people running the Supreme Court are concerned, would you say you have a great deal of confidence, only some confidence, or hardly any confidence at all in them?"

(percent of people aged 18 or older responding by sex, race, age, and education, 1978–98)

	a great deal			only some			hardly any		
	1998	1988	1978	1998	1988	1978	1998	1988	1978
Total	**31%**	**35%**	**28%**	**50%**	**50%**	**53%**	**14%**	**11%**	**15%**
Men	34	39	32	47	47	50	15	10	16
Women	28	31	25	52	53	55	13	11	14
Black	24	25	20	49	57	62	21	9	13
White	33	36	28	50	49	52	13	11	15
Aged 18 to 29	38	45	27	45	44	57	14	8	13
Aged 30 to 39	30	37	31	52	50	55	13	9	12
Aged 40 to 49	27	29	30	55	60	53	15	8	16
Aged 50 to 59	32	33	31	49	52	51	16	11	15
Aged 60 to 69	29	27	24	51	53	48	13	15	16
Aged 70 or older	31	29	22	45	45	47	13	17	18
Not a high school graduate	26	27	22	40	50	51	19	12	17
High school graduate	27	34	27	54	51	56	15	12	15
Bachelor's degree	39	43	43	50	48	49	9	8	9
Graduate degree	49	49	45	47	43	45	4	6	8

Note: Numbers may not add to 100 because "don't know" is not shown.
Source: General Social Survey, National Opinion Research Center, University of Chicago; calculations by the author

Confidence in Education

Few Americans have a great deal of confidence in educational leaders.

The majority of adults (55 percent) say they have only some confidence in the leaders of the nation's education system. Twenty-seven percent have a great deal of confidence, while 17 percent have only some. The figures are essentially unchanged from 1978.

Whites have less confidence than blacks in education. Only one-quarter of whites have a great deal of confidence in educational leaders compared with 38 percent of blacks. Women are slightly more likely than men to have a great deal of confidence in educators (29 versus 25 percent).

Parents of school-age children are least likely to have a great deal of confidence in educational leaders. Only 21 to 25 percent of people aged 30 to 59 have a great deal of confidence in them. The oldest and the youngest adults are most likely to have a great deal of confidence. Thirty-seven percent of people aged 70 or older and 31 percent of those under age 30 have a great deal of confidence in educational leaders.

Ironically, people who did not complete high school are the ones most likely to have a great deal of confidence in educational leaders. Forty percent feel this way compared with 22 to 29 percent of people with more education.

Confidence in Education, 1978 to 1998

"As far as people running education are concerned, would you say you have a great deal of confidence, only some confidence, or hardly any confidence at all in them?"

(percent of people aged 18 or older responding by sex, race, age, and education, 1978-98)

	a great deal			only some			hardly any		
	1998	**1988**	**1978**	**1998**	**1988**	**1978**	**1998**	**1988**	**1978**
Total	**27%**	**29%**	**28%**	**55%**	**60%**	**55%**	**17%**	**9%**	**15%**
Men	25	28	29	57	62	55	17	9	16
Women	29	31	28	54	58	55	16	9	15
Black	38	30	40	46	58	45	15	10	13
White	24	29	27	57	61	56	17	8	15
Aged 18 to 29	31	32	27	56	61	58	12	6	15
Aged 30 to 39	25	28	24	55	61	62	19	10	14
Aged 40 to 49	22	29	31	58	61	55	20	9	13
Aged 50 to 59	21	28	31	58	62	54	20	8	14
Aged 60 to 69	29	25	25	56	61	54	14	11	20
Aged 70 or older	37	33	37	48	53	38	11	10	19
Not a high school graduate	40	30	32	43	53	47	13	13	18
High school graduate	24	30	27	57	60	56	19	8	16
Bachelor's degree	22	29	23	62	63	69	15	8	9
Graduate degree	29	25	31	63	71	66	8	2	2

Note: Numbers may not add to 100 because "don't know" is not shown.
Source: General Social Survey, National Opinion Research Center, University of Chicago; calculations by the author

Confidence in Executive Branch of Government

Americans thought less highly of the executive branch in 1998 than they did in 1978.

When the economy is booming, the president usually gets most of the credit—whether deserved or not. But so far, the nation's unprecedented economic boom has done nothing to halt the declining confidence in the executive branch of the federal government. More than one-third of Americans now say they have hardly any confidence in the executive branch, up from one-quarter who felt this way in 1978. Only 14 percent have a great deal of confidence in the executive branch, a proportion essentially unchanged from 1978.

Men are slightly more likely than women to say they have hardly any confidence in the executive branch of the federal government. For both men and women, the percentages of those who have hardly any confidence is higher than it was in 1978.

Although both blacks and whites express a more negative view of the executive branch now than in 1978, blacks still hold it in higher regard. More than half of blacks (53 percent) have some confidence in the executive branch of government compared with 46 percent of whites. Thirty-eight percent of whites have hardly any confidence compared with a smaller 27 percent of blacks. Historically, the executive branch has been an important force in remedying much of the discrimination suffered by blacks.

People aged 70 or older are most likely to have a great deal of confidence in the executive branch (20 percent compared with 16 percent or fewer among younger age groups). People in their forties are most likely to say they have hardly any confidence in the executive branch (42 percent compared with 36 percent or fewer among other age groups).

The most and the least educated Americans have more confidence in the executive branch of government. Twenty percent of people with a graduate degree and 21 percent of those who did not complete high school have a great deal of confidence in this branch of government compared with 12 percent of high school graduates and 11 percent of people with a bachelor's degree.

Confidence in Executive Branch of Government, 1978 to 1998

"As far as people running the executive branch of the federal government are concerned, would you say you have a great deal of confidence, only some confidence, or hardly any confidence at all in them?"

(percent of people aged 18 or older responding by sex, race, age, and education, 1978–98)

	a great deal			only some			hardly any		
	1998	*1988*	*1978*	*1998*	*1988*	*1978*	*1998*	*1988*	*1978*
Total	**14%**	**16%**	**13%**	**48%**	**53%**	**59%**	**35%**	**27%**	**25%**
Men	14	19	14	46	51	58	38	28	26
Women	13	14	12	49	55	60	33	26	24
Black	16	12	15	53	47	62	27	37	21
White	13	17	12	46	54	59	38	26	25
Aged 18 to 29	15	19	14	48	54	57	33	23	28
Aged 30 to 39	12	21	11	54	48	65	32	29	23
Aged 40 to 49	11	14	12	45	51	60	42	33	24
Aged 50 to 59	16	13	11	47	57	63	36	26	22
Aged 60 to 69	13	12	10	49	58	60	35	26	24
Aged 70 or older	20	17	16	41	55	48	33	24	28
Not a high school graduate	21	13	13	40	53	54	30	25	26
High school graduate	12	17	12	47	52	61	39	28	25
Bachelor's degree	11	14	11	56	63	69	31	21	19
Graduate degree	20	24	18	55	45	56	25	31	24

Note: Numbers may not add to 100 because "don't know" is not shown.
Source: General Social Survey, National Opinion Research Center, University of Chicago; calculations by the author

Confidence in the Military

The World War II generation has the highest confidence in the military.

Although confidence in the leaders of many institutions has declined considerably over the past few decades, the military has gained ground. In 1978, 30 percent of Americans had a great deal of confidence in the nation's military leaders. By 1998, the figure had grown to 36 percent. Only 12 percent say they have hardly any confidence, while half say they have some confidence in the military.

Men are more likely to feel confident about military leaders. Forty-three percent of men, but only 31 percent of women, have a great deal of confidence in the military. The proportion of men feeling very confident in military leaders was a much smaller 32 percent in 1978.

Whites are more likely than blacks to say they have a great deal of confidence in the military (37 versus 32 percent). Both blacks and whites are more likely to have a great deal of confidence today than in 1978.

The generations that experienced World War II are most likely to say they have a great deal of confidence in the military. Nearly half (48 percent) of people aged 70 or older have a great deal of confidence in the military as do 40 percent of people in their sixties. Among younger aged groups, a smaller 30 to 35 percent have a great deal of confidence in the military.

Confidence in military leaders declines with education. While 49 percent of people who did not complete high school have a great deal of confidence, the proportion drops to 35 percent among high school graduates and 28 percent among college graduates.

Confidence in the Military, 1978 to 1998

"As far as people running the military are concerned, would you say you have a great deal of confidence, only some confidence, or hardly any confidence at all in them?"

(percent of people aged 18 or older responding by sex, race, age, and education, 1978–98)

	a great deal			only some			hardly any		
	1998	*1988*	*1978*	*1998*	*1988*	*1978*	*1998*	*1988*	*1978*
Total	**36%**	**34%**	**30%**	**49%**	**49%**	**54%**	**12%**	**13%**	**13%**
Men	43	37	32	44	47	54	12	14	12
Women	31	32	28	52	51	54	13	13	13
Black	32	31	28	50	54	57	15	10	13
White	37	35	30	49	48	54	12	14	13
Aged 18 to 29	35	41	28	46	45	52	16	12	18
Aged 30 to 39	34	27	25	52	50	60	11	20	13
Aged 40 to 49	34	33	28	49	51	55	14	14	13
Aged 50 to 59	30	36	33	54	49	55	14	12	8
Aged 60 to 69	40	30	36	47	54	49	10	11	8
Aged 70 or older	48	35	33	42	50	48	6	9	11
Not a high school graduate	49	40	38	34	44	46	10	10	10
High school graduate	35	36	29	50	49	55	13	12	13
Bachelor's degree	28	22	17	56	57	64	13	20	19
Graduate degree	28	24	15	57	49	65	15	25	15

Note: Numbers may not add to 100 because "don't know" is not shown.
Source: General Social Survey, National Opinion Research Center, University of Chicago; calculations by the author

Confidence in the Press

Confidence in the news media has gone from bad to worse.

In 1978, only 20 percent of Americans had a great deal of confidence in the people running the media. By 1998, an even smaller 9 percent had a great deal of confidence in the press. Fully 42 percent have hardly any confidence in the press—up from 20 percent who felt that way in 1978.

People who did not graduate from high school are most likely to have a great deal of confidence in the press. But even in this segment, only 15 percent have a great deal of confidence. High school graduates and people with a bachelor's degree are more likely than other educational groups to say they have hardly any confidence in the media.

Similar percentages of men and women have hardly any confidence in the press (43 and 42 percent, respectively). Men are slightly more likely than women to have a great deal of confidence in the media (12 versus 7 percent).

The media have not lost as much ground with blacks as with whites. In 1978, 17 percent of blacks had a great deal of confidence in the press, a figure that had dropped to 13 percent by 1998. Among whites, however, the proportion of those who had a great deal of confidence in the press plummeted from 20 to 8 percent during those years. Forty-three percent of whites and 41 percent of blacks have hardly any confidence in the media, up from 19 and 22 percent, respectively, in 1978.

The middle-aged are most critical of the press. Forty-seven percent of people in their forties and 45 percent of those in their fifties have hardly any confidence in it. The oldest and the youngest adults have the most confidence in the press. Among people under age 30 and those aged 60 or older, 11 to 12 percent have a great deal of confidence in the media compared with 7 to 8 percent of other age groups.

Confidence in the Press, 1978 to 1998

"As far as people running the press are concerned, would you say you have a great deal of confidence, only some confidence, or hardly any confidence at all in them?"

(percent of people aged 18 or older responding by sex, race, age, and education, 1978–98)

	a great deal			only some			hardly any		
	1998	*1988*	*1978*	*1998*	*1988*	*1978*	*1998*	*1988*	*1978*
Total	**9%**	**18%**	**20%**	**46%**	**53%**	**58%**	**42%**	**25%**	**20%**
Men	12	20	21	44	50	58	43	28	19
Women	7	17	19	48	56	58	42	23	20
Black	13	30	17	45	47	58	41	20	22
White	8	17	20	46	54	58	43	26	19
Aged 18 to 29	12	25	22	46	50	58	40	22	19
Aged 30 to 39	8	18	19	47	53	57	42	26	22
Aged 40 to 49	8	18	25	43	54	58	47	27	15
Aged 50 to 59	7	16	18	46	62	62	45	19	19
Aged 60 to 69	12	13	18	53	55	57	35	30	21
Aged 70 or older	11	17	16	43	53	60	41	26	21
Not a high school graduate	15	24	24	41	45	54	37	24	19
High school graduate	9	17	17	46	54	60	44	26	22
Bachelor's degree	8	16	23	46	59	60	44	24	16
Graduate degree	5	14	23	60	57	65	34	29	11

Note: Numbers may not add to 100 because "don't know" is not shown.
Source: General Social Survey, National Opinion Research Center, University of Chicago; calculations by the author

Confidence in Science

College graduates have the most confidence in the scientific community.

Confidence in the scientific community has grown slightly over the past few decades. In 1978, 36 percent of Americans said they had a great deal of confidence in the leaders of the scientific community, while 48 percent had only some confidence. In 1998, a smaller 45 percent had only some confidence while a larger 40 percent had a great deal of confidence.

Men are far more likely than women to have a great deal of confidence in the scientific community. Forty-six percent of men, but only 35 percent of women, have a great deal of confidence in science.

There is also a large difference of opinion by race. While 43 percent of whites say they have a great deal of confidence in the scientific community, only 25 percent of blacks agree. The gap was wider in 1998 than in 1978, when 38 percent of whites and 23 percent of blacks had a great deal of confidence in the scientific community.

Not surprisingly, people with a college degree (many of whom work in the sciences) are much more likely than those with less education to say they have a great deal of confidence in the scientific community. Fully 55 to 60 percent of college graduates have a great deal of confidence compared with only 28 to 35 percent of people with a high school diploma or less education. Among those who did not graduate from high school, 14 percent say they have no confidence in the scientific community compared with 9 percent or fewer of people with more education.

Confidence in Science, 1978 to 1998

"As far as people running the scientific community are concerned, would you say you have a great deal of confidence, only some confidence, or hardly any confidence at all in them?"

(percent of people aged 18 or older responding by sex, race, age, and education, 1978–98)

	a great deal			only some			hardly any		
	1998	**1988**	**1978**	**1998**	**1988**	**1978**	**1998**	**1988**	**1978**
Total	**40%**	**39%**	**36%**	**45%**	**48%**	**48%**	**8%**	**6%**	**7%**
Men	46	46	43	40	42	45	8	6	6
Women	35	33	31	49	52	51	8	5	8
Black	25	37	23	53	47	51	13	5	15
White	43	40	38	44	47	48	6	6	6
Aged 18 to 29	46	47	35	42	41	51	7	8	9
Aged 30 to 39	43	43	41	44	46	49	7	6	6
Aged 40 to 49	34	36	39	50	55	47	9	4	6
Aged 50 to 59	38	33	42	48	53	47	8	3	5
Aged 60 to 69	36	33	30	47	51	47	7	5	7
Aged 70 or older	38	32	26	38	45	46	9	6	11
Not a high school graduate	28	22	24	40	51	49	14	9	12
High school graduate	35	41	36	49	47	52	9	6	6
Bachelor's degree	55	45	60	38	52	36	4	1	3
Graduate degree	60	61	61	39	35	37	1	4	0

Note: Numbers may not add to 100 because "don't know" is not shown.
Source: General Social Survey, National Opinion Research Center, University of Chicago; calculations by the author

Confidence in Organized Labor

American opinion of organized labor is improving.

Although it is hardly a ringing endorsement, the proportion of Americans who have little confidence in organized labor fell from 38 percent in 1978 to 29 percent in 1998. The proportion of those who they have only some confidence in organized labor rose from 46 to 52 percent. But there was no change in the proportion of those who had a great deal of confidence in labor's leaders (11 percent).

One-third of men say they have hardly any confidence in organized labor compared with one-quarter of women. Thirty-one percent of whites, but only 26 percent of blacks, have hardly any confidence in union leaders. The proportion of blacks who have a great deal of confidence in labor fell from 22 percent in 1978 to just 10 percent in 1998.

The youngest and the oldest adults have the most confidence in organized labor. Fourteen percent of people under age 30 and 18 percent of those aged 70 or older have a great deal of confidence in labor leaders compared with 10 percent or fewer of other age groups. Between 1978 and 1998, confidence in labor leaders improved in every age group, as fewer said they had hardly any confidence and more said they had some confidence.

The proportion of people saying they have a great deal of confidence in organized labor declines with education. Seventeen percent of people who did not complete high school have a great deal of confidence compared with 10 percent of high school graduates and 6 to 8 percent of college graduates. The majority of people with at least a high school diploma have only some confidence in labor leaders.

Confidence in Organized Labor, 1978 to 1998

"As far as people running organized labor are concerned, would you say you have a great deal of confidence, only some confidence, or hardly any confidence at all in them?"

(percent of people aged 18 or older responding by sex, race, age, and education, 1978–98)

	a great deal			only some			hardly any		
	1998	*1988*	*1978*	*1998*	*1988*	*1978*	*1998*	*1988*	*1978*
Total	**11%**	**10%**	**11%**	**52%**	**50%**	**46%**	**29%**	**35%**	**38%**
Men	11	12	13	51	46	44	33	38	40
Women	11	8	9	53	54	48	26	32	36
Black	10	16	22	52	59	49	26	18	23
White	11	9	10	51	48	46	31	38	40
Aged 18 to 29	14	16	14	60	59	51	18	20	30
Aged 30 to 39	10	8	7	54	52	52	27	36	38
Aged 40 to 49	9	8	8	50	50	46	33	39	43
Aged 50 to 59	7	10	11	50	52	45	36	33	39
Aged 60 to 69	8	7	13	51	44	37	35	42	43
Aged 70 or older	18	7	12	40	36	35	30	47	40
Not a high school graduate	17	13	16	45	45	40	25	31	34
High school graduate	10	11	10	52	52	49	30	33	38
Bachelor's degree	8	3	5	57	55	52	27	39	42
Graduate degree	6	4	6	55	35	56	36	59	34

Note: Numbers may not add to 100 because "don't know" is not shown.
Source: General Social Survey, National Opinion Research Center, University of Chicago; calculations by the author

Afraid in Own Neighborhood?

Americans are less fearful than they were in 1977.

Fear of crime can be both real and imagined. People who live in a high-crime neighborhood (as many of the poor do) have reason to be afraid. But even if they live in a relatively safe neighborhood, many people are still fearful because they feel personally vulnerable to crime.

Forty-one percent of Americans say there is an area within a mile of their home where they would be afraid to walk alone at night. The oldest Americans are more likely to feel this way than younger people. Older people know they are less able to defend themselves, and this reduced capacity creates a sense of vulnerability that keeps many in their home at night. People aged 40 or older are less likely to be fearful than they were in 1977, however.

Many women, like the elderly, feel vulnerable to crime. More than half of women (52 percent) are afraid to walk alone at night in their neighborhood. In contrast, only 26 percent of men are afraid. The proportion of women who are fearful in their neighborhood is down from 63 percent in 1977, while the proportion of men who say they are afraid rose slightly over the same period.

Blacks and people of "other" race, who are disproportionately poor, are more likely than whites to be afraid to walk alone at night in their neighborhood. Forty percent of whites are afraid compared with 47 to 48 percent of blacks and other races. Blacks are far less likely to be afraid in their neighborhood than they were in 1977, when 63 percent were fearful. The declining crime rate plays a role, but increasing affluence among blacks is also a factor, enabling many to move to safer neighborhoods.

Afraid in Own Neighborhood? 1998

"Is there any area right around here—that is, within a mile— where you would be afraid to walk alone at night?"

(percent of people aged 18 or older responding by sex, race, age, and education, 1998)

	yes	no
Total	**41%**	**57%**
Men	26	74
Women	52	46
Black	47	51
White	40	59
Other	48	52
Aged 18 to 29	42	57
Aged 30 to 39	42	57
Aged 40 to 49	35	65
Aged 50 to 59	38	60
Aged 60 to 69	43	55
Aged 70 or older	51	45
Not a high school graduate	46	50
High school graduate	40	58
Bachelor's degree	39	60
Graduate degree	36	64

Note: Numbers may not add to 100 because "don't know" is not shown.
Source: General Social Survey, National Opinion Research Center, University of Chicago; calculations by the author

Afraid in Own Neighborhood? 1977 to 1998

"Is there any area right around here—that is, within a mile— where you would be afraid to walk alone at night?"

(percent of people aged 18 or older responding by sex, race, age, and education, 1977–98)

	yes			no		
	1998	*1988*	*1977*	*1998*	*1988*	*1977*
Total	**41%**	**40%**	**45%**	**57%**	**59%**	**55%**
Men	26	17	23	74	83	76
Women	52	57	63	46	42	37
Black	47	51	63	51	47	37
White	40	39	43	59	60	57
Aged 18 to 29	42	36	40	57	63	59
Aged 30 to 39	42	32	44	57	68	56
Aged 40 to 49	35	34	38	65	66	62
Aged 50 to 59	38	46	42	60	53	57
Aged 60 to 69	43	49	56	55	51	43
Aged 70 or older	51	58	61	45	41	38
Not a high school graduate	46	46	50	50	53	49
High school graduate	40	41	43	58	59	56
Bachelor's degree	39	39	33	60	60	66
Graduate degree	36	20	43	64	75	57

Note: Numbers may not add to 100 because "don't know" is not shown.
Source: General Social Survey, National Opinion Research Center, University of Chicago; calculations by the author

Are the Courts Too Harsh?

Fewer people think the courts are not harsh enough.

Few topics concern Americans more than crime. When asked whether their local courts are too harsh or not harsh enough with criminals, 74 percent of Americans say they are not harsh enough. After years of tougher laws and longer sentences, there has been a shift in attitudes, however. The proportion of people who think the courts are not harsh enough has fallen by 11 percentage points in the past two decades. The proportion of those who say they are too harsh doubled, from 3 to 6 percent, while the share of those who gave the unprompted response that the courts were about right rose from 7 to 13 percent.

Majorities of all races think the courts are not harsh enough. Fifteen percent of blacks, however, say the courts are too harsh compared with only 5 to 8 percent of whites and "other" races. Blacks are disproportionately likely to be caught up in the criminal justice system, which is one reason for this difference of opinion.

Note that substantial percentages of respondents volunteered that their local courts are "about right" in their handling of criminals. If the question included "about right" as a standard response choice, the percentage saying the courts are not harsh enough might have been lower.

Are the Courts Too Harsh? 1998

"In general, do you think the courts in this area deal too harshly or not harshly enough with criminals?"

(percent of people aged 18 or older responding by sex, race, age, and education, 1998)

	too harshly	not harshly enough	about right*	don't know
Total	**6%**	**74%**	**13%**	**6%**
Men	7	72	15	6
Women	6	76	12	7
Black	15	72	10	4
White	5	75	13	7
Other	8	69	17	5
Aged 18 to 29	10	70	12	8
Aged 30 to 39	6	75	12	7
Aged 40 to 49	8	75	12	5
Aged 50 to 59	4	78	14	4
Aged 60 to 69	3	80	12	6
Aged 70 or older	4	70	19	7
Not a high school graduate	9	74	11	6
High school graduate	6	76	12	6
Bachelor's degree	7	69	17	7
Graduate degree	5	64	21	10

* Volunteered response.
Source: General Social Survey, National Opinion Research Center, University of Chicago; calculations by the author

Are the Courts Too Harsh? 1978 to 1998

"In general, do you think the courts in this area deal too harshly or not harshly enough with criminals?"

(percent of people aged 18 or older responding by sex, race, age, and education, 1978–98)

	too harshly			not harshly enough			about right*		
	1998	*1988*	*1978*	*1998*	*1988*	*1978*	*1998*	*1988*	*1978*
Total	**6%**	**4%**	**3%**	**74%**	**82%**	**85%**	**13%**	**10%**	**7%**
Men	7	5	3	72	79	87	15	13	7
Women	6	3	2	76	83	83	12	8	7
Black	15	8	6	72	75	84	10	11	8
White	5	3	2	75	83	85	13	10	7
Aged 18 to 29	10	8	5	70	78	81	12	9	9
Aged 30 to 39	6	3	4	75	80	85	12	12	5
Aged 40 to 49	8	2	1	75	83	85	12	10	7
Aged 50 to 59	4	3	1	78	77	88	14	16	7
Aged 60 to 69	3	2	1	80	86	89	12	8	5
Aged 70 or older	4	2	1	70	86	87	19	5	8
Not a high school graduate	9	3	3	74	84	82	11	6	9
High school graduate	6	4	2	76	83	88	12	9	6
Bachelor's degree	7	4	4	69	76	83	17	12	5
Graduate degree	5	3	3	64	69	69	21	20	16

* Volunteered response.
Note: Numbers may not add to 100 because "don't know" is not shwon.
Source: General Social Survey, National Opinion Research Center, University of Chicago; calculations by the author

Death Penalty

Blacks are least likely to support the death penalty.

About two-thirds of Americans support the death penalty—about the same level of support as in 1978, but down from 71 percent in 1988. One-quarter oppose the death penalty, and 8 percent are unsure about it.

There is some variation in the level of support for the death penalty by demographic characteristic. Men are more likely than women to support the death penalty, as was the case in 1978. Three-quarters of men, but a smaller 63 percent of women, favor government-sanctioned executions.

The death penalty garners the least support among blacks. Only 45 percent of blacks favor capital punishment, while an equal percentage oppose it. Whites are most likely to support the death penalty (72 percent) while "other" races fall in the middle (58 percent).

People aged 70 or older are slightly less likely than younger people to support the death penalty. Among people under age 70, 67 to 70 percent favor it compared with 64 percent of the oldest Americans.

Support for executions is lowest among people who did not complete high school (60 percent) and those with a graduate degree (58 percent). Seventy-percent of high school graduates and 66 percent of people with a bachelor's degree favor the death penalty. People with a graduate degree are most likely to oppose it (36 percent compared with 22 to 29 percent of people with less education).

Substantial percentages of people say they don't know whether they favor or oppose the death penalty, reflecting the difficulty Americans have in reconciling their concerns about crime with their ethical and moral beliefs. Blacks, the elderly, and people who did not graduate from high school are most likely to say they don't know whether they favor or oppose the death penalty.

Death Penalty, 1998

"Do you favor or oppose the death penalty for persons convicted of murder?"

(percent of people aged 18 or older responding by sex, race, age, and education, 1998)

	favor	oppose	don't know
Total	**68%**	**25%**	**8%**
Men	74	20	6
Women	63	28	9
Black	45	45	10
White	72	20	7
Other	58	34	8
Aged 18 to 29	67	27	6
Aged 30 to 39	70	22	8
Aged 40 to 49	67	25	7
Aged 50 to 59	67	25	8
Aged 60 to 69	69	24	7
Aged 70 or older	64	25	11
Not a high school graduate	60	29	11
High school graduate	70	22	8
Bachelor's degree	66	26	8
Graduate degree	58	36	5

Source: General Social Survey, National Opinion Research Center, University of Chicago; calculations by the author

Death Penalty, 1978 to 1998

"Do you favor or oppose the death penalty for persons convicted of murder?"

(percent of people aged 18 or older responding by sex, race, age, and education, 1978–98)

	favor			oppose			don't know		
	1998	1988	1978	1998	1988	1978	1998	1988	1978
Total	**68%**	**71%**	**66%**	**25%**	**22%**	**28%**	**8%**	**7%**	**6%**
Men	74	77	74	20	18	24	6	5	3
Women	63	66	61	28	26	31	9	8	8
Black	45	44	43	45	47	51	10	9	6
White	72	76	69	20	18	25	7	6	6
Aged 18 to 29	67	71	64	27	25	31	6	4	5
Aged 30 to 39	70	74	66	22	20	28	8	6	5
Aged 40 to 49	67	69	68	25	21	28	7	10	5
Aged 50 to 59	67	68	68	25	25	27	8	7	5
Aged 60 to 69	69	72	72	24	21	20	7	8	8
Aged 70 or older	64	68	64	25	21	27	11	10	9
Not a high school graduate	60	65	59	29	26	33	11	9	8
High school graduate	70	74	71	22	20	24	8	6	5
Bachelor's degree	66	69	66	26	24	29	8	7	5
Graduate degree	58	66	58	36	28	37	5	6	5

Source: General Social Survey, National Opinion Research Center, University of Chicago; calculations by the author

Gun Control

The overwhelming majority of Americans favor requiring a permit to purchase a gun.

The killing of school children by classmates has made the issue of gun control a top priority for many Americans. Legislators may be reluctant to pass significant gun control legislation, but the public has been ready for it for at least two decades. In 1977, 72 percent of Americans said they would favor a law requiring people to obtain a police permit before purchasing a gun. By 1998, the overwhelming 82 percent majority were in favor of permits.

Women are more supportive than men of gun control (86 versus 76 percent). The rift between men and women was also evident in 1976. Since then, greater numbers of both men and women have come to support gun control. Only twenty-two percent of men and 12 percent of women oppose requiring a police permit for gun purchasers.

Whites are less likely than blacks and "other" races to favor requiring gun permits, although the proportion of those who favor permits is high in every racial group. Eighty percent of whites favor gun control compared with 88 to 89 percent of blacks and other races.

Strong majorities of all age groups support requiring a police permit before purchasing a gun. The level of support for gun permits varies by education, however. Among college graduates, 87 to 88 percent favor requiring permits compared with a smaller 79 to 80 percent of people with less education. The gap was much wider in 1978, but since then the percentage of people with a high school diploma or less education who favor gun permits rose sharply.

Gun Control, 1998

"Would you favor or oppose a law which would require a person to obtain a police permit before he or she could buy a gun?"

(percent of people aged 18 or older responding by sex, race, age, and education, 1998)

	favor	oppose
Total	**82%**	**16%**
Men	76	22
Women	86	12
Black	88	10
White	80	18
Other	89	9
Aged 18 to 29	82	16
Aged 30 to 39	82	15
Aged 40 to 49	82	17
Aged 50 to 59	82	16
Aged 60 to 69	80	18
Aged 70 or older	81	15
Not a high school graduate	80	15
High school graduate	79	19
Bachelor's degree	87	12
Graduate degree	88	10

Note: Numbers may not add to 100 because "don't know" is not shown.
Source: General Social Survey, National Opinion Research Center, University of Chicago; calculations by the author

Gun Control, 1977 to 1998

"Would you favor or oppose a law which would require a person to obtain a police permit before he or she could buy a gun?"

(percent of people aged 18 or older responding by sex, race, age, and education, 1977–98)

	favor			oppose		
	1998	*1988*	*1977*	*1998*	*1988*	*1977*
Total	**82%**	**74%**	**72%**	**16%**	**24%**	**27%**
Men	76	66	64	22	33	35
Women	86	79	78	12	17	19
Black	88	79	80	10	20	18
White	80	73	70	18	24	28
Aged 18 to 29	82	73	71	16	26	27
Aged 30 to 39	82	74	71	15	25	27
Aged 40 to 49	82	70	68	17	28	30
Aged 50 to 59	82	77	72	16	21	27
Aged 60 to 69	80	77	73	18	21	24
Aged 70 or older	81	74	77	15	17	19
Not a high school graduate	80	70	73	15	27	25
High school graduate	79	72	69	19	25	29
Bachelor's degree	87	78	76	12	21	24
Graduate degree	88	88	82	10	11	14

Note: Numbers may not add to 100 because "don't know" is not shown.
Source: General Social Survey, National Opinion Research Center, University of Chicago; calculations by the author

Should Marijuana Be Legal?

Most Americans would not legalize marijuana.

Two-thirds of Americans are against the legalization of marijuana, the same proportion as in 1978. There was a brief upswing in support for legalization in 1988, and it is likely opinions on this issue will continue to waver as the public debates the pros and cons of the medical use of marijuana.

Generational differences have always been evident on this issue, but the gap is smaller now than it was 20 years ago. In 1978, half of people under age 30 supported legalizing marijuana, and support fell to just 13 percent among people aged 70 or older. In 1998, a much smaller 34 percent of young adults supported legalization compared with 16 percent of people aged 60 or older.

Men are more likely than women to believe marijuana should be legal (34 versus 22 percent). Fully 71 percent of women oppose legalization compared with 60 percent of men.

By education, support for legalizing marijuana is highest among college graduates. Only 21 to 26 percent of people without a college degree think marijuana should be legal compared with 31 to 35 percent of college graduates. But the percentage of adults who want to make it legal was lower in 1998 than in 1978 among all but the least educated Americans.

Should Marijuana Be Legal? 1998

"Do you think the use of marijuana should be made legal or not?"

(percent of people aged 18 or older responding by sex, race, age, and education, 1998)

	should	should not	don't know
Total	28%	66%	6%
Men	34	60	6
Women	22	71	6
Black	24	71	5
White	28	65	6
Other	26	67	7
Aged 18 to 29	34	60	6
Aged 30 to 39	29	63	8
Aged 40 to 49	32	64	4
Aged 50 to 59	29	66	6
Aged 60 to 69	16	77	6
Aged 70 or older	16	78	6
Not a high school graduate	21	72	7
High school graduate	26	68	6
Bachelor's degree	35	59	6
Graduate degree	31	61	7

Source: General Social Survey, National Opinion Research Center, University of Chicago; calculations by the author

Should Marijuana Be Legal? 1978 to 1998

"Do you think the use of marijuana should be made legal or not?"

(percent of people aged 18 or older responding by sex, race, age, and education, 1978–98)

	should			should not		
	1998	*1988*	*1978*	*1998*	*1988*	*1978*
Total	**28%**	**17%**	**30%**	**66%**	**79%**	**67%**
Men	34	21	34	60	74	63
Women	22	14	27	71	82	71
Black	24	19	39	71	74	60
White	28	17	29	65	80	68
Aged 18 to 29	34	23	49	60	71	49
Aged 30 to 39	29	20	34	63	77	64
Aged 40 to 49	32	17	21	64	80	76
Aged 50 to 59	29	15	18	66	83	78
Aged 60 to 69	16	13	18	77	85	79
Aged 70 or older	16	9	13	78	86	82
Not a high school graduate	21	15	19	72	82	79
High school graduate	26	16	31	68	79	66
Bachelor's degree	35	24	49	59	75	48
Graduate degree	31	18	46	61	73	49

Note: Numbers may not add to 100 because "don't know" is not shown.
Source: General Social Survey, National Opinion Research Center, University of Chicago; calculations by the author

Political Party Identification

Independents outnumber Democrats and Republicans.

The Democrats win the White House. The Republicans win Congress. Neither party wins the loyalty of the American electorate. In 1998, the largest proportion of people identified themselves as independents (38 percent). Thirty-four percent are Democrats, down from 40 percent in 1978. Republicans claim 25 percent of adults, little changed from 1978.

Blacks are the strongest Democratic supporters. Fully 63 percent consider themselves Democrats compared with only 29 percent of whites and 33 percent of "other" races. One-third of blacks, but only 10 percent of whites and other races, say they are strong Democrats. Thirty percent of whites are Republicans compared with 8 to 9 percent of blacks and other races.

Women are more likely than men to be Democrats. Among women, 39 percent are Democrats, 37 percent are independents, and 23 percent are Republicans. Democrats and Republicans each claim 29 percent of men, but 40 percent of men are independents. Among men, there has been a substantial shift from Democrat to Republican since 1978.

People under age 50 are more likely to be independents than Republicans or Democrats. The proportion of people who are Democrats rises with age, reaching 45 percent among people aged 70 or older. Although older generations are also more likely to be Republican, the difference is smaller. Among people aged 60 or older, 29 percent are Republican, compared with 21 to 27 percent of younger adults.

The Democrats have the most support among those who did not complete high school (43 percent compared with 31 to 35 percent of people with more education). Only 17 percent of the least educated Americans identify themselves as Republicans compared with 26 to 31 percent of people with at least a high school diploma.

Political Party Identification, 1998

"Generally speaking, do you usually think of yourself as a Republican, Democrat, independent, or what?"

(percent of people aged 18 or older responding by sex, race, age, and education, 1998)

	Democrat	independent	Republican
Total	**34%**	**38%**	**25%**
Men	29	40	29
Women	39	37	23
Black	63	29	8
White	29	39	30
Other	33	54	9
Aged 18 to 29	29	47	21
Aged 30 to 39	31	41	25
Aged 40 to 49	33	38	27
Aged 50 to 59	37	36	25
Aged 60 to 69	39	32	29
Aged 70 or older	45	26	29
Not a high school graduate	43	38	17
High school graduate	33	39	26
Bachelor's degree	31	35	31
Graduate degree	35	35	28

Note: Numbers may not add to 100 because "other party" and "don't know" are not shown.
Source: General Social Survey, National Opinion Research Center, University of Chicago; calculations by the author

Strength of Political Party Identification, 1998

"Generally speaking, do you usually think of yourself as a Republican, Democrat, Independent, or what? If Republican or Democrat, would you call yourself a strong Republican/Democrat or not a very strong Republican/Democrat? If independent, do you think of yourself as closer to the Republican or Democratic party?"

(percent of people aged 18 or older responding by sex, race, age, and education, 1998)

| | Democrat | | independent | | | Republican | |
	strong	not very strong	lean Democrat	neither	lean Republican	strong	not very strong
Total	13%	21%	12%	17%	9%	17%	8%
Men	11	18	14	16	10	19	10
Women	15	24	11	18	8	15	8
Black	33	30	14	13	2	6	2
White	10	19	12	17	10	20	10
Other	10	23	14	30	10	7	2
Aged 18 to 29	10	19	17	22	8	17	4
Aged 30 to 39	10	21	12	19	10	18	7
Aged 40 to 49	13	20	12	18	8	17	10
Aged 50 to 59	15	22	12	14	10	16	9
Aged 60 to 69	14	25	11	12	9	19	10
Aged 70 or older	23	22	9	11	6	15	14
Not a high school graduate	18	25	11	21	6	11	6
High school graduate	13	20	12	18	9	18	8
Bachelor's degree	10	21	12	12	11	19	12
Graduate degree	15	20	15	10	10	17	11

Note: Numbers may not add to 100 because "other party" and "don't know" are not shown.
Source: General Social Survey, National Opinion Research Center, University of Chicago; calculations by the author

Political Party Identification, 1978 to 1998

"Generally speaking, do you usually think of yourself as a Republican, Democrat, independent, or what?"

(percent of people aged 18 or older responding by sex, race, age, and education, 1978–98)

	Democrat			independent			Republican		
	1998	*1988*	*1978*	*1998*	*1988*	*1978*	*1998*	*1988*	*1978*
Total	**34%**	**37%**	**40%**	**38%**	**34%**	**36%**	**25%**	**28%**	**23%**
Men	29	32	37	40	38	40	29	29	21
Women	39	41	41	37	31	33	23	28	25
Black	63	67	64	29	26	29	8	6	7
White	29	32	37	39	35	37	30	33	25
Aged 18 to 29	29	29	32	47	42	49	21	28	18
Aged 30 to 39	31	39	41	41	35	40	25	26	19
Aged 40 to 49	33	36	43	38	39	34	27	25	22
Aged 50 to 59	37	47	43	36	26	28	25	27	28
Aged 60 to 69	39	41	44	32	30	30	29	29	26
Aged 70 or older	45	39	42	26	22	21	29	39	37
Not a high school graduate	43	45	46	38	32	31	17	23	23
High school graduate	33	36	38	39	33	37	26	30	24
Bachelor's degree	31	30	33	35	37	44	31	32	23
Graduate degree	35	34	31	35	40	44	28	25	23

Note: Numbers may not add to 100 because "other party" and "don't know" are not shown.
Source: General Social Survey, National Opinion Research Center, University of Chicago; calculations by the author

Political Leanings

Americans tilt slightly to the right.

Americans range across the entire political spectrum, although they tilt slightly to the right. Thirty-five percent consider themselves moderate, one-third say they are conservative, and 27 percent consider themselves liberal.

The gender gap often found in elections is evident in the answers to this question. Men are more likely than women to say they are conservative (37 versus 30 percent). Women are more likely to be moderate or liberal.

Whites are more likely than blacks and "other" races to say they are conservative (35 percent compared with 26 percent of blacks and 21 percent of other races). While only 26 percent of whites and 29 percent of blacks are liberal, a larger 34 percent of other races place themselves in the liberal camp.

If the definition of a conservative is "a liberal who has been mugged," there are quite a few crime victims among the baby-boom generation. In 1978, only 22 percent of 18-to-29-year-old boomers identified themselves as conservative while 39 percent said they were liberal. In 1998, fully 35 percent of 40-to-49-year-old boomers identified themselves as conservative while 29 percent held on to the liberal label.

Despite the conversion of some boomers, younger generations are still more likely than their elders to identify themselves as liberal. One-third of people under age 30 and 27 to 29 percent of those aged 30 to 59 say they are liberal. The proportion drops to 20 to 21 percent among people aged 60 or older. Interestingly, people aged 40 or older were more likely to say they were liberal in 1998 than in 1978.

The most educated Americans are most likely to be liberal. Thirty-seven percent of people with a graduate degree are liberals compared with 25 to 29 percent of people with less education. Only 27 percent of people who did not complete high school consider themselves conservative compared with 39 percent of people with a bachelor's degree.

Political Leanings, 1998

"We hear a lot of talk these days about liberals and conservatives. On a seven-point scale from extremely liberal to extremely conservative, where would you place yourself?"

(percent of people aged 18 or older responding by sex, race, age, and education, 1998)

	extremely liberal	liberal	slightly liberal	moderate, middle of the road	slightly conservative	conservative	extremely conservative
Total	2%	13%	12%	35%	15%	15%	3%
Men	2	11	12	34	18	16	3
Women	2	14	12	36	13	14	3
Black	2	14	13	41	13	12	1
White	2	12	12	34	16	16	3
Other	4	16	14	36	11	7	3
Aged 18 to 29	3	17	14	36	14	10	1
Aged 30 to 39	2	13	13	33	17	14	3
Aged 40 to 49	3	13	13	33	17	15	3
Aged 50 to 59	1	12	14	36	14	15	4
Aged 60 to 69	3	7	10	38	13	20	4
Aged 70 or older	1	10	10	37	14	19	3
Not a high school graduate	4	9	12	37	11	12	4
High school graduate	2	11	12	38	15	14	3
Bachelor's degree	1	14	14	29	19	17	3
Graduate degree	5	21	11	30	16	14	0

Note: Numbers may not add to 100 because "don't know" is not shown.
Source: General Social Survey, National Opinion Research Center, University of Chicago; calculations by the author

Political Leanings, 1978 to 1998

"We hear a lot of talk these days about liberals and conservatives. On a seven-point scale from extremely liberal to extremely conservative, where would you place yourself?"

(percent of people aged 18 or older responding by sex, race, age, and education, 1978–98)

	liberal (slightly to extremely)			moderate			conservative (slightly to extremely)		
	1998	1988	1978	1998	1988	1978	1998	1988	1978
Total	27%	27%	27%	35%	35%	36%	33%	34%	32%
Men	25	28	30	34	31	33	37	38	34
Women	28	26	25	36	38	39	30	32	31
Black	29	45	35	41	28	38	26	22	20
White	26	25	26	34	36	37	35	36	33
Aged 18 to 29	34	32	39	36	36	35	25	28	22
Aged 30 to 39	28	33	28	33	31	37	34	34	33
Aged 40 to 49	29	32	24	33	30	35	35	37	37
Aged 50 to 59	27	27	24	36	34	32	33	35	40
Aged 60 to 69	20	18	13	38	42	45	37	36	35
Aged 70 or older	21	12	18	37	40	37	36	40	33
Not a high school graduate	25	23	24	37	37	39	27	30	26
High school graduate	25	26	24	38	37	39	32	34	34
Bachelor's degree	29	31	41	29	26	25	39	42	33
Graduate degree	37	45	43	30	20	20	30	35	38

Note: Numbers may not add to 100 because "don't know" is not shown.
Source: General Social Survey, National Opinion Research Center, University of Chicago; calculations by the author

Does Government Do Too Much?

Growing numbers of Americans believe government does too much.

For many years politicians have been successfully running on a platform of "less government," but the plurality of Americans (39 percent) place themselves in the middle of a scale ranging from "government does too much" to "government does too little." Almost one-quarter say government should do more to solve the country's problems, while one-third believe it is doing too many things that should be left to individuals and private businesses.

Attitudes have changed substantially since 1975. In that year, more than one-third of the public believed government needed to do more to solve the nation's problems. Only 28 percent believed government was doing too many things best left to business and individuals.

Far more men than women think government is doing too much. Only 28 percent of women think so compared with 38 percent of men. Women are more likely than men to think government should do more to solve the country's problems (25 versus 19 percent). In 1975, both women and men were much more likely to think government should do more.

Blacks are far more likely than whites to say government should do more. Only 18 percent of whites believe more government action is needed compared with 39 percent of blacks. Thirty-seven percent of whites say government is doing too much, but only 15 percent of blacks agree.

People under age 40 are slightly more likely than their elders to think government needs to do more to solve problems. Pluralities of most age groups place themselves in the middle of the scale, however. People in their forties and sixties are most likely to think government does too much.

People with at least a high school diploma are more likely than those with less education to think government takes on too many things that should be up to business and individuals—34 to 39 percent compared with 21 percent of people who did not complete high school. But the gap was much wider in 1975, when 45 percent of people who did not complete high school thought government should do more compared with only 26 to 31 percent of college graduates.

Does Government Do Too Much? 1998

"Some people think that the government in Washington is trying to do too many things that should be left to individuals and private businesses. Others disagree and think that the government should do even more to solve our country's problems. Still others have opinions somewhere in between. Where would you place yourself on a scale of 1 to 5 or haven't you made up your mind on this?"

(percent of people aged 18 or older responding by sex, race, age, and education, 1998)

	government should do more 1	2	agree with both 3	4	government is doing too much 5
Total	11%	12%	39%	18%	15%
Men	8	11	39	20	18
Women	12	13	39	16	12
Black	21	18	39	6	9
White	8	10	39	21	16
Other	16	18	41	10	7
Aged 18 to 29	11	14	43	17	9
Aged 30 to 39	10	15	39	20	11
Aged 40 to 49	14	10	36	19	18
Aged 50 to 59	9	10	39	18	17
Aged 60 to 69	8	12	37	23	17
Aged 70 or older	10	10	41	11	21
Not a high school graduate	18	11	42	9	12
High school graduate	11	12	38	18	16
Bachelor's degree	6	13	37	25	14
Graduate degree	8	15	37	20	17

Note: Numbers may not add to 100 because "don't know" is not shown.
Source: General Social Survey, National Opinion Research Center, University of Chicago; calculations by the author

Does Government Do Too Much? 1975 to 1998

"Some people think that the government in Washington is trying to do too many things that should be left to individuals and private businesses. Others disagree and think that the government should do even more to solve our country's problems. Still others have opinions somewhere in between. Where would you place yourself on a scale of 1 to 5 or haven't you made up your mind on this?"

(percent of people aged 18 or older responding by sex, race, age, and education, 1975–98)

	government should do more (1 and 2)			agree with both (3)			government is doing too much (4 and 5)		
	1998	1988	1975	1998	1988	1975	1998	1988	1975
Total	23%	28%	36%	39%	39%	29%	33%	27%	28%
Men	19	26	35	39	39	25	38	30	35
Women	25	29	37	39	39	32	28	24	23
Black	39	52	61	39	31	21	15	11	9
White	18	24	33	39	40	30	37	30	30
Aged 18 to 29	25	33	46	43	37	29	26	23	21
Aged 30 to 39	25	32	34	39	33	31	31	31	28
Aged 40 to 49	24	26	31	36	39	31	37	30	32
Aged 50 to 59	19	30	32	39	45	29	35	19	33
Aged 60 to 69	20	19	34	37	46	29	40	30	32
Aged 70 or older	20	21	28	41	44	24	32	25	30
Not a high school graduate	29	28	45	42	45	26	21	19	18
High school graduate	23	29	31	38	38	31	34	27	33
Bachelor's degree	19	20	26	37	36	38	39	39	34
Graduate degree	23	25	30	37	33	28	37	39	38

Note: Numbers may not add to 100 because "don't know" is not shown.
Source: General Social Survey, National Opinion Research Center, University of Chicago; calculations by the author

Should Government Reduce Income Differences?

The general sentiment is that it should.

Americans lean toward wanting the government to reduce the income disparity between rich and poor. Forty-two percent think income differences should be reduced (choosing 1 through 3 on a 7-point scale), while 35 percent believe government should not be involved in this task (choosing 5 through 7). Twenty-one percent place themselves in the middle. Although the plurality still leans toward government intervention, the proportion is lower than it was in 1978.

Forty-three percent of women believe the government should reduce income differences compared with 39 percent of men. The gap between men and women was larger in 1978, however, when a 51 percent majority of women wanted the government to reduce income differences compared with 44 percent of men.

Blacks are far more likely than whites or "other" races to say government should reduce income disparities. One-quarter of blacks strongly believe it should compared with 13 percent of whites and 18 percent of other races.

People aged 60 or older are less likely than younger people to believe income differences should be reduced (36 to 37 percent compared with 43 to 44 percent of people under age 60). This is a substantial change from 1978, when more than half of people aged 60 or older believe government should reduce income differences.

College graduates are much more likely than those with less education to believe government should not get involved in leveling the income distribution. This group is much more likely to be on the upper end of the income scale. Only 24 percent of people who did not complete high school and 34 percent of high school graduates think the government should not try to reduce income disparities compared with 43 to 44 percent of college graduates.

Should Government Reduce Income Differences? 1998

"Some people think that the government in Washington ought to reduce the income differences between the rich and the poor, perhaps by raising the taxes of wealthy families or by giving income assistance to the poor. Others think that the government should not concern itself with reducing this income difference between the rich and the poor. Here is a card with a scale from 1 to 7. Think of a score of 1 as meaning that the government ought to reduce the income differences between rich and poor, and a score of 7 meaning that the government should not concern itself with reducing income differences. What score between 1 and 7 comes closest to the way you feel?"

(percent of people aged 18 or older responding by sex, race, age, and education, 1998)

	should reduce differences 1	2	3	4	5	6	should not reduce differences 7
Total	**15%**	**10%**	**17%**	**21%**	**11%**	**8%**	**16%**
Men	13	9	17	19	11	9	19
Women	16	10	17	23	11	8	13
Black	24	14	15	24	7	4	8
White	13	9	18	21	12	9	18
Other	18	8	20	18	12	8	11
Aged 18 to 29	12	12	20	26	13	8	8
Aged 30 to 39	14	10	19	19	12	9	14
Aged 40 to 49	16	10	17	18	10	7	21
Aged 50 to 59	19	8	16	19	11	8	18
Aged 60 to 69	10	8	19	26	11	8	17
Aged 70 or older	17	8	11	24	9	9	18
Not a high school graduate	28	10	13	22	8	5	11
High school graduate	15	10	17	23	11	8	15
Bachelor's degree	8	8	20	18	14	11	18
Graduate degree	10	10	21	15	15	12	17

Note: Numbers may not add to 100 because "don't know" is not shown.
Source: General Social Survey, National Opinion Research Center, University of Chicago; calculations by the author

Should Government Reduce Income Differences? 1978 to 1998

"Some people think that the government in Washington ought to reduce the income differences between the rich and the poor, perhaps by raising the taxes of wealthy families or by giving income assistance to the poor. Others think that the government should not concern itself with reducing this income difference between the rich and the poor. Here is a card with a scale from 1 to 7. Think of a score of 1 as meaning that the government ought to reduce the income differences between rich and poor, and a score of 7 meaning that the government should not concern itself with reducing income differences. What score between 1 and 7 comes closest to the way you feel?"

(percent of people aged 18 or older responding by sex, race, age, and education, 1978–98)

	should reduce income differences (1 through 3)			4			should not reduce income differences (5 through 7)		
	1998	1988	1978	1998	1988	1978	1998	1988	1978
Total	**42%**	**47%**	**47%**	**21%**	**20%**	**21%**	**35%**	**31%**	**31%**
Men	39	42	44	19	20	18	39	36	37
Women	43	51	51	23	20	24	32	27	23
Black	53	65	68	24	21	17	19	13	11
White	40	44	44	21	20	21	39	34	33
Aged 18 to 29	44	52	52	26	14	21	29	33	27
Aged 30 to 39	43	51	40	19	16	24	35	32	36
Aged 40 to 49	43	46	41	18	23	23	38	29	35
Aged 50 to 59	43	46	48	19	17	11	37	37	38
Aged 60 to 69	37	46	51	26	24	21	36	26	26
Aged 70 or older	36	37	53	24	29	22	36	28	20
Not a high school graduate	51	51	59	22	20	18	24	25	18
High school graduate	42	49	44	23	21	23	34	29	34
Bachelor's degree	36	33	39	18	18	19	43	46	42
Graduate degree	41	39	37	15	18	16	44	43	47

Note: Numbers may not add to 100 because "don't know" is not shown.
Source: General Social Survey, National Opinion Research Center, University of Chicago; calculations by the author

Who Should Help the Poor?

Most people think a combination of government and individual effort is the answer.

Politicians have succeeded in reducing government aid to the poor. But while Americans are less likely today than they were in 1975 to believe government is the answer, they haven't yet embraced an every-man-for-himself philosophy.

The plurality (43 percent) of Americans believe responsibility for improving the lot of the poor lies with both government and the individual. Almost equal numbers believe government should do whatever is needed to help the poor (26 percent) and that people should take care of themselves (29 percent).

Americans were less likely in 1998 than in 1975 to think government alone should help the poor and more likely to believe it should be a combined effort of government and individuals. The proportion of adults who say government is the answer fell in every demographic segment.

The largest difference of opinion is by race. Forty-three percent of blacks feel government should be responsible for helping the poor, but only 21 percent of whites agree. Thirty-one percent of whites say people should get along without government help compared with 14 percent of blacks.

Men are much more likely than women to think people should take care of themselves (34 versus 24 percent). Women are more likely to take the middle ground or look to the government to help the poor.

College graduates are more likely than those with less education to believe people should take care of themselves (33 to 38 percent compared with 28 percent of high school graduates and 18 percent of those with less education). Only 21 to 25 percent of people with a high school diploma or higher education think government should do whatever is necessary to help the poor compared with 34 percent of people who did not complete high school. The least educated are also the ones most likely to be poor and in need of government assistance.

Who Should Help the Poor? 1998

"Some people think that the government in Washington should do everything possible to improve the standard of living of all poor Americans; they are at Point 1. Other people think it is not the government's responsibility, and that each person should take care of himself; they are at Point 5. Where would you place yourself on this scale?"

(percent of people aged 18 or older responding by sex, race, age, and education, 1998)

	government (strongly agree) 1	2	agree with both 3	4	take care of self (strongly agree) 5
Total	13%	13%	43%	17%	12%
Men	10	13	40	20	15
Women	15	12	45	14	10
Black	27	16	39	9	5
White	9	12	44	18	13
Other	16	12	43	12	12
Aged 18 to 29	13	18	40	16	10
Aged 30 to 39	12	13	41	21	9
Aged 40 to 49	16	11	41	17	13
Aged 50 to 59	13	10	44	16	12
Aged 60 to 69	8	11	50	15	14
Aged 70 or older	12	10	47	10	18
Not a high school graduate	25	9	43	7	11
High school graduate	11	14	44	15	13
Bachelor's degree	8	13	40	27	11
Graduate degree	11	10	45	23	10

Note: Numbers may not add to 100 because "don't know" is not shown.
Source: General Social Survey, National Opinion Research Center, University of Chicago; calculations by the author

Who Should Help the Poor? 1975 to 1998

"Some people think that the government in Washington should do everything possible to improve the standard of living of all poor Americans; they are at Point 1. Other people think it is not the government's responsibility, and that each person should take care of himself; they are at Point 5. Where would you place yourself on this scale?"

(percent of people aged 18 or older responding by sex, race, age, and education, 1975–98)

	government (1 and 2)			agree with both (3)			take care of self (4 and 5)		
	1998	*1988*	*1975*	*1998*	*1988*	*1975*	*1998*	*1988*	*1975*
Total	**26%**	**30%**	**39%**	**43%**	**44%**	**35%**	**29%**	**23%**	**23%**
Men	23	29	37	40	40	33	35	28	28
Women	27	31	41	45	47	36	24	20	20
Black	43	57	67	39	32	23	14	10	7
White	21	26	36	44	46	36	31	26	25
Aged 18 to 29	31	32	44	40	46	36	26	21	17
Aged 30 to 39	25	33	39	41	40	34	30	23	24
Aged 40 to 49	27	31	33	41	45	37	30	23	27
Aged 50 to 59	23	34	37	44	39	37	28	25	24
Aged 60 to 69	19	20	42	50	54	29	29	22	27
Aged 70 or older	22	27	34	47	41	34	28	28	28
Not a high school graduate	34	31	49	43	47	31	18	19	15
High school graduate	25	29	34	44	44	36	28	25	28
Bachelor's degree	21	29	30	40	43	36	38	24	34
Graduate degree	21	24	28	45	47	48	33	27	24

Note: Numbers may not add to 100 because "don't know" is not shown.
Source: General Social Survey, National Opinion Research Center, University of Chicago; calculations by the author

Should Government Provide Jobs?

The demographic segments with the highest unemployment rates are most likely to think the government should provide jobs.

The percentage of people who believe it is the government's responsibility to make sure all Americans have a job has fallen since 1989. In that year, 44 percent of adults said it should be the government's responsibility. By 1998, however, only 36 percent still felt that way while 58 percent said it should not be the government's responsibility to provide jobs.

The biggest difference of opinion on this question is by race. Only 29 percent of whites think it should be the government's responsibility to provide jobs compared with a much larger 61 to 62 percent of blacks and people of "other" race. It's not hard to determine the reason for this difference of opinion: whites have a lower rate of unemployment than blacks and other races.

Forty percent of women believe government should make sure everyone has a job compared with only 31 percent of men. The proportion of both men and women who feel this way was lower in 1998 than in 1978.

Young adults, who are just entering the labor market, are more likely than their elders to believe government should provide jobs (50 percent compared with 28 to 34 percent of people aged 30 or older).

The more education people have, the more employable they are. In today's economy, people who did not complete high school are especially disadvantaged in the labor market. Fully 51 percent of this group believe government should make sure everyone has a job compared with a much smaller 28 to 34 percent of people with more education.

Should Government Provide Jobs? 1998

"On the whole, do you think it should or should not be the government's responsibility to provide a job for everyone who wants one?"

(percent of people aged 18 or older responding by sex, race, age, and education, 1998)

	definitely should be	probably should be	probably should not be	definitely should not be	can't choose	should be, total	should not be, total
Total	**12%**	**24%**	**25%**	**33%**	**7%**	**36%**	**58%**
Men	10	21	25	39	5	31	64
Women	14	26	26	27	8	40	53
Black	33	29	21	11	6	62	32
White	8	21	27	37	7	29	64
Other	19	42	17	16	5	61	33
Aged 18 to 29	17	33	26	20	4	50	46
Aged 30 to 39	11	21	28	35	6	32	63
Aged 40 to 49	9	24	28	34	5	33	62
Aged 50 to 59	13	21	24	35	8	34	59
Aged 60 to 69	11	18	20	39	11	29	59
Aged 70 or older	9	19	22	40	10	28	62
Not a high school graduate	22	29	16	21	13	51	37
High school graduate	11	22	27	33	6	33	60
Bachelor's degree	8	26	26	37	4	34	63
Graduate degree	9	19	29	41	2	28	70

Source: General Social Survey, National Opinion Research Center, University of Chicago; calculations by the author

Should Government Provide Jobs? 1989 and 1998

"On the whole, do you think it should or should not be the government's responsibility to provide a job for everyone who wants one?"

(percent of people aged 18 or older responding by sex, race, age, and education, 1989–98)

	should be		should not be	
	1998	**1989**	**1998**	**1989**
Total	**36%**	**44%**	**58%**	**49%**
Men	31	40	64	55
Women	40	48	53	45
Black	62	76	32	19
White	29	40	64	54
Aged 18 to 29	50	52	46	42
Aged 30 to 39	32	46	63	49
Aged 40 to 49	33	37	62	57
Aged 50 to 59	34	41	59	54
Aged 60 to 69	29	42	59	50
Aged 70 or older	28	46	62	47
Not a high school graduate	51	57	37	34
High school graduate	33	44	60	50
Bachelor's degree	34	30	63	67
Graduate degree	28	33	70	67

Note: Numbers may not add to 100 because "can't choose" is not shown.
Source: General Social Survey, National Opinion Research Center, University of Chicago; calculations by the author

Phase Out or Continue Social Security?

Younger generations are most likely to want to privatize Social Security.

Most Americans (55 percent) want to continue the Social Security system much as it is now. One-third of Americans, however, would like to phase out the nation's current Social Security system and replace it with mandatory private retirement accounts. Many advocates of change are motivated not by concerns about the health of the current system, but by the belief that they can get a higher rate of return by investing the money themselves.

Men are more likely than women to want to opt out of Social Security. Thirty-eight percent of men, but only 29 percent of women, favor replacing the current system with private retirement accounts. Women are more likely to want to leave the system as it is or to say they don't know.

Sixty-four percent of blacks think Social Security should continue as it is compared with 53 to 54 percent of whites and "other" races. Thirty-five percent of whites think the current system should be privatized compared with 21 percent of blacks and 29 percent of other races.

Older Americans are most supportive of the current system. More than three-quarters favor continuing it much as it is now. Today's elderly remember the nation's economic ups and downs while younger generations tend to believe the economy—and more important, the stock market—can only go up. This is why fully 44 percent of people in their forties and 39 to 37 percent of people aged 18 to 39 favor privatizing Social Security. Fewer than half the people in these age groups would keep the system as it is now.

College graduates are divided on whether it would be better to keep the current Social Security system or privatize it. People with less education, however, are much more likely to want to keep the system as it is. Educated Americans are better equipped to navigate the complexities of the stock market and other investment opportunities. People with less education would be more vulnerable to bad choices and unscrupulous financial advisors.

Phase Out or Continue Social Security? 1998

"Do you think it would be better to phase out Social Security and require people to take what they and their employers now pay into Social Security and invest it in mandatory private retirement accounts, or do you think Social Security should continue much as it is now?"

(percent of people aged 18 or older responding by sex, race, age, and education, 1998)

	phase out	*continue as is*	*don't know*
Total	**33%**	**55%**	**13%**
Men	38	52	10
Women	29	57	15
Black	21	64	15
White	35	53	12
Other	29	54	17
Aged 18 to 29	37	47	16
Aged 30 to 39	39	47	14
Aged 40 to 49	44	48	8
Aged 50 to 59	29	56	15
Aged 60 to 69	15	74	11
Aged 70 or older	10	78	12
Not a high school graduate	13	69	18
High school graduate	32	57	12
Bachelor's degree	44	46	10
Graduate degree	41	41	18

Source: General Social Survey, National Opinion Research Center, University of Chicago; calculations by the author

How Serious Is the Social Security Problem?

Baby boomers are most likely to think the Social Security system is in big trouble.

Americans are very concerned about the Social Security system. Half think major changes are required to solve its problems. Twenty-seven percent think the system has only minor problems or none at all. Only 16 percent believe the system is too broken to be fixed and should be replaced.

More than half of whites (55 percent) think Social Security has serious problems which require major changes to fix compared with 40 to 41 percent of blacks and "other" races. Only 25 percent of whites believe the Social Security program has no serious problems or only minor problems compared with 34 percent of blacks and 32 percent of other races. Among blacks and whites, 15 to 16 percent think the current system should be replaced compared with a larger 20 percent of other races.

Not surprisingly, current Social Security recipients are most likely to believe there is little wrong with the Social Security system. Only 44 percent of people aged 70 or older think the current system needs major changes or needs to be replaced. Forty-seven percent say the system has no real problems or requires only minor changes. Among people in their sixties, 54 percent think Social Security needs a major overhaul or should be replaced, while 39 percent think it has only minor problems.

People aged 30 to 49 are most concerned about the health of the Social Security system. Most people in this age group are baby boomers, and they know their generation's retirement will stress the system. Nearly three-quarters of people in their thirties and fully 81 percent of those in their forties believe the system will need major changes or will have to be replaced entirely. Nearly one-quarter of people in their forties think the system needs to be replaced.

College graduates are more likely than people with less education to believe Social Security needs major changes (61 to 62 percent compared with 51 percent of high school graduates and 38 percent of those with less education). Thirty-six percent of people who did not complete high school (many of whom are older Americans) believe the system has only minor problems, as do 27 percent of high school graduates. Just 16 to 20 percent of college graduates agree.

How Serious Is the Social Security Problem? 1998

"Please tell me which of the following statements comes closest to your opinion about the Social Security program. The Social Security program has no serious problems, certainly none that require changing the current system. Social Security has minor problems that can be fixed with minor changes to the current system. Social Security's problems are serious and can be fixed only with major changes to the current system. Social Security's problems are so bad that the current system should be replaced."

(percent of people aged 18 or older responding by sex, race, age, and education, 1998)

	no problems	minor problems	need major changes	should replace current system
Total	**5%**	**22%**	**52%**	**16%**
Men	5	21	51	19
Women	5	23	52	14
Black	6	28	40	15
White	4	21	55	16
Other	13	19	41	20
Aged 18 to 29	4	22	48	19
Aged 30 to 39	4	18	54	19
Aged 40 to 49	1	16	58	23
Aged 50 to 59	5	19	56	13
Aged 60 to 69	4	35	48	6
Aged 70 or older	13	34	40	4
Not a high school graduate	12	24	38	10
High school graduate	3	24	51	17
Bachelor's degree	4	16	61	16
Graduate degree	3	13	62	16

Note: Numbers may not add to 100 because "don't know" is not shown.
Source: General Social Survey, National Opinion Research Center, University of Chicago; calculations by the author

Tax Level Appropriate?

Not surprisingly, most Americans think their taxes are too high.

Americans have been complaining of high taxes for a long time, although federal income taxes are much lower now than they were a few decades ago. In 1977, 67 percent of Americans said their taxes were too high. By 1998, the proportion had dropped only slightly, to 63 percent. Thirty-one percent believe taxes are at about the right level. Only 1 percent say their taxes are too low.

Similar percentages of people by race think their taxes are about right. Among blacks and whites, 63 to 64 percent think their taxes are too high compared with 58 percent of "other" races.

Only 49 percent of people aged 70 or older say their taxes are too high, while 41 percent think they are about right. At this age, most people are retired and are in a lower tax bracket than they were when they were working. Similarly, because young adults just starting a career have relatively low wages (and taxes), only 59 percent of them think their taxes are too high. People aged 30 to 59 earn more than older and younger Americans and are more likely to complain that their taxes are too high (67 to 71 percent).

People who did not complete high school—who tend to earn less than those with more education—are least likely to believe their taxes are too high. Only half say so compared with 62 to 65 percent of people with at least a high school diploma.

Tax Level Appropriate? 1998

"Do you consider the amount of federal income tax which you have to pay as too low, about right, or too high?"

(percent of people aged 18 or older responding by sex, race, age, and education, 1998)

	too low	about right	too high	don't know
Total	**1%**	**31%**	**63%**	**5%**
Men	1	31	65	3
Women	1	31	62	7
Black	1	29	64	7
White	1	32	63	4
Other	1	31	58	10
Aged 18 to 29	0	35	59	6
Aged 30 to 39	1	27	67	5
Aged 40 to 49	1	27	71	1
Aged 50 to 59	2	28	68	3
Aged 60 to 69	1	37	54	8
Aged 70 or older	1	41	49	9
Not a high school graduate	1	34	50	15
High school graduate	1	30	66	4
Bachelor's degree	1	33	62	3
Graduate degree	2	31	65	1

Source: General Social Survey, National Opinion Research Center, University of Chicago; calculations by the author

Tax Level Appropriate? 1977 to 1998

"Do you consider the amount of federal income tax which you have to pay as too low, about right, or too high?"

(percent of people aged 18 or older responding by sex, race, age, and education, 1977–98)

	too low			about right			too high		
	1998	1988	1977	1998	1988	1977	1998	1988	1977
Total	**1%**	**1%**	**1%**	**31%**	**40%**	**28%**	**63%**	**56%**	**67%**
Men	1	1	1	31	46	31	65	53	67
Women	1	1	1	31	35	27	62	58	67
Black	1	2	1	29	30	18	64	63	70
White	1	1	1	32	42	30	63	54	66
Aged 18 to 29	0	1	1	35	45	29	59	52	66
Aged 30 to 39	1	0	1	27	36	29	67	62	68
Aged 40 to 49	1	2	0	27	33	23	71	64	74
Aged 50 to 59	2	2	0	28	28	27	68	69	68
Aged 60 to 69	1	0	1	37	46	25	54	50	69
Aged 70 or older	1	2	0	41	49	39	49	35	47
Not a high school graduate	1	2	0	34	41	30	50	51	60
High school graduate	1	1	1	30	35	28	66	61	71
Bachelor's degree	1	0	1	33	47	26	62	53	71
Graduate degree	2	5	3	31	49	31	65	45	65

Note: Numbers may not add to 100 because "don't know" is not shown.
Source: General Social Survey, National Opinion Research Center, University of Chicago; calculations by the author

Cheating on Taxes

Younger generations are less ethical than their elders on the issue of taxes.

No one likes paying taxes, but Americans do not believe this dislike means it's okay to cheat on their taxes. Fully 81 percent say it is wrong or seriously wrong to underreport income in order to pay less income tax. Thirty-one percent think it is seriously wrong. Only 5 percent say it is not wrong.

Men are a little more comfortable than women with the idea of cheating on their taxes. Eighteen percent of men say it is not wrong or only a bit wrong compared with 13 percent of women. One-third of women think it is seriously wrong compared with 28 percent of men.

Blacks are less likely than whites and "other" races to say it is seriously wrong to cheat on taxes (26 percent compared with 31 to 32 percent of whites and other races). Seventeen percent of blacks and 19 percent of other races think it is not wrong or only a bit wrong to conceal income to lower the tax bill compared with 14 percent of whites.

Younger generations are less ethical than their elders on this issue. Only 23 percent of people aged 18 to 29 think it is seriously wrong to cheat on taxes compared with a larger 30 to 35 percent of older people. The proportion of people who say they don't think it is really wrong to cheat drops sharply with age. Fully 22 percent of people under age 30 think it is not wrong or only a bit wrong to under-report income, but the figure falls to just 7 percent among people aged 70 or older.

Among college graduates, 36 to 37 percent believe it is seriously wrong to cheat on taxes compared with 30 percent of high school graduates and 12 percent of people who did not complete high school. Twenty-one percent of the least-educated Americans, however, say they don't know if it is wrong.

Cheating on Taxes, 1998

"Do you feel it is wrong or not wrong if a taxpayer does not report all of his income in order to pay less income taxes?"

(percent of people aged 18 or older responding by sex, race, age, and education, 1998)

	not wrong	a bit wrong	wrong	seriously wrong	can't choose
Total	**5%**	**10%**	**50%**	**31%**	**5%**
Men	6	12	49	28	6
Women	4	9	50	33	5
Black	5	12	51	26	6
White	4	10	50	31	5
Other	7	12	41	32	9
Aged 18 to 29	7	15	47	23	9
Aged 30 to 39	5	11	50	30	4
Aged 40 to 49	4	11	47	35	4
Aged 50 to 59	5	7	51	35	2
Aged 60 to 69	3	7	53	32	5
Aged 70 or older	2	5	54	32	7
Not a high school graduate	5	7	55	21	12
High school graduate	6	11	48	30	5
Bachelor's degree	1	10	50	36	3
Graduate degree	2	7	52	37	1

Source: General Social Survey, National Opinion Research Center, University of Chicago; calculations by the author

Lying to Obtain Benefits

The more education people have, the more they believe it is wrong to lie to obtain benefits.

The majority of the public believes it is seriously wrong for someone to give incorrect information to obtain government benefits to which the person is not entitled. Americans apparently make a distinction between different kinds of lying, however. They are more likely to say it is seriously wrong to lie to obtain government benefits than to cheat on taxes.

There is no difference of opinion between men and women on this issue. There is some disagreement by race, however. While 42 percent of blacks think it is seriously wrong to lie to obtain benefits, a larger 54 to 55 percent of whites and "other" races agree. Only 3 percent of whites say it is not wrong or only a bit wrong to give false information to obtain government benefits compared with 8 percent of blacks and 10 percent of other races.

Among people aged 70 or older, only 48 percent say it is seriously wrong to lie to obtain benefits while majorities of younger adults think it is (52 to 55 percent). Nine percent of young adults (under age 30) say it is not wrong or only a bit wrong to lie for benefits compared with 2 to 4 percent of older people.

The percentage of people who say it is seriously wrong to lie to obtain benefits increases with education. Thirty-seven percent of people who did not complete high school say it is seriously wrong, but the proportion rises to 67 percent among people with a graduate degree. Eight percent of the least educated think it is not wrong or only a bit wrong compared with 1 percent of college graduates.

Lying to Obtain Benefits, 1998

"Do you feel it is wrong or not wrong if a person gives the government incorrect information about himself to get government benefits that he is not entitled to?"

(percent of people aged 18 or older responding by sex, race, age, and education, 1998)

	not wrong	a bit wrong	wrong	seriously wrong	can't choose
Total	**2%**	**3%**	**41%**	**53%**	**2%**
Men	2	3	40	52	2
Women	1	2	41	53	2
Black	4	4	45	42	5
White	1	2	41	54	1
Other	3	7	30	55	4
Aged 18 to 29	2	7	32	55	5
Aged 30 to 39	2	2	42	52	1
Aged 40 to 49	1	2	40	55	1
Aged 50 to 59	2	1	44	53	1
Aged 60 to 69	2	2	44	53	0
Aged 70 or older	1	1	46	48	5
Not a high school graduate	4	4	48	37	7
High school graduate	2	3	41	53	1
Bachelor's degree	0	1	39	58	2
Graduate degree	1	0	32	67	0

Source: General Social Survey, National Opinion Research Center, University of Chicago; calculations by the author

Technology and Government Secrecy

Most Americans think some technology should be kept secret.

As the Internet links individuals and businesses across the globe, the issue of technology and secrecy is likely to heat up. The government is looking carefully at products such as encryption software, which may have military use, and in some cases banning their export. To date, the public supports maintaining secrecy around technology with military use. Seven in ten Americans support keeping such technology secret, while only 15 percent oppose it.

Men are much more likely than women to think some technology should be kept secret. Fully 42 percent of men say they strongly agree compared with 25 percent of women. Among whites, 72 percent think technology with military use should be kept secret compared with 59 percent of blacks and 63 percent of "other" races.

Similar percentages of people aged 30 or older think technology with military applications should be kept secret (67 to 72 percent), but people under age 30 are slightly less likely to agree (63 percent). People who did not complete high school are least likely to support keeping some technology secret (61 percent), while those with a bachelor's degree are most likely to support secrecy (77 percent).

Technology and Government Secrecy, 1998

"In order to maintain America's leadership in the world, the government should maintain a high level of secrecy surrounding technology with military uses. Do you agree or disagree?"

(percent of people aged 18 or older responding by sex, race, age, and education, 1998)

	strongly agree	agree	neither	disagree	strongly disagree	don't know	agree, total	disagree, total
Total	**32%**	**37%**	**12%**	**11%**	**4%**	**4%**	**69%**	**15%**
Men	42	34	9	10	3	2	76	13
Women	25	39	13	12	4	6	64	16
Black	28	31	16	15	4	8	59	19
White	34	38	11	11	3	3	72	14
Other	22	41	11	9	8	8	63	17
Aged 18 to 29	23	40	15	14	5	3	63	19
Aged 30 to 39	32	35	14	12	3	4	67	15
Aged 40 to 49	35	37	11	12	3	2	72	15
Aged 50 to 59	34	38	9	9	4	6	72	13
Aged 60 to 69	34	38	9	9	3	6	72	12
Aged 70 or older	37	35	7	8	5	8	72	13
Not a high school graduate	33	28	13	11	5	10	61	16
High school graduate	31	38	12	12	4	4	69	16
Bachelor's degree	38	39	11	10	2	1	77	12
Graduate degree	24	44	15	9	5	3	66	14

Source: General Social Survey, National Opinion Research Center, University of Chicago; calculations by the author

Government Keeps Too Many Documents Secret

Most Americans think fewer documents should be classified as secret.

America is one of the most open societies in the world, and Americans like it that way. While most people would agree the government must maintain some secrets, the majority of the public (54 percent) believe too many documents are classified as secret. This suspicion has been borne out from time to time when declassified documents revealed that, rather than protecting national security, the government was trying to protect itself from embarrassment.

Half of women agree that the government classifies too many documents as secret compared with a larger 59 percent of men. Women are more likely to say they don't know or neither agree nor disagree.

Most whites say the government keeps too many documents secret (56 percent). Pluralities of blacks and "other" races agree (48 and 49 percent, respectively), but substantial percentages say they don't know or neither agree nor disagree.

Majorities of people under age 70 think the government keeps too many secrets. People under age 30 and those aged 70 or older are most likely to disagree that too much information is classified as secret.

Half of people who did not complete high school think the government keeps too many secrets, as do 56 percent of high school graduates, 52 percent of people with a bachelor's degree, and 60 percent of those with a graduate degree. The least educated Americans are most likely to say they don't know.

Government Keeps Too Many Documents Secret, 1998

"Given the world situation, the government protects too many documents by classifying them as 'secret' or 'top secret.' Do you agree or disagree?"

(percent of people aged 18 or older responding by sex, race, age, and education, 1998)

	strongly agree	agree	neither	disagree	strongly disagree	don't know	agree, total	disagree, total
Total	16%	38%	18%	16%	4%	8%	54%	20%
Men	19	40	16	16	4	6	59	20
Women	14	36	20	16	4	10	50	20
Black	16	32	21	16	3	13	48	19
White	17	39	17	16	4	7	56	20
Other	17	32	25	14	1	11	49	15
Aged 18 to 29	17	36	17	19	4	7	53	23
Aged 30 to 39	17	38	22	11	3	9	55	14
Aged 40 to 49	17	43	18	15	3	4	60	18
Aged 50 to 59	17	36	16	15	5	10	53	20
Aged 60 to 69	13	40	21	15	4	7	53	19
Aged 70 or older	15	32	10	23	4	15	47	27
Not a high school graduate	17	33	15	16	4	16	50	20
High school graduate	18	38	19	15	4	7	56	19
Bachelor's degree	13	39	20	17	4	7	52	21
Graduate degree	18	42	15	18	1	7	60	19

Source: General Social Survey, National Opinion Research Center, University of Chicago; calculations by the author

5

Race

On racial issues, we are a nation divided—not just by race, but by sex, age, and educational attainment. While people's attitudes about most of the racial issues examined here have changed substantially over the past two decades, gaps between groups remain.

Few Americans believe there should be laws against interracial marriage or agree that blacks should not push where they are not wanted. But people are divided on the reasons for the lower socioeconomic status of blacks, with similar percentages attributing it to lack of education and lack of motivation.

Although overt racism is relatively rare now, stereotypes of blacks and whites persist. More people say blacks are lazy than say whites are lazy. A larger percentage say most whites are intelligent than say most blacks are intelligent. The majority of adults oppose affirmative action and believe blacks should work their way up without special favors.

Blacks and whites have sharply different opinions on most race issues. Whites are far more likely than blacks to attribute the lower socioeconomic status of blacks to lack of motivation and to say that conditions for black people have improved in the last few years. Blacks are more likely to support affirmative action and to attribute socioeconomic differences to discrimination and lack of education. Blacks make similar assessments of the work habits and intelligence of blacks and whites, while whites are more likely to rate whites higher than blacks on both of these characteristics.

Women tend to be more liberal than men on many issues, including race. Women are more likely than men to believe discrimination and a lack of education are behind socioeconomic differences between whites and blacks. Men are more likely to oppose affirmative action and to believe the government has no obligation to help improve the living standards of blacks, despite past discrimination.

On many questions of race, the generations disagree at least as strongly as people by race do. It is important to remember when examining attitudes by age that each successive age group is more racially diverse. Fully 85 percent of people aged 65 or older are white, compared with only about 70 percent of people in their twenties. Consequently, in younger generations whites have a smaller statistical dominance than among older generations. In addition, the attitudes of young whites are influenced by the greater racial diversity of their peer group.

The older people are, the more likely they are to believe blacks should not push where they are not wanted, to believe conditions for blacks have improved in the past few years, and to think blacks should work their way up without special favors. The percentage of people saying most blacks are lazy also rises with age. The younger people are, the more inclined they are to say it is unlikely that a white person will be passed over for a job or promotion while an equally or less qualified black person gets one instead.

On some questions, the oldest Americans stand distinctly apart from younger age groups. People aged 70 or older are far more likely to believe most blacks are unintelligent, to support laws against interracial marriage, and to blame the lower socioeconomic status of blacks on an innate inability to learn.

Education has a strong influence on attitudes toward racial issues. There is, however, considerable overlap between age and education because younger generations are better educated than older ones. Because of this overlap, it is not always clear whether education or age has a greater influence on attitudes.

People who did not complete high school are more likely than those with more education to favor laws against interracial marriage and to believe it is very likely that whites will suffer "reverse discrimination" in the workplace. They are also considerably more likely to think most blacks are unintelligent. The more education people have, the less likely they are to agree that blacks should not push where they are not wanted or to believe that most blacks are lazy.

There is a distinct divide between college graduates and those with less education on many questions. College graduates are most likely to blame a lack of education for the socioeconomic differences between blacks and whites, while those with less education blame a lack of motivation. People with a graduate degree are most likely to support affirmative action and least likely to say blacks should work their way up without special favors.

Changes in Conditions for Blacks

Whites are almost twice as likely as blacks to believe conditions for blacks have improved.

Sixty-three percent of Americans say conditions for blacks have improved in the past few years. Only 5 percent believe things have gotten worse.

Blacks and "other" races disagree sharply with whites on this question. Forty-two percent of blacks and 49 percent of other races say conditions have improved. In contrast, fully 67 percent of whites say conditions for blacks are better now than in the past.

The older people are, the more likely they are to believe conditions for blacks have improved. Among people under age 40, 55 to 58 percent say conditions for blacks have improved in the past few years. But a much larger 73 percent of people aged 60 or older believe things have gotten better. Although the question specifically asked about changes in conditions in the past few years, it is possible that many older people are comparing conditions today with conditions from many years ago.

Changes in Conditions for Blacks, 1998

"In the past few years, do you think conditions for black people have improved, gotten worse, or stayed about the same?"

(percent of people aged 18 or older responding by sex, race, age, and education, 1998)

	improved	stayed the same	gotten worse	don't know
Total	63%	28%	5%	5%
Men	63	28	5	5
Women	63	27	5	5
Black	42	44	11	3
White	67	24	4	5
Other	49	39	4	8
Aged 18 to 29	58	30	6	5
Aged 30 to 39	55	35	6	4
Aged 40 to 49	62	30	5	3
Aged 50 to 59	65	24	6	5
Aged 60 to 69	73	18	2	7
Aged 70 or older	73	19	2	5
Not a high school graduate	61	28	3	7
High school graduate	64	26	5	4
Bachelor's degree	58	30	7	5
Graduate degree	61	32	3	3

Source: General Social Survey, National Opinion Research Center, University of Chicago; calculations by the author

Should Blacks "Push Where They're Not Wanted"?

The young and old disagree on this question.

Few Americans today would publicly state that blacks should not push themselves where they are not wanted, but many whites (and some blacks) frequently made this argument during the 1960s. While growing racial sensitivity has made Americans more careful of what they say, it hasn't completely changed attitudes. Even today, 39 percent of Americans agree at least slightly with this statement.

Forty-one percent of whites agree that blacks should not push where they are not wanted compared with 31 percent of "other" races and a surprisingly high 35 percent of blacks. The percentages of whites and other races who agree, however, has fallen markedly since 1977. (Blacks were not asked this question in that year.)

Americans are worlds apart on this question by education. Only 29 percent of people with a bachelor's degree and 16 percent of those with a graduate degree say blacks should not push, compared with 41 percent of high school graduates and 53 percent of people who did not graduate from high school.

Agreement with this statement fell in every demographic segment between 1977 and 1998. The strongest sign that it will continue to decline is the large proportion of younger people who disagree. Among people under aged 40, 63 to 65 percent disagree with the idea that blacks shouldn't push, compared with only 33 to 39 percent of people aged 60 or older.

Should Blacks "Push Where They're Not Wanted"? 1998

"Here is an opinion other people have expressed in connection with black-white relations: 'Blacks shouldn't push themselves where they're not wanted.' How do you feel about that statement?"

(percent of people aged 18 or older responding by sex, race, age, and education, 1998)

	agree strongly	agree slightly	disagree slightly	disagree strongly	don't know	agree, total	disagree, total
Total	**14%**	**25%**	**23%**	**33%**	**6%**	**39%**	**56%**
Men	14	27	25	30	5	41	55
Women	13	24	21	35	7	37	56
Black	15	20	18	43	5	35	61
White	14	27	24	30	6	41	54
Other	7	24	20	40	9	31	60
Aged 18 to 29	9	20	25	40	6	29	65
Aged 30 to 39	9	23	23	40	5	32	63
Aged 40 to 49	13	22	22	37	6	35	59
Aged 50 to 59	14	28	25	28	7	42	53
Aged 60 to 69	21	34	17	22	6	55	39
Aged 70 or older	25	35	21	12	6	60	33
Not a high school graduate	22	31	22	17	7	53	39
High school graduate	15	26	25	29	5	41	54
Bachelor's degree	8	21	20	44	7	29	64
Graduate degree	4	12	22	54	8	16	76

Source: General Social Survey, National Opinion Research Center, University of Chicago; calculations by the author

Should Blacks "Push Where They're Not Wanted"? 1977 to 1998

"Here is an opinion other people have expressed in connection with black-white relations: 'Blacks shouldn't push themselves where they're not wanted.' How do you feel about that statement?"

(percent of people aged 18 or older responding by sex, race, age, and education, 1977–98)

	agree strongly or slightly			disagree strongly or slightly		
	1998	1985	1977	1998	1985	1977
Total	**39%**	**57%**	**71%**	**56%**	**41%**	**27%**
Men	41	60	74	55	38	24
Women	37	55	69	56	43	28
Black	35	46	*	61	48	*
White	41	59	71	54	39	27
Aged 18 to 29	29	43	61	65	56	38
Aged 30 to 39	32	48	61	63	51	39
Aged 40 to 49	35	65	73	59	31	24
Aged 50 to 59	42	68	79	53	30	19
Aged 60 to 69	55	71	84	39	28	13
Aged 70 or older	60	64	86	33	33	11
Not a high school graduate	53	71	82	39	26	16
High school graduate	41	59	73	54	39	25
Bachelor's degree	29	40	44	64	58	55
Graduate degree	16	36	49	76	61	50

* Question not asked of blacks in 1977.
Note: Numbers may not add to 100 because "don't know" is not shown.
Source: General Social Survey, National Opinion Research Center, University of Chicago; calculations by the author

Interracial Marriage

Changing times are reflected in views of young and old.

Regardless of whether they personally approve of interracial marriage, few Americans believe it should be illegal. As on other racial issues, opinions about interracial marriage have changed substantially in the past two decades. By 1998, only 11 percent of the public still supported laws against interracial marriage compared with 28 percent in 1977.

Thirteen percent of whites, but only 4 percent of blacks and 5 percent of "other" races, believe interracial marriage should be illegal. The percentage of whites saying this is down from 28 percent in 1977, however.

Differences of opinion on this question are greatest by age. Only 5 to 9 percent of people under age 50 favor laws against marriage between blacks and whites compared with 19 percent of people in their sixties and 30 percent of those aged 70 or older.

The less educated are much more likely than those with more education to believe interracial marriage should be illegal. Only 3 percent of college graduates want to outlaw marriages between blacks and whites compared with 12 percent of people with a high school diploma and 23 percent of those who did not complete high school.

Interracial Marriage, 1998

"Do you think there should be laws against marriages between blacks and whites?"

(percent of people aged 18 or older responding by sex, race, age, and education, 1998)

	yes	no	don't know
Total	**11%**	**86%**	**3%**
Men	11	87	2
Women	11	86	3
Black	4	94	2
White	13	85	3
Other	5	94	2
Aged 18 to 29	5	95	1
Aged 30 to 39	5	93	2
Aged 40 to 49	9	90	1
Aged 50 to 59	9	88	2
Aged 60 to 69	19	75	5
Aged 70 or older	30	62	8
Not a high school graduate	23	72	6
High school graduate	12	86	3
Bachelor's degree	3	95	2
Graduate degree	3	96	1

Source: General Social Survey, National Opinion Research Center, University of Chicago; calculations by the author

Interracial Marriage, 1977 to 1998

"Do you think there should be laws against marriages between blacks and whites?"

(percent of people aged 18 or older responding by sex, race, age, and education, 1977–98)

	yes			no			don't know		
	1998	*1988*	*1977*	*1998*	*1988*	*1977*	*1998*	*1988*	*1977*
Total	**11%**	**22%**	**28%**	**86%**	**75%**	**71%**	**3%**	**3%**	**2%**
Men	11	20	26	87	77	72	2	3	1
Women	11	23	29	86	74	69	3	3	2
Black	4	5	*	94	92	*	2	3	*
White	13	25	28	85	72	70	3	3	2
Aged 18 to 29	5	13	12	95	84	87	1	3	1
Aged 30 to 39	5	9	17	93	88	82	2	3	1
Aged 40 to 49	9	20	26	90	79	72	1	1	2
Aged 50 to 59	9	21	33	88	79	65	2	0	2
Aged 60 to 69	19	40	51	75	58	47	5	2	2
Aged 70 or older	30	44	51	62	48	45	8	8	4
Not a high school graduate	23	39	50	72	56	48	6	5	2
High school graduate	12	20	20	86	77	79	3	2	1
Bachelor's degree	3	8	8	95	91	92	2	1	1
Graduate degree	3	5	10	96	94	90	1	2	0

* *Question not asked of blacks in 1977.*
Source: General Social Survey, National Opinion Research Center, University of Chicago; calculations by the author

Work Habits of Blacks and Whites

Whites are more likely than blacks to be considered hard working.

On a scale of 1 (almost all are hard working) to 7 (almost all are lazy), Americans are more likely to say whites are hard working and blacks are lazy. Despite a decline in overt racism, substantial numbers of people still cling to racial stereotypes.

Forty-five percent of people place both blacks and whites in the middle of the scale. The differences are at the extremes. Forty percent say most whites are hard working (1 to 3 on the scale) but only 20 percent say most blacks are hard working. Only 12 percent think most whites are lazy (5 to 7 on the scale), but 31 percent say most blacks are lazy.

Blacks assess the work habits of blacks and whites the same, but whites do not. Thirty-nine percent of whites think most whites are hard working, but only 18 percent make the same assessment of blacks. In contrast, 33 percent of whites say most blacks are lazy, but only 10 percent think most whites are lazy. Among people of "other" races, 35 percent think most blacks are lazy compared with only 10 percent who say this of whites. Whites now are less likely to say blacks are lazy than they were in 1990, however, when 45 percent felt that way.

The older people are, the more likely they are to believe most blacks are lazy. Only 26 percent of people under age 30 say this, but the proportion rises to 38 to 39 percent among people aged 60 or older.

Education also plays a role in the degree to which people stereotype blacks. As the level of education rises, the tendency to believe blacks are lazy declines. Among people who did not complete high school, 38 percent say most blacks are lazy, but the figure drops to only 20 percent among people with a graduate degree.

Work Habits of Blacks, 1998

"A score of 1 means you think almost all of the people in that group are hard-working. A score of 7 means that you think almost all of the people in the group are lazy. How would you rate blacks on this scale?"

(percent of people aged 18 or older responding by sex, race, age, and education, 1998)

	hard working	2	3	4	5	6	lazy
Total	2%	5%	13%	45%	19%	9%	3%
Men	2	4	14	44	21	8	2
Women	2	5	13	45	18	9	3
Black	8	10	15	42	14	5	3
White	1	4	13	46	21	9	3
Other	2	5	16	38	15	13	7
Aged 18 to 29	2	8	14	49	16	8	2
Aged 30 to 39	2	3	14	49	18	7	3
Aged 40 to 49	2	4	13	46	19	9	2
Aged 50 to 59	1	5	13	43	21	7	4
Aged 60 to 69	2	5	10	41	23	10	6
Aged 70 or older	3	4	12	37	22	13	3
Not a high school graduate	5	8	10	36	22	10	6
High school graduate	2	5	13	44	20	10	3
Bachelor's degree	2	4	15	49	17	8	1
Graduate degree	1	4	17	55	17	2	1

Note: Numbers may not add to 100 because "don't know" is not shown.
Source: General Social Survey, National Opinion Research Center, University of Chicago; calculations by the author

Work Habits of Blacks, 1990 and 1998

**"A score of 1 means you think almost all of the people in that group are hard-working.
A score of 7 means that you think almost all of the people in the group are lazy.
How would you rate blacks on this scale?"**

(percent of people aged 18 or older responding by sex, race, age, and education, 1990–98)

	1 to 3 (hard working)		4		5 to 7 (lazy)	
	1998	*1990*	*1998*	*1990*	*1998*	*1990*
Total	**20%**	**20%**	**45%**	**34%**	**31%**	**42%**
Men	20	21	44	33	31	43
Women	20	19	45	35	30	42
Black	33	39	42	37	22	18
White	18	17	46	35	33	45
Aged 18 to 29	24	20	49	41	26	36
Aged 30 to 39	19	23	49	38	28	37
Aged 40 to 49	19	20	46	35	30	43
Aged 50 to 59	19	20	43	31	32	43
Aged 60 to 69	17	14	41	33	39	48
Aged 70 or older	19	18	37	19	38	54
Not a high school graduate	23	22	36	20	38	50
High school graduate	20	18	44	36	33	43
Bachelor's degree	21	21	49	40	26	37
Graduate degree	22	22	55	38	20	36

Note: Numbers may not add to 100 because "don't know" is not shown.
Source: General Social Survey, National Opinion Research Center, University of Chicago; calculations by the author

Work Habits of Whites, 1998

"A score of 1 means you think almost all of the people in that group are hard-working. A score of 7 means that you think almost all of the people in the group are lazy. How would you rate whites on this scale?"

(percent of people aged 18 or older responding by sex, race, age, and education, 1998)

	hard working	2	3	4	5	6	lazy
Total	**5%**	**11%**	**24%**	**45%**	**8%**	**3%**	**1%**
Men	4	10	26	43	10	3	1
Women	5	12	22	47	7	3	1
Black	5	7	20	42	13	5	4
White	4	11	24	47	7	3	0
Other	9	14	28	34	6	2	2
Aged 18 to 29	6	11	27	43	7	2	2
Aged 30 to 39	4	10	24	49	7	3	0
Aged 40 to 49	4	9	24	48	8	3	1
Aged 50 to 59	4	11	18	47	13	1	1
Aged 60 to 69	4	15	25	39	10	4	1
Aged 70 or older	5	13	23	40	6	4	1
Not a high school graduate	10	12	16	41	10	5	2
High school graduate	4	12	23	45	8	3	1
Bachelor's degree	4	10	27	47	6	1	0
Graduate degree	1	7	25	53	9	2	0

Note: Numbers may not add to 100 because "don't know" is not shown.
Source: General Social Survey, National Opinion Research Center, University of Chicago; calculations by the author

Work Habits of Whites, 1990 and 1998

"A score of 1 means you think almost all of the people in that group are hard-working. A score of 7 means that you think almost all of the people in the group are lazy. How would you rate whites on this scale?"

(percent of people aged 18 or older responding by sex, race, age, and education, 1990–98)

	1 to 3 (hard working)		4		5 to 7 (lazy)	
	1998	*1990*	*1998*	*1990*	*1998*	*1990*
Total	**40%**	**55%**	**45%**	**36%**	**12%**	**6%**
Men	40	53	43	36	14	8
Women	39	57	47	35	11	5
Black	32	52	42	32	22	10
White	39	55	47	37	10	5
Aged 18 to 29	44	51	43	42	11	5
Aged 30 to 39	38	55	49	35	10	8
Aged 40 to 49	37	55	48	36	12	6
Aged 50 to 59	33	54	47	34	15	7
Aged 60 to 69	44	56	39	37	15	4
Aged 70 or older	41	62	40	28	11	4
Not a high school graduate	38	58	41	29	17	7
High school graduate	39	56	45	35	12	7
Bachelor's degree	41	49	47	46	7	3
Graduate degree	33	52	53	41	11	3

Note: Numbers may not add to 100 because "don't know" is not shown.
Source: General Social Survey, National Opinion Research Center, University of Chicago; calculations by the author

Intelligence of Blacks and Whites

Stereotypes persist about the relative intelligence of blacks and whites.

Few Americans are overtly racist these days, but negative stereotypes about blacks persist. When asked to rate the intelligence of blacks and whites on a scale from 1 (most are unintelligent) to 7 (most are intelligent), fully 43 percent think most whites are intelligent (5 or higher on the scale), but only 30 percent say most blacks are intelligent. Only 9 percent think most whites are unintelligent (1 to 3 on the scale), but 16 percent say most blacks are unintelligent. The share of those who now feel that way about blacks is considerably smaller, however, than the 27 percent who felt this way in 1990.

Not surprisingly, blacks and whites differ widely in their responses to this question. Similar percentages (43 to 48 percent) of whites, blacks, and "other" races say most whites are intelligent. But while 42 percent of blacks think most blacks are intelligent, only 27 percent of whites and 31 percent of other races agree.

Every age group rates the intelligence of whites higher than that of blacks. Older people are more likely to think most blacks are unintelligent. Only 14 to 15 percent of people under age 60 say this compared with 22 percent of those aged 70 or older.

Twenty-three percent of people who did not complete high school rate the intelligence of blacks at 1 to 3 on the scale compared with 12 to 15 percent of people with more education. The least educated are also more likely to believe most whites are intelligent. Half of people who did not complete high school say most whites are intelligent compared with 43 percent of people with a high school diploma and 35 to 38 percent of college graduates.

Intelligence of Blacks, 1998

"A score of 1 means you think almost all of the people in that group are unintelligent. A score of 7 means that you think almost all of the people in that group are intelligent. How would you rate blacks?"

(percent of people aged 18 or older responding by sex, race, age, and education, 1998)

	unintel-ligent	2	3	4	5	6	intelligent
Total	1%	4%	11%	50%	19%	8%	3%
Men	1	5	11	51	19	6	2
Women	1	3	11	49	18	9	4
Black	2	2	8	43	26	7	9
White	1	4	11	52	17	8	2
Other	1	6	15	40	20	7	4
Aged 18 to 29	1	3	10	52	17	10	5
Aged 30 to 39	1	4	10	52	21	6	3
Aged 40 to 49	1	3	10	53	18	8	2
Aged 50 to 59	0	4	11	51	17	7	3
Aged 60 to 69	0	3	14	48	19	10	2
Aged 70 or older	0	6	16	40	18	9	2
Not a high school graduate	2	7	14	38	20	10	3
High school graduate	1	4	10	49	19	9	4
Bachelor's degree	0	1	12	59	15	5	2
Graduate degree	0	3	9	54	21	6	3

Note: Numbers may not add to 100 because "don't know" is not shown.
Source: General Social Survey, National Opinion Research Center, University of Chicago; calculations by the author

Intelligence of Blacks, 1990 and 1998

"A score of 1 means you think almost all of the people in that group are unintelligent. A score of 7 means that you think almost all of the people in that group are intelligent. How would you rate blacks?"

(percent of people aged 18 or older responding by sex, race, age, and education, 1990–98)

| | 1 to 3 (unintelligent) | | 4 | | 5 to 7 (intelligent) | |
	1998	1990	1998	1990	1998	1990
Total	16%	27%	50%	45%	30%	23%
Men	17	31	51	42	27	23
Women	15	24	49	47	31	23
Black	12	11	43	42	42	41
White	16	29	52	46	27	20
Aged 18 to 29	14	23	52	49	32	23
Aged 30 to 39	15	28	52	47	30	23
Aged 40 to 49	14	26	53	48	28	24
Aged 50 to 59	15	33	51	38	27	24
Aged 60 to 69	17	28	48	45	31	23
Aged 70 or older	22	32	40	35	29	23
Not a high school graduate	23	28	38	36	33	26
High school graduate	15	29	49	45	32	23
Bachelor's degree	13	25	59	51	22	21
Graduate degree	12	17	54	55	30	23

Note: Numbers may not add to 100 because "don't know" is not shown.
Source: General Social Survey, National Opinion Research Center, University of Chicago; calculations by the author

Intelligence of Whites, 1998

"A score of 1 means you think almost all of the people in that group are unintelligent. A score of 7 means that you think almost all of the people in that group are intelligent. How would you rate whites?"

(percent of people aged 18 or older responding by sex, race, age, and education, 1998)

	unintel-ligent	2	3	4	5	6	intelligent
Total	**0%**	**2%**	**7%**	**42%**	**22%**	**15%**	**6%**
Men	0	3	7	43	24	15	4
Women	1	2	8	42	20	15	7
Black	1	4	8	39	24	10	10
White	0	2	7	44	22	16	5
Other	2	3	5	37	17	18	13
Aged 18 to 29	1	3	10	41	19	17	6
Aged 30 to 39	0	2	7	45	24	14	5
Aged 40 to 49	1	2	7	46	23	11	5
Aged 50 to 59	0	2	8	43	22	13	6
Aged 60 to 69	1	3	3	40	23	21	6
Aged 70 or older	0	2	9	33	20	19	7
Not a high school graduate	1	2	5	36	17	19	14
High school graduate	0	3	9	40	23	15	5
Bachelor's degree	1	2	7	48	24	11	3
Graduate degree	0	1	5	54	19	12	4

Note: Numbers may not add to 100 because "don't know" is not shown.
Source: General Social Survey, National Opinion Research Center, University of Chicago; calculations by the author

Intelligence of Whites, 1990 and 1998

"A score of 1 means you think almost all of the people in that group are unintelligent. A score of 7 means that you think almost all of the people in that group are intelligent. How would you rate whites?"

(percent of people aged 18 or older responding by sex, race, age, and education, 1990–98)

	1 to 3 (unintelligent)		4		5 to 7 (intelligent)	
	1998	*1990*	*1998*	*1990*	*1998*	*1990*
Total	**9%**	**7%**	**42%**	**33%**	**43%**	**56%**
Men	10	9	43	32	43	57
Women	11	6	42	34	42	56
Black	13	12	39	29	44	53
White	9	6	44	34	43	57
Aged 18 to 29	14	8	41	38	42	50
Aged 30 to 39	9	9	45	36	43	53
Aged 40 to 49	10	5	46	39	39	54
Aged 50 to 59	10	6	43	31	41	60
Aged 60 to 69	7	6	40	25	50	65
Aged 70 or older	11	6	33	21	46	65
Not a high school graduate	8	8	36	21	50	63
High school graduate	12	8	40	31	43	59
Bachelor's degree	10	4	48	45	38	48
Graduate degree	6	5	54	52	35	39

Note: Numbers may not add to 100 because "don't know" is not shown.
Source: General Social Survey, National Opinion Research Center, University of Chicago; calculations by the author

Causes of Socioeconomic Differences

Americans are divided on the cause of socioeconomic differences between blacks and whites.

Most people are aware that, on average, blacks have worse jobs, incomes, and housing than whites. But Americans are divided on the reason for those differences. Is it due to discrimination, a lack of educational opportunity, a lack of will or motivation, or a lack of ability to learn?

Overall, people are most likely to cite lack of education or lack of motivation as causes for the lower socioeconomic status of blacks. Women most often cite education as the reason, while men most often blame lack of motivation. Blacks are most likely to say discrimination is the cause. College graduates blame a lack of education, while those with less education are most inclined to believe it is a lack of motivation. The only segments in which substantial percentages think blacks have less ability to learn are the oldest and least educated, groups with considerable overlap.

Discrimination

A minority of adults (35 percent) believes the lower socioeconomic status of blacks is due to discrimination. While 39 percent of women believe discrimination is the main reason, only 30 percent of men agree. Far more striking is the racial difference. Fifty-nine percent of blacks, but only 30 percent of whites, believe discrimination is behind the differences in socioeconomic status between blacks and whites.

The proportion of people who believe discrimination is to blame has declined in most demographic segments since 1977, although the drop is relatively small in many segments. The biggest changes are among blacks, people under age 40, and those with a bachelor's degree. The proportion of blacks blaming discrimination fell from 76 percent in 1988 to 59 percent in 1998. In 1977, half of people with a bachelor's degree said discrimination was the reason blacks were disadvantaged, but by 1998 only 35 percent agreed.

Lack of Education

Forty-three percent of adults say lack of education is to blame for differences between blacks and whites in jobs, incomes, and housing. The majority of blacks (56 percent) believe lack of education is the primary cause, as do the majority of people with a graduate degree. In fact, there is a bigger difference of opinion by education than by race. Only 39 percent of people without a college degree believe lack of education is behind the difference in socioeconomic status. In contrast, 49 percent of people with a bachelor's degree and 61 percent of those with a graduate degree believe education is the key.

Lack of Will or Motivation

Americans are far less likely now than in decades past to believe a lack of will or motivation is the cause of differences in socioeconomic status between blacks and whites. In 1977, fully 62 percent of people blamed a lack of motivation, but by 1998 only 42 percent still believed that to be true.

Only 36 percent of blacks, compared with 43 percent of whites, consider lack of motivation a cause of blacks' lower socioeconomic status. Younger respondents are less likely than older ones to believe blacks lack motivation.

The largest difference of opinion exists by educational attainment. Most of the least educated Americans believe blacks lack the will or motivation to succeed. But opinions are sharply different among the college educated. Only 33 percent of people with a bachelor's degree and 22 percent of those with a graduate degree believe lack of motivation is the cause.

Less Ability to Learn

Only 10 percent of Americans believe blacks are innately less able to learn than whites. Even in 1977, only one-quarter of whites believed this was a reason for blacks' lower socioeconomic status.

Older Americans and those with the least education are most likely to believe that blacks have less innate ability to learn. Fewer than 10 percent of people under age 60 believe blacks have less ability compared with 14 percent of people in their fifties and 21 percent of those aged 70 or older.

Education also strongly shapes opinions on this issue. Twenty-two percent of people who did not complete high school believe blacks have less inborn ability to learn, but the figure drops to only 9 percent among high school graduates. Only 3 to 5 percent of college graduates agree.

Causes of Socioeconomic Differences, 1998

"On the average, blacks have worse jobs, income, and housing than white people. What do you think these differences are mainly due to?"

(percent of people aged 18 or older responding by sex, race, age, and education, 1998)

	discrimination		lacking chance for education		lack of will or motivation		less ability to learn	
	yes	no	yes	no	yes	no	yes	no
Total	**35%**	**58%**	**43%**	**52%**	**42%**	**49%**	**10%**	**86%**
Men	30	64	39	58	44	48	11	86
Women	39	54	46	48	42	50	9	86
Black	59	35	56	41	36	58	9	89
White	30	64	41	54	43	49	10	86
Other	48	43	42	50	52	38	10	81
Aged 18 to 29	37	58	40	55	42	52	6	91
Aged 30 to 39	32	63	41	56	39	54	6	90
Aged 40 to 49	34	62	42	54	40	54	7	91
Aged 50 to 59	39	54	49	47	46	46	10	87
Aged 60 to 69	31	61	46	49	44	47	14	79
Aged 70 or older	38	50	44	47	51	34	21	67
Not a high school graduate	37	52	39	55	53	35	22	66
High school graduate	34	60	39	56	45	46	9	88
Bachelor's degree	35	59	49	47	33	61	5	94
Graduate degree	38	56	61	35	22	70	3	95

Note: Numbers may not add to 100 because "don't know" is not shown.
Source: General Social Survey, National Opinion Research Center, University of Chicago; calculations by the author

Causes of Socioeconomic Differences: Discrimination, 1977 to 1998

"On the average, blacks have worse jobs, income, and housing than white people. Do you think these differences are mainly due to discrimination?"

(percent responding by sex, race, age, and education, 1977–98)

	yes			no			don't know		
	1998	*1988*	*1977*	*1998*	*1988*	*1977*	*1998*	*1988*	*1977*
Total	**35%**	**42%**	**39%**	**58%**	**53%**	**56%**	**6%**	**5%**	**4%**
Men	30	38	36	64	58	60	6	3	4
Women	39	46	42	54	49	53	7	6	5
Black	59	76	*	35	19	*	6	5	*
White	30	37	39	64	58	56	6	4	4
Aged 18 to 29	37	49	49	58	48	48	5	4	3
Aged 30 to 39	32	41	43	63	53	55	5	6	2
Aged 40 to 49	34	42	31	62	55	63	4	2	5
Aged 50 to 59	39	43	32	54	52	64	7	4	5
Aged 60 to 69	31	37	35	61	58	61	8	5	4
Aged 70 or older	38	37	41	50	56	47	12	7	12
Not a high school graduate	37	46	37	52	48	55	11	6	8
High school graduate	34	41	38	60	55	59	6	4	3
Bachelor's degree	35	40	50	59	56	47	5	5	4
Graduate degree	38	38	44	56	52	54	6	10	1

* Question not asked of blacks in 1977.
Source: General Social Survey, National Opinion Research Center, University of Chicago; calculations by the author

Causes of Socioeconomic Differences: Lack of Education, 1977 to 1998

"On the average, blacks have worse jobs, income, and housing than white people. Do you think these differences are because most blacks don't have the chance for education that it takes to rise out of poverty?"

(percent of people aged 18 or older responding by sex, race, age, and education, 1977–98)

	yes			no			don't know		
	1998	*1988*	*1977*	*1998*	*1988*	*1977*	*1998*	*1988*	*1977*
Total	**43%**	**52%**	**49%**	**52%**	**44%**	**48%**	**5%**	**4%**	**4%**
Men	39	47	47	58	49	50	3	4	3
Women	46	56	50	48	40	46	6	4	4
Black	56	67	*	41	31	*	3	2	*
White	41	50	49	54	46	48	5	4	4
Aged 18 to 29	40	52	53	55	45	45	5	3	3
Aged 30 to 39	41	53	51	56	46	48	3	1	1
Aged 40 to 49	42	57	43	54	41	52	4	2	5
Aged 50 to 59	49	54	45	47	40	51	4	6	4
Aged 60 to 69	46	48	53	49	48	42	5	4	5
Aged 70 or older	44	47	45	47	43	48	9	10	7
Not a high school graduate	39	43	42	55	50	53	6	7	5
High school graduate	39	50	48	56	47	49	5	3	3
Bachelor's degree	49	67	70	47	31	28	4	2	2
Graduate degree	61	71	61	35	26	35	4	3	4

* Question not asked of blacks in 1977.
Source: General Social Survey, National Opinion Research Center, University of Chicago; calculations by the author

Causes of Socioeconomic Differences: Lack of Motivation, 1977 to 1998

"On the average, blacks have worse jobs, income, and housing than white people. Do you think these differences are because most blacks just don't have the motivation or will power to pull themselves up out of poverty?"

(percent of people aged 18 or older responding by sex, race, age, and education, 1977–98)

	yes			no			don't know		
	1998	*1988*	*1977*	*1998*	*1988*	*1977*	*1998*	*1988*	*1977*
Total	**42%**	**55%**	**62%**	**49%**	**40%**	**32%**	**8%**	**5%**	**6%**
Men	44	56	65	48	39	30	9	4	5
Women	42	54	59	50	41	34	8	6	7
Black	36	32	*	58	64	*	6	4	*
White	43	58	62	49	37	32	9	5	6
Aged 18 to 29	42	49	52	52	48	43	7	3	4
Aged 30 to 39	39	53	60	54	45	37	7	2	3
Aged 40 to 49	40	52	65	54	42	27	7	6	8
Aged 50 to 59	46	54	63	46	41	30	8	4	7
Aged 60 to 69	44	66	69	47	26	25	10	8	6
Aged 70 or older	51	63	73	34	28	20	15	9	7
Not a high school graduate	53	62	70	35	30	24	12	8	6
High school graduate	45	57	63	46	39	32	8	4	5
Bachelor's degree	33	45	47	61	52	49	6	3	4
Graduate degree	22	38	35	70	59	53	8	3	13

* Question not asked of blacks in 1977.
Source: General Social Survey, National Opinion Research Center, University of Chicago; calculations by the author

Causes of Socioeconomic Differences: Less Innate Ability, 1977 to 1998

"On the average, blacks have worse jobs, income, and housing than white people. Do you think these differences are because most blacks have less inborn ability to learn?"

(percent of people aged 18 or older responding by sex, race, age, and education, 1977–98)

| | yes | | | no | | | don't know | | |
	1998	1988	1977	1998	1988	1977	1998	1988	1977
Total	**10%**	**18%**	**25%**	**86%**	**78%**	**70%**	**4%**	**4%**	**5%**
Men	11	19	28	86	79	68	3	3	4
Women	9	18	22	86	77	72	5	5	6
Black	9	8	*	89	90	*	2	2	*
White	10	20	25	86	76	71	4	4	5
Aged 18 to 29	6	13	12	91	84	85	2	3	3
Aged 30 to 39	6	14	15	90	85	82	4	0	3
Aged 40 to 49	7	10	25	91	85	69	1	5	6
Aged 50 to 59	10	21	27	87	76	68	3	3	5
Aged 60 to 69	14	28	46	79	66	45	7	6	9
Aged 70 or older	21	33	44	67	57	49	12	10	7
Not a high school graduate	22	28	38	66	65	54	13	8	8
High school graduate	9	19	21	88	78	75	3	4	4
Bachelor's degree	5	8	12	94	90	88	1	2	1
Graduate degree	3	8	10	95	90	82	2	2	8

* Question not asked of blacks in 1977.
Source: General Social Survey, National Opinion Research Center, University of Chicago; calculations by the author

Blacks Should Work Their Way Up

Most people say blacks should work their way up without special favors.

Seven out of ten people agree that blacks should work their way up as immigrants have done, without special favors. Forty-two percent strongly agree. But there are differences of opinion on this question within all demographic segments.

Three-quarters of whites believe blacks should work their way up without special favors as do 70 percent of "other" races. But only 47 percent of blacks agree. Twenty-nine percent of blacks, but only 12 to 13 percent of whites and other races disagree with the statement.

Older people are more likely to say blacks should work their way up. Among people aged 60 or older, 75 to 78 percent say blacks should work their way up without special favors compared with 68 to 71 percent of people under age 60.

Not quite half of people with a graduate degree believe blacks should work their way up without special favors. Among people with a bachelor's degree, 65 percent agree. The least educated are the most likely to agree. Three-quarters of people without a college degree believe blacks should work their way up as other groups did.

Blacks Should Work Their Way Up, 1998

"Do you agree or disagree with this statement: Irish, Italians, Jews and many other minorities overcame prejudice and worked their way up. Blacks should do the same without special favors."

(percent of people aged 18 or older responding by sex, race, age, and education, 1998)

	agree strongly	agree slightly	neither	disagree slightly	disagree strongly	don't know	agree, total	disagree, total
Total	**42%**	**29%**	**12%**	**9%**	**6%**	**2%**	**71%**	**15%**
Men	45	29	12	8	5	1	74	13
Women	40	29	12	9	7	3	69	16
Black	23	24	19	12	17	5	47	29
White	45	30	11	8	4	2	75	12
Other	42	28	13	7	6	4	70	13
Aged 18 to 29	36	32	14	8	8	2	68	16
Aged 30 to 39	43	28	11	12	5	2	71	17
Aged 40 to 49	41	28	12	9	7	2	69	16
Aged 50 to 59	45	25	14	7	7	2	70	14
Aged 60 to 69	44	34	10	7	4	2	78	11
Aged 70 or older	48	27	12	5	4	4	75	9
Not a high school graduate	49	27	9	5	5	6	76	10
High school graduate	46	29	12	6	6	2	75	12
Bachelor's degree	33	32	15	12	7	2	65	19
Graduate degree	23	26	19	22	9	1	49	31

Source: General Social Survey, National Opinion Research Center, University of Chicago; calculations by the author

Should Government Help Blacks?

Half of Americans say blacks should not get special treatment despite past discrimination.

Only 17 percent of Americans believe that government has a special obligation to improve the living standards of blacks because of historical discrimination (1 and 2 on a 5-point scale). About half believe government should not give blacks special treatment (4 and 5 on the scale). The percentage of those who say government should help has declined since 1975, but the share who say they should not receive special treatment is almost unchanged.

The sharpest disagreement on this question is by race. Twenty percent of blacks strongly agree that government should help blacks because of past discrimination, but only 4 percent of whites and "other" races agree. The proportion of blacks who say they believe government should help (1 and 2 on the scale) fell from 66 percent in 1975 to only 38 percent in 1998, however. Thirty-one percent of whites strongly believe the government should not give blacks special treatment, as do 23 percent of other races. In contrast, only 12 percent of blacks agree.

Men are more likely than women to say blacks should not receive special treatment (52 versus 46 percent). The proportion of men and women who think government should help blacks fell from about one-quarter in 1975 to only 17 percent in 1998.

The percentage of people saying government should help blacks fell among all age groups between 1975 and 1998. But the percentage of those who say they should not receive special treatment also fell among people under age 50 and those in their sixties. Among people in their fifties, the share of those who say blacks should not get special treatment remained about the same between 1975 and 1998, while the percentage of people aged 70 or older who agree increased.

High school graduates and people with a bachelor's degree are more likely than both those with more and those with less education to say blacks should not receive special treatment, while those with the highest and lowest levels of education are more likely to say the government should help. College graduates were considerably less likely in 1998 than in 1975 to say government should help blacks because of past discrimination.

Should Government Help Blacks? 1998

"Some people think that blacks have been discriminated against for so long that the government has a special obligation to help improve their living standards. Others believe that the government should not be giving special treatment to blacks. Where would you place yourself on a scale of 1 to 5 or haven't you made up your mind on this?"

(percent of people aged 18 or older responding by sex, race, age, and education, 1998)

	government should help (strongly agree) 1	2	agree with both 3	4	no special treatment 5	don't know
Total	**7%**	**10%**	**31%**	**21%**	**28%**	**4%**
Men	6	11	28	21	31	3
Women	7	10	34	21	25	4
Black	20	18	40	7	12	3
White	4	9	29	24	31	3
Other	4	8	39	16	23	9
Aged 18 to 29	6	13	33	18	25	5
Aged 30 to 39	6	12	29	25	24	4
Aged 40 to 49	7	8	33	20	30	3
Aged 50 to 59	8	10	26	24	29	3
Aged 60 to 69	6	8	36	22	25	2
Aged 70 or older	6	9	30	17	34	4
Not a high school graduate	11	9	32	12	29	7
High school graduate	6	9	30	21	30	4
Bachelor's degree	3	14	29	26	24	3
Graduate degree	10	19	35	23	13	1

Source: General Social Survey, National Opinion Research Center, University of Chicago; calculations by the author

Should Government Help Blacks? 1975 to 1998

"Some people think that blacks have been discriminated against for so long that the government has a special obligation to help improve their living standards. Others believe that the government should not be giving special treatment to blacks. Where would you place yourself on a scale of 1 to 5 or haven't you made up your mind on this?"

(percent of people aged 18 or older responding by sex, race, age, and education, 1975–98)

	government should help (1 and 2)			agree with both (3)			no special treatment (4 and 5)		
	1998	1988	1975	1998	1988	1975	1998	1988	1975
Total	**17%**	**17%**	**25%**	**31%**	**29%**	**21%**	**49%**	**51%**	**52%**
Men	17	16	25	28	30	18	52	52	55
Women	17	19	24	34	28	23	46	50	49
Black	38	57	66	40	29	15	19	11	15
White	13	12	20	29	28	22	55	57	56
Aged 18 to 29	19	20	25	33	32	24	43	47	49
Aged 30 to 39	18	18	25	29	26	19	49	52	53
Aged 40 to 49	15	24	24	33	24	20	50	49	55
Aged 50 to 59	18	17	21	26	33	24	53	49	54
Aged 60 to 69	14	9	28	36	29	16	47	57	54
Aged 70 or older	15	14	25	30	28	20	51	55	45
Not a high school graduate	20	17	29	32	26	18	41	53	48
High school graduate	15	16	18	30	28	23	51	53	57
Bachelor's degree	17	23	33	29	36	21	50	38	45
Graduate degree	29	18	40	35	31	26	36	47	34

Source: General Social Survey, National Opinion Research Center, University of Chicago; calculations by the author

Affirmative Action for Blacks

Blacks and whites are sharply divided on preferential hiring.

Seventy-eight percent of Americans are opposed to preferential hiring and promotion of blacks. Over half are strongly opposed. But blacks and whites are miles apart on this issue.

An overwhelming majority of whites and "other" races are opposed to preferential hiring and promotion of blacks. Fully 83 percent of whites oppose affirmative action, and 60 percent say they are strongly opposed. A much smaller 53 percent of blacks say they oppose affirmative action, while one-third favor it. Twenty-one percent of blacks strongly favor affirmative action.

One-quarter of people with a graduate degree favor affirmative action compared with 12 to 18 percent of people with less education. But two-thirds of people with graduate degrees oppose affirmative action, as do 81 percent of both high school graduates and people with a bachelor's degree. A smaller 64 percent of people who did not complete high school oppose affirmative action, but 18 percent say they don't know.

Affirmative Action for Blacks, 1998

"Some people say that because of past discrimination, blacks should be given preference in hiring and promotion. Others say that such preference is wrong because it discriminates against whites. Are you for or against preferential hiring and promotion of blacks?"

(percent of people aged 18 or older responding by sex, race, age, and education, 1998)

	favor strongly	favor slightly	oppose slightly	oppose strongly	don't know	favor, total	oppose, total
Total	**8%**	**6%**	**23%**	**55%**	**8%**	**14%**	**78%**
Men	7	6	24	57	6	13	81
Women	8	7	22	54	9	15	76
Black	21	13	21	32	12	34	53
White	5	5	23	60	7	10	83
Other	9	9	27	44	10	18	71
Aged 18 to 29	9	7	29	48	7	16	77
Aged 30 to 39	6	6	21	60	6	12	81
Aged 40 to 49	10	6	21	56	7	16	77
Aged 50 to 59	9	6	23	56	6	15	79
Aged 60 to 69	4	6	23	58	8	10	81
Aged 70 or older	6	6	20	52	15	12	72
Not a high school graduate	9	9	24	40	18	18	64
High school graduate	7	5	23	58	6	12	81
Bachelor's degree	7	6	26	55	6	13	81
Graduate degree	12	12	18	49	9	24	67

Source: General Social Survey, National Opinion Research Center, University of Chicago; calculations by the author

Discrimination against Whites?

Most people think "reverse discrimination" is at least somewhat likely.

There's little support for affirmative action these days. One reason for this is fear among whites of losing a job or promotion solely on the basis of race. Most Americans believe it is at least somewhat likely that a white person won't get a job or promotion while an equally or less qualified black person gets one. In 1990, one-quarter of people believed this was very likely. By 1998, only 19 percent still felt this way. Among most demographic segments the percentage of those who say it is very likely has fallen since 1990.

People who did not complete high school or have only a high school diploma are more inclined than college graduates to believe that a white person is very likely to be passed over for a job or promotion in favor of an equally or less qualified black person. Only 11 percent of graduate students and 16 percent of people with a bachelor's degree believe it is very likely that a white person will lose a job or promotion to a black person. But among those without a college degree, 20 to 21 percent feel it is very likely. Historically, blacks have competed primarily with less educated whites for jobs, so it is no surprise that this group would feel more vulnerable to affirmative action.

Not surprisingly, blacks and whites disagree on this issue. Fifty-nine percent of blacks, but only 26 percent of whites, say it is not very likely that a white person will be passed over for an equally or less qualified black person. One-third of "other" races believe it is not very likely. Twenty-one percent of whites and 19 percent of other races say it is very likely, but only 11 percent of blacks agree.

Discrimination against Whites? 1998

"What do you think the chances are these days that a white person won't get a job or promotion while an equally or less qualified black person gets one instead?"

(percent of people aged 18 or older responding by sex, race, age, and education, 1998)

	very likely	somewhat likely	not very likely	don't know
Total	**19%**	**46%**	**31%**	**3%**
Men	20	46	32	2
Women	19	47	30	4
Black	11	26	59	5
White	21	51	26	2
Other	19	39	34	7
Aged 18 to 29	15	46	37	2
Aged 30 to 39	18	46	33	3
Aged 40 to 49	21	46	32	1
Aged 50 to 59	23	45	30	3
Aged 60 to 69	23	47	23	7
Aged 70 or older	19	52	24	5
Not a high school graduate	20	39	35	6
High school graduate	21	46	30	2
Bachelor's degree	16	49	32	3
Graduate degree	11	49	37	2

Source: General Social Survey, National Opinion Research Center, University of Chicago; calculations by the author

Discrimination against Whites? 1990 and 1998

"What do you think the chances are these days that a white person won't get a job or promotion while an equally or less qualified black person gets one instead?"

(percent of people aged 18 or older responding by sex, race, age, and education, 1990–98)

	very likely		somewhat likely		not very likely	
	1998	*1990*	*1998*	*1990*	*1998*	*1990*
Total	**19%**	**25%**	**46%**	**39%**	**31%**	**34%**
Men	20	26	46	40	32	33
Women	19	25	47	39	30	35
Black	11	8	26	24	59	67
White	21	28	51	42	26	29
Aged 18 to 29	15	18	46	42	37	40
Aged 30 to 39	18	26	46	40	33	33
Aged 40 to 49	21	28	46	42	32	30
Aged 50 to 59	23	29	45	31	30	39
Aged 60 to 69	23	28	47	39	23	31
Aged 70 or older	19	25	52	37	24	35
Not a high school graduate	20	28	39	31	35	38
High school graduate	21	28	46	40	30	31
Bachelor's degree	16	17	49	43	32	40
Graduate degree	11	14	49	47	37	39

Note: Numbers may not add to 100 because "don't know" is not shown.
Source: General Social Survey, National Opinion Research Center, University of Chicago; calculations by the author

6

Religion

Most Americans are religious, but there is a great deal of diversity in religious attitudes and practices, and this diversity is increasing. The percentages of people identifying themselves as Protestant, Catholic, or Jewish were stable or fell slightly during the past two decades, while the percentages of those saying they observe another religion or have no religious preference rose.

On basic issues, most Americans are solidly religious. The majority believe in God without a doubt. Most believe in heaven, hell, and life after death. Most say they try to carry their religious beliefs over into all other dealings in their life.

Americans are not religious zealots, however. Pluralities say they are only moderately religious or spiritual. Most say there are basic truths in many religions. Nearly half think people with very strong religious beliefs are too often intolerant of others.

The sizable majority of Americans believe that to be a good Christian or Jew, one must believe in God, but only a few more than half say it is important to follow the teachings of one's church or synagogue. Fewer than half believe it is important to attend services regularly. This opinion isn't surprising given that most people do not attend religious services regularly.

Confidence in religious leaders fell during the 1980s thanks largely to scandals involving well-known religious figures. The proportion of Americans who say they have a great deal of confidence in leaders has grown since then, but most people still have only "some" confidence in them. This lack of trust is probably one reason why few people believe religious leaders should try to influence elections or government decisions.

In spite of frequent calls by some religious leaders and politicians to reinstate prayer in public schools, people are more likely today to approve of the Supreme Court's ruling against prayer in schools than they were 20 years ago.

Women are more religious than men in both belief and practice, although the differences by gender are not as great as the differences by age and education. Women are less likely than men to say they have no religious preference. They are more likely than men to say they are very spiritual and very religious. Women are also more likely to say they carry their religious beliefs over into other dealings in their life.

Women are more actively religious than men as well. They are more likely to say a daily prayer and attend religious services regularly. Women are more likely to believe in God without a doubt and to believe in heaven, hell, and miracles. They are more likely to believe the Bible should be interpreted literally, whereas men are more likely to say the Bible is simply an ancient book of fables, legends, and history.

By some measures, men have a more negative opinion of religion. Men are more likely than women to say very religious people are often too intolerant of others and to believe that religion brings more conflict than peace. More men than women think religious leaders should abstain from influencing elections and government decisions.

Religion plays a larger role in the lives of blacks than of whites or people of "other" race. Blacks are most likely to pray at least once a day and to attend religious services regularly. They are more likely than whites and other races to believe in heaven, hell, and religious miracles, and to carry their religious beliefs into other dealings in their lives. Blacks are far more likely to believe in God without a doubt, whereas whites and other races are more likely to have some doubts. Over half of blacks, but only a little more than one-third of whites and other races, have had a religious or spiritual experience that changed their lives.

Blacks are also more inclined to take a stricter approach to religion. They are more likely than whites or other races to say that to be a good Christian or Jew it is very important to believe in God without question, to attend religious services, and to follow faithfully the teachings of their church or synagogue. They are less likely to say it is very important to follow one's own conscience even if it means going against the church's teachings. Blacks are far more likely than whites and other races to view the Bible as the word of God, meant to be interpreted literally.

Whites are most likely to disapprove of the commercial use of religious images. Whites and other races are more likely than blacks to approve of the Supreme Court's decision prohibiting public school prayer. They are also more likely to believe that religion can have a negative influence. Whites and other races are more likely than blacks to say people with strong religious beliefs are often too intolerant of others, and to believe that religion brings more conflict than peace to the world. They are also more inclined to want to limit religious influence in the public arena. People of other race are least likely, and blacks most likely, to think religious leaders should try to influence government decisions. Whites and other races are most likely to believe churches have too much power, while blacks are most likely to believe they have too little power.

The generations show distinct differences in religious beliefs and practices. The solid majority of older Americans are Protestant, but in younger age groups diversity is the rule. People under age 50 are less likely than their elders to be Protestant and more likely to be Catholic, to adhere to some other religion (such as Islam), or to have no religious preference.

Younger generations are considerably less likely than older Americans to attend religious services regularly or to pray every day. They are more likely than older people to approve of the Supreme Court ruling on school prayer. Older generations are more likely to believe the Bible is the literal word of God, while boomers and younger generations are more likely to say that it is the inspired word of God, not to be taken literally, or that it is simply an ancient book.

The older people are, the more likely they are to disapprove of the use of religious images to sell commercial products, to disapprove of the Supreme Court's ruling that school prayer is unconstitutional, and to carry their religious beliefs over into other dealings in life. Older generations are more likely to believe that to be a good Christian or Jew it is very important to attend religious services and to follow faithfully the religious teachings of their church or synagogue. Age also is a factor in beliefs about God. The proportion of people saying they believe in God without a doubt rises with age, from a little more than half of people under age 30 to nearly three-quarters of those aged 70 or older.

The oldest Americans have the most confidence in the leaders of organized religion. Fewer than one-quarter of people under age 50 have a great deal of confidence in religious leaders compared with nearly half of people aged 70 or older. But this confidence doesn't mean older people want to see religious leaders involved in politics. Older people are more likely than younger adults to say religious leaders should abstain from influencing elections and government. Younger generations are more likely to fail to take a position on the question of religious influence in politics.

Some of the largest differences of opinion regarding religion are by education. The more education people have, the less likely they are to believe that to be a good Christian or Jew it is very important to believe in God without question, to attend religious services, and to follow faithfully the teachings of one's church or synagogue. People with a graduate degree are most likely to say it is very important to follow one's own conscience regardless of what the churches or synagogues say. They are also most likely to think churches in the U.S. have too much power.

Education also increases the likelihood that people will agree with the Supreme Court decision prohibiting public school prayer. College graduates are more likely than those with less education to believe there are basic truths in many religions and that people with strong religious beliefs are often too intolerant of others.

The less education people have, the more likely they are to think we trust too much in science and not enough in religious faith and to believe the Bible should be interpreted literally. People who did not complete college are more likely to say they definitely believe in heaven and hell and to believe the Bible is meant to be interpreted literally. People who did not complete high school are most likely to have a great deal of confidence in the leaders of organized religion.

Religious Preference

Religious diversity is increasing.

The religious makeup of America has been changing for decades. In 1998, barely half of Americans identified themselves as Protestant compared with 64 percent in 1978. The proportion of those who say they have no religious preference rose from 8 percent in 1978 to 14 percent in 1998. Only 2 percent of Americans identified themselves as Jews, a figure that hasn't changed since 1978. One percent belonged to another religion (such as Islam, Hinduism, or Buddhism) in 1978 and the figure quadrupled to 4 percent by 1998.

The religious composition of the population will change even more as younger generations replace older ones. Among people aged 70 or older, 69 percent are Protestant, but among people under age 30, only 44 percent are. Nearly one-quarter of people under age 30 have no religious preference. Some will adopt a religion as they grow older, but many will continue to seek spiritual fulfillment outside a particular religious faith. Among people in their forties, 14 percent say they have no religious preference.

There are sharp differences in religious preference by race. Three-quarters of blacks are Protestant compared with only 53 percent of whites. Nearly half the people of "other" races (largely Hispanics) are Catholic, while only one-quarter are Protestant.

Religious Preference, 1998

"What is your religious preference? Is it Protestant, Catholic, Jewish, some other religion, or no religion?"

(percent of people aged 18 or older responding by sex, race, age, and education, 1998)

	Protestant	Catholic	Jewish	other	none
Total	**54%**	**25%**	**2%**	**4%**	**14%**
Men	50	25	2	5	18
Women	58	26	2	4	11
Black	76	7	0	6	11
White	53	26	2	4	14
Other	24	48	0	11	18
Aged 18 to 29	44	25	1	6	24
Aged 30 to 39	49	29	0	7	15
Aged 40 to 49	57	22	2	4	14
Aged 50 to 59	58	26	3	4	10
Aged 60 to 69	61	27	2	2	9
Aged 70 or older	69	22	3	0	6
Not a high school graduate	57	28	0	2	13
High school graduate	57	24	1	4	14
Bachelor's degree	49	25	3	7	16
Graduate degree	52	22	7	5	13

Note: Numbers may not add to 100 because "don't know" is not shown.
Source: General Social Survey, National Opinion Research Center, University of Chicago; calculations by the author

Religious Preference, 1978 to 1998

"What is your religious preference? Is it Protestant, Catholic, Jewish, some other religion, or no religion?"

(percent of people aged 18 or older responding by sex, race, age, and education, 1978–98)

	Protestant			Catholic			Jewish			other			none		
	1998	1988	1978	1998	1988	1978	1998	1988	1978	1998	1988	1978	1998	1988	1978
Total	54%	61%	64%	25%	26%	25%	2%	2%	2%	4%	3%	1%	14%	8%	8%
Men	50	58	62	25	25	23	2	2	3	5	4	2	18	12	11
Women	58	64	66	26	27	26	2	2	1	4	2	1	11	5	6
Black	76	80	89	7	9	5	0	0	0	6	4	1	11	8	4
White	53	59	61	26	28	27	2	2	2	4	2	1	14	8	8
Aged 18 to 29	44	55	58	25	28	26	1	1	1	6	2	2	24	13	12
Aged 30 to 39	49	58	61	29	26	27	0	2	2	7	4	1	15	9	9
Aged 40 to 49	57	58	63	22	30	26	2	2	2	4	2	1	14	8	8
Aged 50 to 59	58	69	66	26	19	27	3	3	1	4	3	1	10	5	4
Aged 60 to 69	61	72	70	27	19	23	2	2	3	2	3	0	9	4	3
Aged 70 or older	69	64	76	22	29	17	3	1	3	0	1	0	6	4	4
Not a high school graduate	57	66	72	28	25	22	0	1	1	2	2	0	13	6	5
High school graduate	57	62	62	24	27	28	1	1	1	4	3	1	14	8	7
Bachelor's degree	49	57	56	25	25	24	3	4	5	7	4	1	16	9	15
Graduate degree	52	46	56	22	21	21	7	10	6	5	9	3	13	13	13

Note: Numbers may not add to 100 because "don't know" is not shown.
Source: General Social Survey, National Opinion Research Center, University of Chicago; calculations by the author

Religious Background

Fewer Americans today were raised as Protestants than in the past.

In 1978, 67 percent of Americans said they were raised as Protestants. By 1998, the share had fallen to 58 percent. Increasing numbers now say they were raised as Catholics or with no particular religious preference.

Blacks are far more likely than whites and other races to have been raised as Protestants (82 percent compared with 58 percent of whites and only 16 percent of "other" races). About three out of five people of other races (primarily Hispanics) say they were raised as Catholics compared with one-third of whites and only 10 percent of blacks.

Younger generations are less likely to have been raised as Protestants than older generations. Two-thirds of people aged 70 or older were raised as Protestants compared with only half of people under age 30. Eleven percent of people under age 30 were raised with no religious preference compared with only 4 percent of people aged 60 or older.

Religious Background, 1998

"In what religion were you raised?"

(percent of people aged 18 or older responding by sex, race, age, and education, 1998)

	Protestant	Catholic	Jewish	other	none
Total	**58%**	**31%**	**2%**	**3%**	**6%**
Men	57	31	2	3	7
Women	59	31	2	3	6
Black	82	10	0	3	6
White	58	32	2	2	6
Other	16	59	0	15	10
Aged 18 to 29	50	31	2	6	11
Aged 30 to 39	52	36	0	4	7
Aged 40 to 49	62	29	2	1	6
Aged 50 to 59	64	28	2	2	3
Aged 60 to 69	62	31	3	1	4
Aged 70 or older	67	25	3	1	4
Not a high school graduate	59	32	0	1	7
High school graduate	61	29	1	3	6
Bachelor's degree	51	34	3	5	7
Graduate degree	55	27	8	3	7

Note: Numbers may not add to 100 because "don't know" is not shown.
Source: General Social Survey, National Opinion Research Center, University of Chicago; calculations by the author

Religious Background, 1978 to 1998

"In what religion were you raised?"

(percent of people aged 18 or older responding by sex, race, age, and education, 1978–98)

	Protestant			Catholic			Jewish			other			none		
	1998	1988	1978	1998	1988	1978	1998	1988	1978	1998	1988	1978	1998	1988	1978
Total	58%	64%	67%	31%	28%	27%	2%	2%	2%	3%	2%	1%	6%	4%	3%
Men	57	63	66	31	28	27	2	2	3	3	3	1	7	4	3
Women	59	65	67	31	28	28	2	2	1	3	2	0	6	3	3
Black	82	89	93	10	6	6	0	0	0	3	1	1	6	3	0
White	58	62	64	32	31	30	2	3	2	2	2	1	6	3	4
Aged 18 to 29	50	58	63	31	32	31	2	2	1	6	3	1	11	6	3
Aged 30 to 39	52	62	64	36	28	31	0	2	2	4	3	1	7	4	2
Aged 40 to 49	62	63	65	29	33	27	2	2	2	1	1	1	6	1	5
Aged 50 to 59	64	71	69	28	21	27	2	3	1	2	3	0	3	3	2
Aged 60 to 69	62	75	69	31	20	24	3	2	3	1	1	0	4	3	4
Aged 70 or older	67	66	77	25	27	17	3	1	3	1	1	0	4	3	3
Not a high school graduate	59	68	73	32	25	22	0	1	1	1	2	0	7	4	4
High school graduate	61	64	64	29	29	30	1	1	2	3	2	1	6	4	3
Bachelor's degree	51	61	64	34	30	29	3	6	4	5	2	1	7	2	2
Graduate degree	55	61	63	27	18	26	8	10	6	3	8	3	7	3	2

Note: Numbers may not add to 100 because "don't know" is not shown.
Source: General Social Survey, National Opinion Research Center, University of Chicago; calculations by the author

Attendance at Religious Services

Fewer than half of Americans attend religious services regularly.

In a busy world, it is not surprising that most Americans do not attend religious services on a weekly basis. Only 32 percent say they attend services at least once a week, although nearly half (48 percent) attend at least once a month.

Thirty-seven percent of women, but only 25 percent of men, attend services at least once a week. Thirty-six percent of men, but only 26 percent of women, attend services less often than once a year.

Blacks are more likely than whites and people of "other" race to attend services regularly. Forty percent say they attend at least once a week compared with 32 percent of whites and 23 percent of others. While attendance among whites decreased slightly since 1978, weekly attendance among blacks rose from 32 percent in that year to 40 percent in 1998.

Many religious institutions have noticed a drop in attendance among younger generations. In 1978, 41 percent of people in their forties attended services weekly. By 1998, only 31 percent did so. Among people under age 30, weekly attendance dropped from 21 percent in 1978 to 16 percent in 1998. Half of people aged 70 or older attend religious services at least weekly, about the same share as in 1978. Attendance by younger generations may increase somewhat as they grow older, but it may never reach the level seen among today's older adults.

Attendance at Religious Services, 1998

"How often do you attend religious services?"

(percent of people aged 18 or older responding by sex, race, age, and education, 1998)

	at least weekly	at least monthly, but less than once a week	once to several times a year	less than once a year or never
Total	**32%**	**16%**	**22%**	**30%**
Men	25	16	23	36
Women	37	16	21	26
Black	40	23	17	20
White	32	15	22	32
Other	23	20	26	31
Aged 18 to 29	16	19	29	37
Aged 30 to 39	29	17	23	30
Aged 40 to 49	31	17	23	28
Aged 50 to 59	38	13	18	30
Aged 60 to 69	39	15	16	30
Aged 70 or older	51	13	13	24
Not a high school graduate	32	15	17	36
High school graduate	29	16	22	32
Bachelor's degree	35	17	23	25
Graduate degree	41	14	22	23

Note: Numbers may not add to 100 because "don't know" is not shown.
Source: General Social Survey, National Opinion Research Center, University of Chicago; calculations by the author

Attendance at Religious Services, 1978 to 1998

"How often do you attend religious services?"

(percent of people aged 18 or older responding by sex, race, age, and education, 1978–98)

	at least weekly			1 to 3 times a month			up to several times a year			less than once a year or never		
	1998	1988	1978	1998	1988	1978	1998	1988	1978	1998	1988	1978
Total	32%	33%	35%	16%	17%	16%	22%	24%	25%	30%	24%	24%
Men	25	27	28	16	16	14	23	25	28	36	31	29
Women	37	38	39	16	18	17	21	24	22	26	19	21
Black	40	32	32	23	24	27	17	26	28	20	18	12
White	32	34	35	15	16	15	22	24	24	32	25	26
Aged 18 to 29	16	22	21	19	20	19	29	29	33	37	29	27
Aged 30 to 39	29	31	33	17	20	18	23	25	24	30	23	25
Aged 40 to 49	31	33	41	17	18	15	23	24	22	28	24	22
Aged 50 to 59	38	33	40	13	21	14	18	27	21	30	19	23
Aged 60 to 69	39	40	39	15	13	13	16	27	23	30	21	24
Aged 70 or older	51	51	49	13	11	13	13	12	16	24	25	22
Not a high school graduate	32	31	35	15	15	13	17	20	25	36	34	27
High school graduate	29	35	34	16	18	18	22	24	26	32	22	23
Bachelor's degree	35	39	37	17	17	17	23	26	24	25	19	21
Graduate degree	41	28	34	14	22	18	22	34	15	23	16	34

Note: Numbers may not add to 100 because "don't know" is not shown.
Source: General Social Survey, National Opinion Research Center, University of Chicago; calculations by the author

Prayer

Most Americans say a daily prayer.

Fifty-five percent of Americans pray at least once a day, a proportion that has changed little since 1988.

Women are much more likely than men to pray frequently. Only 43 percent of men pray at least once a day compared with 64 percent of women. Nearly one-third of men say they pray less often than once a week compared with only 14 percent of women.

Fully three-quarters of blacks say a daily prayer compared with half of whites and "other" races. While the proportion of whites who pray at least once a day has changed little since 1988, the proportion of blacks who pray daily rose from 62 percent in that year. Only 10 percent of blacks pray less often than once a week, compared with about one-quarter of whites and other races.

The proportion of people who pray at least once a day rises with age. Only 39 percent of people under age 30 say a daily prayer, but the figure rises to 71 percent among people aged 70 or older.

Prayer, 1998

"About how often do you pray?"

(percent of people aged 18 or older responding by sex, race, age, and education, 1998)

	several times a day	once a day	several times a week	once a week	less than once a week	never
Total	25%	30%	14%	8%	22%	2%
Men	17	26	14	9	31	2
Women	31	33	14	6	14	1
Black	39	36	12	3	10	0
White	23	28	15	8	23	2
Other	19	33	9	12	27	0
Aged 18 to 29	15	24	16	11	31	3
Aged 30 to 39	23	30	16	8	22	1
Aged 40 to 49	24	33	15	8	19	1
Aged 50 to 59	27	30	14	6	22	1
Aged 60 to 69	29	30	10	6	23	2
Aged 70 or older	38	33	11	4	12	2
Not a high school graduate	27	32	13	8	18	1
High school graduate	23	30	15	7	22	1
Bachelor's degree	25	28	13	8	24	2
Graduate degree	25	31	9	5	27	3

Source: General Social Survey, National Opinion Research Center, University of Chicago; calculations by the author

Prayer, 1988 and 1998

"About how often do you pray?"

(percent of people aged 18 or older responding by sex, race, age, and education, 1988–98)

	daily or more		once to several times a week		less than once a week		never	
	1998	*1988*	*1998*	*1988*	*1998*	*1988*	*1998*	*1988*
Total	**55%**	**54%**	**22%**	**23%**	**22%**	**22%**	**2%**	**0%**
Men	43	40	23	28	31	32	2	0
Women	64	65	20	20	14	15	1	0
Black	75	62	15	24	10	15	0	0
White	51	54	23	23	23	23	2	0
Aged 18 to 29	19	39	27	30	31	31	3	1
Aged 30 to 39	53	47	24	27	22	26	1	0
Aged 40 to 49	57	53	23	24	19	23	1	0
Aged 50 to 59	57	61	20	22	22	17	1	0
Aged 60 to 69	59	66	16	19	23	14	2	0
Aged 70 or older	71	77	15	10	12	11	2	0
Not a high school graduate	59	62	21	19	18	17	1	0
High school graduate	53	55	22	24	22	21	1	0
Bachelor's degree	53	45	21	25	24	29	2	1
Graduate degree	56	40	14	23	27	38	3	0

Source: General Social Survey, National Opinion Research Center, University of Chicago; calculations by the author

Belief about God

Most Americans believe in God.

A 63 percent majority of Americans say they believe in God without any doubt. Another 15 percent are believers, but have some doubts. Ten percent say they believe in some type of Higher Power, but not a personal God.

Men and women differ in their beliefs about God. Sixty-eight percent of women believe in God without a doubt, compared with a smaller 56 percent of men. Men are more likely than women to say they believe in a Higher Power (13 versus 8 percent).

Blacks are most likely to say they believe in God and have no doubts about it (86 percent compared with 59 percent of whites and 63 percent of "other" races). Whites and people of other race are more likely to say they believe with some doubts, or they believe in a Higher Power.

The proportion of people who say they believe in God rises with age. Only 55 percent of people under age 30 believe in God without a doubt compared with 73 percent of those aged 70 or older. Young adults' belief in God may grow as they get older, but not necessarily. Some cohorts have shown a slight increase in the proportion of absolute believers over the past decade, but in other cohorts the proportion has remained unchanged.

The proportion of people saying they believe in a Higher Power rather than God increases with education. Only 6 percent of people who did not complete high school say they believe in a Higher Power compared with 16 percent of people with a graduate degree. Conversely, the proportion of those who believe in God without a doubt falls with education, from 68 percent among people who did not complete high school (who tend to be older people) to only 54 percent of those with a graduate degree.

Belief about God, 1998

"Please tell me which of these statements comes closest to expressing what you believe about God.
I don't believe in God.
I don't know whether there is a God and I don't believe there is any way to find out.
I don't believe in a personal God, but I do believe in a Higher Power of some kind.
I find myself believing in God some of the time, but not at others.
While I have doubts, I feel that I do believe in God.
I know God really exists and I have no doubts about it."

(percent of people aged 18 or older responding by sex, race, age, and education, 1998)

	don't believe	don't know, no way to find out	believe in Higher Power	believe only some of the time	believe, but have doubts	believe, have no doubts
Total	3%	5%	10%	5%	15%	63%
Men	5	6	13	4	15	56
Women	2	4	8	5	14	68
Black	2	2	4	3	3	86
White	3	5	11	5	16	59
Other	4	3	11	0	18	63
Aged 18 to 29	4	6	14	2	19	55
Aged 30 to 39	4	5	10	4	16	61
Aged 40 to 49	4	6	8	6	14	63
Aged 50 to 59	3	3	11	5	11	67
Aged 60 to 69	1	3	8	6	16	65
Aged 70 or older	3	4	5	8	7	73
Not a high school graduate	2	5	6	7	13	68
High school graduate	2	4	10	5	15	64
Bachelor's degree	7	6	10	2	17	59
Graduate degree	4	9	16	1	16	54

Note: Numbers may not add to 100 because "don't know" is not shown.
Source: General Social Survey, National Opinion Research Center, University of Chicago; calculations by the author

Belief about God, 1988 and 1998

"Please tell me which of these statements comes closest to expressing what you believe about God. I don't believe in God. I don't know whether there is a God and I don't believe there is any way to find out. I don't believe in a personal God, but I do believe in a Higher Power of some kind. I find myself believing in God some of the time, but not at others. While I have doubts, I feel that I do believe in God. I know God really exists and I have no doubts about it."

(percent of people aged 18 or older responding by sex, race, age, and education, 1988–98)

	don't believe		don't know, no way to find out		believe in Higher Power		believe only some of the time		believe, but have doubt		believe, have no doubts	
	1998	1988	1998	1988	1998	1988	1998	1988	1998	1988	1998	1988
Total	3%	1%	5%	4%	10%	8%	5%	4%	15%	19%	63%	64%
Men	5	2	6	5	13	11	4	5	15	21	56	55
Women	2	1	4	3	8	5	5	4	14	17	68	70
Black	2	1	2	4	4	6	3	2	3	13	86	75
White	3	1	5	4	11	8	5	4	16	20	59	62
Aged 18 to 29	4	1	6	4	14	8	2	6	19	24	55	56
Aged 30 to 39	4	2	5	6	10	7	4	2	16	20	61	62
Aged 40 to 49	4	1	6	4	8	10	6	6	14	16	63	63
Aged 50 to 59	3	2	3	3	11	8	5	5	11	17	67	65
Aged 60 to 69	1	1	3	3	8	8	6	3	16	16	65	69
Aged 70 or older	3	1	4	2	5	6	8	3	7	14	73	73

(continued)

(continued from previous page)

	don't believe		don't know, no way to find out		believe in Higher Power		believe only some of the time		believe, but have doubt		believe, have no doubts	
	1998	1988	1998	1988	1998	1988	1998	1988	1998	1988	1998	1988
Not a high school graduate	2%	1%	5%	2%	6%	6%	7%	5%	13%	14%	68%	72%
High school graduate	2	1	4	3	10	7	5	5	15	19	64	66
Bachelor's degree	7	4	6	7	10	14	2	4	17	20	59	50
Graduate degree	4	5	9	11	16	10	1	3	16	24	54	47

Note: Numbers may not add to 100 because "don't know" is not shown.
Source: General Social Survey, National Opinion Research Center, University of Chicago; calculations by the author

God Is Concerned with Individuals

Education makes a difference in people's views of God.

Most Americans believe God is personally concerned with every individual human being. Forty percent strongly agree with this statement, and another 30 percent agree. There are significant differences of opinion, however, by demographic characteristic.

The more education people have, the less likely they are to believe God is concerned with each person. Seventy-one percent of people with a high school education or less believe God is personally concerned with individuals, but this share drops to 67 percent among college graduates and 56 percent among those with a graduate degree. One-third of the most educated Americans say they disagree with this statement.

Over half of blacks strongly agree that God is personally concerned with individuals compared with 39 percent of whites and 33 percent of "other" races. Overall, 82 percent of blacks agree with the statement compared with 71 percent of others and 69 percent of whites.

Women are more likely than men to believe God is concerned with individual human beings—44 percent of women believe so compared with 35 percent of men.

God Is Concerned with Individuals, 1998

"There is a God who concerns Himself with every human being personally. Do you agree or disagree?"

(percent of people aged 18 or older responding by sex, race, age, and education, 1998)

	strongly agree	agree	neither	disagree	strongly disagree	can't choose	agree, total	disagree, total
Total	**40%**	**30%**	**12%**	**9%**	**5%**	**4%**	**70%**	**14%**
Men	35	30	13	10	8	4	65	18
Women	44	30	10	8	4	4	74	12
Black	53	29	6	5	1	7	82	6
White	39	30	13	9	6	3	69	15
Other	33	38	10	8	5	7	71	13
Aged 18 to 29	33	31	15	11	5	6	64	16
Aged 30 to 39	43	27	14	8	5	3	70	13
Aged 40 to 49	41	30	9	10	6	4	71	16
Aged 50 to 59	42	33	8	7	8	3	75	15
Aged 60 to 69	46	29	11	6	4	4	75	10
Aged 70 or older	39	32	10	9	4	6	71	13
Not a high school graduate	40	31	11	6	2	9	71	8
High school graduate	42	30	13	8	4	3	72	12
Bachelor's degree	38	29	10	12	7	3	67	19
Graduate degree	34	22	8	16	17	3	56	33

Source: General Social Survey, National Opinion Research Center, University of Chicago; calculations by the author

Life after Death

Most people believe life continues after death.

Most Americans take comfort in the belief in an afterlife. Seventy-two percent say they believe in life after death, a proportion that has remained essentially unchanged over the past two decades. During this time, the percentage of people who do not believe in life after death has declined. In 1978, 21 percent of people said they did not believe life continued after death. The figure dropped to 16 percent in 1998. There was a corresponding increase in the proportion of those who say they are undecided.

Women are slightly more likely than men to believe in life after death (74 versus 69 percent). People in their forties are more likely than other age groups to believe in life after death, although the differences by age are small.

Life after Death, 1998

"Do you believe there is a life after death?"

(percent of people aged 18 or older responding by sex, race, age, and education, 1998)

	yes	no	undecided
Total	**72%**	**16%**	**12%**
Men	69	19	13
Women	74	14	11
Black	71	17	12
White	72	16	12
Other	70	16	13
Aged 18 to 29	69	18	13
Aged 30 to 39	74	16	11
Aged 40 to 49	76	14	10
Aged 50 to 59	69	18	13
Aged 60 to 69	68	17	16
Aged 70 or older	72	15	13
Not a high school graduate	68	19	13
High school graduate	72	16	12
Bachelor's degree	75	15	11
Graduate degree	69	18	14

Source: General Social Survey, National Opinion Research Center, University of Chicago; calculations by the author

Life after Death, 1978 to 1998

"Do you believe there is a life after death?"

(percent of people aged 18 or older responding by sex, race, age, and education, 1978–98)

	yes			no			undecided		
	1998	*1988*	*1978*	*1998*	*1988*	*1978*	*1998*	*1988*	*1978*
Total	**72%**	**74%**	**70%**	**16%**	**19%**	**21%**	**12%**	**7%**	**9%**
Men	69	72	67	19	21	24	13	7	8
Women	74	75	72	14	18	19	11	7	9
Black	71	71	72	17	21	20	12	8	8
White	72	74	55	16	18	32	12	7	13
Aged 18 to 29	69	72	65	18	20	25	13	8	9
Aged 30 to 39	74	74	72	16	20	21	11	6	8
Aged 40 to 49	76	78	68	14	15	23	10	7	9
Aged 50 to 59	69	73	76	18	17	15	13	10	8
Aged 60 to 69	68	73	73	17	20	18	16	8	9
Aged 70 or older	72	71	68	15	22	21	13	7	11
Not a high school graduate	68	69	68	19	22	22	13	8	11
High school graduate	72	76	71	16	18	21	12	7	8
Bachelor's degree	75	78	70	15	18	21	11	4	10
Graduate degree	69	63	66	18	22	23	14	15	11

Source: General Social Survey, National Opinion Research Center, University of Chicago; calculations by the author

Believe in Heaven and Hell

Americans are more likely to believe in heaven than hell.

The solid majority of Americans say they believe heaven definitely or probably exists (81 percent), but fewer believe in hell (68 percent). Only 13 percent say there is definitely or probably not a heaven, but 23 percent do not believe in hell.

Education makes the biggest difference in beliefs about heaven and hell. Among people with a high school education or less, 65 to 69 percent say they definitely believe in heaven, but the figure drops to 56 percent among people with a bachelor's degree and to only 48 percent among those with a graduate degree. While 54 to 55 percent of people with a high school degree or less say hell definitely exists, only 41 percent of people with a bachelor's degree and 37 percent of those with a graduate degree agree. College graduates are also more likely than those with less education to say they definitely do not believe in heaven or hell.

Women are more likely than men to believe in heaven and hell. Blacks are more likely than whites and people of "other" race to believe in heaven, and they are far more likely to believe in hell. Fully 71 percent of blacks say they definitely believe in hell compared with 49 percent of whites and 44 percent of others.

Believe in Heaven, 1998

"Do you believe in Heaven?"

(percent of people aged 18 or older responding by sex, race, age, and education, 1998)

	yes, definitely	yes, probably	no, probably not	no, definitely not	can't choose	yes, total	no, total
Total	**63%**	**18%**	**7%**	**6%**	**6%**	**81%**	**13%**
Men	57	20	8	9	6	77	17
Women	67	17	7	4	5	84	11
Black	76	13	5	2	4	89	7
White	61	19	8	6	6	80	14
Other	60	19	5	9	7	79	14
Aged 18 to 29	58	19	7	8	7	77	15
Aged 30 to 39	66	17	7	5	5	83	12
Aged 40 to 49	62	18	9	7	4	80	16
Aged 50 to 59	62	19	7	6	7	81	13
Aged 60 to 69	68	21	7	3	2	89	10
Aged 70 or older	62	17	6	6	9	79	12
Not a high school graduate	69	16	4	2	8	85	6
High school graduate	65	17	7	5	6	82	12
Bachelor's degree	56	19	9	11	7	75	20
Graduate degree	48	25	8	17	2	73	25

Source: General Social Survey, National Opinion Research Center, University of Chicago; calculations by the author

Believe in Hell, 1998

"Do you believe in Hell?"

(percent of people aged 18 or older responding by sex, race, age, and education, 1998)

	yes, definitely	yes, probably	no, probably not	no, definitely not	can't choose	yes, total	no, total
Total	**51%**	**17%**	**12%**	**11%**	**8%**	**68%**	**23%**
Men	49	17	13	14	7	66	27
Women	53	18	12	9	8	71	21
Black	71	12	5	7	5	83	12
White	49	18	14	12	8	67	26
Other	44	23	10	11	11	67	21
Aged 18 to 29	50	16	13	11	9	66	24
Aged 30 to 39	55	20	11	8	6	75	19
Aged 40 to 49	51	16	16	10	6	67	26
Aged 50 to 59	48	18	11	13	9	66	24
Aged 60 to 69	52	17	9	15	7	69	24
Aged 70 or older	47	17	9	13	13	64	22
Not a high school graduate	54	18	9	10	10	72	19
High school graduate	55	16	12	8	9	71	20
Bachelor's degree	41	18	16	18	8	59	34
Graduate degree	37	17	17	27	2	54	44

Source: General Social Survey, National Opinion Research Center, University of Chicago; calculations by the author

Believe in Miracles

More women than men believe in religious miracles.

Most Americans (72 percent) believe religious miracles definitely or probably occur. Twenty percent say they do not believe in miracles.

Women are considerably more likely than men to say they definitely believe in miracles (52 versus 41 percent). Twenty-four percent of men say they do not believe in miracles compared with only 16 percent of women.

Fully 80 percent of blacks believe in miracles compared with 71 percent of whites and 69 percent of "other" races. People under age 30 are less likely than older age groups to say they definitely believe in miracles.

The proportion of people who believe in miracles does not differ much by education, but the most educated are most likely to say they do not believe in miracles. Eighteen percent of people with a graduate degree say they definitely do not believe in religious miracles compared with 10 percent of people with a bachelor's degree and 7 percent of those with a high school diploma or less education.

Believe in Miracles, 1998

"Do you believe in religious miracles?"

(percent of people aged 18 or older responding by sex, race, age, and education, 1998)

	yes, definitely	yes, probably	no, probably not	no, definitely not	can't choose	yes, total	no, total
Total	**47%**	**25%**	**12%**	**8%**	**8%**	**72%**	**20%**
Men	41	26	14	10	9	67	24
Women	52	24	10	6	8	76	16
Black	55	25	5	8	7	80	13
White	46	25	12	8	9	71	20
Other	47	22	13	11	8	69	24
Aged 18 to 29	40	28	15	8	9	68	23
Aged 30 to 39	48	27	13	6	5	75	19
Aged 40 to 49	52	18	12	9	10	70	21
Aged 50 to 59	48	27	10	8	7	75	18
Aged 60 to 69	49	26	9	9	7	75	18
Aged 70 or older	48	22	7	10	13	70	17
Not a high school graduate	48	24	9	7	12	72	16
High school graduate	48	25	12	7	8	73	19
Bachelor's degree	46	24	13	10	8	70	23
Graduate degree	47	23	9	18	3	70	27

Source: General Social Survey, National Opinion Research Center, University of Chicago; calculations by the author

What Is the Bible?

Most say it is inspired by God, but not to be taken literally.

Nearly half of Americans view the Bible as "the inspired word of God," not to be taken literally. Only 31 percent say it should be taken literally. Sixteen percent believe it is an ancient book of fables and stories, "recorded by men." Since 1988, the proportion of those who accept a literal interpretation of the Bible has fallen in most demographic segments, while the proportion of those who say the Bible is inspired by God or simply a book written by people has grown.

Disagreements about how the Bible should be interpreted are found within every demographic segment. Women are more likely than men to say the Bible is to be interpreted literally (33 versus 27 percent). Men are more likely than women to believe it is simply an ancient book (20 versus 13 percent).

There is sharper disagreement by race. Half of blacks, but only 27 percent of whites and 32 percent of "other" races, believe the Bible is the literal word of God. The percentage of blacks saying the Bible should be taken literally has increased since 1988, when 44 percent felt this way. Whites are less likely to say the Bible should be taken literally now than they were in 1988.

Generational differences of opinion were more pronounced in 1988 than in 1998. The percentage of people aged 60 or older who believe the Bible is the actual word of God has declined slightly since 1988, but older Americans are still more likely to say this than younger generations.

The biggest difference of opinion is found by education. Nearly half of people who did not complete high school believe the Bible should be taken literally, but only 12 percent of those with a graduate degree feel that way. Just 12 to 14 percent of people with a high school degree or less education believe the Bible is simply an ancient book, compared with 23 percent of people with a bachelor's degree and 31 percent of those with a graduate degree.

What Is the Bible? 1998

**"Which of these statements comes closest to describing your feelings about the Bible?
a) The Bible is the actual word of God and is to be taken literally, word for word;
b) The Bible is the inspired word of God but not everything in it
should be taken literally, word for word; or
c) The Bible is an ancient book of fables, legends, history,
and moral precepts recorded by men?"**

(percent of people aged 18 or older responding by sex, race, age, and education, 1998)

	actual word	inspired word	ancient book
Total	**31%**	**49%**	**16%**
Men	27	48	20
Women	33	50	13
Black	51	37	9
White	27	52	17
Other	32	43	20
Aged 18 to 29	30	47	21
Aged 30 to 39	30	49	16
Aged 40 to 49	27	53	17
Aged 50 to 59	28	53	17
Aged 60 to 69	39	49	10
Aged 70 or older	38	45	13
Not a high school graduate	49	35	12
High school graduate	33	51	14
Bachelor's degree	17	55	23
Graduate degree	12	54	31

Note: Numbers may not add to 100 because "other" and "don't know" are not shown.
Source: General Social Survey, National Opinion Research Center, University of Chicago; calculations by the author

What Is the Bible? 1988 and 1998

"Which of these statements comes closest to describing your feelings about the Bible?
a) The Bible is the actual word of God and is to be taken literally, word for word;
b) The Bible is the inspired word of God but not everything in it
should be taken literally, word for word; or
c) The Bible is an ancient book of fables, legends, history,
and moral precepts recorded by men?"

(percent of people aged 18 or older responding by sex, race, age, and education, 1988–98)

	actual word		inspired word		ancient book	
	1998	1988	1998	1988	1998	1988
Total	**31%**	**34%**	**49%**	**47%**	**16%**	**16%**
Men	27	28	48	49	20	20
Women	33	39	50	46	13	13
Black	51	44	37	39	9	14
White	27	33	52	49	17	16
Aged 18 to 29	30	30	47	49	21	18
Aged 30 to 39	30	30	49	50	16	17
Aged 40 to 49	27	31	53	48	17	19
Aged 50 to 59	28	33	53	50	17	13
Aged 60 to 69	39	41	49	40	10	16
Aged 70 or older	38	45	45	41	13	11
Not a high school graduate	49	52	35	33	12	12
High school graduate	33	35	51	50	14	13
Bachelor's degree	17	13	55	58	23	27
Graduate degree	12	10	54	50	31	35

Note: Numbers may not add to 100 because other and "don't know" are not shown.
Source: General Social Survey, National Opinion Research Center, University of Chicago; calculations by the author

Importance of Believing in God

Most Americans say it is very important to believe in God without question.

Fifty-nine percent of Americans say that in order to be a good Christian or Jew, it is very important to believe in God without question. In most demographic segments, the proportion of those who believe this is very important has increased slightly during the past 10 years.

Fully 80 percent of blacks say it is very important to believe in God without question, compared with 55 percent of whites and 60 percent of people of "other" races. Sixty-three percent of women, but only 53 percent of men, say an unquestioned belief in God is very important.

The most interesting change has occurred by education. People who did not complete high school were slightly less likely to say it was very important to believe in God without question in 1998 than in 1988, while the opposite trend occurred among people with more education. This change narrowed the gap by education, but those with more education are still less likely to say that believing in God without question is important. Fully 69 percent of people who did not complete high school say unquestioned belief is very important, but the figure drops to just 37 percent among people with a graduate degree. □

Importance of Believing in God, 1998

"People have many differing views about what makes a person a good Christian or Jew. Please tell me how important it is (on a scale of 1 to 5) to believe in God without question or doubt."

(percent of people aged 18 or older responding by sex, race, age, and education, 1998)

	very important 1	2	3	4	not very important 5
Total	**59%**	**15%**	**12%**	**5%**	**8%**
Men	53	17	12	5	10
Women	63	13	12	4	7
Black	80	10	5	1	4
White	55	16	13	5	9
Other	60	11	13	4	10
Aged 18 to 29	53	16	16	5	10
Aged 30 to 39	59	17	11	4	7
Aged 40 to 49	58	14	13	5	9
Aged 50 to 59	61	12	12	5	9
Aged 60 to 69	58	13	9	10	8
Aged 70 or older	66	16	8	1	6
Not a high school graduate	69	10	10	3	5
High school graduate	62	15	11	3	7
Bachelor's degree	48	18	16	6	9
Graduate degree	37	18	13	12	19

Note: Numbers may not add to 100 because "don't know" is not shown.
Source: General Social Survey, National Opinion Research Center, University of Chicago; calculations by the author

Importance of Believing in God, 1988 and 1998

"People have many differing views about what makes a person a good Christian or Jew. Please tell me how important it is (on a scale of 1 to 5) to believe in God without question or doubt."

(percent of people aged 18 or older responding by sex, race, age, and education, 1988–98)

	important (1 and 2)		(3)		not important (4 and 5)	
	1998	*1988*	*1998*	*1988*	*1998*	*1988*
Total	**74%**	**72%**	**12%**	**12%**	**13%**	**15%**
Men	70	67	12	13	15	19
Women	76	75	12	12	11	12
Black	90	85	5	6	5	8
White	71	70	13	13	14	17
Aged 18 to 29	69	71	16	13	15	15
Aged 30 to 39	76	70	11	12	11	17
Aged 40 to 49	72	66	13	13	14	20
Aged 50 to 59	73	71	12	13	14	15
Aged 60 to 69	71	76	9	13	18	12
Aged 70 or older	82	79	8	8	7	12
Not a high school graduate	79	83	10	8	8	8
High school graduate	77	74	11	12	10	14
Bachelor's degree	66	60	16	15	15	24
Graduate degree	55	40	13	21	31	37

Note: Numbers may not add to 100 because "don't know" is not shown.
Source: General Social Survey, National Opinion Research Center, University of Chicago; calculations by the author

Importance of Attending Religious Services

Opinions differ depending on educational attainment.

Americans are somewhat divided on how important attending religious services is to being a good Christian or Jew. A small plurality (30 percent) says it is very important to attend services, while 24 percent of Americans say it is not very important. Some segments of the population, however, are considerably more likely to say it is very important.

Forty-six percent of blacks say it is very important to attend religious services compared with only 27 percent of whites and 34 percent of "other" races. The proportion of blacks saying it is important (1 and 2 on a five-point scale) has grown slightly since 1988.

The older people are, the more likely they are to believe that attending services is very important. Nearly half (47 percent) of people aged 70 or older say it is very important compared with only 20 percent of people under age 30. This difference in attitude is probably more generational than based on lifestage, since only 32 percent of people in their sixties say it is very important to attend services.

The more education people have, the less likely they are to believe attending religious services is very important. Only 24 percent of people with a college degree believe it is very important compared with 41 percent of those who did not complete high school (many of whom are older Americans). One-third of people with a graduate degree say it is not very important, but the figure drops to only 19 percent among people who did not complete high school.

Importance of Attending Religious Services, 1998

**"People have many differing views about what makes a person a good Christian or Jew.
Please tell me how important it is (on a scale of 1 to 5)
to attend regularly religious services at church or synagogue."**

(percent of people aged 18 or older responding by sex, race, age, and education, 1998)

	very important 1	2	3	4	not very important 5
Total	30%	13%	20%	11%	24%
Men	26	12	21	11	28
Women	33	13	20	11	21
Black	46	12	21	7	13
White	27	13	20	12	26
Other	34	12	24	7	20
Aged 18 to 29	20	13	22	17	25
Aged 30 to 39	26	15	24	14	20
Aged 40 to 49	28	11	22	9	27
Aged 50 to 59	35	10	21	8	24
Aged 60 to 69	32	15	16	7	29
Aged 70 or older	47	13	12	6	21
Not a high school graduate	41	9	21	7	19
High school graduate	30	12	20	11	25
Bachelor's degree	24	12	24	12	26
Graduate degree	24	21	13	9	32

Note: Numbers may not add to 100 because "don't know" is not shown.
Source: General Social Survey, National Opinion Research Center, University of Chicago; calculations by the author

Importance of Attending Religious Services, 1988 and 1998

**"People have many differing views about what makes a person a good Christian or Jew.
Please tell me how important it is (on a scale of 1 to 5)
to attend regularly religious services at church or synagogue."**

(percent of people aged 18 or older responding by sex, race, age, and education, 1988–98)

	important (1 and 2)		(3)		not important (4 and 5)	
	1998	1988	1998	1988	1998	1988
Total	**43%**	**43%**	**20%**	**20%**	**35%**	**36%**
Men	38	40	21	19	39	40
Women	46	46	20	21	32	33
Black	58	54	21	19	20	26
White	40	42	20	21	38	37
Aged 18 to 29	33	36	22	25	42	38
Aged 30 to 39	41	38	24	23	34	39
Aged 40 to 49	39	41	22	17	36	42
Aged 50 to 59	45	48	21	19	32	32
Aged 60 to 69	47	49	16	22	36	29
Aged 70 or older	60	60	12	11	27	28
Not a high school graduate	50	56	21	14	26	30
High school graduate	42	42	20	23	36	34
Bachelor's degree	36	34	24	20	38	45
Graduate degree	45	26	13	24	41	48

Note: Numbers may not add to 100 because "don't know" is not shown.
Source: General Social Survey, National Opinion Research Center, University of Chicago; calculations by the author

Importance of Following Religious Teachings

College graduates are less likely to believe adherence is very important.

Only one-third of Americans believe that it is very important to follow faithfully the teachings of their church or synagogue. Slightly more than half say it is important (i.e., chose 1 or 2 on a five-point scale).

There are differences of opinion by demographic characteristic. Only 28 percent of men say it is very important to follow religious teachings compared with 35 percent of women. Forty-four percent of blacks, but only 29 percent of whites and 38 percent of "other" races say it is very important. The proportion of blacks saying it is important increased from 60 to 66 percent between 1988 and 1998.

Older people are more likely than younger generations to believe it is very important to follow religious teachings. Nearly half (46 percent) of people aged 70 or older say so compared with only 25 percent of people under age 30.

The widest gap in opinions on this issue is by education. Among people who did not complete high school (many of whom are older people), 44 percent say it is very important to follow religious teachings. The proportion falls to 19 percent among people with a graduate degree. Twenty-one percent of people with a graduate degree say it is not very important compared with 12 to 14 percent of those with less education.

Importance of Following Religious Teachings, 1998

"People have many differing views about what makes a person a good Christian or Jew. Please tell me how important it is (on a scale of 1 to 5) to follow faithfully the teachings of their church or synagogue."

(percent of people aged 18 or older responding by sex, race, age, and education, 1998)

	very important 1	2	3	4	not very important 5
Total	**32%**	**21%**	**23%**	**9%**	**13%**
Men	28	21	24	10	15
Women	35	20	23	8	12
Black	44	22	18	10	5
White	29	21	25	9	14
Other	38	15	20	6	17
Aged 18 to 29	25	19	28	12	14
Aged 30 to 39	31	22	24	9	14
Aged 40 to 49	29	23	23	7	16
Aged 50 to 59	32	22	20	11	12
Aged 60 to 69	37	16	27	9	10
Aged 70 or older	46	17	18	5	11
Not a high school graduate	44	13	19	9	12
High school graduate	33	21	25	7	13
Bachelor's degree	23	23	27	11	14
Graduate degree	19	25	19	16	21

Note: Numbers may not add to 100 because "don't know" is not shown.
Source: General Social Survey, National Opinion Research Center, University of Chicago; calculations by the author

Importance of Following Religious Teachings, 1988 and 1998

"People have many differing views about what makes a person a good Christian or Jew. Please tell me how important it is (on a scale of 1 to 5) to follow faithfully the teachings of their church or synagogue."

(percent of people aged 18 or older responding by sex, race, age, and education, 1988–98)

	important (1 and 2)		(3)		not important (4 and 5)	
	1998	*1988*	*1998*	*1988*	*1998*	*1988*
Total	53%	54%	23%	24%	22%	21%
Men	49	49	24	26	25	24
Women	55	58	23	23	20	19
Black	66	60	18	22	15	17
White	50	53	25	24	23	22
Aged 18 to 29	44	49	28	29	26	22
Aged 30 to 39	53	51	24	24	23	24
Aged 40 to 49	52	46	23	28	23	25
Aged 50 to 59	54	58	20	24	23	16
Aged 60 to 69	53	62	27	19	19	19
Aged 70 or older	63	69	18	16	16	15
Not a high school graduate	57	67	19	16	21	17
High school graduate	53	53	25	27	20	19
Bachelor's degree	46	48	27	25	25	25
Graduate degree	44	35	19	28	37	36

Note: Numbers may not add to 100 because "don't know" is not shown.
Source: General Social Survey, National Opinion Research Center, University of Chicago; calculations by the author

Importance of Following Own Conscience

The youngest adults are least likely to believe it is important to follow one's own conscience.

A plurality of Americans (40 percent) believe that in order to be a good Christian or Jew, one must follow one's own conscience even if it means going against what the churches or synagogues say and do. But the percentage of those who say following one's own conscience is important (i.e., chose 1 or 2 on a five-point scale) declined between 1988 and 1998 in every demographic segment.

Only 31 percent of blacks say it is important to follow one's own conscience, compared with 42 percent of whites and 40 percent of people of "other" race. There are surprising generational differences on this question as well. Only 32 percent of people under age 30 say it is very important to follow one's own conscience compared with more than 40 percent of older Americans.

College graduates are considerably more likely than those with less education to believe one should follow one's own conscience. More than half (56 percent) of people with a graduate degree say this is important. The figure declines to 42 percent among people with a bachelor's degree and to only 38 to 39 percent among people with a high school diploma or less.

Importance of Following Own Conscience, 1998

"People have many differing views about what makes a person a good Christian or Jew. Please tell me how important it is (on a scale of 1 to 5) to follow one's own conscience even if it means going against what the churches or synagogues say and do."

(percent of people aged 18 or older responding by sex, race, age, and education, 1998)

	very important 1	2	3	4	not very important 5
Total	**40%**	**16%**	**22%**	**6%**	**10%**
Men	40	18	23	7	9
Women	41	15	21	6	10
Black	31	15	26	7	12
White	42	16	21	6	10
Other	40	18	21	8	4
Aged 18 to 29	32	19	29	7	8
Aged 30 to 39	40	17	20	6	11
Aged 40 to 49	41	18	21	9	8
Aged 50 to 59	45	13	24	4	7
Aged 60 to 69	44	16	22	1	10
Aged 70 or older	43	11	13	8	14
Not a high school graduate	39	11	22	7	14
High school graduate	38	17	23	7	10
Bachelor's degree	42	24	19	6	5
Graduate degree	56	11	17	5	8

Note: Numbers may not add to 100 because "don't know" is not shown.
Source: General Social Survey, National Opinion Research Center, University of Chicago; calculations by the author

Importance of Following Own Conscience, 1988 and 1998

"People have many differing views about what makes a person a good Christian or Jew. Please tell me how important it is (on a scale of 1 to 5) to follow one's own conscience even if it means going against what the churches or synagogues say and do."

(percent of people aged 18 or older responding by sex, race, age, and education, 1988–98)

	important (1 and 2)		(3)		not important (4 and 5)	
	1998	*1988*	*1998*	*1988*	*1998*	*1988*
Total	**56%**	**64%**	**22%**	**21%**	**16%**	**14%**
Men	58	64	23	19	16	15
Women	56	64	21	22	16	13
Black	46	57	26	21	19	20
White	58	65	21	21	16	13
Aged 18 to 29	51	60	29	26	15	14
Aged 30 to 39	57	64	20	20	17	15
Aged 40 to 49	59	72	21	18	17	9
Aged 50 to 59	58	66	24	20	11	11
Aged 60 to 69	60	62	22	21	11	16
Aged 70 or older	54	63	13	18	22	16
Not a high school graduate	50	59	22	21	21	18
High school graduate	55	62	23	22	17	14
Bachelor's degree	66	76	19	14	11	10
Graduate degree	67	79	17	16	13	2

Note: Numbers may not add to 100 because "don't know" is not shown.
Source: General Social Survey, National Opinion Research Center, University of Chicago; calculations by the author

Carry Religious Beliefs into Other Areas of Life

Most Americans do not separate their religious feelings from other areas of their life.

Seven out of ten Americans say they try to carry their religious beliefs into other dealings in their life. Those who do differ markedly from those who do not.

Fully 83 percent of blacks say they try to carry their religious beliefs into other areas of their life, compared with a smaller 71 percent of whites and 66 percent of "other" races. Forty-one percent of blacks say they strongly agree with this statement compared with only 25 percent of whites and 30 percent of other races.

While 78 percent of women try to carry their religious beliefs into other areas, a smaller 65 percent of men agree. One-third of women, but only 22 percent of men, strongly agree.

The youngest adults are least likely to say they carry their religious beliefs into other areas. Only 61 percent of adults under age 30 agree with the statement compared with 70 percent of people in their thirties and 75 to 79 percent of older Americans. The proportion of those who strongly agree rises steadily with age, from just 19 percent among 18-to-29-year-olds to 36 to 37 percent among people aged 60 or older.

Carry Religious Beliefs into Other Areas of Life, 1998

"I try hard to carry my religious beliefs over into all my other dealings in life. Do you agree or disagree?"

(percent of people aged 18 or older responding by sex, race, age, and education, 1998)

	strongly agree	agree	disagree	strongly disagree	agree, total	disagree, total
Total	**27%**	**44%**	**20%**	**7%**	**71%**	**27%**
Men	22	43	25	9	65	34
Women	32	46	16	6	78	22
Black	41	42	14	3	83	17
White	25	46	21	8	71	29
Other	30	36	24	9	66	33
Aged 18 to 29	19	42	30	8	61	38
Aged 30 to 39	24	46	21	9	70	30
Aged 40 to 49	28	47	18	6	75	24
Aged 50 to 59	30	47	15	7	77	22
Aged 60 to 69	37	40	17	6	77	23
Aged 70 or older	36	43	14	6	79	20
Not a high school graduate	30	41	22	5	71	27
High school graduate	27	44	22	7	71	29
Bachelor's degree	28	43	18	10	71	28
Graduate degree	30	49	10	11	79	21

Note: Numbers may not add to 100 because "don't know" is not shown.
Source: General Social Survey, National Opinion Research Center, University of Chicago; calculations by the author

Consider Self a Religious or Spiritual Person?

Few Americans consider themselves "very" religious or spiritual.

Americans are slightly more likely to consider themselves "very" spiritual than "very" religious. The latter usually involves beliefs and practices associated with organized religion, while the former involves personal feelings and expressions of belief that are not necessarily part of an organized religion. Overall, 19 percent of Americans consider themselves very religious, while 22 percent say they are very spiritual.

Younger generations and the well-educated are especially likely to feel spiritual rather than religious. Twenty-two percent of people in their forties say they are very religious, but a larger share of 29 percent say they are very spiritual. Among people with a graduate degree, 21 percent say they are very religious while 31 percent say they are very spiritual.

Blacks are considerably more likely than whites or "other" races to say they are very religious or very spiritual. Thirty-two percent say they are very religious compared with 16 percent of whites and 20 percent of other races. Thirty-five percent of blacks say they are very spiritual versus only 20 percent of whites and 23 percent of other races.

Consider Self a Spiritual Person? 1998

"To what extent do you consider yourself a spiritual person?"

(percent of people aged 18 or older responding by sex, race, age, and education, 1998)

	very spiritual	moderately spiritual	slightly spiritual	not spiritual at all
Total	**22%**	**40%**	**26%**	**12%**
Men	18	39	28	15
Women	26	41	24	9
Black	35	38	20	8
White	20	41	26	12
Other	23	29	31	17
Aged 18 to 29	16	33	37	14
Aged 30 to 39	22	41	25	12
Aged 40 to 49	29	39	21	11
Aged 50 to 59	25	38	28	8
Aged 60 to 69	23	43	22	11
Aged 70 or older	16	50	15	17
Not a high school graduate	24	33	27	15
High school graduate	19	41	28	12
Bachelor's degree	24	44	21	10
Graduate degree	31	39	21	9

Note: Numbers may not add to 100 because "don't know" is not shown.
Source: General Social Survey, National Opinion Research Center, University of Chicago; calculations by the author

Consider Self a Religious Person? 1998

"To what extent do you consider yourself a religious person?"

(percent of people aged 18 or older responding by sex, race, age, and education, 1998)

	very religious	moderately religious	slightly religious	not religious at all
Total	**19%**	**42%**	**23%**	**15%**
Men	15	41	25	19
Women	22	44	22	12
Black	32	44	15	9
White	16	43	24	16
Other	20	30	32	18
Aged 18 to 29	11	37	29	23
Aged 30 to 39	17	42	23	19
Aged 40 to 49	22	40	25	12
Aged 50 to 59	21	44	25	10
Aged 60 to 69	21	50	17	12
Aged 70 or older	24	49	16	11
Not a high school graduate	23	38	24	14
High school graduate	17	45	25	14
Bachelor's degree	19	39	22	20
Graduate degree	21	43	20	16

Note: Numbers may not add to 100 because "don't know" is not included.
Source: General Social Survey, National Opinion Research Center, University of Chicago; calculations by the author

Religious Experience Changed Life

Most people have not had a life-changing religious or spiritual experience.

The majority of Americans (61 percent) say they have not had a life-changing religious or spiritual experience. Although women and men often differ on questions of religion, the proportions of women and men who say they have had a life-changing experience are about the same. Differences by education are small as well. There are larger differences by race and age, however.

Blacks are far more likely than whites or "other" races to say they have had a religious or spiritual experience that changed their lives. Over half of blacks (56 percent) have had such an experience compared with only 37 percent of whites and 33 percent of other races.

People in their forties and fifties are more likely than other age groups to say they have had a religious or spiritual experience that changed their lives. Forty-eight percent of people in their forties and 43 percent of those in their fifties have had a life-changing religious experience. In contrast, only 39 percent of people in their thirties, 36 percent of those in their sixties and under age 30, and 26 percent of people aged 70 or older have had such an experience.

Religious Experience Changed Life, 1998

"Did you ever have a religious or spiritual experience that changed your life?"

(percent of people aged 18 or older responding by sex, race, age, and education, 1998)

	yes	no
Total	**39%**	**61%**
Men	40	60
Women	38	62
Black	56	44
White	37	63
Other	33	66
Aged 18 to 29	36	64
Aged 30 to 39	39	60
Aged 40 to 49	48	52
Aged 50 to 59	43	57
Aged 60 to 69	36	63
Aged 70 or older	26	73
Not a high school graduate	35	64
High school graduate	39	61
Bachelor's degree	41	59
Graduate degree	41	59

Note: Numbers may not add to 100 because "don't know" is not shown.
Source: General Social Survey, National Opinion Research Center, University of Chicago; calculations by the author

Confidence in the Leaders of Organized Religion

Religious leaders have regained much of their lost credibility.

Scandals involving well-known religious figures damaged their credibility during the 1980s. Since then, however, the proportion of people saying they have a great deal of confidence in the leaders of organized religion has grown, rising from 20 to 27 percent between 1988 and 1998. The 1998 figure was still lower than the 31 percent share expressing a great deal of confidence in religious leaders in 1978, however. The proportion of those who say they have hardly any confidence declined from 31 percent in 1988 to 19 percent in 1998—about the same proportion as in 1978.

The oldest Americans are far more likely than younger generations to have a great deal of confidence in religious leaders. Forty-six percent of people aged 70 or older feel a great deal of confidence compared with 31 percent of people in their sixties and one-quarter or fewer of those younger.

Age may also play a role in the difference of opinion by education. Thirty-six percent of people who did not complete high school, a group that includes a disproportionately large number of older Americans, feel a great deal of confidence in religious leaders. Only about one-quarter of people with at least a high school diploma agree.

Confidence in the Leaders of Organized Religion, 1998

"As far as the people running organized religion are concerned, would you say you have a great deal of confidence, only some confidence, or hardly any confidence at all in them?"

(percent of people aged 18 or older responding by sex, race, age, and education, 1998)

	a great deal	only some	hardly any
Total	**27%**	**51%**	**19%**
Men	25	52	20
Women	29	51	18
Black	28	52	17
White	27	50	19
Other	22	58	16
Aged 18 to 29	23	53	21
Aged 30 to 39	24	52	20
Aged 40 to 49	22	55	21
Aged 50 to 59	25	56	17
Aged 60 to 69	31	50	15
Aged 70 or older	46	35	15
Not a high school graduate	36	38	19
High school graduate	24	54	19
Bachelor's degree	25	57	16
Graduate degree	26	59	15

Note: Numbers may not add to 100 because "don't know" is not shown.
Source: General Social Survey, National Opinion Research Center, University of Chicago; calculations by the author

Confidence in the Leaders of Organized Religion, 1978 to 1998

"As far as the people running organized religion are concerned, would you say you have a great deal of confidence, only some confidence, or hardly any confidence at all in them?"

(percent of people aged 18 or older responding by sex, race, age, and education, 1978–98)

	a great deal			only some			hardly any		
	1998	1988	1978	1998	1988	1978	1998	1988	1978
Total	**27%**	**20%**	**31%**	**51%**	**46%**	**47%**	**19%**	**31%**	**18%**
Men	25	20	30	52	41	48	20	35	19
Women	29	20	31	51	50	47	18	28	17
Black	28	27	30	52	48	48	17	22	18
White	27	19	34	50	46	46	19	33	17
Aged 18 to 29	23	23	25	53	45	53	21	32	20
Aged 30 to 39	24	17	25	52	52	50	20	30	22
Aged 40 to 49	22	15	35	55	49	45	21	34	16
Aged 50 to 59	25	17	37	56	53	46	17	23	14
Aged 60 to 69	31	22	32	50	38	46	15	35	17
Aged 70 or older	46	26	39	35	40	35	15	30	15
Not a high school graduate	36	23	35	38	43	38	19	29	19
High school graduate	24	21	30	54	46	51	19	31	17
Bachelor's degree	25	14	23	57	50	55	16	34	21
Graduate degree	26	16	34	59	51	50	15	33	15

Note: Numbers may not add to 100 because "don't know" is not shown.
Source: General Social Survey, National Opinion Research Center, University of Chicago; calculations by the author

Religious Leaders' Political Influence

Most people think religion and politics should not mix.

Most Americans believe in the separation of church and state. Sixty-five percent agree that religious leaders should not try to influence votes, and 58 percent say they should not try to influence government decisions. A substantial percentage of Americans agree strongly with both statements.

Although women tend to be more religious than men, they also are more likely to believe religious leaders should not influence elections or government decisions. While similar percentages of people of difference races believe religious leaders should not try to influence elections, they disagree on whether or not religious leaders should be involved in government decisions. Only 46 percent of blacks say religious leaders should stay out of government decisions compared with 59 percent of whites and 66 percent of "other" races.

Older generations are more likely to think religious leaders should not influence the vote or the government, while younger people are more likely to say they neither agree nor disagree.

Should Religious Leaders Influence Elections? 1998

"Religious leaders should not try to influence how people vote in elections. Do you agree or disagree?"

(percent of people aged 18 or older responding by sex, race, age, and education, 1998)

	strongly agree	agree	neither	disagree	strongly disagree	agree, total	disagree, total
Total	36%	29%	17%	12%	4%	65%	16%
Men	34	27	20	13	6	61	19
Women	37	32	14	11	3	69	14
Black	23	37	17	15	4	60	19
White	38	28	17	12	4	66	16
Other	37	29	13	11	9	66	20
Aged 18 to 29	34	25	20	14	3	59	17
Aged 30 to 39	34	30	19	12	4	64	16
Aged 40 to 49	33	28	18	15	5	61	20
Aged 50 to 59	35	35	14	9	5	70	14
Aged 60 to 69	48	28	12	6	6	76	12
Aged 70 or older	39	31	11	11	7	70	18
Not a high school graduate	28	33	14	11	7	61	18
High school graduate	40	30	16	10	4	70	14
Bachelor's degree	34	24	20	17	4	58	21
Graduate degree	32	24	22	20	2	56	22

Note: Numbers may not add to 100 because "don't know" is not shown.
Source: General Social Survey, National Opinion Research Center, University of Chicago; calculations by the author

Should Religious Leaders Influence Government? 1998

"Religious leaders should not try to influence government decisions. Do you agree or disagree?"

(percent of people aged 18 or older responding by sex, race, age, and education, 1998)

	strongly agree	agree	neither	disagree	strongly disagree	agree, total	disagree, total
Total	**29%**	**29%**	**18%**	**16%**	**5%**	**58%**	**21%**
Men	28	26	20	17	6	54	23
Women	31	31	16	15	5	62	20
Black	16	30	24	20	5	46	25
White	31	28	17	16	5	59	21
Other	32	34	15	9	8	66	17
Aged 18 to 29	30	22	22	15	5	52	20
Aged 30 to 39	27	31	19	16	5	58	21
Aged 40 to 49	26	28	18	19	6	54	25
Aged 50 to 59	30	31	18	12	8	61	20
Aged 60 to 69	37	26	16	13	5	63	18
Aged 70 or older	33	33	10	17	5	66	22
Not a high school graduate	23	33	15	13	7	56	20
High school graduate	32	30	18	14	5	62	19
Bachelor's degree	28	21	21	22	7	49	29
Graduate degree	27	25	20	21	6	52	27

Note: Numbers may not add to 100 because "don't know" is not shown.
Source: General Social Survey, National Opinion Research Center, University of Chicago; calculations by the author

Do Churches Have Too Much Power?

Most Americans think religious organizations have the right amount of power.

Nearly half of Americans (48 percent) say churches and religious organizations have about the right amount of power in this country. The proportions of those who say they have too much power and those who say they have too little power are about the same (20 versus 19 percent).

One-third of blacks, however, say churches and religious organizations have too little power, compared with only 17 percent of whites and 19 percent of "other" races. Only 11 percent of blacks believe churches are too powerful compared with 22 percent of whites and 27 percent of other races.

Adults under age 30 and people in their forties are slightly more likely than other age groups to believe churches and religious organizations have too much power. People with a graduate degree are also more likely to believe churches are too powerful (27 percent compared with 18 to 21 percent of people with less education).

Do Churches Have Too Much Power? 1998

"Do you think that churches and religious organizations in this country have too much power or too little power?"

(percent of people aged 18 or older responding by sex, race, age, and education, 1998)

	far too much	too much	about right	too little	far too little	don't know	too much, total	too little, total
Total	5%	15%	48%	15%	4%	13%	20%	19%
Men	6	15	50	12	4	12	21	16
Women	5	15	46	17	4	13	20	21
Black	4	7	44	25	7	14	11	32
White	6	16	49	13	4	12	22	17
Other	8	19	40	17	2	13	27	19
Aged 18 to 29	7	17	45	15	4	12	24	19
Aged 30 to 39	5	15	51	14	4	12	20	18
Aged 40 to 49	4	19	44	16	4	13	23	20
Aged 50 to 59	6	11	52	14	5	11	17	19
Aged 60 to 69	8	13	49	14	3	13	21	17
Aged 70 or older	4	12	48	15	4	18	16	19
Not a high school graduate	5	13	40	15	5	22	18	20
High school graduate	6	14	47	16	4	13	20	20
Bachelor's degree	6	15	54	14	4	10	21	18
Graduate degree	3	24	57	8	2	5	27	10

Note: Numbers may not add to 100 because "don't know" is not shown.
Source: General Social Survey, National Opinion Research Center, University of Chicago; calculations by the author

Do Religions Bring More Conflict Than Peace?

More people disagree than agree.

A plurality of Americans (42 percent) say they do not believe religion brings more conflict than peace in the world. But one-third say they believe the opposite is true.

Only 30 percent of women believe religion is more likely to bring conflict than peace compared with 39 percent of men. People aged 70 or older are more likely than younger generations to believe religion brings more conflict, while adults under age 30 are more likely to say they neither agree nor disagree.

Forty-six percent of people with a graduate degree think religion brings more conflict than peace, as do 36 percent of people who did not complete high school and 38 percent of those with a bachelor's degree. A smaller 31 percent of high school graduates agree.

Blacks are considerably less likely than whites or people of "other" race to agree that religion brings more conflict than peace. Only 28 percent of blacks agree with the statement compared with 35 percent of whites and 40 percent of others.

Do Religions Bring More Conflict than Peace? 1998

"Do you agree or disagree with the following statement? Looking around the world, religions bring more conflict than peace."

(percent of people aged 18 or older responding by sex, race, age, and education, 1998)

	strongly agree	agree	neither	strongly disagree	disagree	can't choose	agree, total	disagree, total
Total	**8%**	**26%**	**21%**	**33%**	**9%**	**3%**	**34%**	**42%**
Men	10	29	20	31	6	3	39	37
Women	6	24	21	34	11	3	30	45
Black	8	20	16	38	17	1	28	55
White	8	27	22	32	8	3	35	40
Other	9	31	13	32	10	4	40	42
Aged 18 to 29	5	28	27	28	8	4	33	36
Aged 30 to 39	11	22	23	35	9	1	33	44
Aged 40 to 49	8	26	18	36	10	2	34	46
Aged 50 to 59	9	28	18	33	9	3	37	42
Aged 60 to 69	9	20	23	31	13	3	29	44
Aged 70 or older	8	34	12	31	9	6	42	40
Not a high school graduate	7	29	21	28	9	7	36	37
High school graduate	8	23	23	34	9	2	31	43
Bachelor's degree	11	27	17	31	10	3	38	41
Graduate degree	12	34	16	32	7	0	46	39

Source: General Social Survey, National Opinion Research Center, University of Chicago; calculations by the author

Religious Intolerance

A plurality of Americans say religious people are often too intolerant.

Nearly half of Americans (47 percent) feel that people with strong religious beliefs are often too intolerant of other people. Only 27 percent disagree. The differences of opinion on this issue by demographic characteristic follow the pattern set by other religious issues. The demographic segments that hold strong religious beliefs are less likely to believe that religious people are intolerant. For example, women tend to be more religious than men, and they are less likely to believe the very religious are often intolerant (43 percent of women compared with 52 percent of men).

College graduates are also more likely to believe the very religious are often too intolerant. Only 40 to 44 percent of people with a high school diploma or less education hold this belief, but the figure rises to 56 percent among people with a bachelor's degree and to 60 percent among those with a graduate degree. One-quarter of those with the highest educational level agree strongly that religious people are often too intolerant.

Whites and blacks are less likely than people of "other" race to agree that people with strong religious beliefs are often too intolerant. Fifty-eight percent of others say religious people are often too intolerant compared with 48 percent of whites and only 33 percent of blacks. Many of those who identify as "other race" are Hispanic and are less likely than blacks or whites to be Protestant, the dominant religious group in the U.S. This difference may contribute to their concern about religious intolerance.

Religious Intolerance, 1998

"Do you agree or disagree with the following statement? People with very strong religious beliefs are often too intolerant of others."

(percent of people aged 18 or older responding by sex, race, age, and education, 1998)

	strongly agree	agree	neither	strongly disagree	disagree	can't choose	agree, total	disagree, total
Total	**12%**	**35%**	**22%**	**22%**	**5%**	**4%**	**47%**	**27%**
Men	15	37	21	20	4	4	52	24
Women	10	33	23	23	6	4	43	29
Black	8	25	25	27	8	7	33	35
White	13	35	21	22	5	4	48	27
Other	12	46	24	10	3	4	58	13
Aged 18 to 29	13	34	27	16	4	7	47	20
Aged 30 to 39	12	33	22	25	5	3	45	30
Aged 40 to 49	11	36	21	23	5	3	47	28
Aged 50 to 59	10	39	21	21	6	3	49	27
Aged 60 to 69	11	36	14	24	8	7	47	32
Aged 70 or older	15	33	20	21	6	5	48	27
Not a high school graduate	10	30	23	19	6	11	40	25
High school graduate	10	34	25	23	5	3	44	28
Bachelor's degree	15	41	14	20	6	3	56	26
Graduate degree	24	36	15	22	2	1	60	24

Source: General Social Survey, National Opinion Research Center, University of Chicago; calculations by the author

One Truth or Many Truths?

Most people believe truth can be found in many religions.

A solid majority of Americans (72 percent) believe there are basic truths in many religions. Only 10 percent believe truth can be found in only one religion. Fourteen percent are uncertain.

Whites are more likely than blacks and "other" races to believe truth can be found in many religions. Three-quarters of whites agree with this sentiment compared with 58 percent of blacks and 55 percent of other races. One-quarter of blacks and others are undecided.

The greatest difference of opinion is by education. Barely half of people who did not complete high school believe there are truths in many religions compared with 73 percent of high school graduates and more than 80 percent of college graduates. Sixteen percent of people without a high school diploma believe truth can be found in only one religion, but the proportion drops to 11 percent among high school graduates, 8 percent among people with a bachelor's degree, and 4 percent among those with a graduate degree.

One Truth or Many Truths? 1998

"Which of the following statements comes closest to your own views?
There is very little truth in any religion.
There are basic truths in many religions.
There is truth in one religion."

(percent of people aged 18 or older responding by sex, race, age, and education, 1998)

	little truth in any religion	truths in many religions	truth in only one religion	can't choose
Total	**3%**	**72%**	**10%**	**14%**
Men	4	71	9	16
Women	3	73	11	13
Black	3	58	15	25
White	3	76	9	12
Other	8	55	11	26
Aged 18 to 29	4	64	11	21
Aged 30 to 39	4	71	12	13
Aged 40 to 49	3	75	9	13
Aged 50 to 59	2	76	10	12
Aged 60 to 69	3	78	9	9
Aged 70 or older	2	73	9	15
Not a high school graduate	6	52	16	26
High school graduate	2	73	11	14
Bachelor's degree	3	80	8	9
Graduate degree	5	82	4	8

Source: General Social Survey, National Opinion Research Center, University of Chicago; calculations by the author

Science versus Religion

Education sharply divides Americans on this issue.

Only 30 percent of Americans agree that we trust too much in science and not enough in religious faith. Forty percent disagree. But there is substantial disagreement on this question within every demographic segment.

Not surprisingly, the sharpest disagreement is by education. People with higher levels of education, who are more likely to have studied the sciences and to be employed in fields requiring scientific expertise, are more likely to trust in science. Fully two-thirds of people with a graduate degree do not believe we trust too much in science and not enough in faith, as do more than half of those with a bachelor's degree. The proportion falls to 37 percent among high school graduates and to only 22 percent among those without a high school diploma. Fewer than 10 percent of those with no more than a high school education disagree, but this share rises to 34 percent among people with a graduate degree.

People aged 70 or older are considerably more likely than younger age groups to believe we favor science over faith too much. There is also a solid racial divide on the question, with more than half of blacks agreeing compared with 26 percent of whites and 35 percent of people of "other" race.

Science versus Religion, 1998

"We trust too much in science and not enough in religious faith—do you agree or disagree?"

(percent of people aged 18 or older responding by sex, race, age, and education, 1998)

	strongly agree	agree	neither	strongly disagree	disagree	can't choose	agree, total	disagree, total
Total	**8%**	**22%**	**26%**	**28%**	**12%**	**3%**	**30%**	**40%**
Men	8	20	26	28	16	3	28	44
Women	9	23	27	28	9	4	32	37
Black	17	35	21	15	6	6	52	21
White	7	19	28	30	14	3	26	44
Other	12	23	22	31	10	1	35	41
Aged 18 to 29	8	20	29	24	16	4	28	40
Aged 30 to 39	7	17	29	32	13	2	24	45
Aged 40 to 49	10	23	22	32	11	2	33	43
Aged 50 to 59	5	25	27	28	12	3	30	40
Aged 60 to 69	12	19	28	30	8	4	31	38
Aged 70 or older	12	29	23	16	12	8	41	28
Not a high school graduate	16	27	26	15	7	9	43	22
High school graduate	9	23	29	28	9	3	32	37
Bachelor's degree	4	18	24	33	20	1	22	53
Graduate degree	2	8	22	33	34	1	10	67

Source: General Social Survey, National Opinion Research Center, University of Chicago; calculations by the author

School Prayer

Support for school prayer is falling.

As the nation becomes more religiously diverse, support for the Supreme Court decision that prohibited the reading of the Lord's Prayer and Bible verses in public schools is growing. In 1977, only one-third of Americans approved of the ruling. By 1998, 43 percent believed it was the right decision.

The majority (53 percent) still disapprove of the ruling, however. Two-thirds of blacks disapprove compared with 51 percent of whites and 48 percent of "other" races. The percentage of blacks saying they disapprove is down from 79 percent in 1977, while the proportion of whites who disapprove has fallen from 63 percent.

Younger generations are considerably more likely to approve of the Court's ruling than older people. Only 29 percent of people aged 70 or older agree with the ruling, but the figure stands at 54 percent among adults under age 30. Not coincidentally, younger generations are also more religiously diverse.

Support for the Court's ruling is strongest among the best-educated Americans. Sixty-four percent of people with a graduate degree and 57 percent of those with a bachelor's degree agree that prayers and Bible verses don't belong in public school. In contrast, only 39 percent of those with only a high school diploma and 26 percent of those who did not complete high school agree.

School Prayer, 1998

"The United States Supreme Court has ruled that no state or local government may require the reading of the Lord's Prayer or Bible verses in public schools. Do you approve or disapprove of the court ruling?"

(percent of people aged 18 or older responding by sex, race, age, and education, 1998)

	approve	disapprove	don't know
Total	**43%**	**53%**	**5%**
Men	45	50	5
Women	41	55	4
Black	30	67	4
White	45	51	4
Other	43	48	9
Aged 18 to 29	54	40	7
Aged 30 to 39	49	48	3
Aged 40 to 49	42	54	3
Aged 50 to 59	35	58	7
Aged 60 to 69	33	64	3
Aged 70 or older	29	65	5
Not a high school graduate	26	69	5
High school graduate	39	56	5
Bachelor's degree	57	39	4
Graduate degree	64	32	4

Note: Numbers may not add to 100 because "don't know" is not shown.
Source: General Social Survey, National Opinion Research Center, University of Chicago; calculations by the author

School Prayer, 1977 to 1998

"The United States Supreme Court has ruled that no state or local government may require the reading of the Lord's Prayer or Bible verses in public schools. Do you approve or disapprove of the court ruling?"

(percent of people aged 18 or older responding by sex, race, age, and education, 1977–98)

	approve			disapprove			don't know		
	1998	*1988*	*1977*	*1998*	*1988*	*1977*	*1998*	*1988*	*1977*
Total	**43%**	**37%**	**33%**	**53%**	**59%**	**64%**	**5%**	**4%**	**2%**
Men	45	40	35	50	56	63	5	4	2
Women	41	35	32	55	61	65	4	3	2
Black	30	34	20	67	62	79	4	3	1
White	45	38	35	51	58	63	4	4	2
Aged 18 to 29	54	48	51	40	49	47	7	4	2
Aged 30 to 39	49	44	36	48	51	62	3	4	1
Aged 40 to 49	42	37	25	54	61	72	3	2	2
Aged 50 to 59	35	32	27	58	64	70	7	3	3
Aged 60 to 69	33	29	24	64	65	74	3	6	2
Aged 70 or older	29	20	21	65	76	73	5	4	5
Not a high school graduate	26	27	26	69	70	72	5	2	2
High school graduate	39	35	34	56	60	64	5	5	1
Bachelor's degree	57	52	46	39	44	50	4	4	4
Graduate degree	64	65	50	32	34	45	4	2	5

Source: General Social Survey, National Opinion Research Center, University of Chicago; calculations by the author

Commercial Use of Religious Images

Americans wholeheartedly disapprove of religious images in advertising.

With almost every area of life now commercialized, Americans want some ground to remain sacred. Sixty-five percent oppose the use of religious images to sell commercial products. Forty-three percent strongly oppose the practice. Only 8 percent approve.

The level of opposition varies by race. Two-thirds of whites oppose the use of religious images in advertising, compared with 59 percent of blacks and 56 percent of "other" races. Forty-four percent of whites are strongly opposed compared with 40 percent of blacks and 38 percent of other races.

Younger generations have grown up in a more ad-soaked culture, which is one reason for the generational difference of opinion on this question. The older people are, the more troubled they are by the use of religious images in ads. While 53 percent of adults under age 30 oppose it, fully 76 percent of those aged 70 or older do. Only 34 percent of adults under age 30 are strongly opposed, but the proportion rises to more than half among people aged 60 or older.

Commercial Use of Religious Images, 1998

"Do you strongly approve of, somewhat approve of, neither approve of nor oppose, somewhat oppose, or strongly oppose the following public expression of religion: The use of religious images in public advertising to sell nonreligious commercial products?"

(percent of people aged 18 or older responding by sex, race, age, and education, 1998)

	strongly approve	somewhat approve	neither	somewhat oppose	strongly oppose	approve, total	oppose, total
Total	2%	6%	22%	22%	43%	8%	65%
Men	2	6	25	20	42	8	62
Women	3	5	20	24	44	8	68
Black	4	7	25	19	40	11	59
White	2	5	22	23	44	7	67
Other	4	9	25	18	38	13	56
Aged 18 to 29	3	7	31	19	34	10	53
Aged 30 to 39	2	6	25	24	38	8	62
Aged 40 to 49	3	3	20	21	47	6	68
Aged 50 to 59	2	7	19	23	44	9	67
Aged 60 to 69	1	5	17	19	53	6	72
Aged 70 or older	3	3	13	25	51	6	76
Not a high school graduate	2	7	21	22	39	9	61
High school graduate	2	5	22	22	45	7	67
Bachelor's degree	3	6	27	21	40	9	61
Graduate degree	1	2	24	25	44	3	69

Note: Numbers may not add to 100 because "don't know" is not shown.
Source: General Social Survey, National Opinion Research Center, University of Chicago; calculations by the author

Athletes' Public Expression of Religion

Most people say it is okay for athletes to thank God during sports events.

Americans do not want religious images used in advertising and would prefer that religious leaders not influence elections or government, but this doesn't mean religious expression has no place in the public arena. Most people approve at least somewhat of professional athletes giving thanks to God during sporting events. Only 11 percent are opposed to this practice, and one-quarter say they neither approve nor oppose it.

Blacks are considerably more likely than whites and "other" races to approve of athletes making a public expression of religion. Seventy-two percent of blacks say they approve (49 percent strongly approve) compared with 59 to 58 percent of whites and other races.

The share of adults who say they approve of athletes publicly thanking God drops with rising educational levels. While 63 to 67 percent of people with a high school diploma or less say they approve, a smaller 52 percent of people with a bachelor's degree and only 41 percent of those with a graduate degree agree. The college educated are slightly more likely to say they are opposed to the practice and are far more likely to say they neither approve of nor oppose the public expression of religion by athletes.

Athletes' Public Expression of Religion, 1998

"Do you strongly approve of, somewhat approve of, neither approve of nor oppose,
somewhat oppose, or strongly oppose the following public expression of religion:
Pro-athletes giving thanks to God during sports events?"

(percent of people aged 18 or older responding by sex, race, age, and education, 1998)

	strongly approve	somewhat approve	neither	somewhat oppose	strongly oppose	approve, total	oppose, total
Total	**36%**	**25%**	**25%**	**6%**	**5%**	**61%**	**11%**
Men	33	27	25	6	6	60	12
Women	38	23	25	7	4	61	11
Black	49	23	20	2	3	72	5
White	33	26	26	7	5	59	12
Other	40	18	19	7	9	58	16
Aged 18 to 29	37	23	29	5	4	60	9
Aged 30 to 39	37	27	25	5	5	64	10
Aged 40 to 49	38	24	24	6	6	62	12
Aged 50 to 59	36	23	25	6	7	59	13
Aged 60 to 69	30	26	26	9	8	56	17
Aged 70 or older	31	27	22	9	5	58	14
Not a high school graduate	41	26	16	5	5	67	10
High school graduate	38	25	25	5	5	63	10
Bachelor's degree	30	22	32	8	6	52	14
Graduate degree	19	22	36	11	7	41	18

Note: Numbers may not add to 100 because "don't know" is not shown.
Source: General Social Survey, National Opinion Research Center, University of Chicago; calculations by the author

7

Sexual Attitudes and Behavior

The sexual mores of Americans have changed dramatically over the past 20 years. The public has grown more accepting of premarital sex, more tolerant of homosexual sex, and more supportive of sex education in the schools. But Americans have not become more permissive on all sexual issues. Most people think adultery is always wrong. Seven out of ten do not think teens should be having sex, although more than half would make birth control available to teens.

Conventional wisdom says men are more libertine than woman, and the attitudes examined here largely support that view. Women are more likely than men to believe it is always wrong for teens to have sex, and they are more likely to want pornography outlawed entirely. Men are far more likely to say there is nothing wrong with premarital sex. They are also more likely than women to have committed adultery and to have exchanged money for sex.

Blacks are more conservative than whites and "other" races about some sexual issues. They are most likely to say homosexual sex and premarital sex are always wrong. Whites are more likely to say pornography should be outlawed entirely, while blacks and other races are more likely to favor restricting its distribution to adults.

The generations differ strongly in their opinions about many sexual issues. They are worlds apart on the issue of homosexual sex, with only 40 percent of the youngest adults, but three-quarters of the oldest, saying it is always wrong. Younger generations are far more likely to see nothing wrong with premarital sex, and they are less likely to believe it is always wrong for teens to have sex. While most people aged 60 or older would outlaw pornography entirely, younger people are far more likely to favor simply restricting it to adults.

The attitudes of college graduates resemble those of younger generations. This similarity is due, in part, to the fact that younger people are overrepresented among college graduates while older generations make up a larger share of the less educated. The percentage of people saying homosexual and premarital sex are always wrong declines with education. College graduates are more likely to favor restricting pornography to adults while those with a high school diploma or less education are more likely to want it outlawed entirely. Most people, regardless of education, believe both adultery and sex between teens are always wrong. But college graduates are less absolute on these issues; a significant share thinks they are almost always wrong rather than always wrong.

Sex Education

The overwhelming majority favors sex education in the public schools.

For a topic that ignites so much controversy, Americans are remarkably united in their opinion about sex education—85 percent favor sex education in the public schools. And, unlike so many of the hot-button issues confronting the nation today, men and women and blacks and whites are in agreement on this topic. Support for sex education in the schools was higher in 1998 than in 1977.

This is not to say there are no dissenters. By age and education, there are differences of opinion on whether schools are the proper arena for teaching young people about sex. The percentage of people who support sex education falls substantially among older Americans. Ninety-three percent of people under age 30 support sex education, as do 87 to 89 percent of those aged 30 to 59. A smaller 77 percent of people in their sixties agree. Least likely to support sex education are those aged 70 or older—only 63 percent favor it.

People who did not complete high school are less likely than those with more education to support sex education. While 87 to 88 percent of people with at least a high school diploma favor sex education, only 73 percent of those who did not complete high school agree.

Sex Education, 1998

"Would you be for or against sex education in the public schools?"

(percent of people aged 18 or older responding by sex, race, age, and education, 1998)

	for	against	don't know
Total	**85%**	**13%**	**2%**
Men	85	13	2
Women	85	13	2
Black	85	13	2
White	85	12	2
Other	83	16	2
Aged 18 to 29	93	6	1
Aged 30 to 39	89	9	1
Aged 40 to 49	87	11	2
Aged 50 to 59	88	10	1
Aged 60 to 69	77	18	5
Aged 70 or older	63	32	5
Not a high school graduate	73	23	4
High school graduate	87	11	2
Bachelor's degree	88	11	1
Graduate degree	87	11	1

Source: General Social Survey, National Opinion Research Center, University of Chicago; calculations by the author

Sex Education, 1977 to 1998

"Would you be for or against sex education in the public schools?"

(percent of people aged 18 or older responding by sex, race, age, and education, 1977–98)

	for			against			don't know		
	1998	1988	1977	1998	1988	1977	1998	1988	1977
Total	**85%**	**85%**	**77%**	**13%**	**13%**	**21%**	**2%**	**3%**	**2%**
Men	85	87	77	13	11	21	2	2	2
Women	85	83	77	13	14	20	2	3	3
Black	85	86	74	13	14	25	2	0	2
White	85	85	77	12	12	21	2	3	2
Aged 18 to 29	93	94	89	6	5	10	1	2	1
Aged 30 to 39	89	92	84	9	7	14	1	0	1
Aged 40 to 49	87	85	75	11	13	21	2	2	4
Aged 50 to 59	88	81	79	10	18	18	1	1	3
Aged 60 to 69	77	79	62	18	14	36	5	7	2
Aged 70 or older	63	64	49	32	29	47	5	7	4
Not a high school graduate	73	70	61	23	26	36	4	4	3
High school graduate	87	88	84	11	9	14	2	3	2
Bachelor's degree	88	92	90	11	7	9	1	1	1
Graduate degree	87	94	92	11	6	8	1	0	0

Source: General Social Survey, National Opinion Research Center, University of Chicago; calculations by the author

Teens and Sex

Most people disapprove of teens having sex before marriage.

Americans are far more accepting of premarital sex than they used to be, but sex between teens has not gained acceptance. Seventy-one percent of adults say it is always wrong for teens aged 14 to 16 to have premarital sex. Another 16 percent say it is almost always wrong. Only 3 percent say it is not wrong at all.

Women are more likely than men to say it is always wrong for teens to have sex (75 versus 65 percent). A larger proportion of blacks (73 percent) than whites (68 percent) and "other" races (68 percent) say it is always wrong. Blacks were more likely to feel this way in 1998 than in 1988.

There is a big difference of opinion by age. Adults closest to their teens, 18-to-29-year-olds, are least likely to say it is always wrong for teens to have sex before marriage (57 percent). The proportion of people saying it is always wrong is highest among Americans aged 60 or older (83 to 85 percent).

The percentage of those who say it is always wrong for teens to have sex declines with education. Among people who did not complete high school, 80 percent believe it is always wrong. The figure falls to 56 percent among people with a graduate degree.

Teens and Sex, 1998

"What about sexual relations before marriage between people in their early teens, say 14 to 16 years old? Is it always wrong, almost always wrong, wrong only sometimes, or not wrong at all?"

(percent of people aged 18 or older responding by sex, race, age, and education, 1998)

	always wrong	*almost always wrong*	*wrong only sometimes*	*not wrong at all*
Total	**71%**	**16%**	**8%**	**3%**
Men	65	17	11	5
Women	75	15	7	2
Black	73	16	7	3
White	70	16	9	3
Other	68	18	9	4
Aged 18 to 29	57	22	14	5
Aged 30 to 39	68	17	10	4
Aged 40 to 49	69	18	8	3
Aged 50 to 59	75	11	6	4
Aged 60 to 69	85	13	3	0
Aged 70 or older	83	10	5	0
Not a high school graduate	80	9	8	2
High school graduate	71	15	9	3
Bachelor's degree	67	19	7	6
Graduate degree	56	26	11	3

Note: Numbers may not add to 100 because "don't know" is not shown.
Source: General Social Survey, National Opinion Research Center, University of Chicago; calculations by the author

Teens and Sex, 1988 to 1998

"What about sexual relations before marriage between people in their early teens, say 14 to 16 years old? Is it always wrong, almost always wrong, wrong only sometimes, or not wrong at all?"

(percent of people aged 18 or older responding by sex, race, age, and education, 1988–98)

	always wrong		almost always wrong		wrong only sometimes		not wrong at all	
	1998	*1988*	*1998*	*1988*	*1998*	*1988*	*1998*	*1988*
Total	**71%**	**69%**	**16%**	**16%**	**8%**	**11%**	**3%**	**3%**
Men	65	63	17	19	11	12	5	5
Women	75	73	15	14	7	10	2	2
Black	73	68	16	9	7	13	3	7
White	70	69	16	17	9	11	3	3
Aged 18 to 29	57	52	22	21	14	23	5	3
Aged 30 to 39	68	62	17	21	10	10	4	5
Aged 40 to 49	69	71	18	16	8	8	3	5
Aged 50 to 59	75	81	11	11	6	4	4	2
Aged 60 to 69	85	81	13	13	3	4	0	1
Aged 70 or older	83	85	10	5	5	6	0	2
Not a high school graduate	80	76	9	7	8	12	2	3
High school graduate	71	68	15	18	9	10	3	3
Bachelor's degree	67	65	19	19	7	11	6	5
Graduate degree	56	53	26	32	11	10	3	5

Note: Numbers may not add to 100 because "don't know" is not shown.
Source: General Social Survey, National Opinion Research Center, University of Chicago; calculations by the author

Birth Control for Teens

Most Americans don't want teenage girls to get pregnant.

Most people do not believe teens should be sexually active, but they feel even more strongly about young girls getting pregnant. More than half of Americans (56 percent) agree that birth control should be available to teenagers aged 14 to 16 even if their parents do not approve. More than one-quarter strongly agree, but a substantial minority (40 percent) disagree.

Women and men are equally likely to support making birth control available to teens. There is no real disagreement by race, either, but the generations are sharply divided on this issue. Fully 73 percent of adults under age 30 think teens should have access to birth control, as do 60 percent of people in their thirties and forties. The proportion drops to barely half among people in their fifties, however. The majority of people aged 60 or older think teens should not have access to birth control. Only 35 to 39 percent of older Americans think they should.

There is a small difference of opinion by education. Just 51 percent of people who did not complete high school think teens should have access to birth control. The proportion rises to 63 percent among people with a graduate degree.

Birth Control for Teens, 1998

"Do you strongly agree, agree, disagree, or strongly disagree that methods of birth control should be available to teenagers between the ages of 14 and 16 if their parents do not approve?"

(percent of people aged 18 or older responding by sex, race, age, and education, 1998)

	strongly agree	agree	disagree	strongly disagree	don't know	agree, total	disagree, total
Total	**26%**	**30%**	**20%**	**20%**	**4%**	**56%**	**40%**
Men	25	31	21	20	3	56	41
Women	27	29	20	21	4	56	41
Black	22	31	24	21	2	53	45
White	26	30	20	20	4	56	40
Other	30	27	20	20	2	57	40
Aged 18 to 29	36	37	14	12	1	73	26
Aged 30 to 39	30	30	19	18	3	60	37
Aged 40 to 49	29	31	16	20	4	60	36
Aged 50 to 59	24	27	24	20	5	51	44
Aged 60 to 69	13	26	27	31	3	39	58
Aged 70 or older	12	23	28	31	7	35	59
Not a high school graduate	24	27	23	20	5	51	43
High school graduate	24	30	21	21	3	54	42
Bachelor's degree	28	31	18	19	4	59	37
Graduate degree	38	25	17	16	5	63	33

Source: General Social Survey, National Opinion Research Center, University of Chicago; calculations by the author

Birth Control for Teens, 1988 and 1998

"Do you strongly agree, agree, disagree, or strongly disagree that methods of birth control should be available to teenagers between the ages of 14 and 16 if their parents do not approve?"

(percent of people aged 18 or older responding by sex, race, age, and education, 1988–98)

	agree/ strongly agree		disagree/ strongly disagree		don't know	
	1998	*1988*	*1998*	*1988*	*1998*	*1988*
Total	**56%**	**56%**	**40%**	**39%**	**4%**	**5%**
Men	56	59	41	36	3	5
Women	56	54	41	42	4	4
Black	53	61	45	38	2	2
White	56	55	40	40	4	5
Aged 18 to 29	73	71	26	27	1	2
Aged 30 to 39	60	61	37	38	3	1
Aged 40 to 49	60	51	36	44	4	5
Aged 50 to 59	51	48	44	48	5	4
Aged 60 to 69	39	48	58	45	3	7
Aged 70 or older	35	41	59	49	7	10
Not a high school graduate	51	46	43	48	5	7
High school graduate	54	57	42	39	3	4
Bachelor's degree	59	60	37	35	4	5
Graduate degree	63	76	33	19	5	5

Source: General Social Survey, National Opinion Research Center, University of Chicago; calculations by the author

Premarital Sex

Fewer than one-quarter of Americans think premarital sex is always wrong.

Since the sexual revolution of the 1960s, attitudes about sex have changed. The plurality of Americans (42 percent) now say there is nothing wrong with sex before marriage. Only one-quarter believe premarital sex is always wrong. In 1978, Americans were more divided on this issue, as 29 percent said premarital sex was always wrong and 38 percent said it was not wrong at all.

Men and women don't entirely agree on this issue. Both sexes were more likely in 1998 than in 1978 to think premarital sex is okay, but women are still less accepting than men. While nearly half of men think it's not wrong, only 36 percent of women agree.

Age is a strong predictor of attitudes about premarital sex. About half of people under age 50 say there is nothing wrong with sex before marriage, but fewer than one-quarter of those aged 60 or older agree. Yet people under age 30 are less likely to agree that premarital sex is not wrong than they were in 1978. The proportion of people aged 30 to 69 who think it is not wrong rose during the period.

There are differences by education in attitudes about premarital sex. The less education people have the more likely they are to believe premarital sex is always wrong. Only 32 percent of people who did not complete high school think premarital sex is not wrong at all compared with 42 to 47 percent of people with more education.

Premarital Sex, 1998

"If a man and woman have sexual relations before marriage, do you think it is always wrong, almost always wrong, wrong only sometimes, or not wrong at all?"

(percent of people aged 18 or older responding by sex, race, age, and education, 1998)

	always wrong	almost always wrong	wrong only sometimes	not wrong at all
Total	**25%**	**9%**	**20%**	**42%**
Men	21	7	19	49
Women	29	10	21	36
Black	35	10	16	37
White	24	8	21	43
Other	21	15	19	41
Aged 18 to 29	18	7	23	50
Aged 30 to 39	21	8	19	49
Aged 40 to 49	23	7	17	51
Aged 50 to 59	27	6	22	39
Aged 60 to 69	32	17	23	24
Aged 70 or older	43	13	21	16
Not a high school graduate	32	11	20	32
High school graduate	27	8	19	42
Bachelor's degree	22	9	22	44
Graduate degree	15	7	27	47

Note: Numbers may not add to 100 because "don't know" is not shown.
Source: General Social Survey, National Opinion Research Center, University of Chicago; calculations by the author

Premarital Sex, 1978 to 1998

"If a man and woman have sexual relations before marriage, do you think it is always wrong, almost always wrong, wrong only sometimes, or not wrong at all?"

(percent of people aged 18 or older responding by sex, race, age, and education, 1978–98)

	always wrong			almost always wrong			wrong only sometimes			not wrong at all		
	1998	1988	1978	1998	1988	1978	1998	1988	1978	1998	1988	1978
Total	25%	26%	29%	9%	10%	11%	20%	22%	20%	42%	40%	38%
Men	21	23	22	7	8	12	19	20	20	49	46	44
Women	29	28	33	10	12	11	21	23	20	36	34	33
Black	35	23	22	10	7	9	16	18	9	37	49	58
White	24	26	30	8	11	12	21	22	21	43	38	35
Aged 18 to 29	18	18	12	7	8	6	23	23	20	50	49	59
Aged 30 to 39	21	15	23	8	4	9	19	27	23	49	53	45
Aged 40 to 49	23	21	30	7	14	16	17	21	19	51	42	32
Aged 50 to 59	27	30	40	6	12	15	22	21	20	39	33	23
Aged 60 to 69	32	34	36	17	14	16	23	21	20	24	23	23
Aged 70 or older	43	50	53	13	15	13	21	13	15	16	18	16
Not a high school graduate	32	37	39	11	11	11	20	16	15	32	34	31
High school graduate	27	23	26	8	11	11	19	23	21	42	40	40
Bachelor's degree	22	24	15	9	8	13	22	21	28	44	46	44
Graduate degree	15	11	16	7	11	16	27	35	24	47	39	44

Note: Numbers may not add to 100 because "don't know" is not shown.
Source: General Social Survey, National Opinion Research Center, University of Chicago; calculations by the author

Extramarital Sex

Americans are more likely now than they were 20 years ago to think extramarital sex is wrong.

On many issues, the sexual mores of Americans are more liberal today than they were a few decades ago. But on one issue, Americans are stricter than ever. They condemned extramarital sexual activity (adultery) more strongly in 1998 than in 1977. More than three-quarters of adults say extramarital sex is always wrong. Only 2 percent say it is not wrong.

Women are more likely than men to think adultery is always wrong (80 versus 75 percent). In 1977 the gap was slightly wider, with 76 percent of women and 68 percent of men saying extramarital sex is always wrong.

By age, there is less disagreement on this issue now than there was in 1977 when only 64 percent of people under age 40 thought adultery was always wrong compared with 90 percent of people aged 70 or older. Over the past two decades, the gap between older and younger adults has narrowed considerably. In 1998, fully 76 to 79 percent of people under age 60 believed extramarital sex to be wrong compared with a slightly larger 82 percent of older adults.

The largest difference of opinion is by education. While 80 to 82 percent of people with a high school diploma or less believe adultery is always wrong, a smaller 72 percent of people with a bachelor's degree agree. Least likely to feel extramarital sex is always wrong are people with a graduate degree, only 64 percent of whom hold this opinion. But another one-quarter of the most educated Americans think extramarital sex is almost always wrong.

Extramarital Sex, 1998

"What is your opinion about a married person having sexual relations with someone other than the marriage partner—is it always wrong, almost always wrong, wrong only sometimes, or not wrong at all?"

(percent of people aged 18 or older responding by sex, race, age, and education, 1998)

	always wrong	almost always wrong	wrong only sometimes	not wrong at all
Total	**78%**	**12%**	**6%**	**2%**
Men	75	13	7	3
Women	80	12	4	2
Black	75	13	6	4
White	79	12	6	2
Other	79	11	4	3
Aged 18 to 29	76	15	6	3
Aged 30 to 39	78	10	7	4
Aged 40 to 49	76	14	7	2
Aged 50 to 59	79	12	4	3
Aged 60 to 69	82	12	4	1
Aged 70 or older	82	10	5	1
Not a high school graduate	82	9	4	2
High school graduate	80	12	5	2
Bachelor's degree	72	14	8	2
Graduate degree	64	23	9	1

Note: Numbers may not add to 100 because "don't know" is not shown.
Source: General Social Survey, National Opinion Research Center, University of Chicago; calculations by the author

Extramarital Sex, 1977 to 1998

"What is your opinion about a married person having sexual relations with someone other than the marriage partner—is it always wrong, almost always wrong, wrong only sometimes, or not wrong at all?"

(percent of people aged 18 or older responding by sex, race, age, and education, 1977–98)

	always wrong			almost always wrong			only sometimes wrong			not wrong at all		
	1998	1988	1977	1998	1988	1977	1998	1988	1977	1998	1988	1977
Total	78%	78%	72%	12%	13%	14%	6%	6%	10%	2%	2%	3%
Men	75	73	68	13	15	15	7	7	13	3	4	4
Women	80	82	76	12	12	13	4	5	8	2	1	2
Black	75	74	63	13	15	10	6	8	18	4	2	7
White	79	79	74	12	13	14	6	5	9	2	2	3
Aged 18 to 29	76	79	64	15	12	19	6	5	13	3	2	4
Aged 30 to 39	78	68	64	10	20	15	7	9	16	4	2	5
Aged 40 to 49	76	77	72	14	11	14	7	7	10	2	4	3
Aged 50 to 59	79	82	75	12	12	13	4	3	7	3	0	3
Aged 60 to 69	82	83	85	12	11	8	4	4	5	1	2	1
Aged 70 or older	82	90	90	10	5	5	5	2	3	1	2	1
Not a high school graduate	82	87	81	9	5	8	4	3	7	2	3	3
High school graduate	80	82	72	12	12	15	5	4	9	2	1	3
Bachelor's degree	72	65	57	14	19	20	8	10	20	2	4	2
Graduate degree	64	49	55	23	32	19	9	17	18	1	0	7

Note: Numbers may not add to 100 because "don't know" is not shown.
Source: General Social Survey, National Opinion Research Center, University of Chicago; calculations by the author

Homosexual Sex

Attitudes about gays are changing.

A slight majority (54 percent) of Americans believe sex between two adults of the same gender is always wrong. But a growing minority says it is not wrong at all. In 1977, only 14 percent of adults said homosexual sex is not at all wrong, but a larger 27 percent felt this way in 1998.

Blacks are most likely to say homosexual sex is always wrong (65 percent compared with 53 percent of whites and 51 percent of "other" races). Within each racial group, the percentage of those who say homosexual sex is always wrong fell between 1977 and 1998.

Strong differences of opinion exist by age. Only 40 percent of people under age 30 believe homosexual sex is always wrong, while 41 percent say it is not wrong at all. Among people in their thirties, half say it is always wrong while 31 percent say it is not wrong. Among people aged 40 to 59, 52 to 55 percent say it is always wrong. The proportion of those who believe it is always wrong rises to 69 percent among people in their sixties and peaks at 75 percent among those aged 70 or older.

The percentage of people saying homosexual sex is always wrong falls sharply with education, while the proportion of those who say it is not at all wrong rises. Fully 74 percent of people who did not complete high school say homosexual sex is always wrong, but the figure drops to just 36 percent among people with a graduate degree. College graduates are most likely to say it is never wrong (37 to 39 percent compared with only 14 percent of those who did not complete high school).

Homosexual Sex, 1998

"What about sexual relations between two adults of the same sex—do you think it is always wrong, almost always wrong, wrong only sometimes, or not wrong at all?"

(percent of people aged 18 or older responding by sex, race, age, and education, 1998)

	always wrong	almost always wrong	wrong only sometimes	not wrong at all
Total	**54%**	**5%**	**6%**	**27%**
Men	57	6	7	25
Women	53	5	6	29
Black	65	6	5	17
White	53	5	7	29
Other	51	6	3	31
Aged 18 to 29	40	5	8	41
Aged 30 to 39	50	5	7	31
Aged 40 to 49	55	6	8	25
Aged 50 to 59	52	6	5	27
Aged 60 to 69	69	4	3	16
Aged 70 or older	75	5	4	12
Not a high school graduate	74	4	2	14
High school graduate	56	6	6	26
Bachelor's degree	41	5	10	37
Graduate degree	36	7	12	39

Note: Numbers may not add to 100 because "don't know" is not shown.
Source: General Social Survey, National Opinion Research Center, University of Chicago; calculations by the author

Homosexual Sex, 1977 to 1998

"What about sexual relations between two adults of the same sex—do you think it is always wrong, almost always wrong, wrong only sometimes, or not wrong at all?"

(percent of people aged 18 or older responding by sex, race, age, and education, 1977–98)

	always wrong			almost always wrong			only sometimes wrong			not wrong at all		
	1998	1988	1977	1998	1988	1977	1998	1988	1977	1998	1988	1977
Total	**54%**	**74%**	**69%**	**5%**	**5%**	**6%**	**6%**	**5%**	**7%**	**27%**	**12%**	**14%**
Men	57	76	67	6	4	6	7	5	7	25	12	16
Women	53	73	70	5	5	5	6	6	7	29	13	13
Black	65	88	73	6	2	6	5	2	5	17	7	12
White	53	72	68	5	5	6	7	6	8	29	14	14
Aged 18 to 29	40	68	57	5	5	8	8	8	10	41	14	23
Aged 30 to 39	50	68	64	5	5	3	7	5	9	31	19	19
Aged 40 to 49	55	71	70	6	5	8	8	8	9	25	12	9
Aged 50 to 59	52	80	74	6	3	5	5	2	5	27	9	11
Aged 60 to 69	69	78	78	4	3	5	3	5	4	16	10	9
Aged 70 or older	75	90	84	5	5	2	4	1	1	12	3	5
Not a high school graduate	74	86	81	4	3	4	2	3	4	14	4	7
High school graduate	56	78	67	6	5	5	6	4	8	26	10	16
Bachelor's degree	41	53	52	5	5	11	10	12	12	37	27	22
Graduate degree	36	49	34	7	5	14	12	12	14	39	29	30

Note: Numbers may not add to 100 because "don't know" is not included.
Source: General Social Survey, National Opinion Research Center, University of Chicago; calculations by the author

Pornography Laws

The generations disagree about legal restrictions on pornography.

The majority of Americans (57 percent) believe the best approach to pornography is simply to keep it out of the hands of children. Another 38 percent support outlawing it entirely. Support for laws against the distribution of pornography to minors has grown slightly since 1978. Few people support no restrictions on the distribution of pornography.

Women are far more likely than men to support making the distribution of pornography illegal (47 versus 27 percent). Men (who are the primary consumers of pornography) are more likely than women to say that only the distribution of pornography to minors should be illegal.

The proportion of people who would outlaw pornography entirely rises sharply with age, from 19 percent of people under age 30 to 64 percent of those aged 70 or older. Younger people are more likely to believe pornography should be restricted to adults rather than outlawed entirely.

By education, those with the least schooling are more supportive of laws making all pornography illegal. Forty-five percent of people who did not complete high school would outlaw it entirely. The proportion drops to 39 percent among high school graduates and to 30 percent among people with a bachelor's degree. However, it rises again among those with the most education—37 percent of people with a graduate degree would make it illegal to distribute pornography to anyone. The gap in attitudes by education was much wider in 1978 when 53 percent of people who did not complete high school favored outlawing pornography entirely compared with only 26 to 28 percent of college graduates.

Pornography Laws, 1998

**"Which of these statements comes closest to your feelings about pornography laws?
There should be laws against the distribution of pornography whatever the age.
There should be laws against the distribution of pornography to persons under 18.
There should be no laws forbidding the distribution of pornography."**

(percent of people aged 18 or older responding by sex, race, age, and education, 1998)

	illegal for all ages	illegal under age 18	legal
Total	**38%**	**57%**	**4%**
Men	27	67	5
Women	47	49	3
Black	33	61	4
White	39	56	4
Other	32	67	2
Aged 18 to 29	19	77	4
Aged 30 to 39	31	66	3
Aged 40 to 49	35	61	3
Aged 50 to 59	44	52	2
Aged 60 to 69	56	37	7
Aged 70 or older	64	28	6
Not a high school graduate	45	48	6
High school graduate	39	56	4
Bachelor's degree	30	67	2
Graduate degree	37	57	6

Note: Numbers may not add to 100 because "don't know" is not shown.
Source: General Social Survey, National Opinion Research Center, University of Chicago; calculations by the author

Pornography Laws, 1978 to 1998

**"Which of these statements comes closest to your feelings about pornography laws?
There should be laws against the distribution of pornography whatever the age.
There should be laws against the distribution of pornography to persons under 18.
There should be no laws forbidding the distribution of pornography."**

(percent of people aged 18 or older responding by sex, race, age, and education, 1978–98)

	illegal for all ages			illegal under age 18			legal		
	1998	*1988*	*1978*	*1998*	*1988*	*1978*	*1998*	*1988*	*1978*
Total	**38%**	**43%**	**43%**	**57%**	**50%**	**49%**	**4%**	**5%**	**7%**
Men	27	33	34	67	59	55	5	6	10
Women	47	51	50	49	43	44	3	4	5
Black	33	35	28	61	58	63	4	7	7
White	39	45	45	56	49	47	4	5	7
Aged 18 to 29	19	27	23	77	67	69	4	5	7
Aged 30 to 39	31	35	37	66	59	55	3	5	7
Aged 40 to 49	35	42	46	61	54	50	3	4	4
Aged 50 to 59	44	53	52	52	40	40	2	4	7
Aged 60 to 69	56	59	62	37	31	24	7	7	12
Aged 70 or older	64	61	67	28	29	23	6	4	7
Not a high school graduate	45	54	53	48	36	38	6	6	7
High school graduate	39	42	42	56	52	51	4	4	6
Bachelor's degree	30	39	28	67	55	63	2	5	9
Graduate degree	37	24	26	57	65	58	6	10	15

Note: Numbers may not add to 100 because "don't know" is not shown.
Source: General Social Survey, National Opinion Research Center, University of Chicago; calculations by the author

Ever Committed Adultery?

Men are more likely than women to say they have had extramarital sex.

Eighteen percent of Americans who are or have been married admit they have committed adultery. As is the case with all sensitive topics, the percentage of people willing to admit an extramarital affair is probably lower than the percentage of those who have had an adulterous affair.

Men are more likely than women to say they have committed adultery. Nearly one-quarter of men (23 percent), but only 15 percent of women, say they have had sex with someone other than their spouse while married.

A similar difference exists by race. Twenty-three percent of blacks admit to having had extramarital sex compared with 17 percent of whites and 15 percent of "other" races.

People aged 40 to 59 are most likely to say they have had sex with someone other than their spouse. Within this age group, 22 to 23 percent admit to having committed adultery. This compares with 16 to 17 percent of people under age 40, 15 percent of those in their sixties, and just 10 percent of people aged 70 or older.

The proportion of people who say they have committed adultery varies slightly by education. Most likely to say they have done so are people with a graduate degree (21 percent) while those with a bachelor's degree are least likely to say so (15 percent). Among people with a high school diploma or less, 18 to 19 percent admit to having had an extramarital affair.

Ever Committed Adultery? 1998

"Have you ever had sex with someone other than your husband or wife while you were married?"

(percent of people aged 18 or older responding by sex, race, age, and education, 1998)

	yes	no
Total	**18%**	**82%**
Men	23	77
Women	15	85
Black	23	77
White	17	83
Other	15	85
Aged 18 to 29	16	84
Aged 30 to 39	17	83
Aged 40 to 49	23	77
Aged 50 to 59	22	78
Aged 60 to 69	15	85
Aged 70 or older	10	90
Not a high school graduate	18	82
High school graduate	19	81
Bachelor's degree	15	85
Graduate degree	21	79

Note: Includes only people who are or have been married.
Source: General Social Survey, National Opinion Research Center, University of Chicago; calculations by the author

Ever Paid or Been Paid for Sex?

Fifteen percent of men admit they have paid for sex.

Only 8 percent of adults admit to having exchanged money for sex at least once since their 18th birthday. It is important to note, however, that on questions about sexual behavior it is not uncommon for people to lie or refuse to answer.

Not surprisingly, the largest difference is found by sex. Only 2 percent of women say they have paid or been paid for sex. A substantial 15 percent of men, however, say they have exchanged money for sex.

Blacks are more likely than whites and "other" races to admit to trading money for sex. Eleven percent of blacks say they have done so compared with 6 to 7 percent of whites and other races.

The youngest and the oldest adults are least likely to admit to exchanging money for sex. Only 4 percent of people aged 18 to 29 and 7 percent of those aged 70 or older said they had done so compared with 8 to 10 percent of other age groups.

Ever Paid or Been Paid for Sex? 1998

"Thinking about the time since your 18th birthday, have you ever had sex with a person you paid or who paid you for sex?"

(percent of people aged 18 or older responding by sex, race, age, and education, 1998)

	yes	no
Total	**8%**	**92%**
Men	15	85
Women	2	98
Black	11	89
White	7	93
Other	6	94
Aged 18 to 29	4	96
Aged 30 to 39	8	92
Aged 40 to 49	10	90
Aged 50 to 59	8	92
Aged 60 to 69	9	91
Aged 70 or older	7	93
Not a high school graduate	8	92
High school graduate	9	91
Bachelor's degree	7	93
Graduate degree	7	93

Source: General Social Survey, National Opinion Research Center, University of Chicago; calculations by the author

Sex Frequency

Frequency of sex diminishes with age.

Forty-three percent of Americans have sex at least once a week. But 18-to-29-year-olds are more sexually active than the average person. Fifty-seven percent of them say they have sex at least weekly. More than one in ten have sex more than three times a week.

Half of people in their forties are having sex once a week or more, but the figure drops to 42 percent among people in their fifties and to 19 percent among those in their sixties. Only 7 percent of people aged 70 or older have sex at least once a week. The great majority (70 percent) of the oldest Americans say they had not had sex in the 12 months prior to the survey. One reason for the lower incidence of sex among the oldest Americans is that many are widowed.

Forty-seven percent of men say they have sex at least once a week compared with 40 percent of women. There are several explanations for this discrepancy, including the fact that the average woman is older and more likely to be widowed than the average man.

The percentage of people saying they did not have sex at all in the 12 months prior to the survey falls with education. Fully 36 percent of people who did not complete high school say so, but the proportion declines to only 14 percent among people with a graduate degree. One reason for the decline is that older people (many of whom are widows) are overrepresented among those with lower levels of education.

Sex Frequency, 1998

"About how often did you have sex during the last 12 months?"

(percent of people aged 18 or older responding by sex, race, age, and education, 1998)

	not at all	once or twice	about once a month	2 to 3 times a month	about once a week	2 to 3 times a week	more than 3 times a week
Total	**22%**	**8%**	**11%**	**15%**	**18%**	**20%**	**5%**
Men	16	9	12	17	20	20	7
Women	27	7	11	14	17	19	4
Black	23	10	8	17	20	17	5
White	22	7	12	16	18	19	5
Other	17	11	8	12	15	31	6
Aged 18 to 29	14	8	7	15	17	28	12
Aged 30 to 39	9	5	13	18	21	27	6
Aged 40 to 49	11	8	12	20	23	22	5
Aged 50 to 59	23	9	13	13	23	16	3
Aged 60 to 69	43	10	16	12	13	4	2
Aged 70 or older	70	9	8	8	5	2	0
Not a high school graduate	36	9	12	13	13	11	5
High school graduate	22	8	10	16	17	21	6
Bachelor's degree	18	6	10	15	23	23	4
Graduate degree	14	8	19	17	23	17	3

Note: Numbers may not add to 100 because "don't know" is not shown.
Source: General Social Survey, National Opinion Research Center, University of Chicago; calculations by the author

Sex Partners in Past Year

Most people have had only one sex partner in the past year.

Two-thirds of Americans had only one sex partner in the 12 months prior to the survey. Twenty-one percent had no sex partners, while 13 percent had two or more. This pattern is only slightly different from the one in 1988, when 23 percent had no partners and 63 percent had one.

Women are considerably more likely than men not to have had a sex partner in the year prior to the survey (26 versus 15 percent). One reason for the difference is that there are far more widowed women than men. Men are much more likely than women to have had more than one sexual partner during the past year (18 versus 9 percent).

Two-thirds of whites and "other" races had only one sex partner in the past year compared with 57 percent of blacks. Blacks are more likely to have had multiple sex partners. Twenty percent of blacks had two or more sex partners compared with 11 percent of whites and 16 percent of other races. Blacks were less likely in 1998 than in 1988 to have had more than one partner, however.

As people get older, the likelihood of not having a sex partner increases. Only 9 to 13 percent of people under age 50 did not have a sex partner in the prior year, but the proportion rises to 23 percent among people in their fifties and to 37 percent among those in their sixties. Nearly two-thirds (65 percent) of people aged 70 or older did not have a sex partner in the past year.

Despite the risk of contracting AIDS or other sexually transmitted diseases, many young adults still have multiple sexual partners. Twenty-seven percent of people under age 30 had more than one partner in the past year. Eleven percent had four or more. Among people aged 30 to 49, 12 to 13 percent had more than one partner. But among those aged 50 or older, only 1 to 4 percent had multiple partners.

While 16 to 17 percent of college graduates had no sex partners in the prior year, the proportion rises to 21 percent among people with a high school diploma and to 34 percent among those who did not complete high school. One reason for the difference by education is that many of the least educated Americans are older widows.

Sex Partners in Past Year, 1998

"How many sex partners have you had in the last 12 months?"

(percent of people aged 18 or older responding by sex, race, age, and education, 1998)

	none	one	two	three	four or more
Total	**21%**	**66%**	**7%**	**2%**	**4%**
Men	15	66	8	4	6
Women	26	65	6	1	2
Black	22	57	12	3	5
White	22	67	6	2	3
Other	16	68	7	2	7
Aged 18 to 29	13	58	13	5	9
Aged 30 to 39	9	77	7	2	3
Aged 40 to 49	12	74	8	2	3
Aged 50 to 59	23	73	2	1	1
Aged 60 to 69	37	60	1	1	0
Aged 70 or older	65	34	0	0	1
Not a high school graduate	34	52	7	2	4
High school graduate	21	65	8	2	4
Bachelor's degree	17	73	6	2	1
Graduate degree	16	77	3	2	3

Note: Numbers may not add to 100 because "don't know" is not shown.
Source: General Social Survey, National Opinion Research Center, University of Chicago; calculations by the author

Sex Partners in Past Year, 1988 and 1998

"How many sex partners have you had in the last 12 months?"

(percent of people aged 18 or older responding by sex, race, age, and education, 1988–98)

	none		one		two		three		four or more	
	1998	1988	1998	1988	1998	1988	1998	1988	1998	1988
Total	21%	23%	66%	63%	7%	6%	2%	4%	4%	4%
Men	15	16	66	65	8	6	4	5	6	8
Women	26	28	65	61	6	6	1	3	2	2
Black	22	15	57	58	12	9	3	7	5	10
White	22	23	67	64	6	5	2	3	3	3
Aged 18 to 29	13	9	58	60	13	12	5	7	9	11
Aged 30 to 39	9	8	77	77	7	5	2	5	3	4
Aged 40 to 49	12	12	74	76	8	5	2	4	3	2
Aged 50 to 59	23	27	73	64	2	4	1	1	1	2
Aged 60 to 69	37	39	60	57	1	2	1	2	0	1
Aged 70 or older	65	67	34	31	0	1	0	0	1	1
Not a high school graduate	34	39	52	48	7	4	2	4	4	5
High school graduate	21	19	65	67	8	7	2	2	4	4
Bachelor's degree	17	13	73	73	6	7	2	4	1	3
Graduate degree	16	14	77	74	3	5	2	6	3	1

Note: Numbers may not add to 100 because "don't know" is not shown.
Source: General Social Survey, National Opinion Research Center, University of Chicago; calculations by the author

Sex Partners in Past Five Years

The majority of young adults had at least two sex partners in the past five years.

More than half of adults had only one sex partner in the past five years. Thirty percent had two or more and 14 percent had none. As in all questions about sex, however, it is difficult to know how honest respondents are in their answers.

Thirty-seven percent of men, but only 25 percent of women, say they had two or more sex partners in the past five years. The discrepancy between men and women is large enough to suggest that some people are not telling the truth.

By race, whites are least likely to have had multiple sex partners. While 40 percent of blacks and 42 percent of "other" races say they had two or more partners in the past five years, only 28 percent of whites say so. Fourteen percent of blacks and whites had no partners during the past five years compared with 8 percent of other races.

The majority (59 percent) of adults under age 30 had two or more sex partners during the past five years. Nearly one-quarter of these young adults say they had at least five partners. The percentage of people who say they had more than one partner drops steadily with age to only 5 percent among those aged 70 or older.

More than one-quarter of people who did not complete high school (many of whom are older adults) had no sex partners during the past five years compared with 8 to 13 percent of those with more education. The majority of people with at least a high school education had only one partner.

Sex Partners in Past Five Years, 1998

"How many sex partners have you had in the past five years?"

(percent of people aged 18 or older responding by sex, race, age, and education, 1998)

	none	one	two	three	four	five to ten	eleven or more
Total	**14%**	**55%**	**10%**	**6%**	**5%**	**6%**	**3%**
Men	9	52	9	7	7	9	5
Women	17	57	11	6	3	4	1
Black	14	42	12	7	8	9	4
White	14	57	9	6	4	6	3
Other	8	49	15	9	5	6	7
Aged 18 to 29	8	31	13	12	11	15	8
Aged 30 to 39	4	61	11	8	6	6	3
Aged 40 to 49	6	63	13	5	4	6	2
Aged 50 to 59	14	68	8	4	2	2	1
Aged 60 to 69	22	69	3	4	0	1	1
Aged 70 or older	52	41	2	1	0	1	1
Not a high school graduate	26	44	8	6	4	6	1
High school graduate	13	54	10	6	5	6	4
Bachelor's degree	10	59	11	6	5	6	2
Graduate degree	8	69	7	6	3	5	2

Note: Numbers may not add to 100 because "don't know" is not shown.
Source: General Social Survey, National Opinion Research Center, University of Chicago; calculations by the author

8

Women's Roles

Attitudes about the roles of women have changed dramatically over the past two decades—perhaps more so than opinions on any other topic. Most Americans no longer believe women should confine themselves to caring for the home and family, leaving business and politics up to men.

Few Americans think women should stay out of politics, although there is a remnant of suspicion that they are less well suited to the political arena than men. Most people do not believe there is something wrong with wives working even if they do not need the money, nor do they think a husband's career is more important than a wife's. Two decades ago, however, most people believed a husband's career came first and that it was better for women to be homemakers and men the breadwinners.

Most people have also come to believe that children do not suffer if their mother is in the labor force. There is disagreement about the effect of working women on family life in general, however.

Although one might assume that women and men would disagree about women's roles, this is the case for only a few of the questions examined here. The opinions of women and men do diverge, for example, on the impact of working mothers on children and family life. Women are less likely than men to believe working mothers harm their children or families.

By race, there are some areas of disagreement. Whites and blacks are slightly more likely than people of "other" race to believe men are better suited emotionally for politics. But blacks and whites are less likely than other races to believe a husband's career is more important than his wife's. Perhaps because black women historically have had to work to help support their families, blacks think more highly of working mothers than people of other race do.

Many older Americans still hold traditional attitudes toward women's roles. In fact, on every question asked, there are substantial differences of opinion by generation. Most people aged 60 or older believe it is better if women take care of the home while men earn the money, an opinion shared by a minority of people under age 50. Most people aged 60 or older believe preschoolers suffer if their mother works.

There is also considerable disagreement about women's roles by education. In general, the college educated are more sympathetic toward working women than those with less education are. People who did not complete high school (a group that includes a dispropor- tionately large number of older people) are especially likely to favor traditional roles for women. This group is far more likely to believe that men are better suited for politics, a traditional division of labor is best, and that a husband's career is more important than his wife's. They are also more likely to believe children suffer if their mother works.

Should Only Men Run the Country?

Few people believe running the country is necessarily a man's job.

Should women stick to running their homes and leave running the country up to men? The majority of Americans (82 percent) say no, up substantially from the 66 percent who said no in 1978.

Men and women are about equally likely to say there is no reason why women can't be in the house—and the Senate. The proportions of both sexes who believe women should leave running the country up to men has declined since 1978.

People aged 60 or older have more difficulty accepting the changing roles of women. While 8 to 13 percent of people under age 60 say women should leave running the country to men, 26 percent of people in their sixties and 35 percent of those aged 70 or older feel that way. Support for the traditional point of view has declined in every age group since 1978, however.

Whites are more likely than blacks or other races to disagree that women should stay out of politics (83 percent compared with 78 percent of blacks and 76 percent of other races). The less education people have the more likely they are to feel government should be the province of males. Thirty-seven percent of people who did not complete high school agree compared with 14 percent of high school graduates and 3 to 8 percent of college graduates.

Should Only Men Run the Country? 1998

"Do you agree or disagree with this statement? Women should take care of running their homes and leave running the country up to men."

(percent of people aged 18 or older responding by sex, race, age, and education, 1998)

	agree	disagree	not sure
Total	**15%**	**82%**	**3%**
Men	14	83	3
Women	16	82	3
Black	18	78	3
White	14	83	3
Other	20	76	3
Aged 18 to 29	8	90	2
Aged 30 to 39	13	85	2
Aged 40 to 49	11	86	2
Aged 50 to 59	10	86	4
Aged 60 to 69	26	71	3
Aged 70 or older	35	61	4
Not a high school graduate	37	58	6
High school graduate	14	83	3
Bachelor's degree	8	90	2
Graduate degree	3	97	1

Source: General Social Survey, National Opinion Research Center, University of Chicago; calculations by the author

Should Only Men Run the Country? 1978 to 1998

"Do you agree or disagree with this statement? Women should take care of running their homes and leave running the country up to men."

(percent of people aged 18 or older responding by sex, race, age, and education, 1978–98)

	agree			disagree			not sure		
	1998	1988	1978	1998	1988	1978	1998	1988	1978
Total	**15%**	**20%**	**31%**	**82%**	**76%**	**66%**	**3%**	**3%**	**3%**
Men	14	21	30	83	75	66	3	4	4
Women	16	20	32	82	77	66	3	3	3
Black	18	24	37	78	73	59	3	3	4
White	14	19	30	83	77	67	3	3	3
Aged 18 to 29	8	10	20	90	88	79	2	2	2
Aged 30 to 39	13	10	23	85	87	74	2	2	3
Aged 40 to 49	11	16	31	86	80	65	2	3	5
Aged 50 to 59	10	24	33	86	72	63	4	3	4
Aged 60 to 69	26	33	38	71	62	57	3	5	5
Aged 70 or older	35	46	62	61	47	36	4	7	2
Not a high school graduate	37	47	51	58	50	44	6	4	4
High school graduate	14	15	26	83	81	71	3	4	3
Bachelor's degree	8	5	7	90	95	93	2	0	0
Graduate degree	3	3	5	97	92	92	1	5	3

Source: General Social Survey, National Opinion Research Center, University of Chicago; calculations by the author

Are Men Better Suited for Politics?

Belief in this idea has slowly declined.

Historically, the supposed excessive emotionalism of women has been used to exclude them from politics. But the public has slowly come around to the idea that women are as well-suited for politics as men. In 1978 a small majority (54 percent) disagreed with the idea that men are better suited for politics. By 1998, a much larger 72 percent majority disagreed. Only 22 percent still believe women are not as well suited for politics as men.

Substantial differences of opinion persist, however, among people of different generations and different levels of education. Thirty percent of people in their sixties and 37 percent of those aged 70 or older still believe women are less well-suited for politics. Among people under age 50, however, fewer than 20 percent agree.

One-third of people who did not complete high school (a disproportionate number of whom are older) believe men are better suited for politics. Only 21 percent of high school graduates and 18 percent of college graduates agree. Those with graduate degrees are least likely to take the traditional point of view (11 percent).

Are Men Better Suited for Politics? 1998

"Most men are better suited emotionally for politics than are most women—do you agree or disagree?"

(percent of people aged 18 or older responding by sex, race, age, and education, 1998)

	agree	disagree	not sure
Total	**22%**	**72%**	**6%**
Men	21	70	9
Women	22	74	4
Black	25	70	5
White	21	73	6
Other	28	65	6
Aged 18 to 29	18	74	8
Aged 30 to 39	19	76	5
Aged 40 to 49	19	76	5
Aged 50 to 59	17	74	8
Aged 60 to 69	30	66	4
Aged 70 or older	37	54	9
Not a high school graduate	32	55	13
High school graduate	21	73	6
Bachelor's degree	18	77	5
Graduate degree	11	87	2

Source: General Social Survey, National Opinion Research Center, University of Chicago; calculations by the author

Are Men Better Suited for Politics? 1978 to 1998

"Most men are better suited emotionally for politics than are most women—do you agree or disagree?"

(percent of people aged 18 or older responding by sex, race, age, and education, 1978–98)

	agree			disagree			not sure		
	1998	1988	1978	1998	1988	1978	1998	1988	1978
Total	**22%**	**32%**	**42%**	**72%**	**64%**	**54%**	**6%**	**3%**	**4%**
Men	21	35	39	70	59	56	9	6	6
Women	22	30	44	74	68	53	4	1	3
Black	25	34	48	70	62	46	5	3	6
White	21	31	41	73	65	55	6	3	4
Aged 18 to 29	18	25	31	74	73	67	8	3	2
Aged 30 to 39	19	23	36	76	73	61	5	3	3
Aged 40 to 49	19	24	50	76	72	47	5	3	4
Aged 50 to 59	17	36	44	74	62	52	8	2	4
Aged 60 to 69	30	43	53	66	54	42	4	4	5
Aged 70 or older	37	57	56	54	38	35	9	5	9
Not a high school graduate	32	52	52	55	44	41	13	4	7
High school graduate	21	29	40	73	68	57	6	3	3
Bachelor's degree	18	19	25	77	80	73	5	2	2
Graduate degree	11	16	32	87	79	66	2	5	2

Source: General Social Survey, National Opinion Research Center, University of Chicago; calculations by the author

Female Presidential Candidate

Only one in ten Americans wouldn't vote for a female presidential candidate.

Elizabeth Dole may not have been able to get the funding to compete effectively as a GOP presidential candidate, but if she had, her gender would not have worked against her. Fully 90 percent of Americans say they would vote for a women if she were their party's nominee for president.

There is solid agreement on this issue among people under age 60, with 92 to 94 percent saying they would vote for a woman for president. But older Americans are not as ready to accept Mrs. President and the First Gentleman. A slightly lower 88 percent of people in their sixties say they would vote for a woman. The proportion drops to 77 percent among people aged 70 or older. But that figure represents a big change in attitude among the oldest Americans since 1978, when only 52 percent said they would vote for a woman.

Education is also a factor in whether or not people would accept a female candidate. More than 90 percent of people with at least a high school diploma say they would vote for a woman. Among those who did not complete high school, a smaller 81 percent agree.

Female Presidential Candidate, 1998

"If your party nominated a woman for president, would you vote for her if she were qualified for the job?"

(percent of people aged 18 or older responding by sex, race, age, and education, 1998)

	yes	no	don't know
Total	**90%**	**6%**	**3%**
Men	91	5	4
Women	90	7	3
Black	90	6	4
White	91	6	3
Other	87	4	9
Aged 18 to 29	94	3	3
Aged 30 to 39	93	4	4
Aged 40 to 49	92	6	2
Aged 50 to 59	93	5	3
Aged 60 to 69	88	9	4
Aged 70 or older	77	17	6
Not a high school graduate	81	15	4
High school graduate	90	6	4
Bachelor's degree	94	3	3
Graduate degree	97	1	3

Source: General Social Survey, National Opinion Research Center, University of Chicago; calculations by the author

Female Presidential Candidate, 1978 to 1998

"If your party nominated a woman for president, would you vote for her if she were qualified for the job?"

(percent of people aged 18 or older responding by sex, race, age, and education, 1978–98)

	agree			disagree			don't know		
	1998	1988	1978	1998	1988	1978	1998	1988	1978
Total	**90%**	**85%**	**79%**	**6%**	**12%**	**18%**	**3%**	**3%**	**3%**
Men	91	88	81	5	10	16	4	2	2
Women	90	84	78	7	13	19	3	3	3
Black	90	85	82	6	12	13	4	2	5
White	91	86	79	6	11	19	3	3	2
Aged 18 to 29	94	91	91	3	7	7	3	1	2
Aged 30 to 39	93	92	87	4	6	11	4	2	2
Aged 40 to 49	92	84	77	6	13	20	2	2	3
Aged 50 to 59	93	83	76	5	10	21	3	7	2
Aged 60 to 69	88	87	72	9	10	25	4	3	3
Aged 70 or older	77	67	52	17	28	42	6	4	6
Not a high school graduate	81	75	68	15	21	29	4	5	4
High school graduate	90	87	84	6	11	14	4	2	2
Bachelor's degree	94	95	87	3	5	11	3	1	2
Graduate degree	97	92	89	1	3	8	3	5	3

Source: General Social Survey, National Opinion Research Center, University of Chicago; calculations by the author

Female Homemakers and Male Breadwinners

Americans have changed their minds about traditional sex roles.

Once upon a time, the world was neatly divided into two separate spheres: his and hers. The woman's domain was the home while the man's was everything else. Most Americans believed this was the best arrangement. In 1977, 65 percent supported separate roles for men and women. By 1998, the 63 percent majority did not.

As with most questions regarding the appropriate roles for men and women, there is little disagreement by sex or race, but there is sharp disagreement by age and education.

The generations could hardly disagree more. Three-quarters of young adults under age 30 do not favor traditional sex roles, nor do 70 to 71 percent of people in their thirties and forties. Among people in their fifties, the proportion of those who disagree with traditional sex roles shrinks to 62 percent. But among people in their sixties, the 51 percent majority thinks that traditional roles are best. Two-thirds of people aged 70 or older believe in traditional sex roles, while only 28 percent disagree.

The majority of people who did not complete high school (many of whom are older) believe traditional sex roles are best, but most of those with at least a high school diploma disagree. Sixty-three percent of high school graduates do not favor traditional roles, nor do nearly three-quarters of college graduates.

Female Homemakers and Male Breadwinners, 1998

"It is much better for everyone involved if the man is the achiever outside the home and the woman takes care of the home and family—do you agree or disagree?"

(percent of people aged 18 or older responding by sex, race, age, and education, 1998)

	strongly agree	agree	strongly disagree	disagree	agree, total	disagree, total
Total	7%	27%	45%	18%	34%	63%
Men	6	29	47	15	35	62
Women	7	26	43	21	33	64
Black	7	25	50	16	32	66
White	7	28	44	19	35	63
Other	7	29	43	19	36	62
Aged 18 to 29	3	17	51	25	20	76
Aged 30 to 39	6	21	51	20	27	71
Aged 40 to 49	6	22	48	22	28	70
Aged 50 to 59	6	31	41	21	37	62
Aged 60 to 69	10	41	41	6	51	47
Aged 70 or older	16	52	24	4	68	28
Not a high school graduate	13	41	34	8	54	42
High school graduate	7	27	47	16	34	63
Bachelor's degree	3	24	45	27	27	72
Graduate degree	3	17	43	32	20	75

Note: Numbers may not add to 100 because "don't know" is not shown.
Source: General Social Survey, National Opinion Research Center, University of Chicago; calculations by the author

Female Homemakers and Male Breadwinners, 1977 to 1998

"It is much better for everyone involved if the man is the achiever outside the home and the woman takes care of the home and family—do you agree or disagree?"

(percent of people aged 18 or older responding by sex, race, age, and education, 1977–98)

	agree/strongly agree			disagree/strongly disagree		
	1998	1988	1977	1998	1988	1977
Total	**34%**	**41%**	**65%**	**63%**	**57%**	**34%**
Men	35	45	68	62	53	31
Women	33	39	62	64	60	36
Black	32	41	61	66	57	37
White	35	41	65	63	57	33
Aged 18 to 29	20	22	45	76	77	54
Aged 30 to 39	27	27	51	71	71	47
Aged 40 to 49	28	37	67	70	62	30
Aged 50 to 59	37	54	79	62	45	21
Aged 60 to 69	51	63	84	47	35	15
Aged 70 or older	68	77	88	28	20	11
Not a high school graduate	54	67	79	42	31	19
High school graduate	34	35	61	63	64	38
Bachelor's degree	27	29	45	72	69	54
Graduate degree	20	27	45	75	69	54

Note: Numbers may not add to 100 because "don't know" is not shown.
Source: General Social Survey, National Opinion Research Center, University of Chicago; calculations by the author

Should Women Work If They Don't Have To?

Most people approve of working women, but support is weaker among older Americans.

The solid majority (81 percent) of Americans say it is fine for a married woman to work even if her husband earns enough to support the family. In 1978, a smaller proportion of people felt this way (72 percent).

The biggest difference of opinion occurs among people of different ages, although the gap is narrower now than it was in 1978. Among people under age 60, 82 to 86 percent approve of married women working whether they need to or not. The proportion of those who approve is somewhat smaller among people in their sixties (77 percent) and considerably smaller among those aged 70 or older (64 percent). Thirty-two percent of the oldest Americans disapprove of women working if they don't have to.

Among people with at least a high school diploma, 82 to 87 percent approve of working wives. Among those who did not complete high school, however, only 68 percent approve and about one-third disapprove.

Should Women Work If They Don't Have To? 1998

"Do you approve or disapprove of a married woman earning money in business or industry if she has a husband capable of supporting her?"

(percent of people aged 18 or older responding by sex, race, age, and education, 1998)

	approve	disapprove
Total	**81%**	**18%**
Men	82	17
Women	81	18
Black	78	20
White	81	17
Other	83	16
Aged 18 to 29	86	13
Aged 30 to 39	83	16
Aged 40 to 49	86	13
Aged 50 to 59	82	17
Aged 60 to 69	77	20
Aged 70 or older	64	32
Not a high school graduate	68	30
High school graduate	82	16
Bachelor's degree	87	13
Graduate degree	85	13

Note: Numbers may not add to 100 because "don't know" is not shown.
Source: General Social Survey, National Opinion Research Center, University of Chicago; calculations by the author

Should Women Work If They Don't Have To? 1978 to 1998

"Do you approve or disapprove of a married woman earning money in business or industry if she has a husband capable of supporting her?"

(percent of people aged 18 or older responding by sex, race, age, and education, 1978–98)

	approve			disapprove		
	1998	**1988**	**1978**	**1998**	**1988**	**1978**
Total	**81%**	**79%**	**72%**	**18%**	**19%**	**26%**
Men	82	80	71	17	18	28
Women	81	78	74	18	20	25
Black	78	76	69	20	23	29
White	81	80	73	17	18	26
Aged 18 to 29	86	80	80	13	19	19
Aged 30 to 39	83	89	81	16	10	17
Aged 40 to 49	86	87	76	13	12	24
Aged 50 to 59	82	75	72	17	21	27
Aged 60 to 69	77	73	61	20	25	38
Aged 70 or older	64	58	46	32	35	52
Not a high school graduate	68	64	56	30	32	42
High school graduate	82	82	77	16	16	22
Bachelor's degree	87	87	87	13	13	12
Graduate degree	85	89	87	13	10	11

Note: Numbers may not add to 100 because "don't know" is not shown.
Source: General Social Survey, National Opinion Research Center, University of Chicago; calculations by the author

Is the Husband's Career More Important?

Older Americans still believe a man's career is more important.

In the past, most Americans assumed the job of a working wife was secondary to that of her husband. In 1977, the majority of Americans (55 percent) agreed that it was more important for a wife to help her husband's career than to have one herself. But by 1998, only 18 percent still held this point of view, while 79 percent disagreed. Increasingly, wives are earning as much or more than their husbands. As this trend continues, the matter of whose career is paramount is likely to be settled on the basis of finances rather than gender.

A substantial proportion of older people still believe a wife's career should take a back seat to her husband's, however. Among people under age 60, fewer than 15 percent agree with the statement compared with 30 percent of those in their sixties and 48 percent of those aged 70 or older. Only 45 percent of people aged 70 or older disagree compared with 84 to 88 percent of people under age 60.

Fewer than 20 percent of people with at least a high school diploma still believe the husband's career is more important than his wife's. Among those with less education, however, 38 percent agree that the husband's career should come first.

Is the Husband's Career More Important? 1998

"It is more important for a wife to help her husband's career than to have one herself—do you agree or disagree?"

(percent of people aged 18 or older responding by sex, race, age, and education, 1998)

	strongly agree	agree	strongly disagree	disagree	agree, total	disagree, total
Total	2%	16%	54%	25%	18%	79%
Men	2	16	59	19	18	78
Women	2	17	50	29	19	79
Black	2	17	54	24	19	78
White	2	16	54	25	18	79
Other	5	22	46	27	27	73
Aged 18 to 29	1	9	55	33	10	88
Aged 30 to 39	3	10	56	29	13	85
Aged 40 to 49	2	12	54	30	14	84
Aged 50 to 59	2	12	59	25	14	84
Aged 60 to 69	2	28	56	11	30	67
Aged 70 or older	6	42	40	5	48	45
Not a high school graduate	5	33	49	9	38	58
High school graduate	2	16	57	23	18	80
Bachelor's degree	3	13	49	33	16	82
Graduate degree	1	5	51	41	6	92

Note: Numbers may not add to 100 because "don't know" is not shown.
Source: General Social Survey, National Opinion Research Center, University of Chicago; calculations by the author

Is the Husband's Career More Important? 1977 to 1998

"It is more important for a wife to help her husband's career than to have one herself—do you agree or disagree?"

(percent of people aged 18 or older responding by sex, race, age, and education, 1977–98)

	agree/strongly agree			disagree/strongly disagree		
	1998	*1988*	*1977*	*1998*	*1988*	*1977*
Total	**18%**	**30%**	**55%**	**79%**	**67%**	**41%**
Men	18	33	50	78	65	45
Women	19	28	59	79	69	38
Black	19	28	53	78	70	44
White	18	30	55	79	68	41
Aged 18 to 29	10	15	36	88	84	63
Aged 30 to 39	13	17	44	85	82	53
Aged 40 to 49	14	25	57	84	73	37
Aged 50 to 59	14	38	65	84	60	32
Aged 60 to 69	30	46	76	67	50	21
Aged 70 or older	48	67	80	45	29	17
Not a high school graduate	38	53	66	58	45	30
High school graduate	18	26	54	80	72	43
Bachelor's degree	16	16	33	82	83	66
Graduate degree	6	18	30	92	82	64

Note: Numbers may not add to 100 because "don't know" is not shown.
Source: General Social Survey, National Opinion Research Center, University of Chicago; calculations by the author

Is a Working Mother Good for Children?

The adult children of working mothers say yes.

Two-thirds of Americans believe a working mother can establish as warm and secure a relationship with her children as a mother who does not work. This opinion was not always prevalent, however. Two decades ago, when mothers of young children were pouring into the labor force for the first time, many Americans worried that children would be neglected. In 1977, people were divided on this issue, with half believing that a working mother's relationship with her children would not be as good as that of a nonworking mother.

Women are more likely than men to believe working mothers can maintain a good relationship with their children (73 versus 58 percent). The gap between the sexes on this question is wider now than it was two decades ago.

Historically, black women have been more likely to work than white women. This fact shapes opinions on this issue by race. Three-quarters of blacks, but only two-thirds of whites and people of other race, say working mothers can maintain as good a relationship with their children as nonworking mothers.

The generation gap on this question is substantial. Three-quarters of adults under age 30, most of whom grew up with working mothers, say a working mother's relationship with her children can be as good as that of a nonworking mother. Nearly seven out of ten people aged 30 to 59 agree. Among people in their sixties, a smaller proportion (59 percent) agrees. Barely half of those aged 70 or older agree, however, while 46 percent disagree.

The college educated are more likely than those with less education to believe having a job doesn't harm a woman's relationship with her children. While 72 to 76 percent of college graduates agree with this opinion, the share drops to 66 percent among high school graduates and to 57 percent among people who did not complete high school.

Is a Working Mother Good for Children? 1998

"A working mother can establish just as warm and secure a relationship with her children as a mother who does not work—do you agree or disagree?"

(percent of people aged 18 or older responding by sex, race, age, and education, 1998)

	strongly agree	agree	strongly disagree	disagree	agree, total	disagree, total
Total	**22%**	**45%**	**25%**	**7%**	**67%**	**32%**
Men	13	45	32	8	58	40
Women	28	45	20	5	73	25
Black	23	51	20	5	74	25
White	22	44	26	7	66	33
Other	22	45	27	5	67	32
Aged 18 to 29	23	51	21	4	74	25
Aged 30 to 39	23	46	23	6	69	29
Aged 40 to 49	27	41	25	6	68	31
Aged 50 to 59	23	46	21	9	69	30
Aged 60 to 69	13	46	34	6	59	40
Aged 70 or older	13	38	34	12	51	46
Not a high school graduate	13	44	32	9	57	41
High school graduate	21	45	26	6	66	32
Bachelor's degree	25	47	22	6	72	28
Graduate degree	33	43	18	6	76	24

Note: Numbers may not add to 100 because "don't know" is not shown.
Source: General Social Survey, National Opinion Research Center, University of Chicago; calculations by the author

Is a Working Mother Good for Children? 1977 to 1998

"A working mother can establish just as warm and secure a relationship with her children as a mother who does not work—do you agree or disagree?"

(percent of people aged 18 or older responding by sex, race, age, and education, 1977–98)

	agree/strongly agree			disagree/strongly disagree		
	1998	*1988*	*1977*	*1998*	*1988*	*1977*
Total	**67%**	**63%**	**48%**	**32%**	**37%**	**50%**
Men	58	55	41	40	44	58
Women	73	69	54	25	30	44
Black	74	69	56	25	30	44
White	66	62	47	33	37	51
Aged 18 to 29	74	69	60	25	31	38
Aged 30 to 39	69	76	61	29	22	38
Aged 40 to 49	68	65	45	31	34	54
Aged 50 to 59	69	50	43	30	50	57
Aged 60 to 69	59	56	32	40	43	66
Aged 70 or older	51	41	30	46	58	68
Not a high school graduate	57	46	37	41	53	61
High school graduate	66	65	52	32	34	47
Bachelor's degree	72	74	61	28	26	39
Graduate degree	76	81	64	24	19	31

Note: Numbers may not add to 100 because "don't know" is not shown.
Source: General Social Survey, National Opinion Research Center, University of Chicago; calculations by the author

Do Young Children Suffer If Mother Works?

The older people are, the more they believe youngsters suffer.

In 1977, two-thirds of Americans believed preschoolers suffered if their mother worked. By 1998, however, only 41 percent held this opinion while the 56 percent majority disagreed.

Women are more likely than men to say they don't believe preschoolers suffer if their mothers work (61 versus 49 percent). The solid majority of blacks (66 percent) say they don't believe young children suffer compared with a smaller 55 percent of whites and 53 percent of other races.

The older people are, the more they agree that young children suffer if their mother works. Among people under age 30, only 31 percent agree with the statement, but among people aged 70 or older, fully 61 percent agree.

Substantial differences of opinion also exist by education. About half of those who did not complete high school say young children suffer if their mother works compared with 38 to 40 percent of people with more education.

Do Young Children Suffer If Mother Works? 1998

"A preschool child is likely to suffer if his or her mother works—do you agree or disagree?"

(percent of people aged 18 or older responding by sex, race, age, and education, 1998)

	strongly agree	agree	strongly disagree	disagree	agree, total	disagree, total
Total	**8%**	**33%**	**46%**	**10%**	**41%**	**56%**
Men	8	39	43	6	47	49
Women	8	28	49	12	36	61
Black	8	25	57	9	33	66
White	9	34	45	10	43	55
Other	6	35	44	9	41	53
Aged 18 to 29	4	27	55	11	31	66
Aged 30 to 39	6	30	51	10	36	61
Aged 40 to 49	8	32	44	14	40	58
Aged 50 to 59	8	35	43	10	43	53
Aged 60 to 69	11	36	48	2	47	50
Aged 70 or older	17	44	29	5	61	34
Not a high school graduate	10	42	40	5	52	45
High school graduate	8	32	47	10	40	57
Bachelor's degree	8	31	46	12	39	58
Graduate degree	8	30	47	13	38	60

Note: Numbers may not add to 100 because "don't know" is not shown.
Source: General Social Survey, National Opinion Research Center, University of Chicago; calculations by the author

Do Young Children Suffer If Mother Works? 1977 to 1998

"A preschool child is likely to suffer if his or her mother works—do you agree or disagree?"

(percent of people aged 18 or older responding by sex, race, age, and education, 1977–98)

	agree/strongly agree			disagree/strongly disagree		
	1998	*1988*	*1977*	*1998*	*1988*	*1977*
Total	**41%**	**47%**	**66%**	**56%**	**51%**	**32%**
Men	47	54	72	49	43	26
Women	36	42	62	61	57	37
Black	33	38	53	66	60	46
White	43	48	68	55	50	30
Aged 18 to 29	31	37	55	66	60	44
Aged 30 to 39	36	32	56	61	67	44
Aged 40 to 49	40	43	69	58	55	29
Aged 50 to 59	43	59	73	53	40	25
Aged 60 to 69	47	58	82	50	40	16
Aged 70 or older	61	76	78	34	20	19
Not a high school graduate	52	62	73	45	35	24
High school graduate	40	44	64	57	55	35
Bachelor's degree	39	40	60	58	57	40
Graduate degree	38	37	55	60	61	39

Note: Numbers may not add to 100 because "don't know" is not shown.
Source: General Social Survey, National Opinion Research Center, University of Chicago; calculations by the author

Do Families Suffer If Women Work?

About half of Americans do not believe families suffer if women work.

Are families harmed when mom goes to work? Undoubtedly, it is easier on other family members if the woman stays home and runs the household. Nevertheless, nearly half (49 percent) of Americans believe family life does not suffer just because a woman has a full-time job. Thirty percent believe family life suffers when mother works full time.

Women are slightly more likely than men to say they don't believe family life suffers when a woman works full time (52 versus 45 percent). As is true with most questions about women's roles, there is much disagreement by generation and education. The proportion of people who say family life suffers rises with age. Only about one-quarter of people under age 40 agree with this statement compared with one-third of those aged 40 to 59 and 41 to 42 percent of people aged 60 or older.

The largest gap is by education. Only 19 percent of people with graduate degrees believe family life suffers if a woman works full time. A larger 26 percent of college graduates and 31 percent of high school graduates agree. Most likely to agree are people who did not complete high school (42 percent).

Do Families Suffer If Women Work? 1998

"All in all, family life suffers when the woman has a full-time job. Do you agree or disagree?"

(percent of people aged 18 or older responding by sex, race, age, and education, 1998)

	strongly agree	agree	neither	disagree	strongly disagree	agree, total	disagree, total
Total	**11%**	**19%**	**19%**	**27%**	**22%**	**30%**	**49%**
Men	12	21	21	28	17	33	45
Women	10	18	18	26	26	28	52
Black	13	18	15	28	23	31	51
White	11	19	20	27	21	30	48
Other	9	23	20	25	24	32	49
Aged 18 to 29	5	18	21	28	25	23	53
Aged 30 to 39	8	16	18	32	26	24	58
Aged 40 to 49	12	21	14	26	25	33	51
Aged 50 to 59	11	21	19	26	21	32	47
Aged 60 to 69	17	25	21	23	13	42	36
Aged 70 or older	21	20	26	21	9	41	30
Not a high school graduate	18	24	21	21	11	42	32
High school graduate	11	20	20	27	20	31	47
Bachelor's degree	9	17	19	29	26	26	55
Graduate degree	5	14	16	28	35	19	63

Note: Numbers may not add to 100 because "can't choose" is not shown.
Source: General Social Survey, National Opinion Research Center, University of Chicago; calculations by the author

Do Families Suffer If Women Work? 1988 and 1998

"All in all, family life suffers when the woman has a full-time job. Do you agree or disagree?"

(percent of people aged 18 or older responding by sex, race, age, and education, 1988–98)

	agree/strongly agree		neither		disagree/ strongly disagree	
	1998	*1988*	*1998*	*1988*	*1998*	*1988*
Total	**30%**	**35%**	**19%**	**15%**	**49%**	**49%**
Men	33	37	21	15	45	48
Women	28	33	18	15	52	51
Black	31	28	15	10	51	61
White	30	35	20	16	48	48
Aged 18 to 29	23	24	21	16	53	59
Aged 30 to 39	24	28	18	13	58	58
Aged 40 to 49	33	30	14	15	51	54
Aged 50 to 59	32	45	19	15	47	40
Aged 60 to 69	42	38	21	18	36	42
Aged 70 or older	41	60	26	14	30	25
Not a high school graduate	42	50	21	12	32	37
High school graduate	31	32	20	16	47	50
Bachelor's degree	26	25	19	15	55	60
Graduate degree	19	17	16	22	63	61

Note: Numbers may not add to 100 because "can't choose" is not shown.
Source: General Social Survey, National Opinion Research Center, University of Chicago; calculations by the author

9

Work and Money

Americans are relatively content with their financial situation. Nearly half say they have average incomes. Few people consider themselves upper or lower class, but instead divide evenly between the working and middle classes. Most still believe the average family can improve its standard of living. Most believe they enjoy a better standard of living than their parents did at their age and that their children will have a better standard of living when they grow up.

Most people say they would continue to work even if they didn't need the money. They wouldn't attribute their success solely to luck, either. The solid majority believe hard work rather than luck enables people to get ahead. Nearly half of Americans believe technology will reduce the number of jobs, but most think it will make work more interesting.

The majority of Americans would rather work for a large firm than a small one and prefer the private sector to government employment. Although relatively few people are self-employed, most say they would like to be.

Most workers say they work as hard as they have to, even if it interferes with other parts of their life. But fewer than one-third think work is a person's most important activity. Most say it is important that a job be interesting and that they have job security. Few Americans worry that their job is not secure, however. This security is fortunate because, if they did lose their job, one-third think it would be difficult to find a new one with comparable pay and benefits.

Working hard has negative side effects, however. Two in five workers say they frequently find their work stressful and often come home from work exhausted. But half of workers are content to keep working the same number of hours for the same pay as they do now. Two in five workers would like to change careers, but fewer than one-third are planning to look for a different job in the near future.

Men are more likely to say they would like to work more hours and earn more pay; women are more likely to say they would like to work less and take home less. One reason for this difference is that women are more likely than men to come home from work exhausted. Women also value work differently than men do. Fewer than half of women, but more than half of men, think work is a person's most important activity.

Job security is the only job characteristic that the majority of men hold important. Among women, the majority rates both job security and interesting work as very important. Women are considerably more likely than men to feel it is important to have job security. They are also more likely than men to say it is important that a job be useful to society and that it enable them to help others.

Men are more likely than women to want to be self-employed, to work in the private sector, and to work for a large employer. Women, on the other hand, are more likely than men to prefer working for someone else, preferably the government or a small firm.

Whites seem to have more positive opinions about their work than blacks or people of "other" race do. Majorities of people of all races would accept a job with higher pay even if it meant leaving their current employer. But whites are more likely than blacks and other races to say they would stay on the job. They are also less likely to want to change the type of work they do. Whites are least likely to think a job is just a way to earn money and are most likely to believe work is a person's most important activity.

Blacks are far more likely than whites and other races to say they would like to work more and earn more money. Whites are more likely to say they would prefer to log fewer hours and take home less pay. It's easy to see why, however. Whites are most likely to say their work is often or always stressful. But both whites and blacks are much less likely than people of other races to say their work is hardly ever or never stressful.

Blacks are far more likely to want to work for a small firm than a large one, while whites are most likely to prefer private-sector over government work. Similar-sized majorities of all races would like to be their own bosses.

Whites are less likely than blacks and other races to say a chance to advance is an important job characteristic. Blacks are most likely to say job security is important. Blacks and other races are more likely than whites to say it is important that a job allow them to help others and that it have a high income.

On many work and money issues, differences in attitudes are strongly associated with age. Behind this association is life stage. Young adults are in entry-level jobs and generally have low incomes. The middle-aged are at the peak of their careers and earnings. Most older Americans are retired and dependent on pensions and Social Security checks.

Since young adults are just beginning their career, it is understandable that they would be the ones least satisfied with their financial situation. But their low-level jobs have at least one benefit. Younger people are more confident than their elders that they could easily find another job with the same pay and benefits.

Many are likely to do just that. Nearly half of workers under age 30 say they may look for a different job in the near future, but fewer than one-third of older workers are likely to do so. The youngest workers also say they would like to work more hours and earn more pay. After age 30, when most workers have young children, the proportion of those who want to work more drops sharply.

Young workers want more money and are willing to work longer hours, but this doesn't mean they are willing to let work interfere with other parts of their life. The proportion of people who say they do the best work they can even if it sometimes interferes with other parts of their life is higher among older workers.

All that hard work takes its toll, however, especially in the peak-earning years. People in their forties and fifties are considerably more likely than younger or older workers to find their work stressful. And the older people are, the more likely they are to say they would quit working if they didn't need the money.

Younger workers are much more likely than older workers to say they would like to have a different type of work. And a substantial pay raise would lure away more workers under age 40 than older workers.

Younger generations are more entrepreneurial than their elders. The proportion of those who would prefer to be self-employed is highest among people under age 40. People under age 50 are more likely than older workers to prefer private-sector over civil-service work. The youngest adults are most likely to say it is important to them that a job be interesting and offer opportunities for advancement. People in their forties are most likely to consider it important to be able to work independently and to have flexible hours. People in their sixties want job security.

Generally, the higher their educational level, the more money people earn. This accounts for the greater financial satisfaction found among the college educated. Higher education also increases the likelihood of obtaining interesting and meaningful work. This is one reason why the percentage of people who would continue to work even if they did not need the money rises sharply with education. Half of people who did not complete high school would jump at the chance to change the type of work they do, but the proportion falls to only 20 percent among people with a graduate degree.

Income differences by education are apparent in the desire to trade extra work hours for more pay. People who did not complete college are more likely to say they would like to work longer hours and earn more money. The percentage of those who say they would like to work fewer hours and earn less money is far higher among people with a graduate degree. People who did not complete high school are the ones most likely to say it would not be easy to find a job with another employer with income and benefits comparable to what they have now.

College graduates are far less likely than those with less education to agree that a job is just a way of earning money. But people who did not complete high school are most likely to believe work is a person's most important activity.

The more education people have, the more likely they are to prefer working for a small firm rather than a large one and to choose private-sector over government work. College graduates are more likely to consider it important that their job be interesting, while those with less education are most likely to consider job security and a high income as important.

Satisfaction with Financial Situation

Americans are neither thrilled nor depressed about their finances.

The nation is enjoying the longest economic boom ever, but this hasn't translated into greater satisfaction with finances. One-quarter of Americans are not at all satisfied with their financial situation, the same proportion as in 1978. Thirty percent are satisfied, down from 34 percent in 1978. The remainder take the middle ground, saying they are more or less satisfied.

One-third of whites say they are satisfied with their financial situation compared with only 19 percent of blacks and 23 percent of "other" races. The percentage of blacks who say they are not at all satisfied fell from 45 percent in 1978 to 39 percent in 1998, however.

The percentage of people who are satisfied with their finances rises with age. This is not surprising since young adults tend to work in lower-wage jobs. Thirty-five percent of people under age 30 are not at all satisfied with their finances (up from 30 percent in 1978), but the proportion drops with age to a low of 10 percent among people aged 70 or older. The oldest Americans are most likely to say they are satisfied with their finances.

Education boosts earnings. This truth explains why the best-educated people are the ones most satisfied with their financial situation. Among college graduates, 41 to 48 percent are satisfied with their finances compared with a much smaller 26 percent of people with less education.

Satisfaction with Financial Situation, 1998

"So far as you and your family are concerned, would you say that you are pretty well satisfied with your present financial situation, more or less satisfied, or not satisfied at all?"

(percent of people aged 18 or older responding by sex, race, age, and education, 1998)

	pretty well satisfied	more or less satisfied	not at all satisfied
Total	**30%**	**44%**	**25%**
Men	30	45	25
Women	30	44	26
Black	19	42	39
White	33	45	22
Other	23	43	34
Aged 18 to 29	21	43	35
Aged 30 to 39	28	43	29
Aged 40 to 49	25	47	27
Aged 50 to 59	36	41	23
Aged 60 to 69	36	47	17
Aged 70 or older	44	45	10
Not a high school graduate	26	43	30
High school graduate	26	46	28
Bachelor's degree	41	40	19
Graduate degree	48	39	13

Note: Numbers may not add to 100 because "don't know" is not shown.
Source: General Social Survey, National Opinion Research Center, University of Chicago; calculations by the author

Satisfaction with Financial Situation, 1978 to 1998

"So far as you and your family are concerned, would you say that you are pretty well satisfied with your present financial situation, more or less satisfied, or not satisfied at all?"

(percent of people aged 18 or older responding by sex, race, age, and education, 1978–98)

	pretty well satisfied			more or less satisfied			not at all satisfied		
	1998	*1988*	*1978*	*1998*	*1988*	*1978*	*1998*	*1988*	*1978*
Total	**30%**	**31%**	**34%**	**44%**	**45%**	**42%**	**25%**	**24%**	**24%**
Men	30	31	35	45	45	41	25	23	23
Women	30	30	33	44	45	43	26	25	24
Black	19	17	23	42	41	32	39	42	45
White	33	33	35	45	45	44	22	22	21
Aged 18 to 29	21	22	26	43	47	44	35	30	30
Aged 30 to 39	28	22	27	43	48	46	29	29	27
Aged 40 to 49	25	26	32	47	41	41	27	33	28
Aged 50 to 59	36	33	40	41	44	43	23	24	17
Aged 60 to 69	36	42	40	47	42	42	17	15	18
Aged 70 or older	44	51	54	45	43	33	10	6	13
Not a high school graduate	26	33	36	43	42	40	30	25	24
High school graduate	26	26	32	46	48	43	28	26	25
Bachelor's degree	41	37	39	40	45	42	19	18	18
Graduate degree	48	54	42	39	33	45	13	13	13

Note: Numbers may not add to 100 because "don't know" is not shown.
Source: General Social Survey, National Opinion Research Center, University of Chicago; calculations by the author

Changes in Financial Situation

There has been little change over the years in the percentage of Americans who say their financial situation is better than a few years ago.

Forty-five percent of Americans say their financial situation has improved. One might assume this optimism stems from the boom times of the late 1990s, but the percentage of those who say their financial situation is improving was only a few points higher in 1998 than in 1988 or 1978.

Similar percentages of men and women say their finances have become worse, improved, or stayed the same. Nearly half of whites (47 percent) say their finances have improved compared with 36 percent of blacks. The proportion of blacks who say their financial situation has deteriorated fell substantially, from 25 percent in 1978 to only 16 percent in 1998.

The percentage of people saying their financial situation has improved falls with age, while the percentage of those who say it has stayed the same rises with age. More than half of people under age 40 say their finances have gotten better, but the proportion falls to only 22 percent among people aged 70 or older. Much of this difference is due to the rising incomes of younger adults as they gain job experience. Most people aged 60 or older, on the other hand, have fixed incomes that, at best, rise at the rate of inflation.

The increasing importance of a college degree is reflected in the changing percentage of people with a bachelor's degree who say their financial situation has improved. In 1978, 44 percent said their finances were getting better. By 1998, the figure had grown to 60 percent. In contrast, 42 percent of people with a high school diploma said their financial situation had improved, down from 48 percent in 1978. Among people who did not complete high school, only 27 percent said their finances were getting better, the same proportion as in 1978.

Changes in Financial Situation, 1998

"During the last few years, has your financial situation been getting better, worse, or has it stayed the same?"

(percent of people aged 18 or older responding by sex, race, age, and education, 1998)

	gotten better	stayed the same	gotten worse
Total	**45%**	**39%**	**16%**
Men	46	39	14
Women	44	39	17
Black	36	47	16
White	47	38	15
Other	42	35	22
Aged 18 to 29	52	31	16
Aged 30 to 39	54	32	13
Aged 40 to 49	46	36	18
Aged 50 to 59	47	38	15
Aged 60 to 69	30	51	18
Aged 70 or older	22	62	15
Not a high school graduate	27	49	23
High school graduate	42	42	16
Bachelor's degree	60	28	12
Graduate degree	57	34	9

Note: Numbers may not add to 100 because "don't know" is not shown.
Source: General Social Survey, National Opinion Research Center, University of Chicago; calculations by the author

Changes in Financial Situation, 1978 to 1998

"During the last few years, has your financial situation been getting better, worse, or has it stayed the same?"

(percent of people aged 18 or older responding by sex, race, age, and education, 1978–98)

	gotten better			stayed the same			gotten worse		
	1998	*1988*	*1978*	*1998*	*1988*	*1978*	*1998*	*1988*	*1978*
Total	**45%**	**40%**	**41%**	**39%**	**41%**	**40%**	**16%**	**18%**	**19%**
Men	46	45	47	39	40	36	14	15	18
Women	44	36	37	39	42	43	17	21	19
Black	36	37	31	47	43	44	16	20	25
White	47	41	43	38	41	39	15	18	18
Aged 18 to 29	52	51	53	31	31	33	16	16	14
Aged 30 to 39	54	50	54	32	33	29	13	16	16
Aged 40 to 49	46	45	42	36	34	39	18	21	19
Aged 50 to 59	47	35	35	38	41	42	15	24	23
Aged 60 to 69	30	21	22	51	57	52	18	22	25
Aged 70 or older	22	20	16	62	65	61	15	15	23
Not a high school graduate	27	25	27	49	53	50	23	22	23
High school graduate	42	41	48	42	39	35	16	20	17
Bachelor's degree	60	55	44	28	32	38	12	13	18
Graduate degree	57	54	58	34	39	26	9	7	16

Note: Numbers may not add to 100 because "don't know" is not shown.
Source: General Social Survey, National Opinion Research Center, University of Chicago; calculations by the author

Social Class

Few people identify with the upper or lower classes.

Regardless of the definitions sociologists and economists use to classify people by economic class, few Americans see themselves as part of the upper or lower class. Instead, most people consider themselves working class (45 percent) or middle class (46 percent). The percentages have changed little during the past two decades.

Whites are most likely to say they are middle class, while blacks and people of "other" races (who generally have lower incomes than whites) are most likely to identify themselves as working class. The percentage of blacks identifying themselves as middle class rose slightly, however, between 1978 and 1998.

There is a decided shift from working class to middle class as people get older. Only 37 percent of people under age 30 feel they are part of the middle class, but the proportion rises to more than half among people aged 60 or older. Conversely, 54 percent of 18-to-29-year-olds say they are in the working class compared with fewer than 30 percent of people aged 70 or older.

The most pronounced disparity is by education. The more educated people are, the higher their incomes. Only 32 percent of people who did not complete high school say they are middle class, but the proportion rises to 75 percent among people with a graduate degree.

Social Class, 1998

"If you were asked to use one of four names for your social class, which would you say you belong in: the lower class, the working class, the middle class, or the upper class?"

(percent of people aged 18 or older responding by sex, race, age, and education, 1998)

	lower class	working class	middle class	upper class
Total	5%	45%	46%	4%
Men	4	45	46	5
Women	6	45	46	3
Black	10	56	31	3
White	4	42	49	4
Other	9	53	34	3
Aged 18 to 29	6	54	37	2
Aged 30 to 39	5	47	46	2
Aged 40 to 49	4	52	41	3
Aged 50 to 59	6	38	49	7
Aged 60 to 69	6	36	54	3
Aged 70 or older	7	30	56	6
Not a high school graduate	15	50	32	4
High school graduate	5	53	40	2
Bachelor's degree	2	27	64	8
Graduate degree	1	14	75	10

Note: Numbers may not add to 100 because "don't know" is not shown.
Source: General Social Survey, National Opinion Research Center, University of Chicago; calculations by the author

Social Class, 1978 to 1998

"If you were asked to use one of four names for your social class, which would you say you belong in: the lower class, the working class, the middle class, or the upper class?"

(percent of people aged 18 or older responding by sex, race, age, and education, 1978–98)

	lower class			working class			middle class			upper class		
	1998	*1988*	*1978*	*1998*	*1988*	*1978*	*1998*	*1988*	*1978*	*1998*	*1988*	*1978*
Total	5%	5%	5%	45%	45%	47%	46%	47%	45%	4%	2%	2%
Men	4	4	5	45	46	47	46	47	45	5	3	2
Women	6	6	6	45	44	46	46	48	46	3	2	2
Black	10	12	13	56	58	58	31	27	27	3	2	3
White	4	4	5	42	42	46	49	51	48	4	3	2
Aged 18 to 29	6	6	5	54	51	56	37	41	39	2	2	0
Aged 30 to 39	5	5	4	47	46	45	46	48	49	2	1	2
Aged 40 to 49	4	4	3	52	46	48	41	46	44	3	4	3
Aged 50 to 59	6	3	6	38	56	48	49	38	43	7	3	4
Aged 60 to 69	6	6	8	36	36	42	54	55	46	3	4	4
Aged 70 or older	7	6	9	30	32	31	56	59	56	6	3	3
Not a high school graduate	15	10	11	50	52	55	32	35	34	4	2	0
High school graduate	5	5	3	53	50	51	40	43	44	2	1	2
Bachelor's degree	2	1	1	27	22	20	64	72	72	8	5	7
Graduate degree	1	0	0	14	4	6	75	85	82	10	10	11

Note: Numbers may not add to 100 because "don't know" is not shown.
Source: General Social Survey, National Opinion Research Center, University of Chicago; calculations by the author

Income Relative to Others'

Education is the biggest factor in income differences.

Americans have a fairly accurate assessment of their income relative to the incomes of other Americans. Nearly half of adults (47 percent) say their income is average, while 29 percent say it is below average and 23 percent say it is above average.

Whites are less likely than blacks and "other" races to believe their income is below average. Forty-one percent of blacks and 33 percent of others say they have a below-average income compared with only 26 percent of whites.

People under age 30 and those aged 60 or older are more likely than other adults to say their income is below average. People in their fifties are most likely to say their income is above average, which is no so surprise since this is the age at which earnings peak for most people.

The largest differences are by education. Well over half of people with a graduate degree say their income is above average, but the proportion falls to only 8 percent among people who did not complete high school. Forty-seven percent of the least educated say their income is below average, but the proportion of those who say this drops to only 13 percent among people with a graduate degree.

Income Relative to Others', 1998

"Compared with American families in general, would you say your family income is far below average, below average, average, above average, or far above average?"

(percent of people aged 18 or older responding by sex, race, age, and education, 1998)

	far below average	below average	average	above average	far above average	below average, total	above average, total
Total	6%	23%	47%	21%	2%	29%	23%
Men	5	22	46	23	3	27	26
Women	7	23	48	19	2	30	21
Black	9	32	47	9	2	41	11
White	5	21	47	24	2	26	26
Other	9	24	49	14	2	33	16
Aged 18 to 29	10	25	49	13	2	35	15
Aged 30 to 39	5	20	53	20	2	25	22
Aged 40 to 49	6	21	45	25	2	27	27
Aged 50 to 59	5	17	42	30	5	22	35
Aged 60 to 69	6	29	43	19	2	35	21
Aged 70 or older	3	30	43	19	1	33	20
Not a high school graduate	11	36	43	7	1	47	8
High school graduate	6	24	51	17	1	30	18
Bachelor's degree	4	13	44	34	4	17	38
Graduate degree	3	10	30	50	6	13	56

Note: Numbers may not add to 100 because "don't know" is not shown.
Source: General Social Survey, National Opinion Research Center, University of Chicago; calculations by the author

Income Relative to Others, 1978 to 1998

"Compared with American families in general, would you say your family income is far below average, below average, average, above average, or far above average?"

(percent of people aged 18 or older responding by sex, race, age, and education, 1978–98)

	far below/below average			average			above/far above average		
	1998	*1988*	*1978*	*1998*	*1988*	*1978*	*1998*	*1988*	*1978*
Total	**29%**	**28%**	**27%**	**47%**	**51%**	**53%**	**23%**	**20%**	**20%**
Men	27	24	26	46	52	47	26	24	27
Women	30	31	28	48	51	57	21	17	14
Black	41	42	47	47	46	39	11	11	13
White	26	25	24	47	52	54	26	22	21
Aged 18 to 29	35	33	29	49	50	56	15	17	15
Aged 30 to 39	25	23	22	53	56	51	22	20	27
Aged 40 to 49	27	24	23	45	47	53	27	29	24
Aged 50 to 59	22	31	23	42	46	53	35	24	24
Aged 60 to 69	35	26	34	43	52	48	21	21	18
Aged 70 or older	33	30	34	43	56	55	20	13	9
Not a high school graduate	47	40	36	43	50	57	8	9	5
High school graduate	30	28	25	51	56	54	18	16	20
Bachelor's degree	17	13	15	44	47	36	38	40	48
Graduate degree	13	12	10	30	24	37	56	64	53

Note: Numbers may not add to 100 because "don't know" is not shown.
Source: General Social Survey, National Opinion Research Center, University of Chicago; calculations by the author

Standard of Living Relative to Parents'

Most people believe they are better off than their parents were at the same age.

Most Americans believe their current standard of living is better than their parents' at the same age. The 64 percent majority say they have a better standard of living, and one-third say it is much better.

People of "other" races are more likely than blacks or whites to say they are much better off than their parents were. One reason for this improvement is that many people of other races are first- or second-generation Americans who came to this country expressly to better their living conditions.

Substantial differences exist among the generations. Forty-six percent of people aged 70 or older and 43 percent of those in their sixties say they are much better off than their parents were at the same age. The proportions fall to only 27 to 28 percent among people under age 40. Most of today's elderly have been spared the poverty experienced by many of the elderly in the past, thanks in large part to Social Security. Current retirees have also benefited from a sharp rise in home values that occurred in the 1970s and 1980s as the baby-boom generation bid up the price of homes. This has left today's older Americans better off in retirement than any previous generation.

Standard of Living Relative to Parents', 1998

"Compared to your parents when they were the age you are now, do you think your own standard of living now is much better, somewhat better, about the same, somewhat worse, or much worse than theirs was?"

(percent of people aged 18 or older responding by sex, race, age, and education, 1998)

	much better	somewhat better	about the same	somewhat worse	much worse	better, total	worse, total
Total	**33%**	**31%**	**21%**	**10%**	**3%**	**64%**	**13%**
Men	33	30	21	11	3	63	14
Women	33	31	22	10	3	64	13
Black	30	32	19	13	4	62	17
White	33	31	22	11	3	64	14
Other	38	31	22	5	2	69	7
Aged 18 to 29	27	34	22	11	2	61	13
Aged 30 to 39	28	30	24	13	4	58	17
Aged 40 to 49	32	30	21	13	4	62	17
Aged 50 to 59	31	34	19	11	4	65	15
Aged 60 to 69	43	31	18	5	2	74	7
Aged 70 or older	46	25	20	5	1	71	6
Not a high school graduate	39	29	19	5	5	68	10
High school graduate	32	31	22	12	3	63	15
Bachelor's degree	33	30	21	11	3	63	14
Graduate degree	25	34	27	10	4	59	14

Note: Numbers may not add to 100 because "don't know" is not shown.
Source: General Social Survey, National Opinion Research Center, University of Chicago; calculations by the author

Children's Future Standard of Living

Most people believe their children will have it better than they themselves do now.

All parents want to believe their children's future will be at least as good as their own. Only 14 percent of adults think their children's future standard of living will be worse than their own is now. Sixty percent believe their children will be better off.

The proportion of people who say their children will enjoy a better standard of living than they themselves do now is greatest among the segments of the population that tend to have a relatively low standard of living. Blacks and "other" races, for example, are more likely than whites to say their children will have a better standard of living. Three-quarters of blacks and 70 percent of others say their children's standard of living will improve at least somewhat compared with a smaller 56 percent of whites.

People with a graduate degree, who command above-average salaries, are least likely to believe their children's standard of living will be better than their own. Only 38 percent of people with a graduate degree expect their children to improve on their own standard of living compared with more than half of people with less education.

Children's Future Standard of Living, 1998

"When your children are at the age you are now, do you think their standard of living will be much better, somewhat better, about the same, somewhat worse, or much worse than yours is now?"

(percent of people aged 18 or older responding by sex, race, age, and education, 1998)

	much better	somewhat better	about the same	somewhat worse	much worse	better, total	worse, total
Total	**24%**	**36%**	**22%**	**10%**	**4%**	**60%**	**14%**
Men	23	35	23	10	4	58	14
Women	26	37	21	10	3	63	13
Black	36	38	10	8	3	74	11
White	20	36	24	11	3	56	14
Other	43	27	14	5	5	70	10
Aged 18 to 29	30	40	18	6	3	70	9
Aged 30 to 39	24	37	21	10	4	61	14
Aged 40 to 49	20	36	22	12	6	56	18
Aged 50 to 59	20	32	23	14	4	52	18
Aged 60 to 69	30	27	28	9	1	57	10
Aged 70 or older	25	36	20	10	1	61	11
Not a high school graduate	32	31	13	9	6	63	15
High school graduate	24	38	20	10	4	62	14
Bachelor's degree	20	36	31	8	1	56	9
Graduate degree	12	26	39	16	3	38	19

Note: Numbers may not add to 100 because "don't know" is not shown.
Source: General Social Survey, National Opinion Research Center, University of Chicago; calculations by the author

Achieving the Good Life

Most Americans believe they can improve their standard of living.

Most people still believe in the American dream of equality of opportunity. Seventy-two percent agree that people like themselves have a good chance of improving their standard of living. Overall, this is the same percentage of people who agree as in 1987, but among some segments of the population there has a been a substantial increase in agreement.

People of "other" races are more likely than whites and blacks to believe they can improve their standard of living. The proportion of blacks who agree increased from 65 percent in 1987 to 71 percent in 1998, making blacks as likely as whites to agree with the statement.

In 1987, older people were more optimistic than the young. By 1998 young adults were the most optimistic. The percentage of people under age 40 who believe they can achieve the good life rose during the decade, while the percentage of people aged 70 or older who agree declined.

College graduates are more optimistic about their chances than those with less education. More than one-quarter of college graduates strongly agree that people like themselves have a good chance of improving their standard of living, but only 16 to 17 percent of people with less education agree. Considering the changes in the economy that make it difficult for those with little education to obtain well-paying jobs, they are probably right.

Achieving the Good Life, 1998

"The way things are in America, people like me and my family have a good chance of improving our standard of living. Do you agree or disagree?"

(percent of people aged 18 or older responding by sex, race, age, and education, 1998)

	strongly agree	agree	neither	disagree	strongly disagree	agree, total	disagree, total
Total	18%	54%	11%	12%	3%	72%	15%
Men	21	54	10	12	3	75	15
Women	16	55	12	12	3	71	15
Black	14	57	12	13	3	71	16
White	18	54	11	12	3	72	15
Other	25	55	8	10	1	80	11
Aged 18 to 29	21	55	13	7	2	76	9
Aged 30 to 39	18	58	11	10	2	76	12
Aged 40 to 49	20	52	11	14	4	72	18
Aged 50 to 59	17	57	7	14	3	74	17
Aged 60 to 69	19	55	12	11	2	74	13
Aged 70 or older	14	49	13	17	2	63	19
Not a high school graduate	17	51	10	15	3	68	18
High school graduate	16	56	11	13	3	72	16
Bachelor's degree	24	53	13	8	2	77	10
Graduate degree	27	51	11	8	3	78	11

Note: Numbers may not add to 100 because "can't choose" is not shown.
Source: General Social Survey, National Opinion Research Center, University of Chicago; calculations by the author

Achieving the Good Life, 1987 and 1998

"The way things are in America, people like me and my family have a good chance of improving our standard of living. Do you agree or disagree?"

(percent of people aged 18 or older responding by sex, race, age, and education, 1987–98)

	agree/ strongly agree		neither		disagree/ strongly disagree	
	1998	1987	1998	1987	1998	1987
Total	**72%**	**71%**	**11%**	**17%**	**15%**	**10%**
Men	75	74	10	15	15	10
Women	71	68	12	20	15	10
Black	71	65	12	19	16	13
White	72	72	11	17	15	10
Aged 18 to 29	76	66	13	23	9	9
Aged 30 to 39	76	66	11	18	12	15
Aged 40 to 49	72	77	11	14	18	9
Aged 50 to 59	74	74	7	14	17	9
Aged 60 to 69	74	80	12	10	13	7
Aged 70 or older	63	68	13	21	19	10
Not a high school graduate	68	68	10	17	18	12
High school graduate	72	70	11	18	16	11
Bachelor's degree	77	78	13	13	10	8
Graduate degree	78	68	11	24	11	8

Note: Numbers may not add to 100 because "can't choose" is not shown.
Source: General Social Survey, National Opinion Research Center, University of Chicago; calculations by the author

Hard Work or Luck?

Most people believe working hard is the key to getting ahead.

Two-thirds of Americans think people get ahead by their own hard work. Only 10 percent believe luck is the key to success, and 22 percent think both hard work and luck play a role.

There are only small differences of opinion on this question, but in 1977 there were larger gaps in opinion by sex, race, and education. Changes in the percentage of those whose say hard work is most important have narrowed the gaps. In 1977, for example, only 50 percent of people with a graduate degree said hard work was the key to getting ahead, while 43 percent said hard work and luck were equally important. In 1998, however, fully 67 percent of people with a graduate degree said people get ahead by hard work, while only 25 percent said luck was just as important. The gap also narrowed between blacks and whites as the percentage of blacks saying hard work is most important increased.

Hard Work or Luck? 1998

"Some people say that people get ahead by their own hard work, others say that lucky breaks or help from other people are more important. Which do you think is most important?"

(percent of people aged 18 or older responding by sex, race, age, and education, 1998)

	hard work	hard work, luck equally important	luck
Total	**67%**	**22%**	**10%**
Men	65	23	12
Women	68	22	10
Black	64	20	14
White	67	23	10
Other	67	22	11
Aged 18 to 29	63	23	13
Aged 30 to 39	72	19	8
Aged 40 to 49	67	20	12
Aged 50 to 59	62	26	11
Aged 60 to 69	62	26	13
Aged 70 or older	69	23	7
Not a high school graduate	70	17	11
High school graduate	68	21	10
Bachelor's degree	60	29	10
Graduate degree	67	25	7

Note: Numbers may not add to 100 because "don't know" is not shown.
Source: General Social Survey, National Opinion Research Center, University of Chicago; calculations by the author

Hard Work or Luck? 1977 to 1998

"Some people say that people get ahead by their own hard work, others say that lucky breaks or help from other people are more important. Which do you think is most important?"

(percent of people aged 18 or older responding by sex, race, age, and education, 1977–98)

	hard work			hard work, luck equally important			luck		
	1998	*1988*	*1977*	*1998*	*1988*	*1977*	*1998*	*1988*	*1977*
Total	**67%**	**67%**	**61%**	**22%**	**21%**	**28%**	**10%**	**12%**	**10%**
Men	65	64	58	23	21	29	12	15	13
Women	68	68	63	22	21	28	10	10	8
Black	64	59	52	20	26	31	14	13	15
White	67	68	62	23	20	28	10	11	10
Aged 18 to 29	63	66	61	23	19	27	13	15	11
Aged 30 to 39	72	67	60	19	24	29	8	9	10
Aged 40 to 49	67	66	60	20	23	28	12	11	11
Aged 50 to 59	62	64	59	26	23	29	11	13	11
Aged 60 to 69	62	69	63	26	20	26	13	10	10
Aged 70 or older	69	69	61	23	16	28	7	15	9
Not a high school graduate	70	73	65	17	16	22	11	10	12
High school graduate	68	66	59	21	21	30	10	13	10
Bachelor's degree	60	60	57	29	24	33	10	15	9
Graduate degree	67	55	50	25	32	43	7	11	7

Note: Numbers may not add to 100 because "don't know" is not shown.
Source: General Social Survey, National Opinion Research Center, University of Chicago; calculations by the author

Likelihood of Losing Job

The tight labor market provides a great deal of job security.

Although the low unemployment rate and booming economy help provide a sense of job security, in most years few people believe they are likely to lose their job. Nine out of ten Americans say it is unlikely that they will be out of work in the near future.

Blacks are less secure than whites and "other" races about their job. While 92 percent of whites and 91 percent of others say they don't think their job is at risk, a smaller 82 percent of blacks feel that way. The gap between blacks and whites was greater in 1978, however, when 93 percent of whites but only 79 percent of blacks felt their job was secure.

In 1978, workers under age 30 and those in their sixties were less likely than people aged 30 to 59 to believe their job was secure. In 1998, the youngest workers were most likely to say their job was secure. This reflects both the current dearth of entry-level workers and the shortage of workers with the technological skills that are second-nature to many young adults.

People who did not complete high school feel more vulnerable than those with a college degree. Only 81 percent of the least educated believe their job is secure compared with 89 to 94 percent of people with at least a high school diploma.

Likelihood of Losing Job, 1998

"Thinking about the next 12 months, how likely do you think it is that you will lose your job or be laid off?"

(percent of people aged 18 or older responding by sex, race, age, and education, 1998)

	very likely	fairly likely	not too likely	not at all likely	likely, total	not likely, total
Total	**4%**	**4%**	**26%**	**64%**	**8%**	**90%**
Men	3	5	25	64	8	89
Women	4	4	27	64	8	91
Black	9	5	27	55	14	82
White	3	4	26	66	7	92
Other	6	3	28	63	9	91
Aged 18 to 29	3	3	33	61	6	94
Aged 30 to 39	4	5	26	64	9	90
Aged 40 to 49	4	4	26	63	8	89
Aged 50 to 59	3	3	23	68	6	91
Aged 60 to 69	2	8	20	70	10	90
Not a high school graduate	3	9	29	52	12	81
High school graduate	5	4	25	64	9	89
Bachelor's degree	3	4	26	66	7	92
Graduate degree	1	3	26	68	4	94

Note: Asked of people currently working. Aged 70 or older not shown because of small sample size. Numbers may not add to 100 because "don't know" is not shown.
Source: General Social Survey, National Opinion Research Center, University of Chicago; calculations by the author

Likelihood of Losing Job, 1978 to 1998

"Thinking about the next 12 months, how likely do you think it is that you will lose your job or be laid off?"

(percent of people aged 18 or older responding by sex, race, age, and education, 1978–98)

	very/fairly likely			not too/not at all likely		
	1998	*1988*	*1978*	*1998*	*1988*	*1978*
Total	**8%**	**8%**	**8%**	**90%**	**90%**	**91%**
Men	8	10	7	89	89	92
Women	8	7	9	91	92	90
Black	14	13	19	82	87	79
White	7	7	7	92	91	93
Aged 18 to 29	6	10	11	94	90	88
Aged 30 to 39	9	6	6	90	92	94
Aged 40 to 49	8	9	6	89	91	91
Aged 50 to 59	6	7	5	91	93	95
Aged 60 to 69	10	12	10	90	84	88
Not a high school graduate	12	14	9	81	82	89
High school graduate	9	10	9	89	89	90
Bachelor's degree	7	4	4	92	95	96
Graduate degree	4	2	4	94	98	96

Note: Asked of people currently working. Aged 70 or older not shown because of small sample size. Numbers may not add to 100 because "don't know" is not shown.
Source: General Social Survey, National Opinion Research Center, University of Chicago; calculations by the author

Ease of Finding a New Job

Young workers are least worried about replacing their current job.

American workers are divided about how easy it would be to find another job with approximately the same income and fringe benefits they have now. Thirty percent believe it would be very easy, 35 percent say it would be somewhat easy, and 33 percent think it would not be easy at all.

Whites and "other" races are more likely than blacks to say it would be very easy to replace their current job. But blacks are far more optimistic than they were in 1978. In that year, more than half of black workers said it would be very hard to find a comparable job, while 17 percent said it would be very easy. By 1998, only 32 percent felt it would be very hard, while 26 percent said it would be very easy.

Younger workers believe they could easily find another job with about the same pay and benefits. They are probably right, given the current high demand for entry-level and tech-savvy workers. Only 18 percent of workers under age 30 think it would not be easy to find a comparable job. As workers get older, however, finding an equivalent job becomes more difficult. Only 27 percent of workers in their forties and 22 percent of those in their fifties believe it would be easy to replace their current pay and benefits. Older workers are more highly paid than younger workers, making it more difficult for them to replace their incomes and fringe benefits.

Not surprisingly, people with marketable skills are more likely to feel they could easily replace their current job. The percentage of those who say it would be very easy rises with education, from only 16 percent among people who did not complete high school to 30 to 33 percent among college graduates. Conversely, the percentage of those who say it would not be easy at all is much higher among people with less education.

Ease of Finding a New Job, 1998

"About how easy would it be for you to find a job with another employer with approximately the same income and fringe benefits you have now?"

(percent of people aged 18 or older responding by sex, race, age, and education, 1998)

	very easy	somewhat easy	not easy at all
Total	**30**%	**35**%	**33**%
Men	30	35	32
Women	30	35	33
Black	26	37	32
White	31	34	33
Other	33	39	27
Aged 18 to 29	35	46	18
Aged 30 to 39	37	34	27
Aged 40 to 49	27	34	36
Aged 50 to 59	22	30	44
Aged 60 to 69	18	22	60
Not a high school graduate	16	32	45
High school graduate	29	33	36
Bachelor's degree	30	42	25
Graduate degree	33	36	29

Note: Asked of people currently working. Aged 70 or older not shown because of small sample size. Numbers may not add to 100 because "don't know" is not shown.
Source: General Social Survey, National Opinion Research Center, University of Chicago; calculations by the author

Ease of Finding a New Job, 1978 to 1998

"About how easy would it be for you to find a job with another employer with approximately the same income and fringe benefits you have now?"

(percent of people aged 18 or older responding by sex, race, age, and education, 1978–98)

	very easy			somewhat easy			not easy at all		
	1998	*1988*	*1978*	*1998*	*1988*	*1978*	*1998*	*1988*	*1978*
Total	**30%**	**27%**	**28%**	**35%**	**36%**	**32%**	**33%**	**34%**	**38%**
Men	30	30	28	35	33	33	32	35	38
Women	30	25	27	35	39	31	33	34	39
Black	26	21	17	37	36	28	32	41	52
White	31	29	29	34	36	32	33	33	37
Aged 18 to 29	35	29	30	46	46	38	18	25	31
Aged 30 to 39	37	26	30	34	46	34	27	26	35
Aged 40 to 49	27	33	28	34	20	33	36	46	36
Aged 50 to 59	22	22	21	30	26	25	44	46	52
Aged 60 to 69	18	16	21	22	21	15	60	51	60
Not a high school graduate	16	27	24	32	29	27	45	42	45
High school graduate	29	26	29	33	33	30	36	38	39
Bachelor's degree	30	34	27	42	44	42	25	20	30
Graduate degree	33	24	28	36	45	43	29	29	30

Note: Asked of people currently working. Aged 70 or older not shown because of small sample size. Numbers may not add to 100 because "don't know" is not shown.
Source: General Social Survey, National Opinion Research Center, University of Chicago; calculations by the author

Would Like Different Work

Americans are split on whether or not they want to change careers.

American workers are divided on whether or not they would like to do something different. Forty percent agree that, given the chance, they would change their present type of work for a different career, while 37 percent disagree and 23 percent neither agree nor disagree.

More men than women would like different work (43 percent of men versus 36 percent of women). Only 36 percent of whites would change careers compared with 51 percent of blacks and 46 percent of "other" races. Twenty-one percent of blacks, but only 12 to 14 percent of whites and others, strongly agree that they would like a career change.

Only 21 percent of the youngest workers (under age 30) have no desire to try a different type of job compared with 36 to 37 percent of workers aged 30 to 49, 46 percent of those in their fifties, and 59 percent of workers in their sixties. It is understandable that this share is rising with age, because older workers have spent years gaining experience and expertise in their current job. Many younger workers, in contrast, are still searching for the career that best matches their interests and abilities.

The less education people have, the fewer their career choices. The least educated workers are generally relegated to work that is not mentally challenging, although it may be physically demanding. Half of workers who did not complete high school would like to change careers, as would 42 percent of those with only a high school diploma. Among people with a bachelor's degree, a smaller 37 percent would like to try a different kind of work. Only 20 percent of people with a graduate degree want to switch careers.

Would Like Different Work, 1998

"To what extent do you agree or disagree with this statement? Given the chance, I would change my present type of work for something different."

(percent of people aged 18 or older responding by sex, race, age, and education, 1998)

	strongly agree	agree	neither	disagree	strongly disagree	agree, total	disagree, total
Total	**14%**	**26%**	**23%**	**26%**	**11%**	**40%**	**37%**
Men	14	29	23	22	9	43	31
Women	13	23	23	29	12	36	41
Black	21	30	20	23	3	51	26
White	12	24	23	27	12	36	39
Other	14	32	28	18	6	46	24
Aged 18 to 29	21	27	31	14	7	48	21
Aged 30 to 39	12	27	23	28	8	39	36
Aged 40 to 49	13	28	20	26	11	41	37
Aged 50 to 59	10	23	19	32	14	33	46
Aged 60 to 69	5	14	19	40	19	19	59
Not a high school graduate	19	31	21	16	10	50	26
High school graduate	14	28	23	27	7	42	34
Bachelor's degree	14	23	22	23	16	37	39
Graduate degree	6	14	21	38	21	20	59

Note: Asked of people currently working. Aged 70 or older not shown because of small sample size. Numbers may not add to 100 because "can't choose" is not shown.
Source: General Social Survey, National Opinion Research Center, University of Chicago; calculations by the author

Likely to Change Jobs

Young workers are most likely to job hop.

Although most workers would take a job with another employer if offered a large pay raise, two-thirds say they are not actively looking for another job. Thirty percent, however, are planning to seek a new job in the near future.

While only 27 percent of whites say they are likely to look for a different job, a larger 39 percent of blacks and 36 percent of "other" races do. Men are slightly more likely than women to be hoping for a change in employers.

Young workers are most likely to job hop as they seek careers that best fit their interests and skills. Nearly half of workers under age 30 (47 percent) are likely to look for work with a different employer in the near future. The proportion drops sharply after age 30. Only 27 to 31 percent of workers aged 30 to 49, 20 percent of those in their fifties, and 11 percent of people in their sixties say they are likely to change jobs soon. The small percentage of those who are looking for a new job among workers aged 50 or older doesn't mean this group is content with their present employer, however. Most are aware that many employers prefer younger workers, and they simply don't want to rock the boat.

Among people with a high school diploma or more education, 30 to 31 percent say they are likely to look for new employment opportunities in the near future. On the other hand, a slightly larger 36 percent of people who did not complete high school hope to change jobs.

Likely to Change Jobs, 1998

"All in all, how likely is it that you will try to find a job with another firm or organization within the next 12 months?"

(percent of people aged 18 or older responding by sex, race, age, and education, 1998)

	very likely	likely	unlikely	very unlikely	likely, total	unlikely, total
Total	**14%**	**16%**	**24%**	**43%**	**30%**	**67%**
Men	13	18	24	41	31	65
Women	14	14	24	44	28	68
Black	19	20	30	26	39	56
White	12	15	23	46	27	69
Other	20	16	20	42	36	62
Aged 18 to 29	22	25	27	24	47	51
Aged 30 to 39	12	15	28	41	27	69
Aged 40 to 49	15	16	22	43	31	65
Aged 50 to 59	11	9	20	55	20	75
Aged 60 to 69	2	9	20	68	11	88
Not a high school graduate	19	17	27	33	36	60
High school graduate	15	15	25	42	30	67
Bachelor's degree	11	20	23	43	31	66
Graduate degree	11	19	19	50	30	69

Note: Asked of people currently working. Aged 70 or older not shown because of small sample size. Numbers may not add to 100 because "can't choose" is not shown.
Source: General Social Survey, National Opinion Research Center, University of Chicago; calculations by the author

Turn Down Higher Pay to Stay with Employer

Higher pay would entice most workers to switch employers.

Money isn't everything, but it is enough to lure most workers away from their job. Only 20 percent of workers would turn down a large pay raise to stay with their current employer, while 52 percent would readily jump ship. A substantial proportion (24 percent) neither agree nor disagree that they would turn down higher pay to stay with their employer.

Twenty-two percent of whites say a substantial raise would not entice them to change employers, while a smaller 16 percent of blacks and 8 percent of "other" races agree. Sixty-one percent of blacks disagree compared with one-half of whites and other races.

Older workers generally have more invested in their jobs and less need of higher incomes than younger workers. Only 17 percent of workers under age 50 would turn down higher pay to stay with their employer compared with 27 percent of workers in their fifties and nearly half (46 percent) of workers in their sixties.

The least-educated workers are most loyal to their current employer. Twenty-eight percent of people who did not complete high school would turn down a higher paying job compared with 17 to 20 percent of workers with more education. Among college graduates, 28 to 32 percent neither agree nor disagree with the proposition, indicating that for these workers money is only one of many factors that determine where they want to work.

Turn Down Higher Pay to Stay with Employer, 1998

"To what extent do you agree or disagree with this statement? I would turn down another job that offered quite a bit more pay in order to stay with this organization."

(percent of people aged 18 or older responding by sex, race, age, and education, 1998)

	strongly agree	agree	neither	disagree	strongly disagree	agree, total	disagree, total
Total	**5%**	**15%**	**24%**	**35%**	**17%**	**20%**	**52%**
Men	6	13	26	35	17	19	52
Women	5	16	23	35	16	21	51
Black	4	12	21	37	24	16	61
White	6	16	24	34	16	22	50
Other	0	8	36	40	12	8	52
Aged 18 to 29	3	14	22	39	20	17	59
Aged 30 to 39	5	12	27	37	16	17	53
Aged 40 to 49	4	13	24	37	17	17	54
Aged 50 to 59	11	16	26	28	15	27	43
Aged 60 to 69	9	37	21	23	7	46	30
Not a high school graduate	10	18	24	23	19	28	42
High school graduate	4	16	21	37	18	20	55
Bachelor's degree	6	13	28	34	16	19	50
Graduate degree	6	11	32	37	11	17	48

Note: Asked of people currently working. Aged 70 or older not shown because of small sample size. Numbers may not add to 100 because "can't choose" is not shown.
Source: General Social Survey, National Opinion Research Center, University of Chicago; calculations by the author

Work Is Most Important Activity

A declining number of Americans agree.

The priorities of Americans seem to be changing. In 1989, 37 percent of Americans agreed that work is a person's most important activity, while 42 percent disagreed. By 1998, however, a smaller 30 percent agreed, while the 51 percent majority disagreed.

Men are more likely than women to say work is a person's most important activity (32 versus 28 percent). More than half of women (54 percent) disagree compared with 45 percent of men.

Whites are less likely than blacks or "other" races to think work is most important. Only 25 percent of whites concur compared with 45 percent of blacks and 49 percent of other races. The proportion of blacks who think work is most important dropped only 5 percentage points between 1989 and 1998, while the proportion of whites who agree dropped 10 percentage points.

In 1989, the percentage of people saying work is most important increased with age. But the percentage of older people who hold this opinion declined substantially. Today, the gap by age is much narrower, but people aged 70 or older are still most likely to believe work is a person's most important activity Least likely to agree are people in their thirties, the age at which most people are busy raising children.

Nearly half of people who did not complete high school think work is most important compared with 22 to 28 percent of people with more education. Only one-third of those with the least education disagree compared with 47 to 55 percent of people with more education.

Work Is Most Important Activity, 1998

"Thinking of work in general, please indicate how much you agree or disagree. Work is a person's most important activity."

(percent of people aged 18 or older responding by sex, race, age, and education, 1998)

	strongly agree	agree	neither	disagree	strongly disagree	agree, total	disagree, total
Total	**8%**	**22%**	**19%**	**36%**	**15%**	**30%**	**51%**
Men	8	24	22	34	11	32	45
Women	8	20	16	37	17	28	54
Black	15	30	18	28	8	45	36
White	6	19	19	38	16	25	54
Other	10	39	14	27	9	49	36
Aged 18 to 29	7	25	18	35	14	32	49
Aged 30 to 39	7	16	19	41	17	23	58
Aged 40 to 49	8	18	20	38	16	26	54
Aged 50 to 59	7	21	23	33	16	28	49
Aged 60 to 69	8	29	17	31	15	37	46
Aged 70 or older	12	33	13	31	7	45	38
Not a high school graduate	16	32	16	23	10	48	33
High school graduate	7	21	18	38	15	28	53
Bachelor's degree	5	17	23	38	17	22	55
Graduate degree	2	22	28	35	12	24	47

Note: Numbers may not add to 100 because "can't choose" is not shown.
Source: General Social Survey, National Opinion Research Center, University of Chicago; calculations by the author

Work Is Most Important Activity, 1989 and 1998

"Thinking of work in general, please indicate how much you agree or disagree. Work is a person's most important activity."

(percent of people aged 18 or older responding by sex, race, age, and education, 1989–98)

	agree/ strongly agree		neither		disagree/ strongly disagree	
	1998	*1989*	*1998*	*1989*	*1998*	*1989*
Total	**30%**	**37%**	**19%**	**21%**	**51%**	**42%**
Men	32	38	22	22	45	39
Women	28	35	16	20	54	44
Black	45	50	18	13	36	36
White	25	35	19	21	54	43
Aged 18 to 29	32	30	18	29	49	41
Aged 30 to 39	23	27	19	23	58	50
Aged 40 to 49	26	30	20	20	54	49
Aged 50 to 59	28	45	23	17	49	36
Aged 60 to 69	37	45	17	19	46	34
Aged 70 or older	45	60	13	9	38	28
Not a high school graduate	48	48	16	15	33	35
High school graduate	28	36	18	22	53	41
Bachelor's degree	22	26	23	26	55	47
Graduate degree	24	33	28	23	47	43

Note: Numbers may not add to 100 because "can't choose" is not shown.
Source: General Social Survey, National Opinion Research Center, University of Chicago; calculations by the author

A Job Is Not Just for Money

Only one-quarter of Americans say a job is just a way to earn a living.

Most people get more out of their job than just a paycheck. Fifty-eight percent of adults disagree that a job is just a way to earn money. Only one-quarter agree.

Blacks are divided on this question, with 41 percent agreeing and 40 percent disagreeing that a job is just a way to earn a living. Only 20 percent of whites and 33 percent of "other" races think a job is just a way to earn money, while 62 percent of whites and 40 percent of others disagree.

People in their forties and fifties, who are at the peak of their career, are most likely to think work is about more than a paycheck. More than 60 percent of people in these age groups think there is more to work, while a smaller 52 to 57 percent of other age groups think so.

Most people pursue higher education to get better-paying and more interesting work. So it is no surprise that the more education people have, the more likely they are to think work offers more than just a means to earn a living. Fully 88 percent of people with a graduate degree believe there is more to work, but the proportion falls to 41 percent among people who did not complete high school. Conversely, for 37 percent of those with the least education work represents nothing more than a paycheck compared with only 7 percent of people with the most education.

A Job Is Not Just for Money, 1998

"Thinking of work in general, please indicate how much you agree or disagree. A job is just a way of earning money—no more."

(percent of people aged 18 or older responding by sex, race, age, and education, 1998)

	strongly agree	agree	neither	disagree	strongly disagree	agree, total	disagree, total
Total	**6%**	**18%**	**17%**	**41%**	**17%**	**24%**	**58%**
Men	5	18	19	39	18	23	57
Women	7	17	15	42	16	24	58
Black	10	31	15	33	7	41	40
White	5	15	16	43	19	20	62
Other	13	20	23	27	13	33	40
Aged 18 to 29	7	17	22	42	10	24	52
Aged 30 to 39	5	19	18	41	15	24	56
Aged 40 to 49	8	18	11	42	20	26	62
Aged 50 to 59	5	16	14	40	23	21	63
Aged 60 to 69	9	16	18	31	22	25	53
Aged 70 or older	3	17	16	41	16	20	57
Not a high school graduate	9	28	16	35	6	37	41
High school graduate	8	19	20	39	12	27	51
Bachelor's degree	3	10	12	45	30	13	75
Graduate degree	2	5	5	44	44	7	88

Note: Numbers may not add to 100 because "can't choose" is not shown.
Source: General Social Survey, National Opinion Research Center, University of Chicago; calculations by the author

A Job Is Not Just for Money, 1989 and 1998

**"Thinking of work in general, please indicate how much you agree or disagree.
A job is just a way of earning money—no more."**

(percent of people aged 18 or older responding by sex, race, age, and education, 1989–98)

	agree/ strongly agree		neither		disagree/ strongly disagree	
	1998	*1989*	*1998*	*1989*	*1998*	*1989*
Total	**24%**	**22%**	**17%**	**18%**	**58%**	**59%**
Men	23	24	19	16	57	59
Women	24	21	15	18	58	59
Black	41	45	15	14	40	39
White	20	19	16	18	62	62
Aged 18 to 29	24	23	22	20	52	56
Aged 30 to 39	24	20	18	16	56	64
Aged 40 to 49	26	16	11	15	62	68
Aged 50 to 59	21	26	14	18	63	55
Aged 60 to 69	25	22	18	21	53	55
Aged 70 or older	20	32	16	14	57	52
Not a high school graduate	37	42	16	15	41	40
High school graduate	27	20	20	21	51	59
Bachelor's degree	13	9	12	11	75	79
Graduate degree	7	9	5	10	88	81

Note: Numbers may not add to 100 because "can't choose" is not shown.
Source: General Social Survey, National Opinion Research Center, University of Chicago; calculations by the author

Would You Work If You Were Rich?

Money isn't the only thing that motivates workers.

Only 30 percent of Americans would log off their computers or hang up their hammers if they had enough money to live comfortably for the rest of their lives. Sixty-nine percent would continue to work even if they didn't need the money. Money may be a major reason for working, but it is clearly not the only one.

In 1977, men were much more likely than women to want to continue working even if they struck it rich (74 versus 62 percent). By 1998, however, the proportions were not far apart, as 70 percent of men and 68 percent of women said they would continue to work even if they did not need the money.

Sixty-three percent of blacks say they would keep working even if they became rich compared with a higher 69 percent of whites and 73 percent of "other" races. The percentage of blacks who say they would keep working has decreased since 1977.

As people accumulate more years in the workforce, their desire to retire grows. Three-quarters of young adults, with the enthusiasm of those just entering the workforce, say they would keep working even if they didn't need the money. The figure stands at a smaller 68 to 70 percent among people aged 30 to 49, and drops to 63 percent among people in their fifties and sixties.

The percentage of those who say they would continue to work rises with education. Only 59 percent of people who did not complete high school say they would work even if they didn't need the money, but the figure rises to 82 percent among people with a graduate degree. Education opens the door not only to higher paying work, but to more interesting work, which explains why the best-educated people are the ones most likely to want to continue to work.

Would You Work If You Were Rich? 1998

"If you were to get enough money to live as comfortably as you would like for the rest of your life, would you continue to work or would you stop working?"

(percent of people aged 18 or older responding by sex, race, age, and education, 1998)

	continue to work	stop working
Total	**69%**	**30%**
Men	70	29
Women	68	31
Black	63	34
White	69	30
Other	73	27
Aged 18 to 29	75	24
Aged 30 to 39	70	28
Aged 40 to 49	68	30
Aged 50 to 59	63	36
Aged 60 to 69	63	36
Not a high school graduate	59	39
High school graduate	66	32
Bachelor's degree	70	29
Graduate degree	82	17

Note: Asked of people currently working or temporarily not at work. Aged 70 or older not shown because of small sample size. Numbers may not add to 100 because "don't know" is not shown.
Source: General Social Survey, National Opinion Research Center, University of Chicago; calculations by the author

Would You Work If You Were Rich? 1977 to 1998

"If you were to get enough money to live as comfortably as you would like for the rest of your life, would you continue to work or would you stop working?"

(percent of people aged 18 or older responding by sex, race, age, and education, 1977–98)

	continue to work			stop working		
	1998	1988	1977	1998	1988	1977
Total	**69%**	**70%**	**69%**	**30%**	**29%**	**30%**
Men	70	74	74	29	25	24
Women	68	67	62	31	32	37
Black	63	68	68	34	30	30
White	69	70	69	30	29	30
Aged 18 to 29	75	77	77	24	23	23
Aged 30 to 39	70	76	73	28	23	26
Aged 40 to 49	68	66	68	30	33	30
Aged 50 to 59	63	64	56	36	34	42
Aged 60 to 69	63	44	64	36	54	36
Not a high school graduate	59	68	67	39	30	31
High school graduate	66	71	68	32	28	31
Bachelor's degree	70	64	70	29	33	28
Graduate degree	82	74	83	17	26	16

Note: Asked of people currently working or temporarily not at work. Aged 70 or older not shown because of small sample size. Numbers may not add to 100 because "don't know" is not shown.
Source: General Social Survey, National Opinion Research Center, University of Chicago; calculations by the author

Prefer to Work More or Less?

Most people would not change their work hours.

It is common to hear people complain that they have too much work. But given a choice, only 9 percent of Americans would choose to work fewer hours if it meant a pay cut. Thirty percent would work more if they could earn more money. Most are content with the hours and earnings they have now.

One-third of men say they would prefer to work more and earn more. Only 26 percent of women would choose this option. Since women still have more household responsibilities than men, working longer hours would be difficult for many of them.

Blacks, who generally earn less than whites, are most likely to want to work more and earn more. Nearly half of blacks (47 percent) would like to work more, compared with 27 percent of whites and 29 percent of "other" races. The percentage of blacks who would like to work more has grown substantially since 1989, when 39 percent felt that way.

The youngest workers are most likely to prefer working longer hours for more pay. They are also less likely to have family responsibilities and more likely to have relatively low paying jobs. Forty-one percent of workers under age 30 would work more compared with 23 to 28 percent of older workers.

The best-educated people are the ones most likely to want to work fewer hours. Nearly 3 out of 10 people with a graduate degree want to work less compared with 10 percent or fewer among people with less education. People who do not have a college degree generally earn less than those with more education. This explains why the less-educated are the ones most likely to say they would choose to work more and earn more.

Prefer to Work More or Less? 1998

"Think of the number of hours you work and the money you earn in your main job, including regular overtime. If you had only one of these three choices, which of the following would you prefer? Work longer hours and earn more money. Work the same number of hours and earn the same money. Work fewer hours and earn less money."

(percent of people aged 18 or older responding by sex, race, age, and education, 1998)

	work more, earn more	stay the same	work less, earn less	can't choose
Total	**30%**	**53%**	**9%**	**9%**
Men	34	51	7	8
Women	26	54	11	9
Black	47	41	3	9
White	27	54	11	8
Other	29	51	2	18
Aged 18 to 29	41	47	4	8
Aged 30 to 39	28	53	11	8
Aged 40 to 49	27	52	9	12
Aged 50 to 59	25	55	13	8
Aged 60 to 69	23	60	14	2
Not a high school graduate	38	53	3	6
High school graduate	34	50	8	9
Bachelor's degree	22	57	10	11
Graduate degree	12	55	29	3

Note: Asked of people working at least ten hours per week. Aged 70 or older not shown because of small sample size.
Source: General Social Survey, National Opinion Research Center, University of Chicago; calculations by the author

Prefer to Work More or Less? 1989 and 1998

"Think of the number of hours you work and the money you earn in your main job, including regular overtime. If you had only one of these three choices, which of the following would you prefer? Work longer hours and earn more money. Work the same number of hours and earn the same money. Work fewer hours and earn less money."

(percent of people aged 18 or older responding by sex, race, age, and education, 1989–98)

	work more, earn more		stay the same		work less, earn less		can't choose	
	1998	*1989*	*1998*	*1989*	*1998*	*1989*	*1998*	*1989*
Total	**30%**	**30%**	**53%**	**57%**	**9%**	**5%**	**9%**	**8%**
Men	34	34	51	53	7	5	8	8
Women	26	25	54	61	11	5	9	9
Black	47	39	41	52	3	3	9	6
White	27	29	54	57	11	5	8	8
Aged 18 to 29	41	37	47	52	4	3	8	8
Aged 30 to 39	28	31	53	56	11	6	8	7
Aged 40 to 49	27	25	52	62	9	5	12	7
Aged 50 to 59	25	30	55	56	13	3	8	12
Aged 60 to 69	23	17	60	66	14	8	2	9
Not a high school graduate	38	36	53	51	3	4	6	8
High school graduate	34	32	50	54	8	5	9	9
Bachelor's degree	22	27	57	56	10	6	11	10
Graduate degree	12	19	55	66	29	10	3	5

Note: Asked of people working at least ten hours per week. Aged 70 or older not shown because of small sample size.
Source: General Social Survey, National Opinion Research Center, University of Chicago; calculations by the author

Work to Live or Live to Work?

Half of Americans allow work to interfere with their life.

Fifty-four percent of Americans say they do the best work they can, even if it sometimes interferes with the rest of their life. Thirty-seven percent say they work hard, but they don't let work interfere with other parts of their life.

Whites are most likely to say they let work interfere with the rest of their life if necessary (57 percent compared with 43 percent of blacks and 38 percent of "other" races). Blacks and other races are more likely than whites to say they work only as hard as they have to.

The older people are, the more likely they are to work as hard as necessary. Two-thirds of workers in their sixties say they work as hard as they have to even if it interferes with their life, but the proportion drops to 46 percent among people under age 30. Younger generations are more likely to say they work hard, but they don't let it interfere with the rest of their life. Fourteen percent of workers under age 30 say they work only as hard as they have to, compared with fewer than 10 percent of older workers.

The percentage of people who say they let work interfere with their life if necessary increases with education. Only 38 percent of workers who did not complete high school put work first if necessary compared with 65 percent of people with a graduate degree. Conversely, those with less education are more likely to say they work hard but don't let it interfere with their life.

Work to Live or Live to Work? 1998

"Which of the following statements best describes your feelings about your job?
I work only as hard as I have to. I work hard, but not so as to interfere with the rest of my life.
I make a point of doing the best work I can, even if it
sometimes does interfere with the rest of my life."

(percent of people aged 18 or older responding by sex, race, age, and education, 1998)

	work only as hard as I have to	work hard, but don't let it interfere with rest of life	do best work I can, even if it interferes with rest of life
Total	**8%**	**37%**	**54%**
Men	10	34	55
Women	7	38	53
Black	18	39	43
White	6	35	57
Other	13	48	38
Aged 18 to 29	14	39	46
Aged 30 to 39	9	41	48
Aged 40 to 49	6	33	59
Aged 50 to 59	4	34	61
Aged 60 to 69	5	27	66
Not a high school graduate	11	41	38
High school graduate	8	38	54
Bachelor's degree	5	36	57
Graduate degree	8	26	65

Note: Asked of people working at least ten hours per week. Aged 70 or older not shown because of small sample size. Numbers may not add to 100 because "can't choose" is not shown.
Source: General Social Survey, National Opinion Research Center, University of Chicago; calculations by the author

Work to Live or Live to Work? 1989 and 1998

**"Which of the following statements best describes your feelings about your job?
I work only as hard as I have to. I work hard, but not so as to interfere with the rest of my life.
I make a point of doing the best work I can, even if it
sometimes does interfere with the rest of my life."**

(percent of people aged 18 or older responding by sex, race, age, and education, 1989–98)

	work only as hard as I have to		work hard, but don't let it interfere with rest of life		do best work I can, even if it interferes with rest of life	
	1998	*1989*	*1998*	*1989*	*1998*	*1989*
Total	**8%**	**8%**	**37%**	**31%**	**54%**	**60%**
Men	10	8	34	28	55	63
Women	7	7	38	34	53	58
Black	18	14	39	34	43	50
White	6	7	35	30	57	62
Aged 18 to 29	14	14	39	36	46	49
Aged 30 to 39	9	7	41	33	48	59
Aged 40 to 49	6	2	33	30	59	66
Aged 50 to 59	4	2	34	23	61	74
Aged 60 to 69	5	15	27	17	66	65
Not a high school graduate	11	18	41	24	38	56
High school graduate	8	8	38	29	54	62
Bachelor's degree	5	3	36	32	57	64
Graduate degree	8	1	26	33	65	65

Note: Asked of people working at least ten hours per week. Aged 70 or older not shown because of small sample size. Numbers may not add to 100 because "can't choose" is not shown.
Source: General Social Survey, National Opinion Research Center, University of Chicago; calculations by the author

Importance of Education in Job

Predictably, college graduates are more likely to say their education prepared them for work.

Every American has heard that education is the key to getting ahead in today's workplace. But how much of a role do schools and universities play in helping people develop the skills they need on the job? Sixty-one percent of workers say their education was important in developing the skills they use at work. Only 23 percent say it was not important.

Blacks are slightly more likely than whites and "other" races to say their education was important in preparing them for their work (66 percent compared with 60 percent of whites and other races). The responses of men and women differ little.

Younger workers are more educated than their elders, but their response to this question does not reflect that fact. Workers in their sixties, not younger workers, are the ones most likely to say education was important in developing the skills needed for their job.

The largest difference of opinion is by education. The 68 percent majority of people with a graduate degree say their education was very important in developing the skills they use in their job. Among those with a bachelor's degree, 42 percent say their education was very important while another 38 percent say it was important. Only 16 to 17 percent of workers with a high school education or less say school was very important in giving them the skills they actually use in the work place. In some cases, this is because the work they do requires little or no education. But it also reflects an unmet need for more specific job-skills training at the high school level.

Importance of Education in Job, 1998

"Now think about the skills that you actually use in your job. How important would you say each of the following was in developing these skills? School, college, or university."

(percent of people aged 18 or older responding by sex, race, age, and education, 1998)

	very important	important	neither	not important	not important at all	impor- tant, total	not impor, tant, total
Total	**27%**	**34%**	**16%**	**13%**	**10%**	**61%**	**23%**
Men	26	35	16	12	9	61	21
Women	27	32	15	13	11	59	24
Black	31	35	15	14	5	66	19
White	26	34	16	13	11	60	24
Other	30	30	14	10	16	60	26
Aged 18 to 29	28	32	18	11	10	60	21
Aged 30 to 39	29	31	15	15	9	60	24
Aged 40 to 49	23	38	16	13	9	61	22
Aged 50 to 59	33	30	14	9	13	63	22
Aged 60 to 69	21	47	9	12	12	68	24
Not a high school graduate	16	21	16	16	21	37	37
High school graduate	17	33	19	18	13	50	31
Bachelor's degree	42	38	10	3	6	80	19
Graduate degree	68	29	2	2	0	97	2

Note: Asked of people currently working. Aged 70 or older is not shown because of small sample size. Numbers may not add to 100 because "can't choose" is not shown.
Source: General Social Survey, National Opinion Research Center, University of Chicago; calculations by the author

Use of Experience and Skills in Job

College graduates are most likely to use their accumulated experience and skills in their current job.

The largest percentage of workers say they are able to use almost all of the experience and skills they gained from past jobs in their current employment. Forty-three percent say they use almost all of their accumulated experience and skills, while 23 percent say they use a lot. Only 11 percent say almost none of their experience and skills are useful in their current job.

Men and women make similar assessments about the use of their skills and experience in their current job. There are pronounced differences by race, however. Nearly half of whites (47 percent) use almost all of their past work experience and skills in their present job compared with one-third of blacks and only one-quarter of "other" races. Only 19 percent of whites and blacks say they use only a little of their accumulated experience and skills compared with 25 percent of other races.

The youngest workers are least likely to say their current work allows them to use the experience and skills they gained in prior employment. This result isn't surprising since young workers have a limited work history and many spend their early working years trying out different types of jobs. Only 28 percent of workers under age 30 use almost all of their experience and skills in their present job compared with 50 to 52 percent of workers aged 40 to 59. Workers in their sixties, however, are far more likely to say they use almost none of their experience and skills (21 versus 12 percent or fewer of younger workers). One reason is that many workers in their sixties have downshifted into less demanding occupations.

College graduates are most likely to say almost all of their past experience and skills are useful in their present job. Only 34 to 38 percent of workers who do not have a college degree use almost all of their experience and skills in their job compared with 47 percent of people with a bachelor's degree and fully 77 percent of those with a graduate degree.

Use of Experience and Skills in Job, 1998

"How much of your past work experience and/or job skills can you make use of in your present job?"

(percent of people aged 18 or older responding by sex, race, age, and education, 1998)

	almost none	a little	a lot	almost all	can't choose	almost none, a little	a lot, almost all
Total	**11%**	**19%**	**23%**	**43%**	**4%**	**30%**	**66%**
Men	10	18	25	43	4	28	68
Women	11	20	22	43	3	31	65
Black	11	19	29	32	9	30	61
White	10	19	22	47	3	29	69
Other	12	25	31	25	6	37	56
Aged 18 to 29	12	31	25	28	5	43	53
Aged 30 to 39	12	19	21	44	5	31	65
Aged 40 to 49	6	16	25	50	3	22	75
Aged 50 to 59	11	14	21	52	2	25	73
Aged 60 to 69	21	5	30	40	5	26	70
Not a high school graduate	6	20	30	34	9	26	64
High school graduate	13	22	22	38	4	35	60
Bachelor's degree	9	16	26	47	2	25	73
Graduate degree	2	6	15	77	0	8	92

Note: Asked of people currently working. Aged 70 or older is not shown because of small sample size.
Source: General Social Survey, National Opinion Research Center, University of Chicago; calculations by the author

Technology Makes Work More Interesting

Americans are optimistic about the impact of technology on work.

Most Americans are optimistic that new technologies will make work more interesting. Overall, 63 percent think it will make work at least a little more interesting. Only 11 percent think work will become less interesting as new technologies are introduced into the workplace.

Interestingly, the generations with the most exposure to new technology are least likely to think it will make work more interesting. Only 26 percent of people under age 40 think technology will make work much more interesting compared with 34 to 35 percent of people aged 60 or older. Younger generations' familiarity with technology explains this attitude. The gee-whiz factor has diminished for generations raised on constantly changing technologies.

Whites are less likely than blacks and "other" races to think technology will make work much more interesting in the near future. Only 27 percent of whites think it will compared with 36 percent of blacks and 34 percent of other races.

Technology Makes Work More Interesting, 1998

"Do you think that the introduction of new technologies in the United States over the next few years will make work much more, a little more, a little less, much less, or neither more nor less interesting?"

(percent of people aged 18 or older responding by sex, race, age, and education, 1998)

	much more	a little more	neither	a little less	much less	can't choose	more, total	less, total
Total	**29%**	**34%**	**19%**	**7%**	**4%**	**7%**	**63%**	**11%**
Men	30	34	19	8	4	5	64	12
Women	28	34	19	7	4	8	62	11
Black	36	31	12	7	4	10	67	11
White	27	35	20	8	4	7	62	12
Other	34	37	17	4	1	6	71	5
Aged 18 to 29	26	36	19	11	4	4	62	15
Aged 30 to 39	26	43	18	5	1	6	69	6
Aged 40 to 49	30	35	19	7	5	5	65	12
Aged 50 to 59	29	30	24	8	5	4	59	13
Aged 60 to 69	34	28	16	7	5	11	62	12
Aged 70 or older	35	21	16	7	4	17	56	11
Not a high school graduate	36	20	14	5	6	19	56	11
High school graduate	26	37	18	8	4	6	63	12
Bachelor's degree	30	37	20	6	2	4	67	8
Graduate degree	34	21	24	13	5	2	55	18

Source: General Social Survey, National Opinion Research Center, University of Chicago; calculations by the author

Will Technology Change the Number of Jobs?

A plurality say jobs will be lost to technology.

Historically, new technologies have eliminated many jobs—but they also create new ones. Forty-six percent of Americans believe that during the next few years the number of jobs will decrease at least slightly because of new technologies, while 35 percent think there will be more jobs. Eleven percent believe technology will have no impact on the number of jobs.

Men are slightly more likely than women to believe jobs will increase because of new technologies. Similar percentages of blacks and whites think jobs will decrease, but people of "other" races are more likely to think there will be more jobs.

Younger generations are more familiar and comfortable with technology, so it is no surprise that they are more likely to believe jobs will increase thanks to new technologies. Among people under age 50, 35 to 40 percent think there will be more jobs, while a smaller 30 to 33 percent of people aged 50 or older agree.

College graduates are more likely than people who did not complete college to believe technology will increase the number of jobs, while those with less education are more likely to believe there will be fewer jobs. About one-third of people who did not complete college say jobs will increase compared with 42 to 44 percent of college graduates. Only 35 percent of college graduates believe there will be fewer jobs compared with 52 percent of high school graduates and 44 percent of those with less education. Sixteen percent of people who did not complete high school say they can't choose.

Will Technology Change the Number of Jobs? 1998

"New kinds of technology are being introduced more and more in the United States: computers, robots, and so on. Do you think these new technologies will over the next few years greatly increase, slightly increase, slightly reduce, greatly reduce, or make no difference to the number of jobs?"

(percent of people aged 18 or older responding by sex, race, age, and education, 1998)

	greatly increase	slightly increase	no difference	slightly decrease	greatly decrease	can't choose	in-crease, total	de-crease, total
Total	**15%**	**20%**	**11%**	**27%**	**19%**	**7%**	**35%**	**46%**
Men	15	23	10	26	19	6	38	45
Women	15	17	11	29	20	8	32	49
Black	17	19	5	23	27	8	36	50
White	14	20	12	28	19	7	34	47
Other	26	19	11	26	11	7	45	37
Aged 18 to 29	20	20	10	30	15	5	40	45
Aged 30 to 39	15	20	13	29	16	6	35	45
Aged 40 to 49	13	25	11	28	17	6	38	45
Aged 50 to 59	13	17	11	28	25	5	30	53
Aged 60 to 69	18	15	10	28	27	3	33	55
Aged 70 or older	13	17	7	19	26	19	30	45
Not a high school graduate	20	12	8	22	22	16	32	44
High school graduate	14	19	9	29	23	6	33	52
Bachelor's degree	20	22	17	27	8	7	42	35
Graduate degree	15	29	16	23	12	5	44	35

Source: General Social Survey, National Opinion Research Center, University of Chicago; calculations by the author

Prefer Self-Employment?

Young adults have the most entrepreneurial spirit.

Few Americans are self-employed, but the entrepreneurial spirit is nonetheless alive. Sixty-three percent say they would rather be self-employed than work as an employee. This share is 6 percentage points greater than in 1989. In fact, within every demographic segment, the percentage of people saying they prefer self-employment rose between 1989 and 1998.

The widest gap on this issue is by age. Fully 71 percent of people under age 30 say they would like to be their own boss, as do 66 percent of those in their thirties. In contrast, a smaller 60 to 61 percent of people aged 40 to 69 and 54 percent of people aged 70 or older say they would choose self-employment over being an employee. Between 1989 and 1998, the proportion of people under age 30 saying they would prefer self-employment rose 12 percentage points.

Women are more likely than men to prefer the security of being an employee (31 versus 20 percent). Men, on the other hand, are far more likely to want to be their own boss (71 versus 58 percent).

A larger share of people with a high school diploma or more education would choose self-employment than of those who did not complete high school. Thirteen percent of the least educated say they can't choose between the two options. Members of this group probably are aware that without even the skills and credentials afforded by a high school diploma, it would be very difficult indeed to make their own way in the work world.

Prefer Self-Employment? 1998

"Suppose you were working and could choose between different kinds of jobs. Which of the following would you personally choose: being an employee or being self-employed?"

(percent of people aged 18 or older responding by sex, race, age, and education, 1998)

	employee	self-employed	can't choose
Total	**26%**	**63%**	**11%**
Men	20	71	9
Women	31	58	12
Black	27	63	10
White	26	63	11
Other	29	66	6
Aged 18 to 29	19	71	11
Aged 30 to 39	22	66	11
Aged 40 to 49	29	61	10
Aged 50 to 59	30	60	10
Aged 60 to 69	30	60	10
Aged 70 or older	33	54	13
Not a high school graduate	31	56	13
High school graduate	25	65	10
Bachelor's degree	27	63	9
Graduate degree	25	67	9

Source: General Social Survey, National Opinion Research Center, University of Chicago; calculations by the author

Prefer Self-Employment? 1989 and 1998

"Suppose you were working and could choose between different kinds of jobs. Which of the following would you personally choose: being an employee or being self-employed?"

(percent of people aged 18 or older responding by sex, race, age, and education, 1989–98)

	employee		self-employed		can't choose	
	1998	*1989*	*1998*	*1989*	*1998*	*1989*
Total	**26%**	**34%**	**63%**	**57%**	**11%**	**9%**
Men	20	27	71	66	9	7
Women	31	39	58	50	12	12
Black	27	35	63	59	10	6
White	26	33	63	57	11	10
Aged 18 to 29	19	30	71	59	11	10
Aged 30 to 39	22	31	66	60	11	9
Aged 40 to 49	29	36	61	58	10	6
Aged 50 to 59	30	33	60	59	10	8
Aged 60 to 69	30	37	60	49	10	13
Aged 70 or older	33	39	54	51	13	10
Not a high school graduate	31	38	56	52	13	11
High school graduate	25	32	65	58	10	10
Bachelor's degree	27	35	63	59	9	6
Graduate degree	25	30	67	58	9	13

Source: General Social Survey, National Opinion Research Center, University of Chicago; calculations by the author

Prefer Government or Private-Sector Work?

Fewer people would choose government employment now than in the past.

Two-thirds of Americans would rather work in the private sector, while only 19 percent would prefer government or civil service work. Thirteen percent say they can't choose. This distribution represents a substantial change from 1989, when a smaller 58 percent said they would choose private-sector work, while a larger 28 percent said they would prefer working for the government.

The government historically has had stronger affirmative action programs than the private sector, and this difference is reflected in the larger proportion of blacks who would rather be government employees. One-third of blacks say they would choose government work compared with only 16 percent of whites and 24 percent of "other" races. But the proportion of blacks who prefer government work is down from 48 percent in 1989.

The percentages of men and women who prefer private-sector work rose between 1989 and 1998, but in both years men were more likely than women to choose the private sector over government. Fully 72 percent of men say they would rather be in the private sector compared with 64 percent of women.

College graduates think their opportunities are better in the private sector. More than three-quarters would choose employment in the private sector compared with two-thirds of high school graduates. Only 53 percent of people who did not complete high school think private-sector work is preferable to government work, while 26 percent would choose government work and 21 percent say they can't choose.

Prefer Government or Private-Sector Work? 1998

"Suppose you were working and could choose between different kinds of jobs. Which of the following would you personally choose: working in a private business or working for the government or civil service?"

(percent of people aged 18 or older responding by sex, race, age, and education, 1998)

	private	government	can't choose
Total	**67%**	**19%**	**13%**
Men	72	17	12
Women	64	21	15
Black	48	34	18
White	71	16	13
Other	63	24	13
Aged 18 to 29	71	18	11
Aged 30 to 39	70	16	13
Aged 40 to 49	70	21	9
Aged 50 to 59	63	20	17
Aged 60 to 69	57	22	21
Aged 70 or older	61	23	16
Not a high school graduate	53	26	21
High school graduate	67	20	13
Bachelor's degree	74	15	11
Graduate degree	77	16	7

Source: General Social Survey, National Opinion Research Center, University of Chicago; calculations by the author

Prefer Government or Private-Sector Work? 1989 and 1998

"Suppose you were working and could choose between different kinds of jobs. Which of the following would you personally choose: working in a private business or working for the government or civil service?"

(percent of people aged 18 or older responding by sex, race, age, and education, 1989–98)

	private		government		can't choose	
	1998	*1989*	*1998*	*1989*	*1998*	*1989*
Total	**67%**	**58%**	**19%**	**28%**	**13%**	**14%**
Men	72	64	17	26	12	9
Women	64	53	21	29	15	18
Black	48	36	34	48	18	15
White	71	61	16	25	13	14
Aged 18 to 29	71	62	18	24	11	14
Aged 30 to 39	70	64	16	22	13	14
Aged 40 to 49	70	60	21	27	9	13
Aged 50 to 59	63	53	20	33	17	14
Aged 60 to 69	57	50	22	35	21	15
Aged 70 or older	61	48	23	36	16	16
Not a high school graduate	53	52	26	30	21	18
High school graduate	67	58	20	29	13	13
Bachelor's degree	74	69	15	18	11	13
Graduate degree	77	55	16	30	7	16

Source: General Social Survey, National Opinion Research Center, University of Chicago; calculations by the author

Prefer Working for Small or Large Firm?

Increasing numbers of Americans want to work for a small firm.

In 1989, 53 percent of Americans said they would rather work for a small firm than a large one. By 1998, a larger 61 percent said they preferred a small firm. During those years, the proportion of those who prefer a large firm fell from 34 to 26 percent.

Women are slightly more likely than men to prefer a small firm, but the proportions of both men and women who prefer a small employer increased between 1989 and 1998.

Whites are much more likely than blacks and people of "other" race to prefer working for a small firm. Sixty-five percent of whites, but only 45 percent of blacks and 40 percent of others would rather work for a small employer. Since 1989, however, the percentage of blacks saying they prefer working for a small firm grew substantially.

Two-thirds of people aged 40 to 49 and of those aged 60 or older would rather work for a small firm. Fifty-nine percent of people in their thirties or forties agree. Young workers are least likely to prefer a small firm. Only 54 percent would rather work for a small firm, while 33 percent would rather be with a large employer.

The percentage of people preferring a small employer rises sharply with education. Only 45 percent of people who did not complete high school would rather work for a small company, but the proportion rises to 77 percent among people with a graduate degree.

Prefer Working for Small or Large Firm? 1998

"Suppose you were working and could choose between different kinds of jobs. Which of the following would you personally choose: working in a small firm or working in a large firm?"

(percent of people aged 18 or older responding by sex, race, age, and education, 1998)

	small firm	large firm	can't choose
Total	**61%**	**26%**	**13%**
Men	59	28	13
Women	62	24	14
Black	45	39	16
White	65	22	13
Other	40	47	13
Aged 18 to 29	54	33	13
Aged 30 to 39	59	29	11
Aged 40 to 49	66	23	11
Aged 50 to 59	59	24	17
Aged 60 to 69	66	17	17
Aged 70 or older	65	21	15
Not a high school graduate	45	34	21
High school graduate	62	26	12
Bachelor's degree	68	21	11
Graduate degree	77	15	9

Source: General Social Survey, National Opinion Research Center, University of Chicago; calculations by the author

Prefer Working for Small or Large Firm? 1989 and 1998

"Suppose you were working and could choose between different kinds of jobs. Which of the following would you personally choose: working in a small firm or working in a large firm?"

(percent of people aged 18 or older responding by sex, race, age, and education, 1989–98)

	small firm		large firm		can't choose	
	1998	*1989*	*1998*	*1989*	*1998*	*1989*
Total	**61%**	**53%**	**26%**	**34%**	**13%**	**14%**
Men	59	51	28	37	13	12
Women	62	54	24	31	14	15
Black	45	32	39	56	16	12
White	65	56	22	30	13	14
Aged 18 to 29	54	45	33	43	13	13
Aged 30 to 39	59	57	29	27	11	16
Aged 40 to 49	66	54	23	32	11	14
Aged 50 to 59	59	54	24	33	17	13
Aged 60 to 69	66	53	17	34	17	13
Aged 70 or older	65	55	21	30	15	14
Not a high school graduate	45	47	34	36	21	17
High school graduate	62	53	26	34	12	13
Bachelor's degree	68	56	21	29	11	14
Graduate degree	77	69	15	22	9	9

Source: General Social Survey, National Opinion Research Center, University of Chicago; calculations by the author

Important Characteristics of a Job

Job security ranks first with most Americans.

Fifty-seven percent of Americans say job security is a very important job characteristic to them personally. Half say an interesting job is very important. Thirty-six percent say a chance for advancement is very important, while fewer than one-third rate high income, ability to work independently, helping others, socially useful work, or flexible hours as very important aspects of a job. People were more likely in 1998 than in 1989 to say an interesting job was very important, while they were less likely to say a chance for promotion was very important.

Women are considerably more likely than men to consider job security, helping others, and work that is socially useful very important. For all three of these job characteristics, the percentage of women saying they are very important increased between 1989 and 1998. The percentages of both women and men saying it is very important that a job be interesting also increased since 1989.

Whites are considerably less likely than blacks or "other" races to say a chance for advancement, helping others, and high income are very important in a job. Blacks are most likely to say it is very important to have job security, to work independently, and to be socially useful.

The youngest workers are most likely to say an interesting job and a chance for advancement are very important. Understandably, the percentage of Americans who regard advancement as very important declines with age. People in their forties are most likely to say flexible hours are very important. This is the age at which most people have school-aged children, and flexible hours come in handy for time-crunched parents.

The college educated are considerably more likely than those with less education to say it is very important that a job be interesting. They are less likely to think job security and high income are very important. Interestingly, people with the least education and those with the most education are the ones most likely to say it is very important that a job allow them to be socially useful and to help others.

Important Characteristics of a Job, 1998

"On the following list there are various aspects of jobs. Please indicate how important you personally consider it is in a job: an interesting job; job security; good opportunities for advancement; a job that allows someone to help other people; a high income; a job that allows someone to work independently; a job that is useful to society; a job with flexible working hours."

(percent of people aged 18 or older responding "very important" by sex, race, age, and education, 1998)

	interesting job	job security	chance to advance	help others	high income	work independently	socially useful	flexible hours
Total	**50%**	**57%**	**36%**	**29%**	**23%**	**28%**	**31%**	**17%**
Men	48	52	35	24	25	27	25	13
Women	52	61	37	33	21	29	35	19
Black	48	61	51	38	38	33	38	21
White	51	57	32	28	19	27	29	16
Other	51	53	54	32	36	29	32	14
Aged 18 to 29	63	57	50	27	26	29	32	17
Aged 30 to 39	48	60	36	29	27	25	30	17
Aged 40 to 49	49	54	35	33	25	33	32	22
Aged 50 to 59	52	58	32	33	20	28	34	13
Aged 60 to 69	42	62	26	26	13	24	31	14
Aged 70 or older	42	54	29	24	16	29	23	12
Not a high school graduate	47	57	38	34	35	36	37	17
High school graduate	48	61	38	27	23	26	28	17
Bachelor's degree	57	49	34	28	14	27	27	16
Graduate degree	65	51	25	43	18	33	44	20

Source: General Social Survey, National Opinion Research Center, University of Chicago; calculations by the author

Important Characteristics of a Job, 1989 and 1998

"On the following list there are various aspects of jobs. Please indicate how important you personally consider it is in a job: an interesting job; job security; good opportunities for advancement; a job that allows someone to help other people; a high income; a job that allows someone to work independently; a job that is useful to society; a job with flexible working hours."

(percent of people aged 18 or older responding very important by sex, race, age, and education, 1989–98)

	interesting job		job security		chance to advance		help others		high income		work independently		socially useful		flexible hours	
	1998	1989	1998	1989	1998	1989	1998	1989	1998	1989	1998	1989	1998	1989	1998	1989
Total	**50%**	**43%**	**57%**	**54%**	**36%**	**41%**	**29%**	**25%**	**23%**	**25%**	**28%**	**27%**	**31%**	**28%**	**17%**	**15%**
Men	48	43	52	52	35	41	24	23	25	25	27	29	25	29	13	15
Women	52	43	61	56	37	41	33	26	21	24	29	25	35	28	19	16
Black	48	41	61	74	51	52	38	25	38	49	33	31	38	33	21	22
White	51	43	57	52	32	39	28	25	19	21	27	26	29	28	16	14
Aged 18 to 29	63	48	57	49	50	42	27	25	26	26	29	27	32	29	17	19
Aged 30 to 39	48	40	60	52	36	41	29	22	27	25	25	27	30	27	17	20
Aged 40 to 49	49	47	54	50	35	37	33	27	25	23	33	31	32	29	22	15
Aged 50 to 59	52	39	58	60	32	41	33	27	20	20	28	24	34	34	13	13
Aged 60 to 69	42	42	62	60	26	40	26	24	13	25	24	20	31	26	14	8
Aged 70 or older	42	40	54	62	29	48	24	25	16	25	29	26	23	28	12	10
Not a high school graduate	47	36	57	66	38	44	34	27	35	36	36	26	37	25	17	19
High school graduate	48	41	61	55	38	42	27	23	23	23	26	23	28	28	17	14
Bachelor's degree	57	53	49	37	34	38	28	29	14	17	27	34	27	34	16	13
Graduate degree	65	60	51	37	25	28	43	25	18	19	33	36	44	35	20	15

Source: General Social Survey, National Opinion Research Center, University of Chicago; calculations by the author

Stressful Work

Two out of five workers frequently find their work stressful.

In a competitive environment, it's a luxury to have a stress-free job. Only 16 percent of workers hardly ever or never find their work stressful. Thirty-nine percent say their work is often or always stressful. The percentage of people with a stressful job did not change much between 1989 and 1998 within most demographic segments.

Whites are more likely than blacks and "other" races to find their work frequently stressful. Forty percent of whites often or always find work stressful compared with 32 percent of blacks and 30 percent of other races. Fifteen percent of whites and blacks hardly ever or never find their work stressful compared with 28 percent of other races.

People in their forties and fifties are most likely to find their work stressful, with 45 to 46 percent saying it is often or always stressful. Only 19 percent of workers in their sixties frequently find their work stressful.

People with a college degree may have more interesting and higher paying jobs, but they pay the price in stress. More than half of people with a graduate degree and 41 percent of those with a bachelor's degree often or always find their work stressful. In contrast, only 34 to 36 percent of people with less education are frequently stressed by their jobs. One-quarter of people who did not complete high school and 19 percent of high school graduates rarely or never find their work stressful compared with just 10 percent or fewer of college graduates.

Stressful Work, 1998

"How often do you find your work stressful?"

(percent of people aged 18 or older responding by sex, race, age, and education, 1998)

	always	often	sometimes	hardly ever	never	always/ often	hardly ever/ never
Total	**11%**	**28%**	**46%**	**11%**	**5%**	**39%**	**16%**
Men	11	28	44	13	4	39	17
Women	10	27	47	10	6	37	16
Black	10	22	53	8	7	32	15
White	11	29	44	11	4	40	15
Other	6	24	43	14	14	30	28
Aged 18 to 29	13	24	47	10	6	37	16
Aged 30 to 39	9	26	50	9	5	35	14
Aged 40 to 49	13	33	42	9	2	46	11
Aged 50 to 59	11	34	35	14	6	45	20
Aged 60 to 69	5	14	61	14	7	19	21
Not a high school graduate	11	23	40	10	15	34	25
High school graduate	11	25	45	13	6	36	19
Bachelor's degree	8	33	49	8	2	41	10
Graduate degree	11	46	34	9	0	57	9

Note: Asked of people working at least ten hours per week. Aged 70 or older not shown because of small sample size. Numbers may not add to 100 because "can't choose" is not shown.
Source: General Social Survey, National Opinion Research Center, University of Chicago; calculations by the author

Stressful Work, 1989 and 1998

"How often do you find your work stressful?"

(percent of people aged 18 or older responding by sex, race, age, and education, 1989–98)

	always/often		sometimes		hardly ever/never	
	1998	*1989*	*1998*	*1989*	*1998*	*1989*
Total	**39%**	**39%**	**46%**	**44%**	**16%**	**17%**
Men	39	40	44	44	17	16
Women	37	38	47	44	16	17
Black	32	30	53	43	15	28
White	40	41	44	44	15	15
Aged 18 to 29	37	39	47	42	16	19
Aged 30 to 39	35	38	50	47	14	14
Aged 40 to 49	46	42	42	47	11	11
Aged 50 to 59	45	43	35	37	20	20
Aged 60 to 69	19	29	61	37	21	33
Not a high school graduate	34	35	40	41	25	23
High school graduate	36	36	45	45	19	19
Bachelor's degree	41	41	49	48	10	10
Graduate degree	57	56	34	33	9	11

Note: Asked of people working at least ten hours per week. Aged 70 or older not shown because of small sample size. Numbers may not add to 100 because "can't choose" is not shown.
Source: General Social Survey, National Opinion Research Center, University of Chicago; calculations by the author

Exhausted after Work

One-third of workers say they often or always come home exhausted.

The homes of Americans aren't as clean as they once were, even though fewer pots and pans are being dirtied to make home-cooked meals. A big reason for our dirtier homes is that many people are simply too tired to tackle household chores when they come home from work. Half of workers say they at least sometimes come home from work exhausted, while 41 percent say they are often or always exhausted after work.

Women are more likely than men to feel exhausted after work (44 verus 38 percent). Ten percent of women say they are always exhausted after work compared with 6 percent of men. Only 9 to 10 percent of whites and blacks say they hardly ever or never come home from work exhausted, compared with fully 20 percent of people of "other" races.

Workers in their sixties seem to have it a little better than younger people. Only 26 percent are often or always exhausted after work compared with 39 to 45 percent of younger workers. Nineteen percent of workers in their sixties say they are hardly ever or never exhausted at the end of the day compared with 12 percent or fewer people under age 60.

The least educated workers are the ones most likely to say they are always exhausted after work (15 versus 10 percent or fewer of more educated workers). But higher education doesn't ensure an easier day at work. Nearly half of people with a graduate degree say they often come home from work exhausted.

Exhausted after Work, 1998

"How often do you come home from work exhausted?"

(percent of people aged 18 or older responding by sex, race, age, and education, 1998)

	always	often	sometimes	hardly ever	never	always/ often	hardly ever/ never
Total	**8%**	**33%**	**48%**	**9%**	**2%**	**41%**	**11%**
Men	6	32	50	10	2	38	12
Women	10	34	46	8	2	44	10
Black	15	28	48	6	3	43	9
White	7	34	48	9	1	41	10
Other	10	25	43	12	8	35	20
Aged 18 to 29	12	31	45	10	2	43	12
Aged 30 to 39	7	32	53	7	1	39	8
Aged 40 to 49	10	35	45	9	0	45	9
Aged 50 to 59	5	39	43	8	4	44	12
Aged 60 to 69	0	26	55	14	5	26	19
Not a high school graduate	15	26	47	8	3	41	11
High school graduate	10	32	47	9	2	42	11
Bachelor's degree	3	36	50	9	1	39	10
Graduate degree	6	48	37	8	0	54	8

Note: Asked of people working at least ten hours per week. Aged 70 or older now shown because of small sample size. Numbers may not add to 100 because "can't choose" is not shown.
Source: General Social Survey, National Opinion Research Center, University of Chicago; calculations by the author

Exhausted after Work, 1989 and 1998

"How often do you come home from work exhausted?"

(percent of people aged 18 or older responding by sex, race, age, and education, 1989–98)

	always/often		sometimes		hardly ever/never	
	1998	1989	1998	1989	1998	1989
Total	**41%**	**36%**	**48%**	**50%**	**11%**	**13%**
Men	38	36	50	52	12	12
Women	44	35	46	49	10	15
Black	43	38	48	48	9	15
White	41	36	48	50	10	13
Aged 18 to 29	43	40	45	44	12	16
Aged 30 to 39	39	39	53	50	8	10
Aged 40 to 49	45	32	45	54	9	14
Aged 50 to 59	44	34	43	55	12	12
Aged 60 to 69	26	29	55	55	19	14
Not a high school graduate	41	36	47	47	11	17
High school graduate	42	37	47	50	11	13
Bachelor's degree	39	26	50	61	10	12
Graduate degree	54	47	37	44	8	9

Note: Asked of people working at least ten hours per week. Aged 70 or older not shown because of small sample size. Numbers may not add to 100 because "can't choose" is not shown.
Source: General Social Survey, National Opinion Research Center, University of Chicago; calculations by the author

Characteristics of Your Job

Most workers say they help others and work independently.

The great majority of people say their job allows them to help other people and to work independently. Solid majorities say their work is interesting and socially useful. Most also believe their job is secure. But only 31 percent say their job offers a chance for advancement, and only 24 percent say they have a high income.

Women are more likely to work in the service industries, which is undoubtedly one reason why they are more likely than men to say their job allows them to help others. Women are also more likely to say their job is secure, while men are more likely to say they have a high income.

Blacks are less likely than whites and "other" races to say their job is interesting and that they can work independently. Whites are most likely to say their job is secure. They are slightly less likely than blacks and other races to say their job is socially useful.

The younger people are, the more likely they are to have a job that offers an opportunity for advancement. While 42 percent of people under age 30 think they have a shot at a promotion, only 12 percent of workers in their sixties agree. Workers in their sixties are most likely to think their job is secure and interesting, however. The older people are, the more likely they are to have a job that allows them to help others.

People who did not complete college are least likely to feel their job is secure. They are probably correct in this assessment since education is increasingly important to getting and keeping a job. College graduates are considerably more likely than those with less education to say their job is interesting and socially useful.

Characteristics of Your Job, 1998

"For each statement, please indicate how much you agree or disagree that it applies to your job: in my job I can help other people; I can work independently; my job is interesting; my job is useful to society; my job is secure; my opportunities for advancement are high; my income is high."

(percent of people aged 18 or older responding "agree" or "strongly agree" by sex, race, age, and education, 1998)

	help others	work independently	interesting job	socially useful	secure job	chance to advance	high income
Total	**80%**	**80%**	**74%**	**70%**	**69%**	**31%**	**24%**
Men	75	80	72	70	67	32	29
Women	84	81	75	70	72	30	21
Black	81	75	63	74	58	37	21
White	79	81	76	69	72	29	25
Other	80	84	73	73	57	39	24
Aged 18 to 29	77	79	67	70	74	42	26
Aged 30 to 39	78	82	75	68	71	36	24
Aged 40 to 49	81	77	74	72	66	27	25
Aged 50 to 59	83	86	75	73	65	21	25
Aged 60 to 69	84	77	86	65	79	12	21
Not a high school graduate	75	65	66	61	59	25	18
High school graduate	79	83	69	68	71	28	20
Bachelor's degree	77	84	80	72	66	38	33
Graduate degree	92	77	91	88	74	28	45

Note: Asked of people working at least ten hours per week. Aged 70 or older not shown because of small sample size. Numbers may not add to 100 because "can't choose" is not shown.
Source: General Social Survey, National Opinion Research Center, University of Chicago; calculations by the author

Characteristics of Your Job, 1989 and 1998

"For each statement, please indicate how much you agree or disagree that it applies to your job: in my job I can help other people; I can work independently; my job is interesting; my job is useful to society; my job is secure; my opportunities for advancement are high; my income is high."

(percent of people aged 18 or older responding "agree" or "strongly agree" by sex, race, age, and education, 1989–98)

	help others		work independently		interesting job		socially useful		secure job		chance to advance		high income	
	1998	1989	1998	1989	1998	1989	1998	1989	1998	1989	1998	1989	1998	1989
Total	80%	76%	80%	77%	74%	76%	70%	68%	69%	75%	31%	36%	24%	26%
Men	75	72	80	77	72	75	70	69	67	76	32	39	29	32
Women	84	80	81	78	75	78	70	67	72	74	30	33	21	19
Black	81	76	75	61	63	63	74	81	58	68	37	36	21	21
White	79	76	81	79	76	78	69	66	72	76	29	36	25	27
Aged 18 to 29	77	67	79	70	67	67	70	59	74	75	42	42	26	20
Aged 30 to 39	78	78	82	79	75	78	68	67	71	75	36	39	24	25
Aged 40 to 49	81	81	77	81	74	80	72	70	66	77	27	34	25	34
Aged 50 to 59	83	77	86	77	75	78	73	79	65	70	21	28	25	26
Aged 60 to 69	84	81	77	80	86	87	65	71	79	79	12	15	21	28
Not a high school graduate	75	72	65	62	66	60	61	65	59	73	25	22	18	17
High school graduate	79	74	83	78	69	74	68	64	71	73	28	37	20	23
Bachelor's degree	77	77	84	81	80	86	72	69	66	83	38	44	33	36
Graduate degree	92	91	77	87	91	91	88	92	74	82	28	38	45	41

Note: Asked of people working at least ten hours per week for pay. Aged 70 or older not shown because of small sample size. Numbers may not add to 100 because "can't choose" is not shown.
Source: General Social Survey, National Opinion Research Center, University of Chicago; calculations by the author

Index

Media, confidence in, 157, 160, 175–176

Medical leaders, confidence in, 39–41

Medicine. *See* Health care.

Men

  as breadwinners, 390–392

  better suited for politics than women, 384–386

  career of, more important than wife's, 396–398

  should run the country, 381–383

Mental health care, limited by HMOs, 62–63

Military, confidence in, 157, 160, 173–174

Miracles, religious, belief in, 297–298

Moderate, politically, consider self, 200–202

Mothers, working

  as good as nonworking, 399–401

  effect on preschoolers, 402–404

Motivation, lack of as cause of lower

      socioeconomic status of

      blacks, 251–253, 256

Municipal government funding for arts

      organizations, 20, 23

Music performance, classical or opera,

      attendance at, 13–14

Obedience, most important quality of children,

      147–149

Opera performance, attendance at, 13–14

Organized labor, confidence in, 157, 159,

      179–180

Parents, standard of living relative to, 425–426

Physician-assisted suicide, 45–47

Physicians

  are not thorough enough, 86–87

  avoid unnecessary health care expenses, 92–93

  avoid unnecessary surgery, 80–81

  don't explain medical problems, 76–77

  don't give all treatment options, 78–79

  HMOs limit, 55, 57, 60–61

  ignore patient history, 74–75

  put cost considerations above care, 90–91

  put medical needs first, 88–89

  rare see same twice, 66–67

  take unnecessary risks, 82–83

  treat patients with respect, 72–73

  trust between, and patient damaged by HMOs,

      53–54

  trust judgment of, 68–69

  trust to reveal mistakes, 70–71

  try not to worry patients, 84–85

Political

  leaning, 200–202

  parties, identification with, 196–199

Politics, men better suited than women for,

      384–386

Poor

  government responsibility to help, 209–211

  reduce income differences between rich and,

      206–208

Popularity, most important quality of children,

      147–149

Pornography, laws against, 365–367

Prayer

  frequency of, 282–284

  in schools, 337–339

Premarital sex, wrong or not, 356–358

Presidential candidate, vote for woman as,

      387–389

Press, confidence in, 157, 160, 175–176

Private-sector versus government employment,

      473–475

Prostitution, ever engaged in, 370–371

Protestant

  as religious preference, 273–275

  raised as, 276–278

Religion

  brings more conflict than peace, 329–330

  truth in one or many, 333–334

  versus science, 335–336

Religious

  background, 276–278

  beliefs carried into other areas, 314–315

  consider self, 316, 318

  experience changed life, 319–320

  expression by athletes, 342–343

  images in advertising, 340–341

  intolerance, 331–332